Hear, O Israel: the Lord our God, the Lord is One.

-Deuteronomy 6:4

THE BIBLE IN RHYME
Published by Minor Planet Press, LLC

For information:
MINOR PLANET PRESS, LLC
13844 BRADSHAW ST.
OVERLAND PARK, KS 66221
www.minorplanetpress.com

Cover design by Timothy McCabe
Internal word clouds developed with Wordle.net
Author photo by MeredithRae Photography

Minor Planet Press books may be purchased for educational, business, or
sales promotional use.

First edition: September 2009
ISBN 978-0-9840920-0-0
Library of Congress Control Number: 2009907812

Printed in the United States of America

1 2 3 4 5 6 7 8 9 10

The Bible In Rhyme

Kyle Holt

Minor Planet Press

CONTENTS

Introduction:
Author's Comments: i
How to Read This Book: iii

THE OLD TESTAMENT

Historical Books:
Genesis: 3
Exodus: 37
Leviticus: 53
Numbers: 57
Deuteronomy: 67
Joshua: 79
Judges: 89
Ruth: 103
I Samuel: 107
II Samuel: 129
I Kings: 141
II Kings: 155
I Chronicles: 169
II Chronicles: 177
Ezra: 189
Nehemiah: 193
Esther: 197

Poetic Books:
Job: 203
Psalms: 221
Proverbs: 243
Ecclesiastes: 261
Song of Songs: 267

Major Prophets:
Isaiah: 273
Jeremiah: 297
Lamentations: 311
Ezekiel: 315
Daniel: 327

Minor Prophets:
Hosea: 337
Joel: 347
Amos: 351
Obadiah: 357
Jonah: 359
Micah: 363
Nahum: 369
Habakkuk: 373
Zephaniah: 377
Haggai: 381
Zechariah: 385
Malachi: 393

THE NEW TESTAMENT

Historical Books:
Matthew: 397
Mark: 439
Luke: 469
John: 505
Acts: 527

The Pauline Epistles to Individuals:
I Timothy: 599
II Timothy: 605
Titus: 609
Philemon: 613

The Pauline Epistles to Churches:
Romans: 549
I Corinthians: 557
II Corinthians: 565
Galatians: 571
Ephesians: 577
Philippians: 583
Colossians: 587
I Thessalonians: 591
II Thessalonians: 595

The General Epistles:
Hebrews: 615
James: 623
I Peter: 629
II Peter: 633
I John: 637
II John: 641
III John: 643
Jude: 645
Revelation: 647

AUTHOR'S COMMENTS

In addition to being the basis of faith for the Judeo-Christian religions, the Bible offers everything a reader could want – action, romance, powerful warriors, beautiful women, palace intrigue, words of wisdom, life after death, and even the end of the world! The Bible is the most revered book on the planet – and yet the vast majority of people, including followers of the Good Book itself, have never read it. Why? Because it is looooooooooooooooooooong and hard to understand.

Actually, the Bible is not a single book. It is sixty-six books by dozens of authors! With thousands of messages that are still applicable to our lives, this is a tome that we should all read, understand, and live by daily. But if we don't know what it says…what it *really* says, not just what we *heard* it says…then how can we embrace it fully?

My goal in writing *The Bible in Rhyme* was to create a portal; something which shares the biblical message and stories, while simultaneously inviting people to open the Bible itself. The rhythmic, rhyming style of this book should allow everyone – children and adults alike – to encounter the scriptures in a fun, easy-to-understand format. Maybe something close to what Shakespeare and Dr. Seuss would have created if they had teamed up to turn the Bible into a rhyming poem!

In modern culture, we do not experience the Bible as they did in ancient Israel. We read quietly and ponder its meaning in silence, but two thousand years ago only an elite few could read and write, so the biblical stories were shared orally. The Bible wasn't quiet. It was LOUD! The stories were shared at dinner time, around campfires, and as entertainment. They even sang about it – hence Psalms. My hope is that *The Bible in Rhyme* is something you will share out loud with friends and family, and that we can recapture and reconnect with our ancestral method of hearing and knowing the Word of God.

In creating this work, I have approached it from a book-by-book, chapter-by-chapter mindset rather than a word-for-word translation (I couldn't have completed Leviticus otherwise!). If you read something that makes you laugh, confuses you, or makes you wonder whether the Bible actually said that, open up the *real* Bible and compare. If you do, then I've done my job right! And if I got something wrong, call me on it. Go to www.thebibleinrhyme.com and leave a comment. I can take criticism – but please, make it constructive.

As my final thought before you enter the text itself, I want to be clear. I did not write this. Men and women who lived 2,000 to 3,500 years ago wrote it. I merely turned their prose into poetry (and sometimes their poetry into poetry!). And I believe that God asked me to write this. Not by speaking out loud to me, but by causing all those sleepless nights where I couldn't stop thinking about this project. The night I finally got out of bed, walked downstairs, and pounded out Genesis 1 will always remain a defining moment in my life. He made this daunting task enjoyable. He gave me the willpower to persevere, and He reminded me to start working again when I procrastinated. He is the originator of all that is awesome. He's the Coolest of the cool. He's Master of the universe. Truly, thank You, Lord, for making this possible. Amen and enjoy!

HOW TO READ THIS BOOK

- Read out loud. It's more fun that way, and it's true to the way that the biblical stories were shared 2,000 years ago!

- ALL are welcome in The Bible in Rhyme! The non, the nominally, and the deeply religious. Whether you're Christian, Jewish, Muslim, Hindu, Buddhist, agnostic, atheist, or something else, I just hope and pray that you find something that draws you closer to God.

- Feel free to skip around – the Bible was not intended to be read front to back, and neither was *The Bible in Rhyme* (you can't ruin the ending by skipping to the back!).

- The rhythm and rhyme scheme (A, A, B, B) is the same throughout the entire book EXCEPT for Psalms. Since the Psalms are so varied in the Bible, each Psalm may have a different rhythm and/or rhyme structure.

- *The Bible in Rhyme* is wonderful to read as a family, but before you read it to young children please check and make sure you're comfortable with the selection. This book is based on the entire Bible, and the Bible is graphic. I did my best to serve the word of God as originally written, so as a warning...some selections may not be suitable for young children.

- Grab a Bible and keep it close by. That way you can compare *The Bible in Rhyme* to the *real* Bible and see what was originally written.

- I recognize that my bias shows up in here, but that was unavoidable. Seriously though! The original authors of the Bible couldn't have been *more* biased in their writings!

THE OLD TESTAMENT

Genesis 1

In the beginning, God created.
The rules were established. The physics translated.
In the nothing, God shouted, "Let there be light."
He created the first day, and thus made the night.
Then the waters, the sky, and the land from the seas
upon which He placed all the seed-bearing trees.
Then the seasons, the stars, the moon and the sun,
then sea creatures, birds; the Lord made each one.
Next came the beasts who covered the land
and all that God saw was as good as He'd planned.
"Though everything here is within My control,
it's missing a piece to make the Earth whole.
A man in My likeness, to rule all the beasts.
To govern the greatest and govern the least."
God took up His dirt, and He took up His dust
and then in the swiftest, most powerful gust
He blew into Adam the Godbreath of life.
But God saw that Adam now needed a wife
to be a companion, for man was alone.
So from His new man, God plucked out a bone.
Then there on the new and glorious Earth,
out in the open, woman was birthed.
And as they lay gasping from being created
unto the woman and man God related,
"This is My Earth, but I give it to you.
It is now yours to rule and subdue...
Multiply, prosper, for I love you best."
He saw it was good, so God took His rest.

Genesis 2 – 3

All was completed, and all was perfected,
not one thing amiss, nor one thing neglected.
The Lord God was pleased, blessing all that He'd made
including the Sabbath on which He had laid
and rested as He saw what He had begun.
On that day we're all to recall what He's done.
But there was no way that the Lord could just rest.
He had to create for the two He loved best
a place of perfection, where humans could live.
A garden called Eden. The best He could give.
So He took the woman and man by the hand
leading them into this beautiful land.
"See the four rivers, the Tigris and Pishon,"
He told them, "and there's the Euphrates and Gihon.
Throughout the whole garden the trees bear good fruit.
But one is not yours. At this be astute.
The tree bearing knowledge of good and of evil
will bring upon both of you chaos, upheaval,
and all of the terrors of which you know naught
so know that if either of you two are caught
with that fruit, then surely the both of you die."
They wanted for nothing, for all was supplied,
so they lived a life that you've never known,
one of pure beauty that they knew alone.
But it wasn't to last. Just ask the asp,
for that slithering serpent would get the last laugh.
In his split-tongue technique, he quickly deceived
the humans. When she was alone, he found Eve.
"Just take one bite," he told her that night.
"God knows keeping knowledge from you isn't right.
He's afraid once you eat it, you'll have all His might
and you will then see what He's kept out of sight."
So she plucked down the fruit which looked quite delicious
(She didn't realize the snake was malicious).
She took it to Adam. They each took a bite,
and then their eyes opened to terror and fright,
and shame, and jealousy, anger and lust.

That moment they knew they had broken God's trust.
And when He came calling, they hid for they feared
God would kill both of them if they appeared.
"What have you done?!"
In fear they confessed.
And God became angry, for those He had blessed
above all the others had just disobeyed
the single, unbreakable rule He had made.
"Cursed is the snake, who tricked you and lied.
If it were your actions, you both should have died.
But as you were foolish, a worse fate I give.
Banishment! Now and as long as you live.
Never will your kind view Eden again.
All are shut out for your cognizant sin.
Man, you shall toil and work in the earth.
And woman, your pain will come giving birth.
You're banished! Get out! All three of you go!"
Then God set a guard at the Tree of Life so
we'd not be let in, but always we'd know
that this was how woman and man fell so low.

Genesis 4 - 5

Adam and Eve had sons, Cain and Abel,
thousands of years 'fore the babe in the stable.
Though they had been banished for what they had done,
the Lord God was pleased with both of their sons.
But humans seek suffering, as they seek joy.
In jealousy Cain went out to destroy
his own flesh and blood. And thus he slew Abel,
for Abel brought more to their family table.
But when God sought Abel, he cried out to Cain,
"Where is your brother?"
"I just work the grain.
And he works the flocks. Must I be his keeper?"
But God knew Cain's anger and sin ran much deeper.
"What have you done? Listen! The sound!
Your brother's blood cries out to Me from the ground!
Again, banishment!"

Cain cried in despair,
"O Lord, Your punishment's too much to bear."
"You'll flee east of Eden, and settle in Nod
And no one shall harm you, for am I not God?
But always you'll wander, always you'll stray,
for this is a sin which you cannot repay."
So Cain was cast out, but his bloodline continued
for Cain's many wives also went into
the wilderness with him. But Adam and Eve
knew Cain would not see their new son conceived.
And thus was born Seth, and more generations.
Among this great line were the leaders of nations.
But God was displeased for all their faith wavered,
except for one, Noah, in whom God found favor.

Genesis 6:1 - 9:17

So God went to Noah, and said, "Build an ark,
upon which your family and you shall embark
on a journey to save all that I have made
that's not turned against Me, for you have not strayed.
Take two of each animal, female and male,
that they may survive, for it's man that has failed.
So take every fruit and each stalk of grain,
for soon, Noah, I will be bringing the rain."
So Noah worked hard to build what he needed
for he knew the word of the Lord should be heeded.
He gathered the beasts and he brought them on board,
just as the clouds began to pour forth.
For forty straight days and forty straight nights,
the flood covered everything in Noah's sight.
The fields and the mountains all disappeared.
The power of God over man was made clear.
And all was destroyed as God made his mark,
except those who sat in the dark of the ark.
And when the rain stopped, the flood still remained.
They floated one hundred and fifty more days.
Then Noah sent forth a dove and a raven,
hoping that God would remember to save them.

The message was clear, though God didn't speak,
an olive branch held in the dove's tiny beak.
"The waters recede!" Noah called to his kin,
and soon they were all out on dry land again.
They bowed down and worshipped the God that they loved;
their Lord who had watched over them from above.
"Noah, as I said to Adam and Eve,
be fruitful and multiply. Man must believe!
I now make a promise to all of your blood,
never again shall I use the flood
to wipe out mankind and each living thing;
the beasts, and the birds, and all your offspring.
When you see a rainbow, that symbol shall be
a reminder of this promise I make with thee."

Genesis 9:18 - 11:32

Of Noah's three sons, two would be blessed,
and the third would be cursed as the scourge of the rest.
From Ham would come Canaan, the bane of the Jews,
as well as Assyria, Babylon too.
So as the descendants of Noah increased,
all spoke the same tongue, as mankind spread east.
Though everyone knew of the things God had spoken,
the men muttered angrily, "Our God is broken!
Why worship Him? Can He not see our power?
We're greater than Him. Come, let's build a tower
and show Him that He should be worshipping us."
But God saw their plan, and was filled with disgust.
"Man never changes, so I must change him."
So he twisted their tongues and confused all of them.
And he scattered mankind, confounding the rabble
and that's why it's called the Tower of Babel.

Genesis 12

The Lord gave His people long lives, but they praised
many false idols. But when the Lord gazed
at all of the people, He found in one man

a faith and a will to do as God planned.
"Abram," God said, "Leave your people and go,
to a land far away, to a place I will show.
I'll curse all who curse you and bless those who bless you.
'The father of many' is how they'll address you."
So Abram arose, took his nephew and wife,
and those three set out for a new, unknown life.
In Canaan, the land that the Lord spoke about,
Abram was shocked to find severe drought.
The people were suffering. Did God intend
that they suffer too? For He didn't amend
His message, so Abram said to his wife,
"We'll leave, but return when this place regains life."
Sarai, his wife, agreed, as did Lot,
the nephew of Abram. They packed what they'd brought
to wait out the famine, until it had passed,
then they'd make Canaan their real home at last.
Until then, to Egypt - but Abram was scared.
He knew what could happen to them over there.
For Sarai had beauty, which caused him to fear,
so he said to his wife, "While we're staying here,
say you're my sister," he said, "not my wife.
For if you do not, I'll be put to the knife.
But if you're my sister, they must let me live,
and unto us treasures the Pharaoh will give."
So when they arrived, Sarai obeyed
and the Pharaoh took her as a concubine maid.
In taking her, though, he paid Abram well.
But God did not like this, so on Pharaoh fell
diseases and plagues. Ten times Sarai's pain
was inflicted on Pharoah while she remained
with him in his house. But Pharaoh found out.
He yelled, "Abram, what is this lie all about?!
You have deceived me and brought this disaster,
delivered from Him, the God you call Master.
Here! Take your wife, and all that you've gained!
But before the night falls, you must leave my domain!"

Genesis 13

And so they left Egypt, as Pharaoh had told,
Abram much richer with silver and gold.
Lot had gained flocks, and his wealth had grown.
He too had been honored by Egypt's great throne.
When they reached Bethel, in Canaan again,
Abram said, "Lot, we have so many men!
It's hard for us both to live so close together.
If we split the land, we both will live better.
Would you have the east, or would you take the west?
I want you to have the one you like best."
Lot looked around, and the east with its towns
seemed far more attractive than just empty ground.
"I'll take the east, Uncle."
"Good! It is settled.
I will stay here, as I'm happy in Bethel."
Lot thought that he'd made a far better deal,
with his land near Sodom, but this he concealed.
When Lot had departed, the Lord came to say,
"Abram, now look out in every way.
To the north and the south, to the east and the west,
it all is for you, and all of it's blessed.
To you and your offspring, the many to come,
so numerous they can't be counted, My son.
This is their home. Let none take away
that which I've given to you on this day."

Genesis 14

After this time, a battle was fought
during which four kings together took Lot
as a captive, and when Abram heard, he made haste,
pursuing them, beating them, and laying waste
to their forces. He rescued his nephew and found
the treasures the kings stole from all of the towns
they had conquered. And as they returned from this trek,
they encountered a king named Melchizedek.
A king and a priest, he brought wine and bread

so Abram and all of his men could be fed.
And there unto Abram, in front of his men,
Melchizedek gave this rare blessing to him.
"Blessed be Abram by our God Most High,
Creator of Earth, and all in the sky.
And blessed is He who delivered your foes,
and kept you from all of your enemy's blows."
Abram gave one-tenth of all he'd recovered
unto this priest-king, for Abram discovered
that God had been watching and caring for him
as he'd gone to battle with hundreds of men.
"The rest of the treasure, I give back completely,
for I'll have no man saying, even discreetly,
'I made Abram rich,' which God would abhor.
Give it to those men who helped me in war.
God is the One who has given me wealth,
my flocks and my servants, my family and health.
It's Him that I worship, for my God is One."
So it was written, and so it was done.

Genesis 15 - 16

The Lord in a vision to Abram declared,
"Good faithful servant, do not be scared,
for I am your shield and your great reward."
"I know," Abram said, "but hear me, O Lord.
Sarai and I do not yet have an heir,
and now my wife has become too old to bear
any children."
"My son, your offspring will be
as numerous as all the stars that you see.
But lo! They will suffer, enslaved and mistreated.
Vain and conceited, they will be defeated.
Hauled off by your foes, long after you die,
but always they will be watched over by I.
And when they are ready, they will be redeemed.
For the one person whom no one had dreamed
will come to their rescue. As I made the flood,
each one of those people will be of your blood."

Now, Abram believed, but Sarai did not.
She said, "This maidservant whom we have bought
will give you a child. So take her." But when
Hagar conceived, she was filled up with sin.
She looked down on Sarai. The servant, now bold,
boasted, "My mistress' womb must be cold."
Sarai was angry and had her dismissed,
but an angel found Hagar and told her, "Desist
from abusing your mistress. You must return
and, Hagar, don't fear, for you won't be spurned.
Get up and go to your mistress and master."
With these next words, homeward he cast her.
"You shall have many descendents who come
from this son who will stand against everyone.
The Lord pitied you as you wept at this well.
Since God heard your cry, call your son Ishmael."

Genesis 17:1 – 18:15

But do not believe that this is the son
that God promised Abram, for he was just one.
Abram and Sarai did not realize
that God was to bring them another surprise.
"Abram," God said, and Abram prostrated
as God, the Almighty Creator then stated,
"You are now 'Abraham,' father of nations,
and you'll be remembered for all generations.
Your wife shall be 'Sarah' and bear you a son.
Abraham laughed, "You're just making fun.
For Sarah is ninety! She is too old."
Abraham could not believe what was told.
"You'll call him Isaac, for 'My servant laughs,'
and through him I promise your bloodline will pass.
As covenant to everything I've foretold,
you'll circumcise all of your men, young and old.
You'll pass this act down, through all of your kin,
as a clear outward sign that you reject sin
and will follow Me always."
And so he obeyed,

and all of them were circumcised on that day.
Not too much later, God came to see
Abraham, taking the shape as if three
separate men traveling together, and when
Abraham saw them, he told them, "Come in."
Then one of them said to him, "Surely next year
you'll have a new son." He spoke loud and clear.
Sarah, who lurked, at that had to smirk
for she was too old for childbearing work.
But when she came in, the Man asked her, "Why
did you laugh at My words?" And so Sarah lied.
"Sir, I did not."
But the Man, with an odd
look said, "You did." And she knew it was God.

Genesis 18:16 - 19:29

When the Lord, who was Three, then got up to leave
He said to Abraham, "Lo, but I grieve,
for Gomorrah and Sodom sin so indiscreetly
that I must destroy both these cities completely."
"But Lord! You are merciful," Abraham said,
"Won't there be those who are faithful left dead?
If there were fifty, would You show them grace?"
"If there were fifty, I'd save the whole place."
"What if there were forty, would You show them grace?"
"If there were forty, I'd save the whole place."
"What if there were thirty, would You show them grace?"
"If there were thirty, I'd save the whole place."
"What if there were twenty, would You show them grace?"
"If there were twenty, I'd save the whole place."
"What if there were ten, would You show them grace?"
"Yes! For the ten, I'd save the whole place.
But you try My patience, and I have been just.
Find Me your ten, or I turn them to dust!"
That evening God's angels went to Sodom's gate,
and there they found Lot, and because it was late,
he invited them all to his home, but they said,
"Thank you, but we will sleep outside instead."

"No!" Lot insisted, and thus he persisted,
for he knew the men of Sodom were twisted.
They would attack and rape any stranger,
and men such as these were in perilous danger.
So they went with him, but word quickly spread
and soon Sodom's men were at Lot's door and said,
"Send out your strangers, we'll rape them and bind them."
The angels used powers to stop them and blind them,
and so they warned Lot, "We're destroying this place,
for they have all turned from the Lord's holy face.
Gather your family before we attack.
Whatever may happen, never look back."
So they fled for safety, and when they were past
the city walls, into the country a blast
rang out as the angels began their assault,
but Lot's wife looked back and turned into salt.
Then the next morning when they looked around,
nothing but smoke remained of the town.

Genesis 19:30 – 19:38

Thus Lot and both of his daughters were saved,
They fled to the mountains and lived in a cave.
Because they were far from all others there were
no men for the girls, and so they conferred.
"Father is old. Let's give him some wine,
that we may lay with him so our family line
continues." And thus they settled their plot.
So they got him drunk and lay down with Lot.
And they became pregnant, both from their father,
and thus out of incest was born to each daughter
a son, and from them two lines born anew:
the Moabites and the Ammonites too.

Genesis 20

Now Abraham moved to the Negev, and when
he was asked about Sarah, he lied once again.
He said to the king, Abimelech, "She

is my sister."
The king lusted for her. When he
took her to his house, God came in a dream
"Abimelech, hear now that Sarah's unclean.
She's married and if you dare touch her, you'll die."
Abimelech cried out, "Tell me God, why?
I have not touched her. I'm innocent! Please!"
"Release her right now and I'll be appeased."
Abimelech went to find Abraham and
he asked, "What is your insidious plan?
Sarah's your wife, so why did you not
tell me this thing?!"
"In your land I thought
that we would be safer by making this claim."
"Take back your wife! Release me from blame.
Take some of my wealth," Abimelech said,
"Because of your lie, I could have been dead.
Go! Live in peace, anywhere in my land.
Now I've fulfilled all of your God's command."

Genesis 21 - 22

So Sarah returned to her husband and bore
a son they named Isaac, just as God swore.
On the eighth day, Isaac was circumcised
so he would be blessed in the Lord's holy eyes.
When Isaac was older, they had a great feast
where Ishmael mocked him, and without the least
hesitation Hagar and he were cast out
of the camp by Sarah to wander about.
Abraham worried, but God assured him
that He would take care of and look after them
"For though it is Isaac that you'll be blessed through,
the offspring of Ishmael will be great too."
With Ishmael gone, and Hagar as well
that left only Isaac to live and to dwell
and Abraham loved him with all of his heart.
But in the Lord's plan, each man plays his part.
One day God said to him, "Come Abraham!"

Abraham called back at once, "Here I am!"
God said, "Take Isaac, your son whom you love,
up and into the mountains above.
Sacrifice him as an offering there
to Me as your Lord in a true, sovereign prayer."
Although it destroyed him and tore him apart,
Abraham held the Lord first in his heart.
Even though it was against his desire,
he bound Isaac up and then built a fire.
Just as he took the knife to his son,
the angel of God said, "Stop, loyal one!
Now I know that you love Me most of all.
Let the boy go. May no ill befall
either of you. Go take up a ram,
and sacrifice it instead, Abraham."

Genesis 23 - 24

When at last Sarah died, Abraham grieved,
for she had believed, and then had conceived
a child and heir, so he bought the land
where she might be buried by her husband's hand.
Once done, he had only one goal in life -
to find his son Isaac a suitable wife.
So he took a servant and said to him, "Come!
And swear you will bring him a woman who's from
our land, and not this one! Don't bring Canaanites,
nor Moabites, Hittites, and no Ammonites."
His servant agreed and offered his hand,
and then he set off for Abraham's land.
The servant arrived and sat down to rest,
and prayed, "God help me succeed in my quest.
Send me a sign. Let the first woman who
offers to give me a drink be from You."
Before he had even finished his prayer,
a girl was approaching him who was both fair
and faithful. She said, "Sir, let me fetch you
a drink for your thirst and for your camels too."
The servant jumped up with the greatest elation,

and said, "Tell me, girl, without hesitation,
your name and if there would be space in the tent
of your father tonight? To him I was sent."
"My name is Rebekah," she said to the slave
and at this the servant then bowed down and gave
her bracelets and rings, all gifts made of gold.
And so she went back to her father and told
of all that had happened, and they fetched the man.
He said, "She's been chosen for my master's hand."
"Wait," they said, "Let her remain ten more days."
"Do not detain me! The Lord has his ways.
She has been chosen. Go ask her so."
"Will you go with this man?" they asked.
"I will go."
And so the men blessed her, and sent her to be
Isaac's new bride, as she had agreed.

Genesis 25

When Abraham died as a very old man,
Isaac and Ishmael went to the land
where Sarah was buried, and buried him there
next to his wife with the greatest of care.
Now Ishmael's sons created much strife
as God had foretold. But when Isaac's wife
felt life within her a struggle began,
for two hearts were beating.
"I don't understand.
What's happening in me?" she cried.
The Lord stated,
"Here is your answer, and know it is fated.
Two nations are in you, and they will be torn.
Your youngest son will come to rule your firstborn."
First Esau was birthed, then Jacob his brother.
Jacob was favored much more by their mother.
Esau was reckless while Jacob was meek,
but do not mistake that as him being weak.
One day when Esau came in from a hunt
famished so greatly he let out a grunt,

"Give me some stew, so I do not die."
"First sell me your birthright, then stew I'll supply.
Swear it."
"My birthright is yours! Give me bread!"
And Jacob remembered what Esau had said.
Although for the moment, the food tasted good,
the youngest gained power, as God said he would.

Genesis 26

Just like his father, Isaac was scared,
for his wife, Rebekah, was often declared
so beautiful, he thought that someone might try
to kill him for her, so he told the same lie.
"She is my sister," he'd say, as his father
had said in his time, so he'd not be bothered.
Abimelech found out his lie, and proclaimed,
"Isaac, you've lied! You should feel ashamed.
No man shall touch this woman, but you
may no longer live here. It is not true
that she is your sister. Go! Leave our land."
So he took his flocks and all his field hands.
He moved to Gerar, then Abimelech came
and said, "You are blessed. We both want the same
peace in our lives, so let us not fight
for God is with you and so is His might."
A treaty was settled, and all were at peace.
Isaac then watched as his great wealth increased.
He knew that the Lord had answered each prayer,
and all that remained was choosing his heir.

Genesis 27:1 - 28:9

When Isaac was old and his vision had failed,
he said, "Esau, come. Before I've exhaled
the last breath God gave me, I want you to be
blessed by my blessing; blessed here by me.
Go out and hunt, and make me a meal
of wild game meats that often appeal

to my appetite, then I will offer my blessing
to you, son, my oldest, the one I'm addressing."
Rebekah heard this and found Jacob quickly.
"Hurry, your father is sounding quite sickly.
Get me some goat meat that I can prepare
so you'll be the son who is blessed by his prayer."
But Jacob said, "Esau is covered in hair.
I am smooth-skinned. If father's aware
of the trick we are playing, I might be caught.
Then I will be cursed, not blessed as we've sought."
Rebekah was sly, so she took the goat skin
and made a coarse beard which would disguise him.
When Jacob took Isaac the meat she'd prepared,
he wore Esau's clothes, and Isaac declared,
"Who's that?"
"It's me, father. Esau, your son.
I've done as you told me. Now sit and eat some."
"My, that was fast, but you do not sound
like Esau, but Jacob. If you're to be crowned,
come closer, my son." And as Jacob neared,
Isaac believed as he felt the fake beard.
"Kiss me my son, if you're the firstborn."
And when Jacob did, Isaac smelled what he'd worn.
"Ah! That's my son who smells of the field.
Come here, my boy." And so Jacob kneeled.
"May Heaven and Earth always bless you divine,
with the best of the grain and the best of the vine.
Lord over your brothers and over all nations,
and may you be blessed in all declarations!"
When it was over and Jacob was gone
Esau came in with a newly-killed fawn.
"Father, I'm here with the game you like best."
"Then who," Isaac asked, "is the man I just blessed?"
"No! You've been tricked! Please, father, bless me!"
"Your brother!" cried Isaac. "Son, I couldn't see.
He came and he fooled me, and he took your blessing.
I'm so sorry, Esau, but Jacob's possessing
all of the things that I would have bestowed
upon you. Now, son, you must bear the load.

You'll serve your brother, just as I've spoken,
but when you grow restless, that yoke will be broken."
So Jacob gained Esau's birthright and blessing,
to which Esau lost all right or redressing.
Now Esau was angry at his younger brother.
He wanted to kill Jacob, but when their mother
heard of the plan, she set up her own
that could kill two birds with one single stone.
She told Isaac, "Hittites fill me with disgust.
Not one of their women is worthy of trust.
If Jacob took one and made her his wife,
I think I'd be better off taking my life."
"Hmm, this is true," her husband replied.
"He needs a wife who is more dignified.
Let's send him back to your father who'll find
a woman of our race, for that's the right kind."
And so it was settled and Jacob was sent.
But when Esau heard about where Jacob went,
he was angry and then in a moment of spite
he went out to marry a Hittite that night.

Genesis 28:10 - 31:55

During his trip, Jacob slept on a stone
and as he lay dreaming, a vision was shone.
A ladder reached up into Heaven from where
he stood on the Earth, and the angels were there.
And God spoke to Jacob, "The land where you sleep
is blessed and your offspring will have it to keep."
When Jacob awoke, he said, "In this place
I have known God, and I saw the Lord's face."
God was with him as he went to find
a wife who was beautiful, gentle, and kind.
And when he arrived in the land of his father
he soon saw his uncle's most beautiful daughter.
Her name was Rachel, and she took him in
to see Uncle Laban and all of his kin.
"Work here!" said Laban. "Just name your fee."
"Rachel," said Jacob.

"To that I'll agree.
Work seven years and she'll be your bride,
to take care of you and stay by your side."
Seven years later, Jacob said, "Time
has passed and now you must give me what's mine."
So they had a feast, but that night instead,
Laban sent Leah into Jacob's bed.
Jacob awoke in a rage and he went
to Laban and yelled at him, "Why have you sent
Rachel's sister to me? You lied and you cheated.
With all of my service, why am I mistreated?"
But Laban said, "Jacob, you don't understand.
The firstborn must marry the first willing man.
Here's what I'll do to fix the mistake.
Spend this week with Leah, then next week we'll make
Rachel your wife. But then in exchange,
I ask only one thing, which isn't so strange.
Seven more years of service. Do we
have a deal?"
"I need Rachel. We are agreed."
So Jacob complied, for he loved Rachel more,
but Leah was fertile and four boys she bore.
First Reuben, then Simeon, Levi, and Judah.
And Rachel had none, so she gave Jacob Bilhah,
her maidservant, saying, "Her children will be
born of my servant, but children from me."
Then Bilhah had Dan and Naphtali too.
Then Leah said, "Here is my own maid for you.
Her sons will be mine, so that you love me more
than Rachel, and I can add them to my four."
So Zilpah bore Gad and Asher as well.
Then Leah saw her belly starting to swell,
bearing Issachar, Zebulun; sons for their father,
and then she bore Dinah, Jacob's first daughter.
Then Rachel gave birth to Joseph, a son,
and Jacob told Laban, "My time here is done."
But Laban said, "No, Jacob! Please, you must stay.
Just name your price and now I will pay."
"Fine," Jacob said, "Give the speckled or spotted

from your flocks to me." And so Laban plotted.
Agreeing, he sent all the spotted away,
but Jacob was quiet and did not dismay,
for God was with Jacob, and when the goats mated
the spotted kids were all the best ones created.
Those became Jacob's, and Jacob grew rich,
while Laban was punished for making the switch.
Laban grew angry, and God said, "Go home,
and know I'll be with you. You're never alone."
So Jacob packed up all his family and wealth
and left Laban's home with the greatest of stealth.
Before they left, Rachel stole her father's gods.
When Laban discovered this, he was at odds
with Jacob and chased him and caught him and said,
"Why have you done this?! I heard that you fled.
You took all my flocks, my daughters, and then
you took all the gods that I kept stored within
my household, but your God came and demanded
that I not attack you. Although I'm commanded,
explain yourself!"
"Laban, I thought you would take
your daughters by force, but make no mistake,
your gods are not here. Go on and look.
If you find them, *then* you may call me a crook."
Laban searched, but Rachel hid them beneath her
where he couldn't see. Jacob said, "I'm no cheater.
I worked twenty years, and I never stole.
When you cheated me, the Lord made me whole."
Laban said, "Let us not argue or fight.
Let us make a covenant, making things right.
Let peace be between us, wherever we roam."
So they sealed their pact, and Laban went home.

Genesis 32 - 33

Jacob was headed back home when he said,
"Last I knew, Esau still wanted me dead."
So he sent a messenger well in advance
to find out if Esau perhaps changed his stance.

The messenger came back, and Jacob was told,
"Esau approaches with four hundred fold!
His army is massive!"
"O Lord, hear my prayer.
You said to return. Though I'm almost there
Would my brother kill me? I have but You
to protect me and mine. I trust You are true."
And then in his cunning, he gathered up gifts
and sent them in waves in the hope that they'd lift
his brother's hostilities; praying he'd spare
his life and his family from death and despair.
Jacob sent all 'cross the stream, but he stayed
in camp to await the upcoming day.
That night when Jacob thought he was alone
a man appeared who was not one of his own.
He wrestled with Jacob. The furious fight
lasted throughout the entire night.
He threw Jacob's hip out, but still couldn't win.
The Man said, "Release Me! This battle must end."
"Not till You bless me."
"Then tell Me your name."
"I'm Jacob."
"No longer! For now I proclaim
you're Israel. Although you're now walking lame,
you struggled with God, and you overcame."
"What's Your name?" Israel called out at once.
"Why ask *My* name?" the Man said in response,
then blessed him, and Israel named the place there
for he'd seen the Lord's face, and he had been spared.
The next day as Israel limped down the road,
weakened from battle and visibly slowed,
he saw Esau coming, so Israel braced
but then was surprised when Esau embraced
and hugged him and cried in the arms of his brother,
glad that they'd once again seen one another.
"Brother," said Esau, "why have you sent
these gifts out before you and into my tent?"
"To find favor," Israel quickly replied.
"I want for nothing. Just you by my side.

I've missed you, dear Jacob. I'm glad you've come back.
It's been twenty years, if I have kept track.
But who are these women and children I see?"
"That, my dear brother, is my family.
God has been good to me, and so I sought
to send you a bit of the greatness God brought.
Please keep the gifts."
"Very well, let us go."
"You go ahead. I have many in tow."
So Esau set off, but Israel went
to a city in Canaan and there pitched his tent
and erected an altar to God who had blessed
his journey back home, where he could then rest.

Genesis 34

Now Dinah, the daughter of Israel, was
a beautiful woman, and Shechem because
he was a prince and a powerful man
raped her. Before a great battle began,
he confessed that he loved her and wanted his father
to talk Israel into giving his daughter
to be Shechem's wife. So the Hivite king went
to talk with her family in Israel's tent.
He said, "My son loves her, despite what he did,
which we're all aware, is strictly forbid.
But give her to us, and we'll give to you
our women and land. You can marry ours too.
Just name your price."
Then one of the boys
said, "Why should we keep what Shechem enjoys?
But you are unclean in God's holy eyes,
all of your men must be circumcised."
"Yes," said another, "our sister may wed
only a circumcised man."
And one said,
"But all of your men must do this or we
must fight for her honor. Will you agree?"
"Yes, that is fair," the Hivite replied.

But he did not know that her brothers had lied.
When all of the Hivites were cut as required,
and lying in pain as the boys had desired,
they took up their swords and went into town
and killed each and every man that they found.
No Hivite could fight, like lambs to the slaughter.
And Israel said, "What you've done for my daughter
could put us at risk in this alien land."
But one of the boys just put up his hand.
"Our sister's no whore! Would you treat her as such?
It's our right to kill them, so we did as much."

Genesis 35 - 36

God came to Israel and said, "Go to Bethel.
Build me an altar, and that's where you'll settle."
And so they lived there for a while but then
they knew that they would have to move once again.
Now Rachel was pregnant again with a son,
but this was to be her very last one,
for when he was born, to give him his life
she died, and Israel mourned for his wife.
So Benjamin was the last of twelve sons.
And they all returned to where he'd begun.
Back to his father, Isaac's household,
though Isaac was now becoming quite old.
When Isaac died, Esau and Israel carried
him out to a site where his body was buried.
Then Esau and Israel took separate lands
so the pastures would meet their flocks' great demands.
The offspring of Esau were many and formed
the base of the Edomite people who swarmed
across the whole country. As God had assigned,
Edom would be against Israel's line.

Genesis 37 - 39

Now Joseph was Israel's favorite son.
His brothers all hated him second to none.

Though favored, he might have escaped so much pain
but he had a talent he could not contain.
For Joseph had dreams that put him above
his brothers, and for it they showed him no love.
"Listen," he said, "to this dream I have had."
They grumbled. His prophecies always were bad.
"In gathering grain, my stalk was the highest..."
"Oh!" they all said, "at least you're not biased!"
"No, brothers! I have no cause to malign.
It's just that your stalks all bowed down to mine."
"You plan to reign over us?! Govern and rule us?
We hate all your dreaming! You cannot fool us."
They wouldn't hear, but the dreams didn't cease,
so he went to his father and said, "Father, peace!
I've had a dream where the moon and the sun
and eleven stars bowed to me all as one."
"What is this talk about?" Israel yelled.
"Suddenly all of us will feel compelled
to bow down before you? Your mother and I?
And I can't imagine your brothers' reply!
Speak not again about your place above us.
Instead be a good son, respect us and love us."
Though Israel kept Joseph's words in his mind,
his brothers were all feeling far more unkind.
One day as the brothers were shepherding, they
saw Joseph approaching and said, "Let's betray
our brother and kill him!"
"No," Reuben said.
"Throw him in this cistern and leave him for dead,
but let us not murder." And so they did not,
but they knew their actions would soon get them caught.
Just then, as they stood around arguing there,
a caravan came by and Judah declared,
"Let's sell him and profit." So Joseph was sold
and they covered his robe in goat's blood and told
their father he'd died. How Israel mourned!
He loved Joseph more than he loved his firstborn.
Meanwhile Joseph was sold to a man
in Egypt who worked in the Pharaoh's command;

not dead, but a slave by his own brothers' schemes,
with nothing but faith, and the signs in his dreams.
(Now Judah, who sold Joseph off as a slave,
showed us exactly how not to behave
when he slept with his daughter-in-law in a veil,
whom he thought was a prostitute. Although that tale's
not really a story for here and for now,
it probably ought to be recognized how
different our Joseph was from the rest
of his brothers, and how he was specially blessed.)
In Egypt, Potiphar, Joseph's new master
found that with Joseph, his wealth could grow faster.
And Potiphar's wife noticed his power
and said, "Come and bed me at this very hour."
"My master has put me in charge of his house,
to govern it all, except for his spouse.
To betray him is sin. Even though you insisted,
I won't!"
But Potiphar's wife still persisted.
"No," Joseph said, as she pulled off his cloak.
He fled, but she went to her husband and spoke,
"Look at this Jew! He has come to defile
myself and our house in the most lurid style.
He came to my bed to sleep with me, and
when I screamed he dropped his cloak and then ran."
So Potiphar's anger burned strong and deep.
He took Joseph down to the prison guard's keep.
But God was with Joseph, and soon he again
was serving a master, the warden, his friend.

Genesis 40

While Joseph was jailed, still serving his time,
a baker and man who served Pharaoh wine
were both thrown in jail for offending their master,
though it was debated what caused such disaster.
Now Joseph attended to each of the men,
and after some time they each asked him, "Friend,
we both had a dream, but who'll comprehend

the dreams that we've had and what they portend."
"Tell me your dreams," Joseph said with a nod,
"Interpretations belong but to God."
The cupbearer said, "In my vision there grew
a vine with three branches and from them I drew
wine from the grapes which I poured in a cup
and offered to Pharaoh, which he then drank up."
"Ah," answered Joseph, "In three days you'll be
restored to your job by the king and made free.
That is good fortune. Remember me when
you're free. Help me leave this cell that I'm in."
When the baker heard this, he said with elation,
"Joseph, give me your interpretation.
In my dream I carried three loaves on my head
in a basket and all of the birds ate the bread."
"Ah," answered Joseph, "In three days you'll be
killed by the Pharaoh and hanged from a tree."
"What?! That's not good. Why is my fortune bad?"
"I'm sorry," said Joseph.
Then just as he had
foretold, the cupbearer was reinstated
and the baker was hanged as Joseph dictated.

Genesis 41

Joseph's predictions were quickly forgot.
For two more long years he was left there to rot.
But then Pharaoh dreamt the strangest of dreams
and no one could tell him what his dream might mean.
The cupbearer said, "My king, when you sent
me to prison I met one who knew what dreams meant."
So Pharaoh called Joseph and said, "You must tell
what my dream means since you interpret so well.
Seven fat cows came out of the Nile
and ate from the reeds, then after awhile
seven thin cows, all ugly and lean
came forth from the river. That's what I've seen.
But wait! There's another dream to explain.
For I saw a stalk with seven large grains

healthy and full, but seven more sprouts
burst forth as if scorched from the wind or from drought."
"Ah," answered Joseph, "they're one and the same.
God has revealed to Pharaoh his aim.
Seven good years of abundance come first,
then seven years follow of famine and thirst."
"God is with you," the Pharaoh discerned,
"and hearing this news I am greatly concerned.
In this land you'll be second only to me,
and through this rough time, you will oversee
the care of our people."
So they set aside
oceans of grain, enough to provide
for Egypt's survival. Pharaoh decreed
"Joseph has saved us. I look around me.
Of all of the countries, Egypt alone
has food to feed each mouth in every man's home."
And so foreign countries came and they bought
their grain all from Egypt, for they all had naught.

Genesis 42 - 43:14

Now Jacob learned Egypt had grain they would sell
so he told his sons, "It would be very well
for you to go buy some grain lest we die."
So all but young Benjamin bid him good-bye.
When they arrived there, Joseph saw them,
but none of his brothers could recognize him.
"Where are you from?" he asked them and they
said, "Canaan. We've come from quite far away."
"You're not! You are spies!" Joseph proclaimed.
"No, we're all brothers. Our father's the same.
At home the youngest of us still remains."
"I still don't believe you, so you'll get no grain.
Until he arrives here, let them be jailed.
Spies in this land should all be impaled."
"We're being punished for selling away
our brother. Our sins are returning today."
Then Joseph told them, "If you will retrieve

your brother then I'd be convinced to believe
your story. Leave one of your number with me.
And take enough grain for your whole family."
So Simeon had to remain in the jail
and soon after they had completed the sale
the brothers went back to their father and learned
that secretly they'd had their money returned.
They feared for their lives, for they didn't know
that Joseph arranged all of this. Even though
they had sold him away, he loved them all still
and did not wish any of his brothers ill.
When they told their father all that occurred
he said to them, "Would you have me lose a third
son to this man? Joseph is dead,
and probably they will take Simeon's head.
I'll not lose my youngest! Benjamin stays!"
For Israel was quite set in his ways.
Soon they ran out of their grain, though, and he
said, "Go get more grain for our family."
"Father, we cannot return empty handed.
Benjamin must come, as that man demanded!"
They argued and finally Israel gave.
"But if he dies, know you sent me to my grave."
"If Benjamin dies we all shoulder the blame,
but wasting more time is a meaningless game.
If we had ignored you like men, not like mice,
we could have gone down there and come back now twice."
"Then go," stated Israel. "Take him some gifts
and pay him twice over, that he would forgive
you leaving the last time and not paying him.
And let's pray he doesn't cut you limb from limb."

Genesis 43:15 - 45:28

They went back to Egypt with Benjamin too,
and when Joseph saw them, he knew what to do.
A servant went to them to escort them back
to Joseph's house, but they all feared an attack.
"He'll harm us," they said, "enslave us or worse."

They said to the servant, "Sir, we'd reimburse
your master, for somehow our silver was still
in our bags and we don't want our brother killed."
"Peace," said the servant. "I know these details."
And then he brought Simeon out of the jail.
He took them to Joseph's where they had a feast
with Joseph. Although the man had released
their brother, no one knew why he treated them
so well. They still were suspicious of him.
And as they were leaving, a servant was told
by Joseph, "These men have paid me their gold,
so fill the men's sacks with plenty of food
and inside those sacks make sure you include
their money, but then place my own silver cup
in the youngest one's sack before tying it up.
After they left, Joseph called to his man
and said, "Be off after them, fast as you can.
They've stolen my vessel." The servant rode hard
and caught them, surrounding them with Joseph's guards.
"Who stole the cup that belongs to my master?"
"Why would we steal? That would be a disaster.
Especially after we just paid him double.
We're honest men, sir. We don't want any trouble.
If someone has stolen, let him be cut down."
"So it shall be. If his cup is found
upon one of you, his life will belong
to my master." And it didn't take very long
before it was found in Benjamin's sack.
Although they were frightened, the brothers went back.
And Joseph said, "Thief! Now you'll be my slave."
"No!" Judah cried, "That would mean the grave
for our father. Take me, for I'll bear the blame
of my brother, for you see, his brother was slain.
And our father loves him far greater than us.
I'll serve you well if you'll just free him, plus
I couldn't bear to return to my land
and witness my poor father's mourning firsthand."
At these words Joseph no longer could keep
control of emotion. He started to weep.

"It is I! It is Joseph! Yes, I am your brother.
Benjamin and I both had the same mother."
At these words, none of the brothers could speak.
"Gather around me, and do not be meek.
I am not angry with any of you
for selling me off, for God led me true.
He placed me before you to save many lives.
God showed me before the great famine arrived.
And now here we are, together at last."
And he told them all of the things that had passed.
When Pharaoh heard Joseph's brothers had come,
he said, "Send them back to where they are from
to summon their father, and I'll give the best
of my land to their family, where they may all rest."
So they loaded up riches the Pharaoh was giving,
and went to the home where their father was living.
"Father!" they cried, "Joseph is still alive!"
And Israel called out, "My heart is revived!
Let's go to this land that God has supplied
so I may see Joseph before I'm to die."

Genesis 46 - 47

So Israel set out with all he possessed.
At Beersheba he stopped to pray and to rest,
and God came to him and said, "Israel,
go on to Egypt, for it will be well.
I'll make you a nation in Egypt and then,
I'll be there when Israel comes back again."
Then Israel stood, praising God up on high,
then set off to see his son with his own eyes.
When he got to Goshen in Egypt, he saw
Joseph, embraced him, and fell down in awe.
"Now I may die, for my son's been delivered
back by the Lord, the greatest of givers."
And Joseph said, "Hear me, my brothers and father,
that you may be fruitful and live here unbothered.
Pharaoh knows you are my family and guests,
and know that in Egypt, the people detest

us shepherds, so you will live here unmolested."
And Pharaoh did just what Joseph requested.
He said, "Let them live in the best of my land.
For in troubled times, you have been my right hand."
They settled, but still the famine persisted.
When money was gone the people insisted,
"Still we need food, or we will be dead."
Joseph said, "Bring me your livestock instead."
When that was gone, there still was demand.
The people said, "All we have left is our land."
So Joseph bought that for seed and for grain,
and all worked for Pharaoh, who sought to maintain
his people and asked for one fifth of their crop.
He knew that without them his kingdom would stop
its growth and its glory. And so by their hands,
they bested the famine that killed nearby lands.

Genesis 48 - 50

Several years later, Joseph was told
his father was ill, for he was quite old.
So he rushed to be next to his father's bed,
and Israel raised himself up as he said,
"God told me that He would make from my line
a nation of peoples, and it's nearly time
for me to be gathered to my God to rest.
Bring me your sons, that they may be blessed."
As Jacob, the younger, was blessed over Esau,
Joseph was not pleased a bit by what he saw
when Israel blessed younger Ephraim in form
before Manasseh, who was the firstborn.
"Father that's wrong," he said to correct,
but Israel said, "I know you expect
the oldest to rule, but that won't be so.
The younger will prosper in ways you don't know."
Then he called all of his sons to his tent,
and said, "Hear my words, for you represent
my blood line and heirs, and so you'll be blessed
despite how these words may cause some unrest.

Reuben, the first born, you have brought shame
by defiling my couch; defiling my name.
You'll never be great, nor will you be the man
who is left after me to head up our clan.
Levi and Simeon live by the sword,
and anger is not something to be adored.
Cursed be your fury, but Judah I praise.
Your brothers will bow down to you all your days.
The scepter shall not leave him until the one
to whom it truly belongs finally comes.
Zebulun, next to the sea you shall stay
becoming a haven for ships, so I say.
Issachar, you will submit to your load
and live your whole life in a servant-like mode.
Dan will serve justice. Gad when attacked,
will surely be right at their heels to strike back.
You, Asher, shall have the best to consume.
Naphtali's line shall be a beautiful bloom.
And Joseph, whose blessings have come from our Lord,
has overcome hardships to reap his reward.
Your blessings exceed the sum here times ten.
A man amongst boys, and a prince amongst men.
And Benjamin, youngest of all of my sons,
you devour your prey, and divide what you've won.
These are your blessings, and though I'll soon die
swear so I'll know by your honest reply
that you'll bury me far from these foreigners' land,
where my people are buried, and by your own hand."
They swore this to him as he breathed his last,
and there with his sons, Israel passed.
They mourned for their father, and Egypt mourned too
at Israel's passing, though he was Jew.
Now Joseph lived long, and saw generations
of Israel's offspring become a great nation,
and when it was time for his expiration
to his brothers he made a last declaration.

"God is with us. He will come to our aid
and take us away, like the oath that He made
to Abraham, Isaac, and Israel too.
God is with me, and God is with you."

Exodus 1 - 2:10

The descendants of Israel spilled 'cross the land,
and his generations saw their lines expand.
But soon a new pharaoh sat up on the throne.
To this man a love for the Jews was unknown.
He cast all the Jews into bondage and chains;
forced to be slaves, to toil and strain.
Although they were stricken, they still multiplied
till Pharaoh said, "Let all their newborn sons die!"
The midwives refused, for God hated such
an abominable action, and they knew as much.
So Pharaoh declared, "People of every town!
Throw the Jews' sons in the Nile to drown!"
During this horror, a baby was born
to two Jewish slaves. His mother was torn.
She couldn't hide her son forever, but she
did not want to give him up so easily.
She kept him three months, but knew that much more
and they'd find him, so she thought a plan up before
they could come. She made a basket to float
down the Nile, and stifled the wail in her throat.
The baby's young sister stood at a distance
unsure of how she could provide him assistance,
and lo! Pharaoh's daughter approached by a path
to enter the Nile where she'd take a bath.
But she saw the basket and heard the sad cries
and her heart was moved as she looked in his eyes.
"He must be a Hebrew," she said to her slave.
"Go fetch a Hebrew to nurse and to save
this sweet little boy." The slave went and found

the baby's own mother, relieved he'd not drowned.
But she remained silent, for it was a crime
to allow Hebrew boys to survive at this time.
But the daughter of Pharaoh could do as she pleased
and now at this joy the mother's heart eased.
"Woman," the princess said, "take this boy
and nurse him. I want him to know only joy.
When he is weaned, I'll adopt him to be
my very own son and a prince by decree.
I'll name him Moses," the princess went on,
"for out of the water my baby was drawn."

Exodus 2:11 - 2:25

Many years later, when he was a man,
Moses went out to survey the land.
There he viewed how the Hebrews were used
and saw one poor slave who was being abused.
He killed the Egyptian who beat on the man
and buried him there just under the sand.
The next day he found that many knew he
had murdered a man, and Pharaoh decreed
that Moses would be arrested and killed.
In this way Egyptian law could be fulfilled.
But Moses escaped before he was found
and traveled until he arrived at a town
called Midian, where some girls with their flock
needed some help as they tended their stock.
For helping them, their father said, "Go invite
this young man to join us for dinner tonight."
And not too much later, Moses was married
to one of the daughters and soon that girl carried
a son he named Gershom just as he'd planned,
"For I've been a stranger, and far from my land."
Many years passed and the old pharaoh died
and God heard the wails as the Hebrew slaves cried
and remembered the promise that He had once made,
the promise for which all of Israel prayed.

Exodus 3 - 4:17

While Moses was leading a flock by the mountain
of Sinai, he saw a flame like a fountain
engulfing a bush, but the bush was not burned,
and rather than running away, Moses turned.
As Moses approached, God called out his name.
"Here I am," Moses replied to the flame.
"Take off your sandals on this holy ground.
I am your God." And Moses bowed down.
"Moses, I've heard the cries from the land
of Egypt, the same cities from which you ran.
I know their oppression, and so I've called you
to lead them from bondage in Egypt onto
the promised land."
"Lord, but I am so low.
How can I go stand before the Pharaoh?"
"I will be with you."
"But they won't believe
that You would send someone as lowly as me.
They'll ask who You are."
"I AM THAT I AM!"
the Lord shouted so that it shook the whole land.
"Tell them I AM sent you. I will be there.
And you'll lead them into the land of their prayers.
Go tell My people what you have seen here,
and then tell the Pharaoh that I have appeared.
But he won't believe you in whole or in part,
so I will reach out and will strike at his heart.
In Egypt, I promise, you will not know harm.
When you leave you'll bear such gifts in your arms
that after I've struck them and My voice has thundered,
your freedom will also leave all Egypt plundered."
But Moses protested, "They'll say I'm a liar
and that You did not appear here in a fire."
"What's in your hand?"
"A staff."
"So then take
and throw it down."

Then it turned into a snake.
Moses was frightened, but then the Lord said,
"Grab it."
Though Moses was filled up with dread,
he picked up the snake and it turned to a rod.
"Do this and then they will know I am God.
If not, take some water that comes from the flood
of the Nile and they will see it turn to blood."
"But God," Moses whined, "my speech is so poor.
Send someone else."
"Resist Me no more!
Who makes a mouth? Don't you know that I do?
But I will send Aaron to go with you too.
He'll be the mouthpiece to say what I say.
So now hurry forth and be on your way."

Exodus 4:18 - 7:7

Then Moses and Aaron traveled to see
the Israelites in their captivity
and when they showed all of the Hebrews the signs,
the slaves cried, "God save us from these wicked times."
So after the Israelites all believed,
they went to the Pharaoh and they were received.
"Pharaoh, God states, 'Let My people go.'"
"Who is this God?" Pharaoh said, "I don't know
a thing about Him. Why should I set free
the hundreds of thousands who're working for me?"
"If you do not, plagues will be delivered.
And His wrath will span the whole Nile River."
"Moses, know now that you made it worse
on all of your people. This lie you've rehearsed
and spread through the land will break the men's backs.
I'll work them all harder and show them no slack.
Now they'll make bricks, but we'll give them no straw.
Perhaps you don't realize that I am the law.
The Hebrews will pay for your words with their hands."
And Pharaoh's decree went out 'cross the land.
"What have you done?" the Israelites moaned.

"God has forsaken us. We are disowned!"
And Moses bowed down and cried, "I implore,
God help us all. It's worse than before."
"Though Pharaoh does not know Me, he will bow down.
Before I am through, every Egyptian town
will see all My acts and then they will know
that I am the Lord. Let My people go."

Exodus 7:8 - 7:25

Moses returned, but Pharaoh just laughed
till he saw the serpent come out of the staff,
but then his magicians said, "Sire, it's fake."
And they also turned their staffs into snakes.
But all of their snakes were quickly devoured
by Moses' snake, but Pharaoh just glowered.
He threw Moses and Aaron out as foretold
for God knew the heart of the Pharaoh was cold.
Then God said to Moses, "Go down to the Nile
and tell Pharaoh he has been wicked and vile.
As you strike your staff in the riverbank mud
all of the Nile will turn into blood."
And when Moses did this, the water did change.
But Pharaoh's magicians said, "That's not so strange."
And using some tricks, they did the same thing
and so Moses did not persuade Egypt's king.
But all of the people across the whole land
could not drink a drop and could not understand
why God was against them, and so the blood stayed
in all of the water for seven full days.

Exodus 8

Then God said, "Tell Pharaoh he must understand.
Let My people go or across the whole land
a plague will descend like the darkest of fogs
and you'll be enshrouded by thousands of frogs."
So Moses told Pharaoh, but Pharaoh just scoffed
till frogs filled their houses.

"Moses, call off
this plague. Pray for us, and rid us of these
creatures that plague us just like a disease.
Then I'll free your people."
And so Moses asked
the Lord to stop sending the frogs and it passed.
But once Pharaoh saw it was as it had been,
he hardened his heart to the Hebrews again.
But God said to Moses, "Do not despair,
for My plague of gnats will soon fill the air."
And when Pharaoh's men could not duplicate
this plague they realized that it was too late.
"This is the finger of God," they all cried.
As the Lord's swarm of gnats spread out far and wide.
"Now Moses," God said, "next shall come flies,
and they'll cover the land as he's covered his eyes.
But this will be different, for in Goshen's land
where My people live I will raise up My hand.
They will not be bothered. This is My accord,
so all of My people will know I am Lord."
And when it was so, the Pharaoh cried out,
"Moses, please stop this. I do not doubt
that your God has sent this. Stop it and know
that I will let all of the Hebrew slaves go."
So Moses went out to the Lord and he prayed,
but Pharaoh had lied, so they were betrayed.
For God had made sure that Pharaoh's heart hardened,
so Egypt was punished before they were pardoned.

Exodus 9

"Next," Moses said, "your livestock will die,
but the Hebrew stock will be healthy and spry."
But still Pharaoh stood unwilling to yield
though all of his cattle were dead in the field.
Then came a plague of boils and rot
that no one could see but everyone caught.
For as God told Moses, "Now all will know
that I am the Lord and now you must go.

Tell them the next plague will be one of hail.
Before this new plague all the others will pale,
for this one will be a storm to behold."
And so Moses went, and Pharaoh was told.
Egyptians now paid a terrible price
as God sent a storm of fire and ice,
which pounded the land and destroyed every crop.
And Pharaoh cried, "Moses, you must make it stop!
The ice and the fire are tearing apart
my land. Take your people and you may depart.
But when the storm stopped its pounding outside,
Pharaoh revealed he'd once again lied.

Exodus 10

"Moses," God spoke, "I said from the start
that I would make sure Pharaoh hardened his heart.
I am not done, and my wrath will persist.
Locusts shall come until Pharaoh desists."
Clouds of those pests then ate and enjoyed
anything that the hail hadn't destroyed,
and so there was nothing in Egypt to eat
but still Egypt's punishment was not complete.
Then came a darkness that covered the land
for three days. A man couldn't see his own hand
in front of his face. And when it was done
finally Egypt again saw the sun.
"Moses, the next time you look in my eye,"
said Pharaoh, "will be the day that you die."
"Pharaoh, this plague will not be the end.
But till you request, I'll not come here again."

Exodus 11 - 12

God spoke to Moses and said, "You should know
that after this plague, you will be let go.
Tell all of My people to gather their gold
and silver for they will be free as foretold.
At midnight tonight, I'll go through the land.

Forever the people shall know that My hand
smote the firstborn of all Egypt's sons,
even the Pharaoh's. Then I'll be done.
Now tell all My children to kill a young lamb.
With blood, mark their doorframes so that the I AM
does not take their child. Instead I shall pass
over them so that their lineage lasts.
Tell them to eat their dinner in haste.
Bread without yeast and herbs that will taste
bitter, with meat cooked over the fire,
for quickness is key and what I desire.
They must all be ready to leave right away
for finally they'll have salvation today.
And celebrate this event each single year
so no one forgets what has happened right here."
And while the Hebrews ate dinner that night
God killed each firstborn Egyptian in sight,
and Egypt awoke with a wail and a moan
for there was a dead son in every home.
Pharaoh called Moses and said, "You must leave.
Because of you, now for my own son I grieve.
Go and go now! I gave my decree."
And so all the Hebrews were finally free.

Exodus 13 - 14

The Lord said to Moses, "This is the day
that I made for you, so do as I say.
As I killed the firstborn of Egypt, agree
to consecrate Israel's firstborn to me.
Remember this day that My mighty hand
brought Israel's people out of Egypt's land.
As you leave I want to make sure that you lead
them out and toward the great Sea of Reeds."
They followed the Lord, for He was a spire
of smoke in the day. By night He was fire.
And He said to Moses, "It soon will be clear
that I am the Lord. My day's drawing near.
We'll wander as if we're confused by the sea

while Pharaoh regrets that he set you all free.
Then he will pursue to the Reed Sea and find
My people and there he will see My last sign."
Just as God said, Pharaoh's heart changed
and he said, "I freed them? I must be deranged!
Gather the army! We go in pursuit.
I'll not lose my slaves in this kind of dispute."
And so Pharaoh's army caught up with the pack
of Hebrews who cried out, "We're under attack!
Pharaoh will kill us. Why did you not leave
us in Egypt's hands? How we've been deceived!"
But Moses replied, "There's no reason to fear,
for all of us see that God is right here
in His pillar of smoke, which moved in between
our army and Pharaoh's, who now has no means
to harm us."
And God said, "Take up your staff.
Point at the sea and make a new path."
So Moses said, "Israel know that our God
is greatest of all," as he stretched out his rod.
Lo, the sea parted and cleared a wide berth.
Between walls of water, there was dry earth,
and Moses led all of the Hebrews across
and though they were scared, they suffered no loss.
The pillar of smoke and fire removed
itself from between them, and Pharaoh pursued.
Before they had made it across the dry ground
God loosed the waters, and Egypt was drowned.
When Israel saw what God did for them
they believed in His miracles and worshipped Him.
They had been saved and set free at last
and they saw God's powers were awesome and vast.

Exodus 15 - 16

Although they were free, they now had no home
and they were not used to a life where they'd roam
without anything upon which to feed.
They said, "Back in Egypt we had all we'd need."

God replied, "I'll rain down bread from above;
this manna for breakfast, to show My true love.
And then in the evening I'll give them all quail
for though they are stubborn, My love does not fail.
But they shouldn't keep today's food till the next."
But many ignored this, and so they were vexed
because when they woke their stores had gone bad.
When Moses learned what they had done he was mad.
"Didn't I tell you what God indicated?
At nighttime did you think that God abdicated?
Have you no faith in the Lord who has come?
You should not act as if He's blind and dumb!
Each day the Lord gives, but He can take away.
Stop acting like He isn't real and obey!"
And for forty years, that's how they ate,
because God provided. Because God is great.

Exodus 17 - 20

Still all the Hebrews questioned who guided
them through the wilderness, though God provided.
If they were thirsty, God gave them water.
In war their enemies always were slaughtered.
Although God was with them, still they complained
and fought with each other, so Moses arranged
a group of the men to judge and to stand
for righteousness. This people without a land
complained and grew restless, so God up on high
told Moses when they had all reached Mount Sinai,
"Moses, this mountain is holy, and here
I'll give you the law for all to adhere.
I am the Lord, and all must agree
that they shall have no other gods before Me.
One who makes idols to bow down before
is sinful, for this is a thing I abhor.
And no one shall curse or misuse My name.
It's holy and it lights your path like a flame.
Remember the Sabbath and sanctify it.
Honor your parents for they are a gift.

Murder is sin; the theft of a life.
Adultery is the theft of a wife.
Theft of all kinds is sinful and so
is bearing false witness. This they should know.
One shall not covet what they don't possess.
All of these sins are to be suppressed.
This is the Law that I give unto you.
Now go tell the people that My Law is true."

Exodus 21 - 23

God said to Moses, "What I commanded
is law, but I know that you'll be demanded
to answer more questions than simply these ten
so here's what to do for all other sins.
Set all of your slaves free after six years,
unless that slave says 'I am happier here,
for my master loves me and gave me a wife.'
In that case the man is a servant for life.
A tooth for a tooth and an eye for an eye.
A life for a life. Every murderer dies.
If an injury happens, one must compensate
the injured man whom he put into that state.
And property must be protected as well.
The man who caused damage, shall thus be compelled
to pay for the losses the other sustained,
whether the loss is in livestock or grain.
Socially there are so many devices
that can lead a man or a woman to vices.
Do not worship gods except for the Lord
and do not do that which I'd find untoward.
Seducing young girls or sex with a beast,
harming those who are considered the least,
like orphans or widows or foreigners who
are wandering alien lands just like you.
These are abhorrent to Me, don't you see?
You are My people. The ones I set free.
Don't lie or take bribes, for then you've denied
the justice and mercy that you should provide.

Honor the Sabbath and celebrate Me
each year at your festivals, numbering three.
And I'll send an angel who'll prepare the way
as long as My people obey what I say.
He'll go before you and I'll be with him.
This, Moses, you are to tell all of them.
You will find enemies in this new land,
But I am your staff and always at hand."

Exodus 24 - 27

Then God said, "Bring all of the elders up here."
And when Moses did, they saw God quite clear.
He stood on a pavement of sapphire stone
and they all bowed down as His radiance shone.
When Moses approached, a cloud then came down
and covered the entire sky and the ground.
The people below said once in the cloud
Sinai looked like a fiery shroud.
Forty long nights and forty long days
passed while Moses was inside the haze
and God told him, "Moses, you must make an ark
to carry the tablets upon which I'll mark
the ten great commandments that all must obey."
And Moses responded, "I'll do what You say."
God relayed to them how it should be built
of acacia wood with a fine golden gilt.
"Along with the ark, My people should tackle
a project of building a great tabernacle.
A place for their worship in various lands,
with a place where the ark of the covenant stands."

Exodus 28 - 32

"Bring Aaron, your brother, and all of his sons.
They will be known as the holiest ones.
The priests for the people, so all will recall
that I am the Lord and Creator of all.
Consecrate them, for only they'll stand

in the Holy of Holies with no other man.
At the altar, they'll worship My might and renown.
But now, Moses, go. It's time to go down."
While Moses was inside the fiery cloud,
panic broke out in the Israelite crowd.
"God is not with us," the people all cried,
"and Moses is gone and has probably died.
Aaron, come quick, and make us some gods.
Something to worship. Some sort of façade."
He melted their gold and took up his staff.
"Now we shall bow down to this golden calf!"
As Moses descended, God said to him,
"So quickly they turn! I will burn against them!"
But Moses said, "Lord, if You smite them all now,
think about all the Egyptians and how
they will scoff at Your name and say You're to blame
for killing their people, then doing the same
to all of the ones You brought out of their land.
Show mercy, Lord, and stay Your great hand."
And so God relented, but when Moses saw
them worship the calf in wonder and awe,
he smashed the stone tablets and screamed, "How you turn
against our true God. This calf has to burn!"
And as it was melted, Moses yelled out
"All who are for our Lord and don't doubt,
rally to me and pick up your sword.
Atonement must be meted out for the Lord."
The Levites all stood by Moses' side,
and that afternoon three thousand souls died
for they turned away, but all was atoned
by sword and by arrow, by blood and by bone.

Exodus 33

After this, God told them, "You must leave here
and I won't be with you, for if I were near
your stubborn complaining as you walk about
might lead Me to wiping all Israel out.
But, lo, do not fear. You won't be alone.

I'll send you an angel, so you will be shown
the way to the land I've promised to you,
and know that My presence is in all you do."
Then Moses said, "Do not send me from this place
unless You allow me to look on Your face."
"No man," God stated, "can see Me and live,
but there is another thing that I can give.
I'll pass by and cover your eyes with My hand
and you'll feel My presence right there where you stand.
I will be with you Moses, My friend,
as you lead your people, till you reach your end."

Exodus 34

Then Moses remade the tablets of stone
which both had been broken when they had been thrown
onto the ground when Moses had found
a golden calf to whom the people bowed down.
When Moses came down from Sinai and showed
the new tablets everyone saw his face glowed,
for God's presence shone in every detail,
and so Moses covered his face with a veil.

Exodus 35 - 40

Moses found craftsmen with hands that were skilled
and told them what God had asked them to build.
Once told, they went to create and provide
the Lord's tabernacle as God specified.
The ark and the table, the altar and lamp stand,
the courtyard, the basin for washing the priests' hands,
and all of the garments the priests were to wear
took everyone's help to make and prepare.
And when it was done, Moses approved
and the glory of God appeared, and He moved
over the tent that they had constructed.
The Lord was pleased, for it was as He'd instructed.

Leviticus 1 - 16

God called to Moses and said, "There will be
particular ways to make offerings to me."
He gave them great detail for beast and for grain,
which Moses passed on for the priests to explain.
God's great commandments would keep man from guilt,
but God knew that wasn't how man had been built.
So God laid the ways in which we'd be restored
through offerings people would give to the Lord.
To help all the people, priests were ordained
and in all the laws, those priests were then trained.
Aaron and his sons were chosen to act
as servants of God to keep faith intact.
God told the priests, "Make an off'ring for all
of the sins of the people, and I'll come to call."
In front of the people, God's fire came down
consuming the offering laid on the ground.
The Lord's explanation of what is unclean
was given for clothing and health and cuisine.
To keep people healthy and keep people pure
in their lives and their faith, the law would ensure.

Leviticus 17 - 20

Then God said, "Now listen so you aren't defiled.
No incest, adultery; both these are vile.
Do not pass your children into Molech's fire
lest you be cast into the muck and the mire.
Honor your parents. Honor your God.
I am true. Idols are just a façade.

Leave grain and leave grapes at the edge of your field
so the poor and the alien share in your yield.
Do not eat meat if the blood still remains.
My name is holy. It shan't be profaned.
No lying, no cheating, no stealing. Be holy.
Don't favor the rich; judge fairly and slowly.
Don't steal or defraud or endanger your neighbor.
Love him as yourself. And you shall not labor
when it is the Sabbath. Observe it in kind.
Don't curse the deaf, nor trip up the blind.
Do not prostitute your daughter, for I
despise a cruel parent. Such parents should die.
If you seek divination or sorcerers, know
that you've turned against Me, for they are My foes.
Don't slander or hate your neighbor or brother.
I want My people to love one another.
You were aliens once, in an alien land.
When foreigners come to you, reach out your hand.
My law is complete. In it is salvation.
But death is the punishment for violation.
I've given the ground upon which you trod.
Know that I am Lord, and I am one God."

Leviticus 21 - 27

God said, "Now priests, be holy and hear
the rules that you'll follow, or My wrath you'll fear.
You represent Me to all of the tribes.
You're holy. Be holy as your Lord prescribes!
Don't be unclean, unkempt, or disgrace
yourself in your life or in My holy place.
Marry a virgin, who's one of your own.
No prostitutes, widows, or someone unknown.
Your daughter must not be a prostitute too.
To disgrace herself does the same thing to you.
Aaron and his sons shall all represent
My will and My way, in act and intent.
Keep offerings holy and acceptable to
the rules I have laid out and given to you.

Honor the Sabbath and all of My feasts.
You're people…My people! Do not act like beasts.
To blaspheme My name is to show Me your back.
Stone all the blasphemers! Show them no slack.
But a Day of Atonement shall be held each year.
If sinners repent, their sin shall be cleared."
Then God said, "Be joyful! Be joyful in Me.
Each fiftieth year shall be Jubilee.
Let property go back to its rightful owner.
Let atonement be given to every atoner.
And if you own slaves who are Israelites,
at Jubilee they will be freed. That's their right.
But if you own slaves of foreign descent,
they're yours and shall be, one hundred percent.
Obedience brings an abundance of joy.
If the people obey, then they will enjoy
rain for their crops and peace in their land.
And when they lie down, they'll know I'm at hand.
But if they do not show the faith I desire,
know that they'll see both the plague and the fire.
Your foes shall defeat you. A famine ensues.
Worship Me only, for if you refuse
I'll knock down your high places and I will set
your corpses upon the false idols you kept.
If you are treacherous, no man shall live.
But if you confess, then your Lord shall forgive.
Give unto Me what is Mine and you'll find
that I am a merciful God who is kind.
Though I brought you out of Egypt, I can
send you back in an instant, each tribe and each clan."

Numbers 1 - 9:14

Two years after Moses brought all
of the Israelites out of Egypt, God called,
and said, "Take a census of every man,
who is older than twenty and able to stand
as an army." So men from each tribe were counted,
and they numbered more than six hundred thousand.
And that counted all, except the Levites,
whom God set aside to perform holy rites.
Then each of the tribes was given a banner,
and they were encamped in appropriate manner.
Divided by tribe and family and clan,
Moses laid out an orderly plan.
Then God came to Moses and said, "Know, as I
struck down the firstborn of Egypt to die,
so each firstborn son of the whole Levite tribe,
are now and forever for Me set aside."
And so God laid out what each Levite clan
was to be in charge of, right down to the man.
And He laid out rules, and offerings too,
that were to be followed by all of the Jews.
Then God's tabernacle and altar were made,
where offerings from all the twelve tribes were laid.
Once all the offering rules had been set,
God said to Moses, "Let no one forget,
that I bought them out of their bondage with blood.
I AM that I AM. The God of the Flood.
So let them each year have a Passover feast,
of lamb, bitter herbs, and bread without yeast."

Numbers 9:15 - 12:16

Then God made a cloud come over the tent,
that burned like a fire wherever it went,
and when it moved on, the Israelites
followed that cloud, by day and by night.
Out of the Sinai all Israel roamed;
a borderless nation in search of a home.
The cloud traveled 'round till it found the sand
of the desert-like wilderness known as Paran.
The people grew restless; sick of maintaining
this wandering life. They started complaining,
so God sent out fire for He had grown tired,
and thought to destroy them. But Moses desired
that they not be killed, and so God relented,
But still all the people complained and lamented.
"Moses," they cried, "we were better off slaves,
for Egypt was better than all that God gave
since we have come out. There's nothing to eat!"
"But you have the manna."
"But we demand meat!"
So God sent them quail and they gathered the birds,
finally grateful for what had occurred.
But God was still angry and sent them a plague,
and those who ate quail all went to their grave.
The attack by the Lord, an assault on their diet,
angered the people, and started a riot.
Then Aaron and his wife began to speak out
in ways that cast Moses' honor in doubt.
God became angry, and in a great cloud,
He came to the tent where they worshipped and vowed,
"To most prophets I send visions and dreams.
But Moses alone is faithful, it seems,
and so do not ask why I speak face to face
with My faithful servant inside of this place.
He sees Me clearly. Why do you mock him?"
The Lord's anger burned, and then just to shock them,
He struck Aaron's wife with leprosy so
her skin looked as white as a new fallen snow.

"No, God!" cried Aaron, "Forgive us our sin!"
"Lord," Moses called to Him, "Please heal her skin."
"Cast her out! In a week, she'll be restored,
and welcomed back knowing that I am the Lord."

Numbers 13 - 14

While in the desert, God said, "Explore
the Canaanite lands that I promised before.
A man from each tribe should be sent to see
the land and the people, the fields and the trees."
And so Moses sent them, and forty days passed.
When they returned, all of Israel asked,
"What was it like?"
"The land and the fruits,
were good, but the people were giants and brutes.
The land can't be taken, we'd die if we tried."
"We can though!" cried Caleb.
"But that's suicide!
If we go to war, we'll all end up dead,
with swords through our bellies or spears in our heads."
So all of the people cried out, "O Lord, why
did you take us from Egypt to this place to die?"
They spoke against Moses and Aaron out loud,
and both men prostrated in front of the crowd.
But Caleb and Joshua stood in defense
and said, "God is good! We must go hence.
He'll give us this new land, just as He said!"
But then the crowd wanted all four of them dead.
The glory of God appeared at the altar,
and He asked, "How long will all of you falter?
I should wipe you out!"
"Please no," Moses pleaded,
"if You plague the people, then You'll have conceded
that You couldn't bring us to our promised land."
Because Moses asked, God held back His hand.
"I will forgive them, but all of their fears
will follow them over the next forty years.
Let them all wander, and not see the land

that I would have given and placed in their hand.
Every adult will die in this waste,
'cept Caleb and Joshua, those two will taste
the milk and the honey. Alone they'll be fed."
When Moses told everyone what the Lord said,
they screamed, "We have sinned. Now let us go to
the place that God spoke of, as God said to do."
"You fools!" Moses screamed, "Our God is against
you all, and you'll lose. Please, someone speak sense."
But they would not listen, so they were defeated,
and ran back to Moses once they had retreated.

Numbers 15 - 19

God knew His people would mutter and whine,
so He set forth rules to keep them in line.
Like keeping the Sabbath to honor the Lord,
so that He is praised and is not ignored.
But still they complained of their wandering fate,
and soon many Levites sought to berate
both Moses and Aaron, and question how they
were set above others. So in great dismay,
Moses said, "Levites! Do you not recall
God gave you dominion and charge over all?
You won't be happy until you all see
Aaron and I fall down on our knees.
So be it! Come with us and bow to the Lord.
Then He will draw to Him of His own accord
the one to be high priest, so ready your gifts!"
The three men who led the group stiffened their lips.
And so they went forth, to the Lord's holy place,
and God said, "Why shouldn't I wipe out this race?
They've never been pleased with all that I give!"
"No," shouted Moses, "Let Your people live!"
The Lord spoke to Moses who turned and then said,
"Back away from these three, for they are all dead."
The earth opened up and swallowed those three
along with their tents and their three families.
Then the earth was sealed over, and everyone cried,

"We've sinned once again! Now we're all going to die!"
A fire burst forth and killed all the men
who had stood against Moses and Aaron, and then
When God was done, he told Aaron, "Now go,
fetch staffs from each of the tribes. Then they'll know
that the staff that sprouts forth is the one who will be
high priest of the people and chosen by Me."
Aaron's staff blossomed, so none could oppose
that Aaron was priest, the one the Lord chose.
Then God spoke to Aaron, "You and your sons
are now and forever your Lord's chosen ones."

Numbers 20 - 21

The Israelites moved along to Kadesh,
where the people cried, "There is no water that's fresh
in this place. It will be the death of our race."
So Moses asked God as he fell on his face,
"What shall I do?"
"You'll take up your rod,
and twice strike a rock. They will know I am God,
because at your strike, the water will flow.
They've forgotten what I promised ages ago."
But miracles only inspired the mass
awhile. For after a brief time had passed,
then they would get restless and want to move on,
but soon all their options for moving were gone.
They would ask countries if they could pass through,
and they would be told, "We'll attack if you do!"
The Israelites were constantly spurned
from seeing the country for which they all yearned.
Then God said, "Take Aaron and his son, then climb
up onto Mount Hor, for it's now Aaron's time
to join me. His son will now be high priest."
And all wept when they heard that he was deceased.
Countries warred with them.
"God, be understanding,"
the Hebrews cried. "We will not leave a brick standing."
And so God was with them, as they laid to waste

all the Canaanite towns that they had to face.
Although they knew victory, they were still kept
from the land they were promised, and all of them slept
in these far foreign lands, knowing they'd never view
the land God would let their offspring subdue.

Numbers 22 - 24

Now Balak of Moab saw Israel fight
and beat both the Canaanites and Amorites,
and he was afraid that he'd not defeat
their army, so he sought to be more discreet.
He sent men to Balaam, a prophet, and asked,
"Will you curse these people and do so en masse?
I'll give to you treasures, just tell me your fee."
Balaam said, "I'll ask what God wants of me."
And God came to Balaam and said, "Do not curse
My people, or unto you I will do worse."
So Balaam declined, but Balak persisted,
"You must curse them, Balaam!"
But still he resisted.
God came again, saying, "Go with these men,
but do only what I command, lest you sin."
And so Balaam got on his donkey and went
with Balak's advisors, but with God's consent.
Now as he was riding, the angel of God
appeared on the road where the donkey had trod.
He drew out his sword, and the ass, in retreat,
three times turned away, and three times was beat.
"Stupid beast," Balaam said, whipping the ass,
"Turn back to the road, and do as I ask!"
Balaam was blind to the angel who showed
himself to the donkey and stood in the road.
God touched the donkey, who opened his mouth.
Not a bray, but the speech of a human came out.
"Why have you beaten me three times already?
Am I not your donkey, both sturdy and steady?"
"I beat you," said Balaam, "because you have strayed."
The angel appeared. Then Balaam, afraid,

said, "I couldn't see you."
The angel said, "Heed,
for you should not beat such a good, faithful steed.
He turned from the path in fear as he should.
Know this, that the path that God gives you is good.
Do only what I instruct you to do.
Now go on your way with your anger subdued."
When Balaam arrived, Balak confronted
the prophet and stormed, "Why have I been affronted,
that you would not hurry? Now curse their whole land."
But Balaam said, "I'll do what my God commands."
So Balak took Balaam to look on the Jews
and said, "Curse them now and do not refuse!"
But Balaam said, "They are all blessed by the Lord,
I cannot speak ill of my own accord."
Four other times, Balak asked for a curse,
but each time instead in beautiful verse
a blessing was given to Israel's nation.
So angrily Balak expressed his frustration.
"I asked you to curse them, but five times they're blest.
Leave, Balaam! You've proved an unwelcome guest."
"Can I," said Balaam, "speak one word that goes
against what God says or what the Lord shows?"
So Balaam left after he'd blessed all the Jews
as God had instructed the prophet to do.
And Balak could not set his great fear aside
for now he knew God was on Israel's side.

Numbers 25 - 36

Midian was full of sin and pollution
where they worshiped Baals and performed prostitution.
and God's anger burned against all of the Jews
who joined in these acts, for they had refused
God's love and protection. Thus Moses was told,
"Round up each person who's acted so bold.
They've turned from My face. Destroy every one
to stay My great anger that blots out the sun."
So Moses told each tribe, "Destroy every man

who has turned from the Lord. This is our God's command."
One man had a pagan wife whom he had wed.
This was not allowed, just as God had said.
So the grandson of Aaron took up his spear
and stabbed them both with it, for God had been clear.
And God said, "Because this man's zealous for Me
he will be priest, for this man believes."
Then God said, "Now do a census again,
and count up my people. Count all of the men
who are older than twenty." And when it was done,
they numbered in thousands, six hundred and one.
Now of all this number, just three men remained
of those who had heard the people complain.
Just Joshua, Caleb, and Moses were left,
and God said to Moses, "You're nearing your death."
"Before I am taken," he asked of the Lord,
"assign a new leader who'll lead them toward
the land You have promised."
Then God said, "You'll make
Joshua leader to follow your wake.
But before you die, let My law be known.
The Midianites must be overthrown.
For they brought the Baals, which turned some away
from My light. So they will not see one more day."
Twelve thousand Hebrews went into the fight,
and defeated and killed each Midianite.
They brought the children and women to be
slaves in their houses, but Moses decreed,
"These are the women who brought us the Baals!
Let none of them live. Let all be impaled!
And each boy as well. And each girl who's been
with a man, lest they lead us back into sin."
And so it was done, to keep their faith pure.
Then God said to Moses, "Now you must ensure
when your people go and take up their land
let no man nor idol remain by their hand.

Though you will not go, make sure that they kill
everyone, leave no survivors who will
tempt them away with false gods and cause
a loss of their faith or a break in My laws."

Deuteronomy 1 - 2

In the last month of the fortieth year,
the Lord said to Moses, "The way is now clear.
Take them into the land I'll bestow.
The place that I promised you two score ago."
So Moses proclaimed to the people he led,
"When we were hungry, by God we were fed.
He was with us as a column of fire.
Your love and your worship was our Lord's desire.
But over and over you showed him your back.
We wanted for nothing, but in faith we lack!
That is why we spent forty years here
in the desert, but now we will leave the frontier.
When we reach the land King Sihon possesses,
we'll have the first of our many successes."
They battled with Sihon when they first arrived,
and they left no man nor woman alive.

Deuteronomy 3 - 5

Then they encountered in Bashan King Og,
but God said, "Fear him no more than a dog,
for I shall give him and his army to you
in total, as you and your people move through."
Again no survivors were left in the land,
as kingdoms were toppled by God's mighty hand.
Kings realized if they decided to battle
with Israel, even the flocks and the cattle
were killed. When they reached the great Jordan River,
God said to Moses, "I will not deliver

you with your people on into that place,
for we both remember when you hid your face
from Mine, and I told you that you will not stand
on one single grain of the sand in that land.
Do not speak of this again, but go out.
Remind everybody they must be devout."
So Moses declared to all Israel, "Hear!
The Lord God is great and His might we must fear.
When we are to enter the land that He gives,
if we should rebel, not one of us lives.
Don't bow to the sun or the moon or a Baal,
but make sure your faith in the Lord does not fail.
Many times we have opposed God and we
have seen that His wrath is mighty indeed.
On Sinai God told us that we're not to stray
from His ten commandments. Do not disobey!
Must I repeat them so you won't forget?
Hasn't each man memorized them all yet?
There's no other God, and do not cast idols.
Honor His name and His Sabbath; that's vital.
Honor your parents. Don't kill, and don't thieve.
Adultery's vile. Don't lie or deceive.
Don't covet the things your neighbor may own.
These are the ten things that God won't condone.
Don't turn away to the left or the right
of God's law. He watches each day and each night."

Deuteronomy 6 - 10

"Hear, oh Israel, second to none!
The Lord is our God, and our God is one!
As you see the land that you all await,
the cities and vineyards you didn't create,
do not forget that it's God who allows
us passage, for we have all taken our vows
to love Him and honor Him, fear Him and serve.
Question if this is a gift you deserve!
When your generations ask of His law
will you respond with appropriate awe?

You are to teach your children and theirs
why God has made us his firstborn; his heirs.
When you go in, drive out the nations.
Stamp out their lines, leave no indication
that they came before you, their sons or their gods
their wives or their daughters, or you'll be at odds
with God who despises these idols for they
are blasphemous things. Wipe them away!
And do not fear nations, their armies, or arms,
for God hands them to you, and you'll know no harm.
Do not forget God, for He knows your face.
Because you love Him, He gives you this place.
When you have eaten and are satisfied
thank Him for everything that He provides.
You didn't make it, nor earn it, but He
gives it you. He gives graciously.
Just as in war, it is the Lord
who puts all your enemies under your sword.
Never forget how you brought forth the wrath
of God as you bowed to the great golden calf.
And how many other times have you aroused
the ire of God before you espoused
that you are believers and worthy to know
the will of the Lord? Still God lets you go
into the promised land, holding the ark
of the covenant built with acacia bark.
Two great stone tablets are held in that chest,
etched by my hand after two that were blessed
and written by God were smashed in the place
that your forefathers built that golden disgrace.
Oh Israel, tremble! May you fear the Lord!
A debt against Him you cannot afford.
Mark your heart circumcised so God may see
that you have been faithful, and always will be."

Deuteronomy 11 - 13

"I can't go with you, but you must obey
the Lord, who swept all the Egyptians away

and brought you all here to give you a gift
of this promised land. Remember to lift
your prayers and your praise and obey His law.
All that you've known and all that you saw
should help you remember the power and might
of God who is with you in every plight.
When you go forth, destroy the high places
where idols were worshipped by those foreign races.
Break down their altars and Asherah poles.
Wipe all the names off of their sacred scrolls.
If, after all of these things have been burned,
a man comes to you and says he has learned
of visions and dreams, but you must defy
the Lord, know then that this man must die.
If your own brother, father, or mother
tells you that you should go worship another,
they're to be stoned, right then and right there.
No one who turns from the Lord shall be spared."

Deuteronomy 14 - 17

"Follow these rules, so you're not obscene.
Eat only meat that the priests declare clean.
Those with a split hoof and those that chew cud
can be eaten, but not with the animal's blood.
Set the first tenth of your harvest aside
for God, and give Him the best as your tithe.
The first fruits and firstborn of beasts and of sons
are the Lord's, for all He has given and done.
Each seven years, cancel your debts,
set your slaves free, and have no regrets.
But do not forsake the poor and the needy
the other six years, for that would be greedy.
Open your hand and do not resist
those who need help whom you can assist.
Don't be tightfisted with all your poor brothers.
Give to the orphans and bless widowed mothers.
Celebrate Passover; all of God's feasts.
You are His people. Do not live as beasts.

His law is first, and it shall not budge.
Assign men to honor His law and to judge.
When you have kings, give them a scroll
with God's law upon it, so that their soul
is pure and adheres to what God has blessed
and stays far away from all things He detests."

Deuteronomy 18 - 19

"That which you offer to God feeds the priests.
They have no lot, so it is the least
that you can do for them as they serve the Lord
upon your behalf and of His accord.
The Levites will keep you upon the right path,
from divination and out of witchcraft,
sorcery, omens, the casting of spells,
and mediums. These actions do not sit well
with God and the prophets that He'll send to show
us what He requires and where we're to go.
Prophets who come for the one true God show
that which is holy, what God would bestow.
Now, hear the law. Murder's forbid,
but if he did not mean to do what he did,
he may take refuge in one of three towns
and won't be arrested, 'less he leaves those grounds.
But if it was malice that drove him to kill,
regardless of fleeing, it is the Lord's will
that he be brought back. A life for a life
to appease the dead's parents, his children and wife.
But one witness is not enough to convict.
More than one witness must see the conflict.
And bearing false witness is one of the ten
commandments God gave us to keep us from sin."

Deuteronomy 20

"As you go into this land and to war,
don't look at their army and say, 'There are more
men than we have. We're doomed.' You forget

that this battle's outcome is already set.
Whenever you come to a city, give them
a chance to have peace if they'll let you in.
If they submit, then they are your slaves.
If they do not, all go to their graves."

Deuteronomy 21 - 26

Moses gave his people quite a long list
of laws so that they might all coexist.
"Listen to me as I speak to you
about what you are and are not to do.
The firstborn's preferred, so honor those rights.
Don't leave a hanged man out overnight.
Sons who rebel are all to be stoned.
Cross-dressing simply will not be condoned.
Take back a donkey or ox to its master.
The tent of assembly is closed to all bastards.
Don't plant two seeds in the place you grow wine.
Eunuchs are not allowed into God's shrine.
Do not weave linen and wool in together.
Don't take another man's wife you like better.
Stone promiscuity out of the tribe.
Shrine prostitutes are strictly proscribed.
Whatever you vow to the Lord you must pay.
One who kidnaps is one you must slay.
Do not remarry her once you've divorced.
As pledge, do not take a man's income source.
Don't send a newlywed man into war.
Don't withhold payment to those who are poor.
When harvesting, leave grain for widows in need.
Let judges mete justice out for wicked deeds.
Be honest in weight, and measure things fair.
Give your first tenth to God, as His share.
Follow these laws, commands, and decrees.
Enjoy the new land, for God set you free."

Deuteronomy 27 - 28

"Remember to always do what God commands,
for I won't go with you into these new lands.
When you are there, the Levites shall curse
deviants who seek the evil, perverse,
malevolent ways that anger our Lord.
Those people must all be put to the sword.
But if you're obedient to the Lord's call,
prosperity will be enjoyed by you all.
The city and country, the flocks and the wombs,
the vineyards and harvests, the homes and the looms
will all become fruitful which you will enjoy.
And God will see to it your foes are destroyed.
But if you break covenant with all you've sworn
you'll soon find a plague where goodness was born.
Your enemies will drive you into the ground
You will be cursed and God's wrath will abound."

Deuteronomy 29 - 30

Moses called out, "Your eyes have all seen
God destroy Egypt and its war machines.
You have borne witness to miracles, feats,
and signs which no human can ever repeat.
God made His covenant not just with you,
but all your descendants who must hold onto
our faith in the Lord. You must tell them!
All I have said and done is for Him.
I can't go with you. I must stay here.
You will have trials. You must persevere.
Do what is right and reap your reward,
but if you do wrong you will see the Lord
strike down upon you with curses and plagues.
Do you not know this? Have I been vague?
You have been given the simplest of terms
and all will be yours if you just affirm.
You do not have to fly through the sky
over the seas or climb up on high

to gain all the joy that God has to give.
Just follow his law each day that you live."

Deuteronomy 31

Then Moses called out, saying, "Joshua, come
and stand by my side. Now everyone, from
this moment and henceforth you shall be led
by Joshua. Soon I will surely be dead.
I disobeyed God on that fateful day
when everyone wanted to turn from His way.
Joshua, though, had faith and he fought
to follow the Lord in action and thought."
Then God said to Moses, "It's nearly time
for your life to cease and to be enshrined.
Alas! My people will seek other gods.
The Israelites and I will be at odds."
Moses told Israel what God had said.
"Not too long after my body is dead,
you'll turn away from the Lord and you'll find
disaster wash over our entire kind.
You'll break the covenant that has been set.
You'll turn from the Lord and you will forget!"
"No!" they replied, "No, you are wrong."
Moses replied to their pleas with a song.

Deuteronomy 32:1 - 32:47

"Listen, oh heavens," Moses sang out,
"I honor God with songs as I shout
Let all my teachings fall just like rain.
everything's perfect within His domain.
He will be scorned by this generation.
We're the most foolish of all of the nations.
He is upright. Our Lord is so just.
Is this how we will return the Lord's trust?
Israel's faith is all that He needs.
Your parents all witnessed the Lord's mighty deeds.
They could affirm, if you would but ask.

He's the Creator. Remember the past.
God shielded Jacob and showed him great care.
He brought forth honey and fruit from nowhere
only as our protecting Lord can.
Only the Lord can watch over each man.
But when they bow down to demons in praise
He hates those idols and our wicked ways.
We shame the Lord and tarnish His name.
He has every right to treat us the same.
He heaps calamities up on our land.
Our foes say, 'See, they die by our hand.'
Enemies trample us without delay.
They do not see that our Lord's turned away.
God is our rock. But we are all flawed.
The truth is that we turned away from our God.
Our Lord will avenge with imminent doom,
and all of our idols the Lord will consume.
Their vine comes from Sodom. Their harvest, Gomorrah.
But God is the maker of fauna and flora.
Even this day that the Lord raises up
He calls, 'I still love you. Just drink from My cup.'
Great is His fury! His arrows and sword
get drunk on His enemy's blood. In the Lord
I acknowledge His glory in all that I see.
God, I am with You! I beg, be with me."

Deuteronomy 32:48 - 34:12

Then God said to Moses, "Go up to the Mount
of Nebo and there I shall make an account
of your days and then, My friend, you shall die."
Before he left, Moses blessed each of the tribes.
He blessed the twelve tribes and then he set out.
There was no asking, for there was no doubt
that he would be staying behind as they went
into the land where they had been sent.

So Moses went up to Moab and died.
The nation mourned greatly and every man cried.
For everyone there had followed that man
from Egypt into the Lord's promised land.

Joshua 1

When Moses had died, the Lord said, "Now then,
Joshua take all these people, and when
you are ready cross over the Jordan and go
into the land I have promised, and lo,
all from the desert to Lebanon and
to the Euphrates is to be your land.
Be strong and courageous and obey My law
and out of My will your strength you shall draw."
So Joshua ordered the people to pack,
that all should be ready to launch the attack.
"As we were with Moses, so we shall be
with you, Joshua. We will all follow thee."

Joshua 2

Then Joshua sent out two spies and they went
to see Jericho with their secret intent.
They were hidden at Rahab's, a prostitute, who
protected them both.
The king told her, "You
must give us the Israelites who have come
to spy on our land."
She said, "Where they're from
is not my concern. They were here, it is true.
But they left before I heard one word from you.
Go ahead. Search! But it's you who will let
them escape. Go now and you may catch them yet."
She'd hidden the spies, for she knew the Lord was
on Israel's side, and also because

she said, "We have heard what your God did when you
were slaves down in Egypt, and now He's come to
take over our land. So please hear my plea
to spare all my family and also spare me."
"Our lives for your lives," they told her.
"Now go
and hide in the hills so that no one will know.
Once the king's men have returned, you may flee
and when you come back, please don't forget me."

Joshua 3 - 4

Knowing the fear of their enemies gave
Joshua strength to go forth and be brave,
and so he told all of his people, "It's time.
Prepare and be ready to form a great line.
We'll follow the Levites who carry the ark,
but do not go near it. Prepare to embark!
I tell you tomorrow the Lord will amaze
you all. Spend tonight in worship and praise."
The next day he told the priests, "You will lead
us into the new land, but first you must heed
what I am to tell you. Take one from each tribe
to carry the ark, so that all may ascribe
the miracle that they will witness is of
the Lord's doing, He who reigns from above.
When the first man's foot touches the flow
the water shall stop, so the people may go.
The Jordan won't flow until everyone's passed.
This way they'll see that the Lord's unsurpassed
in His might and glory, and that we'll succeed
in all our endeavors with Him in the lead."
And so it was done, and though all had thought
they'd be soaked in crossing, not one single drop
touched them the whole time the ark stood in place
proving that Israel stood in God's grace.
That night they took up twelve stones and they made
a memorial there at the place that God stayed
the water when Israel crossed to the land

that God had promised them. Then every man
exalted the Lord and Joshua too.
Any who doubted before then now knew
that the Lord was with Joshua, just as He'd been
with Moses before, and they honored him.

Joshua 5:1 - 5:12

When the kings in the land heard the Jordan had stopped
so that Israel could come across, their hearts dropped.
And God said to Joshua, "None of your men
are circumcised. Restart this custom again."
For since they had been in the desert, no man
had circumcised his son. So by their own hand
they fulfilled the sign of God's covenant and
honored the Lord, since it was His command.
They named the place Gilgal, and stayed there to heal.
During that time, the Passover meal
was eaten by all in great celebration
for they knew that this was the great culmination
of why they'd been freed. The last generation
had not known this land or felt the elation
of reaching the goal. With great supplication
they honored the Lord as one congregation.
That day they ate their last manna, for God
had given them manna wherever they trod.
But now they would eat of Canaan's great yield,
for God was with Israel's sword and its shield.

Joshua 5:13 - 6:27

Near Jericho, Joshua saw a man who
stood square in their path, so Joshua drew.
"Are you with or against us when you raise your sword?"
"Neither, for I command all that's the Lord's."
Then Joshua fell at the angel's feet and
he said, "Tell me what is my Great God's command?"
"Take off your sandals. You're on holy ground."
He did so. The angel said, "Now look around.

Jericho's closed up its gate for it fears
the Lord, who cannot be harmed by their spears.
Listen, for I'll tell you what you must do
to conquer the city and its armies too.
March all your men one time 'round the town
each day for six days. On the seventh march 'round
seven whole times as the priests' trumpets sound,
then shout at the walls. They'll come tumbling down!"
So Joshua told all the people the plan.
They did as he said, for they knew the Lord's hand
was at work in their actions. The seventh day came,
and Joshua said, "We go in the name
of the Lord. When I tell you, shout out at the wall.
Destroy everything when you see the wall fall.
But do not harm Rahab, for she is the one
who gave us this day. The time has now come."
So just as the angel of God had declared,
they shouted, the walls fell and no one was spared
except for the family of Rahab who earned
a place in the tribes as Jericho burned.

Joshua 7

The word of this siege spread far and spread wide,
but some amongst Israel did not abide
by the word of the Lord. When they went to Ai
they were routed and many of Israel died.
Then Joshua fell on his face and he cried,
"Why, Lord, oh why are we now denied?
Now others will hear that we lost in disgrace
and they shall bring armies to wipe out our race."
"Stand up!" said the Lord, "Why are you on the ground?
Some in your midst have sinned. You were bound
to follow My law, which some have ignored.
They worshipped false idols, things I abhorred.
That's why you lost! And if you do not
destroy what I tell you, more pain shall be wrought
on the entire people. Do as I desire.
Send every man forward. I'll judge them with fire.

I'll show who it is. Destroy him and all
you should have when I toppled Jericho's wall."
In front of God each and every man came
and it was discovered Achan was to blame.
"Why have you done this?" Joshua cried.
"I saw the gold and thought I could hide
the treasures I'd found with the greatest of stealth.
In doing so I would increase my own wealth."
"The Lord must now judge you," Joshua said,
"Stone him and his family till they are dead."
And so they were stoned and burned so the tribe
would know the Lord's anger when He was denied.

Joshua 8

The Lord was appeased, saying, "Go back to Ai
and take it this time, for you won't be denied."
They laid out a plan to ambush the men
which worked, for the tribes had been cleansed of their sin.
They killed every woman, each child, each man.
The cattle and livestock all fell by their hand.
Not one living thing was left to deface
the Lord, for they left it a desolate place.
Twelve thousand died, and they burned the whole town
till every last building collapsed to the ground.
Then they worshipped the Lord with reverence and awe
as Joshua read every word of His law.

Joshua 9

When the other kings heard what had happened at Ai
they wanted the Israelites all to die.
They united; the Jebusites, Amorites, Hittites,
and Canaanites, Perizzites, also the Hivites.
All but the Gibeons. They played a trick.
They took moldy bread that was hard as a brick.
They wore shoddy robes. Their sandals were cracked.
They asked Joshua before he attacked,
"Make treaties with us. We are from far away.

We heard of your glories and came here today
to join with you now."
"But where are you from?"
"Oh, quite far away! See how far we've come.
Our bread is all moldy. Our sandals are worn.
We're tired from travel. Our robes are all torn."
So it was agreed, and an oath was declared
that they would be allies, but tempers soon flared
when the Israelites learned that Gibeon was
a neighbor. But they could not fight them because
they'd sworn an oath in the name of the Lord.
They could not put Gibeon under the sword.
So Joshua went to Gibeon's king
and said, "You have done a most heinous thing.
We shall let you live, but you're cursed to be
servants of ours, since we were deceived.
You'll do the worst deeds, you snakes and you worms.
If you want to live, then these are our terms."
"In fear we have lied. We accept your demands."
Thus Gibeon was spared from Joshua's hands.

Joshua 10 - 19

The king of Jerusalem heard of these things
and feared what this treaty between them might bring,
so he and four kings joined forces to fight
and thus destroy Gibeon with all their might.
So Gibeon called, "Save your servants, lest we
are destroyed at the hands of this great enemy."
The Lord said to Joshua, "Go to their lands.
I'll place all the enemies into your hands."
So they marched all night, surprising their foes,
routing and driving them back up the roads.
Then hailstones rained down on their lot, thus the Lord
killed more with His hail than those killed by the sword.
The sun then stood still in the sky a full day,
and the moon stopped as well, as the records all say.
Now the five kings had fled to Makkedah where
they hid in a cave, but they were found there.

They were killed, then Joshua took up his men
and conquered Makkedah. When they went in,
they killed everyone. And then they moved on
to Libnah and Lachish. When this war was done,
there was not a survivor remaining, for they
had destroyed them as Jericho was wiped away.
The army of Gezer, the city of Eglon
were put to the sword, then the city of Hebron.
Then Debir, the mountains, the Negev, and hills
were subdued and all whom had lived there were killed.
The kings of the north made a pact to wipe out
the Israelites who'd been storming about
in the south of their lands. But then the Lord said
to Joshua, "Fear not, for they shall be dead
by this time tomorrow."
So Joshua slew
their armies and then killed their citizens too.
Thirty-one kings fell under his sword
as Joshua cut down the foes of the Lord.
The land was divided so each tribe might gain
the promised land God had placed in their domain.
When Joshua was a very old man,
Caleb came to him and said, "As I stand,
I've had eighty-five years on the Earth, and when I
was a young man, Moses sent me as a spy.
I came back and told everyone what I saw,
but our brothers were frightened, and frankly in awe
of the size of the brutes who had lived in this land.
As you know I put all my faith in God's hand.
Moses said then that the land I was on
would be my inheritance once he was gone."
So Joshua gave Caleb all of the land
of Hebron that it might be in his command.

Joshua 20 - 22

The Lord said to Joshua, "Cities must be
set aside so that any man who must flee
after killing a man accidentally, can go.

They'll have sanctuary. Let everyone know
that there they may live without persecution
and without the fear of a tribe's retribution."
The cities were set and all men were pleased,
for eleven tribes held the land they had seized.
But one tribe, the Levites, were not pleased at all,
for when God had asked, they had answered the call
to be the Lord's priests. They said, "Give us land.
Do not make us live in the wild or sand."
So it was done, and the tribes all returned.
Finally they had the land they had yearned
and waited upon. The Lord had brought them
to the land He had promised, and they worshipped Him.

Joshua 23 - 24

Now they had peace, and Joshua said,
"Through all of these years, the Lord clothed and fed
our people, and finally this land became ours.
He's loved us the most under all of His stars.
Be strong in your faith, and always obey
the law Moses gave us. Do not turn away!
Nations will tempt you with false gods. Do not
stray from His path in deed or in thought.
If you turn away, you will find there are snares
to trap you and whip you, for no god compares
to the Lord of our fathers. I shall soon die.
Continue to lift up your prayers to the sky.
God said to Abraham, I'll make your line
a nation of greatness, and He sent us signs.
Moses was shown them and freed everyone
from the bondage of Egypt, but when he was done
we turned on the Lord. We wandered, but then
He gave us the land He had promised us when
He first spoke to Abraham. Now you must say
you'll follow Him always."
"We'll serve and obey!"

So everyone swore that they'd follow the Lord,
and Joshua died in peace. By the sword
he'd taken the land as the Lord said he would.
So they honored him, for his life had been good.

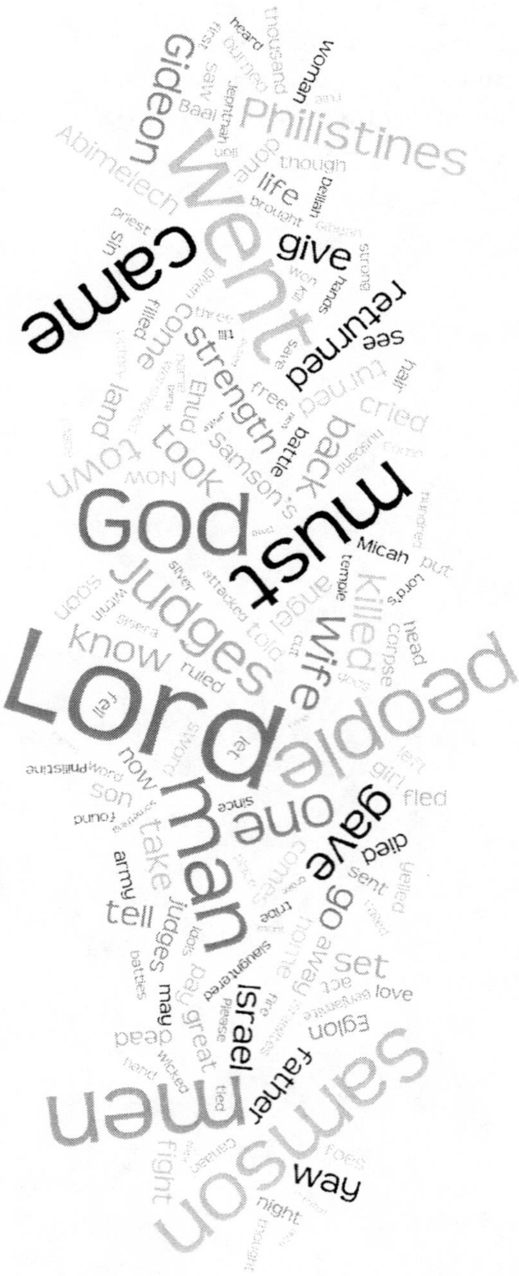

Judges 1 - 2

When Joshua died, the Simeonites
joined with Judah's army to fight Canaanites.
They toppled Bezek, and then they attacked
Jerusalem. They won, the city was sacked,
then burned to the ground. The battles continued.
The Lord was with Israel. In every venue,
although they succeeded, the Jews couldn't blot
out the people of Canaan, despite how they fought.
After awhile a new generation
of men who did not serve with true dedication
to God in their lives ruled Israel and
they made the Lord angry at all in the land.
They turned from the Lord, and bowed down to Baal.
Soon in their battles, they could not prevail
for God was against them. Then He raised up men
as leaders and judges to keep them from sin.
But they turned away from the judges and sought
all that was evil. The Lord's judges brought
prosperity, but all the people ignored
the judges' commands and the word of the Lord.

Judges 3

So Israel's enemies lived in their land,
because the Jews did not obey God's command.
The Israelites and the foreigners wed.
They worshipped false idols, and they were misled.
Then Eglon, the Moabite king, took the land
in battle away from Israel's hands.

The people all lifted a plea, and God heard
their cries, and He sent them a man of His word.
Ehud, a left-handed man, went and gave
a tribute to Eglon, so that he might save
his people, but he had a secret plan too.
He said, "Eglon, I have a message for you.
May we have some privacy?"
Eglon sent all
of his servants and slaves away from the hall.
Ehud said, "This message comes from the Lord,"
Then in Eglon's belly, Ehud shoved his sword.
As he left, he locked all the doors and he fled,
for nobody else knew that Eglon was dead.
The king's servants waited for him to come out
until they succumbed to their fears and their doubts.
The corpse was inside, but Ehud was gone.
He'd run to the Israelites, with his sword drawn
and said, "Come and fight! For Moab is ours.
The Lord has shown us His will and His powers."
The Hebrews went down to meet Moab's might,
and they slaughtered everyone within their sight.
They struck down the Moabite people and gained
an eighty year peace in which Israel reigned.

Judges 4

When Ehud had died, they turned to the ways
they'd followed before in their darkest of days.
The Lord's fury raged. He gave them again
to Canaan because they had turned against Him.
Then Deborah, a prophetess leading them, said,
"Barak, take your men and let them be led
against our oppressors."
He said, "I will go
if you will go with me."
"So be it, but know
that since you're afraid, the glory will not
be yours but a woman's."
So their army fought

against Canaan's army, led by the great
general, Sisera, who until late
had won with his chariots. Now, though, the Lord
declared He'd put Sisera onto His sword.
Canaan was beaten. With his soldiers dead,
Sisera, fearing for his life, then fled.
He went to Jael's tent, for she was the wife
of a friend, saying, "Please, you must help me. My life
is in danger."
"Come in," she said, "You can hide.
Just rest here and I will stand guard right outside."
But when he had fallen asleep, she went in
and hammered a peg through his temple. So when
Barak came to her, she said, "Won't you see
the corpse of their leader."
And so they were free.

Judges 5 - 6

They worshipped the Lord with songs of great praise,
but soon they went back to idolatrous ways.
So Midian came and ravaged their land,
till the angel of God came down to a man
who was threshing some wheat. The angel said, "Lo,
you are a warrior. I tell you now, go!
For you shall free Israel from Midian."
The man he spoke to was named Gideon.
Gideon said, "But my clan is weak."
"Your victory has been assured. As I speak,
My word and My will is set on your side.
All that you need, your Lord shall provide."
So Gideon offered the Lord meat and bread,
and a fire consumed it, which filled him with dread.
The angel of God in a flash disappeared,
then Gideon cried, "The Lord has been here!"
The Lord said to him, "Go tear down the Baals."
When he had done this, the town let out wails
demanding his life. His father said, "No!
If Baal is so great, he'll already know.

And he can then come for my son."
So they said,
"Yes! If Baal wants him, then he'll soon be dead."
But Baal was not real, and couldn't lay claim
to Gideon, who basked within the Lord's name.

Judges 7 - 8

Gideon called all the men to go fight
and destroy their oppressors, the Midianites.
Thirty-two thousand came with their swords,
but God said, "So everyone knows that the Lord
has given them victory, send some men back."
So only ten thousand stayed to attack.
But God said, "No, there still are too many men.
Take only three hundred with you and you'll win.
The battle is yours. I'll give you your foe,
so when you have won, My people shall know."
So Gideon, with only three hundred swords
defeated the Midianites through the Lord.
When they gathered up all the plunder, they said,
"Rule us, oh Gideon. Take up the head
of our people."
But he said, "I won't, but I will
take one golden earring from your treasure's fill."
So each man gave Gideon one earring from
their plunder and when he had melted the sum
he made a gold ephod, but those of his town
prostituted themselves. The people bowed down
to worship the garment. This was a snare
for Gideon's line, for while he was there
they worshipped the Lord, but as soon as he died
they returned to idolatry and sinful pride.

Judges 9

Abimelech, one of Gideon's sons,
said, "Wouldn't the people prefer if just one
ruled over them? I shall go take up the throne

from all of my brothers. I must rule alone."
He went to their homes and slaughtered them all.
Except for one brother who jumped the town wall.
Jotham, the youngest, escaped the bloodshed,
but when he heard they'd placed the crown on the head
of Abimelech, he climbed a mountain to shout
to the citizens. "My father brought you all out
of oppression, and now you have slaughtered his sons.
But if you were faithful in what you have done,
may Abimelech bless you. Let all your lines bloom.
If not, then let fire both doom and consume
your households, and then strike Abimelech dead."
With this curse, Jotham turned and he fled.
God cursed Abimelech's name, so the hearts
of his people were turned against him, and in parts
of his kingdom the people rebelled, so he went
to battle the ones who created dissent.
One town he burned, killing thousands, but when
he besieged another, he paid for his sin.
For during a siege, a woman had thrown
a rock on his head, but it wasn't the stone
that killed Abimelech. To save his pride
he had a man stab him so when he had died,
no one could say that a woman had killed
Abimelech. His death was as the Lord willed.

Judges 10 - 11

More leaders and judges ruled Israel. They
continued to go back to idols to pray.
God said, "Have I not been there every time
to save you, only to witness your crime
of turning against Me again and again?"
"Lord," they cried out, "we've committed a sin.
But let us not be oppressed by our foes."
Again God relented when He heard their woes.
So God gave them Jephthah, a warrior, to fight
and defeat the armies of the Ammonites.
He said, "God, if you put them onto my sword,

then when I return I will give to You, Lord,
the first thing that comes out from my own door."
So Ammon was left as fire and gore.
When Jephthah returned to his home from the slaughter
the first thing he saw was his very own daughter.
Jephthah fell down, beginning to weep,
for he knew the promise he'd made he must keep.
When he told the girl, she said, "I beg you
to give me two months to mourn. Then I'll do
whatever you ask."
He did and when she
returned, he sacrificed her as decreed.
From this comes the custom where young women go
to remember the sacrifice that the girl showed.

Judges 12 - 14

Then twenty-five years of peace passed, until
the Philistines came. The land was then filled
with their idols and people. An angel appeared
to a woman and said, "The way has been cleared.
You'll soon bear a son."
"I'm barren and can't."
"The Lord has decided you will. He shall grant
a son of great strength, and he will relieve
the land from its foes. You shall conceive.
But do not drink wine, for you must be clean.
And don't cut his hair, for it must be seen
that he's set aside as a Nazarite man."
She said to the angel, "I understand."
Then she told her husband, and he was surprised,
but didn't believe till he saw with his eyes
when the angel returned and told him that he
would have a son who would set their nation free.
So she bore a son, named Samson, who grew
in strength and in size until he said, "You
must get me a wife. There's a Philistine girl.
The only one pleasing to me in the world."
So when Samson and his father went down

to Timnah to see her, a lion came round.
While he was alone, it came to kill him.
With bare hands he tore the beast limb from limb.
The power God gave him was far greater than
the strength that is found in a typical man.
But he didn't tell his parents what he
had done, and was glad that they didn't see.
Then he met the girl and liked her, so they
decided to marry. But then on his way
back home, he went to the lion that he
had killed. In its corpse was a hive full of bees.
He plucked out the hive and took back the comb
to his parents who ate it along their way home.
When they had returned, a party was held
and though they were Philistines, he was compelled
to say, "I shall tell you a riddle. If you
solve it within the next week, I'll come to
you each and give you a garment so fine
that people will gawk. So put down your wine.
'Out of the eater comes something to eat.
Out of the strong comes something so sweet.'"
Then all of the men who were there on that eve
struggled, for not one of them could conceive
what this riddle meant. So they found his wife
and said, "You must tell us or we'll take your life.
We'll set you ablaze and your father's house too.
So she went to Samson and said, "Why won't you
tell me the answer? You must hate me!"
She nagged till he broke down and said, "Leave me be!
I'll tell you."
And when he had done so she went
to the men. So then they approached Samson's tent
and said, "What is sweeter than honey which came
from the heart of a lion?"
"You all are to blame.
You cheated by using my wife, but I still
will pay on my debt."
He went down and killed
thirty young men in Ashkelon, then

he stripped them of clothes. Returning again,
he threw all the clothes of the dead men to those
who had cheated him. Now they were not friends but foes.
His wife was then given to Samson's best man,
for they thought he hated her. Thus understand
that God had created this problem between
His Israelites and all Philistines.

Judges 15

But Samson returned, demanding his wife.
Her father said, "No. I thought in my life
you'd never come back, so I gave her away."
"Because of this all Philistia shall pay."
So Samson caught three hundred foxes and tied
them up into pairs and set them outside
with a torch on their tails. He set them in fields
of the Philistine crops and burned up their yields.
"Who did this?!" they yelled.
"It's Samson. He came
for his wife, but I gave her away. He's to blame."
The Philistines went and burned her alive
as well as her father. When Samson arrived,
he said, "You disgust me. Is this how you act?
I'll have my vengeance."
And then he attacked.
He killed many men, then fled to a cave.
The Philistines went to Judah and raved.
"Give us this Samson, so that we may do
to him what he's done!"
So men went up to
where Samson was hiding and said, "You attacked
the Philistines! Do you not know we must act
carefully for they rule over us now?"
"Swear not to kill me, and I will allow
you men to hand me over to them."
"We will not kill you," the people told him.
The Philistines came, but then Samson's chains
fell off as the Spirit of God filled his veins.

He picked up a jawbone that lay in the dust,
and killed more than one thousand men in his lust
for blood and revenge, and there in that place
he freed all his people and saved his whole race.
"God gave me victory, now quench my thirst."
Water poured forth, since he put the Lord first.

Judges 16

Samson fell deeply in love, but he chose
the wrong woman, for when approached by his foes,
they said, "Now, Delilah, we'll pay you if you
can find Samson's weakness. Do what you must do."
So she went to Samson and said, "Tell me why
you are so strong."
He told her, "If I
am bound up with seven strong strings that aren't dried,
then I will be weakened."
So that night she tied
him up with the thongs, and cried out in dread,
"The Philistines come!"
He jumped from the bed
and the cords fell apart.
"Samson! You lied!
Why don't you trust me, my love?" the girl cried.
"If I am tied up with new ropes, then I
cannot break or snap the ties that will bind."
So she tried again, and when she cried out
he burst through the ropes.
"What's this all about?"
she yelled. "You must hate me! What must I do
to prove that I love you, and earn trust from you?"
"Delilah, why must you know how to make
me weak? Do you want to see your man break?"
"No, love. I just want to know you believe
in me."
"My strength leave is you take and weave
my hair in a loom."
So that night as he

was sleeping she did, but again he broke free.
"You lied to me, Samson."
"Why must you press
this issue?"
For weeks she whined her bequest,
"Please, Samson, tell me," so much that he caved.
When she asked again, he finally gave
the secret to her.
"If my hair is shaved
then there is no way that I can be saved.
I'll be overtaken by weakness, for then
I won't be a Nazarite. I will have sinned."
Delilah then called for the Philistines and
said, "I will give Samson now into your hand."
So she shaved his head and called out in fright,
"The Philistines!"
But when he went out to fight
his strength had dissolved. His holiness gone,
he could not defend himself when set upon.
They gouged out his eyes and shackled his arms,
and took him with plans to do him more harm.
But soon Samson's hair began to grow in,
so when the crowd went to humiliate him
they brought Samson into their temple and he
prayed to the Lord, "Please, Lord, give to me
my strength once again so in my final act
I may do Your will, though I won't come back."
He emerged and braced his body against
the pillars. Before anybody had sensed
what he was to do, he pushed and the walls
of the temple came down and crushed one and all.
The Philistine deaths from this act were more
than Samson had killed in all battles before.
With the strength God had given, he killed all their kings.
This is the punishment that the Lord brings
upon those who injure His people. They pay
for tearing the people of God from His way.

Judges 17 - 18

After this happened, God left them because
they would not acknowledge He is and He was
and will be forever their Lord. In one case,
a man took some silver from his mother's place.
But then this man, Micah, confided, "It's me
who took all your silver."
"A good thief!" said she.
"I'll give you my silver since you said what's true.
Now make a great idol for us to bow to."
So he cast an idol, and then went to see
a Levite and said, "Be priest over me
and all of my family."
That man agreed,
so Micah thought he had all that he would need,
his priest and some gods - but Danites came down,
entered his house and invaded his town.
They took all his gods and his priest as well,
and Micah said, "This is my home where I dwell!
You took everything! Now nothing remains."
"Silence!" they yelled, "or you shall know pain!"
To Micah's gods they became prostitutes,
and Micah, in total, was left destitute.

Judges 19 - 21

A Levite had taken a concubine who
was unfaithful to him and so she fled to
her father, then when the husband returned
he took back the wife for whom he had yearned.
On the way home, the party was tired,
and one slave saw Jebus and said, "We'll retire
when we reach that city."
His master said, "No.
Onto an Israelite town we will go."
When they came to Gibeah, he stated, "Here.
A Benjamite town. Have no more fear.
Someone will welcome us."

But they did not,
until a man saw that the travelers sought
a place for the night.
"Come here," the man said.
"Eat of my food and sleep in my bed."
But that night the wicked men of the town came
and yelled to the old man, calling his name.
"Bring out the foreigner, so that he may
be raped by us, so he knows we rule this way!"
"No!" cried the old man. "Here, take his wife.
But spare my companion. Do not take his life."
They sent out the concubine to the crazed men
who abused her and raped her again and again.
She died on the doorstep. When her husband found
her body, he picked it up, taking it down
to where he was from. Then with his own hands
he cut up her corpse to send to the lands
of Israel, so they would know what transpired
in Gibeah and how his wife had expired.
Then all of the tribes but the Benjamites came
to fight against Gibeah. They all proclaimed,
"The wicked must pay."
Then they all went
to battle. First in the fray the Lord sent
Judah's tribe, and forty thousand were killed
by the Benjamite army, but as the Lord willed
they bested the tribe of Benjamin and
the Lord gave the wicked men into their hand.
After this war, the tribes all agreed
that they would not give any daughters to be
married to Benjamite men, even though
they wept at this fact. "God, must it be so
that we cut off the tribe of Benjamin's men?"
This was a time that was filled up with sin,
for Israel was not yet ruled by a king,
and wickedness flourished in everything.

Ruth 1

In the days of the judges, a famine broke out.
Elimelech took his whole family from drought
in Bethlehem off to Moab. But there
he died, leaving his wife and two sons to fare
for themselves. So Naomi, his wife, found two wives,
for her boys, but then both of her sons lost their lives.
So now with two daughters-in-law she was left
in a land far from home, in a state quite bereft.
She said to the women, "Go back to the home
of your families. You two should not be alone.
Find a new husband."
Then they wept aloud.
"We'll both stay with you," the two women vowed.
"No," said Naomi. "I'm old, but you're young.
Go home, I say. Find a husband among
your people."
So one girl went home, but the other,
named Ruth, told Naomi, "Now you are my mother.
Let your people be my people, and let
your God be my God."
Ruth was so set,
Naomi did not argue so they left for
Bethlehem husbandless, homeless, and poor.

Ruth 2 - 3

When they had arrived, Ruth said, "Let me
go to a field and gather such seed
as should fall to the ground."

So Ruth worked the land
of Boaz, a kind and generous man.
He said to her, "Woman, I've heard what you've done.
You stayed with your mother-in-law when her son
had died. I would like it if you would stay here.
The men here won't touch you, so do not have fear."
"Thank you, my lord."
Then he said to his men,
"Drop a few stalks when she harvests again."
When that day was finished, she took all she'd gained
to Naomi who saw all the good stalks of grain.
Naomi said, "Tell me where you worked today,
and bless the man who gave so much grain away
to widows like us."
"In Boaz's field."
"Bless him! Let God more than double his yield."
Naomi said, "Daughter, I'll find you a home.
Go back and find Boaz when he is alone
on the threshing floor where he is working and when
he is tired, go to him, for he is the kin
of my husband who died. He'll know what to do.
Do anything Boaz requires of you."
So Ruth went to him when he was asleep,
and when he awoke, he found at his feet
the woman. He said, "Who is this?"
"It is Ruth.
Cover me, master."
"Though it is the truth
that I am your kinsman, a kinsman of mine
has precedence over you. If he'd decline
I'd make you my wife. On this very day,
I'll go and find out what my kinsman would say.
You could have picked someone much younger than I,
but I'm grateful you came. I will get his reply."

Ruth 4

Boaz sought out his kinsman and found
the man and he said, "Let us both sit down.

Naomi is selling our dead kinsman's land,
and you're first in line. Behind you, I stand.
Would you redeem it?"
"I would," the man said.
"But then," Boaz said, "the wife of the dead
shall now becomes yours; the Moabitress."
"Then I cannot do it, for I'd make a mess
of my own estate. You take it. I can't."
And so they were witnessed. No man could recant.
The deal had been sealed, and so it was done.
So Boaz took Ruth, and she bore him a son.
Obed, their son, was to carry the line
of kings who'd be blessed by God the Divine.
For his son was Jesse, whose son would be King
David, the one of whom Israel sings.

Lord Saul Samuel God David

Philistines son people man king Israel went told men army sons one know Now father knew

Jonathan Eli

kill set must Philistine cursed Saul's killed returned fight land came back away sword battle done King just friend Goliath died

I Samuel 1

A man had two wives, one who bore sons
and one who was barren, and since she had none
her rival would ridicule her till she wept.
Although she was barren, her husband still kept
her with him and loved her. She went and she prayed,
"God, if You'll give me a son, he'll be saved,
and set aside for You." And when she conceived,
she praised the Lord for the gift she'd received.
She said to her husband, "He'll live with the priests,
for God gave him to me, though I am the least
of all of His servants."
And so she endowed
Samuel, her son, to the Lord as she'd vowed.

I Samuel 2

The priest's sons were wicked, and they were a source
of anger. They stole and took things by force.
They slept with the women who tended the tent,
and sinned against God wherever they went.
But Samuel, who lived with these fools was a fair
and honest boy in both his worship and prayer.
When Eli, the priest, heard what they had done,
he said, "I'm ashamed of all of my sons.
They have sinned against God."
A prophet told him,
"The Lord is appalled at your sons. All of them
have cursed Him. Since humankind first begun,
we've been told not to do all these things they have done.

God has declared that your sons shall both die
on the same exact day. Then He'll raise upon high
a priest for His nation. And your line shall bow
down at his feet, for he keeps the Lord's vow."

I Samuel 3

One night as Samuel slept close to the ark,
the voice of the Lord called out in the dark.
Samuel ran quickly to Eli and said,
"You called?"
"I did not. Now go back to bed."
When Samuel lay down to sleep, God again
called out to him, "Samuel!"
So Samuel ran in
to Eli again, and then Samuel said,
"You called?"
"I did not. Now go back to bed."
Then Samuel went back, but only to hear
the Lord's voice again, quite strong and quite clear.
So he went to Eli, and Eli realized
that God had called Samuel. Though he was surprised,
he knew what to do.
"Go back and lie still
and listen to God, and follow His will."
So Samuel laid down, and when God appeared,
he said, "Here I am, Lord. Your servant is here."
The Lord said to Samuel, "As I have proclaimed,
the priest's sons shall die, for they cursed My name.
And all that I've said that would come to pass,
shall happen, and you will be high priest at last."
Samuel was scared of what the Lord spoke,
but Eli came to him when he had awoke.
Eli said, "Tell me all that you have heard."
When Samuel was done, he said, "It's God's word."

I Samuel 4

The Israelites took the ark out to fight
the Philistine army to show them God's might.
But they were defeated and Eli's sons died.
The ark was then stolen. All Israel cried.
When Eli heard this he fell and he broke
his neck and he died. Then this news provoked
his daughter-in-law into labor. She then
gave birth and said to her people, "We've sinned.
I've named my son Ichabod. Glory is gone
from Israel. Our holy Lord has withdrawn.
The ark has been taken. Now we are bereft
for God has deserted us. Nothing is left."

I Samuel 5 - 6

The Philistines took the ark to their land.
Where they set their idol, Dagon, to stand,
they set the ark too. But the next morning they
saw Dagon had fallen face down. There he lay
in front of the ark. They replaced him but when
they woke the next morning, he'd fallen again,
but this time his limbs and head had been split.
The Philistines realized God wouldn't submit
to any false idol. Then He sent them sores
and tumors that covered the Philistine hordes.
So they said, "Let's send the ark on to Gath."
But then the Lord showered that city in wrath.
They sent it to Ekron, but those people cried,
"Take it away!"
But still many died.
"What shall we do?" they yelled.
"We must send
it back to the Hebrews. Then this curse will end."
So they sent it back. When it was discovered,
Israel cheered that the ark was recovered.
A few men opened the ark and looked in,
and they were destroyed by God for their sin.

I Samuel 7

Samuel told Israel, "If we're to be
free from the Philistines, listen to me.
Tear down your idols. Then offer your hearts
to God. If you do this, then He'll do His part."
So they all confessed their sins to the Lord,
and when they attacked, the Lord's fury roared
against the whole Philistine army. They'd seen
their victory come when the Lord intervened.

I Samuel 8

When Samuel was old, the people said, "Give
a new king to us, for you will not live
much longer. It's known that your sons don't walk
with God like you do."
So he went to talk
with God, for he did not like what they'd said,
but God said, "It's Me, not you who is dead
in the hearts of these people. I have been rejected.
It's just as it always has been. It's expected.
For I am their King, but they want a man.
Now go tell My people so they understand,
a human king will make them slaves, but through Me
I will lighten their burden and set them all free."
When Samuel told all of the people these things,
they shouted, "We don't care! Give us a king!"
Then God said to Samuel, "So it shall be.
Once again Israel has turned from Me."

I Samuel 9 - 10

A Benjamite, Saul, who was handsome and tall,
was chosen to be the king over all
of Israel. Samuel was told by the Lord,
"Tomorrow I'll send you of My own accord,
the man who will lead all of Israel's tribes,

its people and priests, its armies and scribes."
Then Saul came to him, and Samuel knew.
He said, "Saul, I have something I must tell you."
Then Samuel took oil and Saul was anointed.
Samuel said, "Saul, you have been appointed
king of all Israel. Now, Saul, your heart
shall be changed by God. You've been set apart."
So Saul then went out, surprised by this news,
while Samuel went forth to the people he'd ruled
and said, "You have asked for a king, for you've turned
your backs on the Lord. Soon you will learn."
Then Samuel said to them, "Now I shall bring
your leader out."
Everyone yelled, "Hail the king!
This is the man who'll save us!"
And they
worshipped a man, not the Lord on that day.

I Samuel 11

The Ammonites went to Jabesh Gilead,
surrounding the city with all that they had.
The Israelites told them, "Let's make a pact.
We'll be your subjects, if you won't attack."
"Only if I get to gouge out the eye
of Israel's men."
They said with a cry,
"If none come to save us within the next week,
then we will submit to the terms that you seek."
When Saul heard the terms the Ammonites set,
he said, "We must go in response to this threat."
With three hundred thousand men he set out,
and slaughtered the Ammonites. After the rout,
the people said, "Whoever doubted this Saul,
must be put to death."
But Saul said to all,
"No one shall be put to death, for the Lord
killed all of our foes with the blade of His sword."

I Samuel 12

Samuel told Israel, "You have your king.
I've lived a long life, and I've done everything
that I can for you, but let me remind
you all what the Lord has done for our kind.
When we were in Egypt, God brought us out.
Our hearts were not true. Our pride and our doubt
destroyed us. Again we all became slaves,
forgetting that only through God are we saved.
We bowed down and worshiped those in our own lands,
and to their false gods, we raised up our hands.
Then we went back to the Lord, and received
judges to guide us. Men who could lead.
But then you begged, 'Samuel, give us a king.'
Though God is the King over everything.
Now Saul is your king. And if you and he
both fear the Lord, then you'll remain free.
But turn away and you'll know nothing but pain.
Now see God is great. Lord, bring us rain."
Then rain started pouring throughout the whole land,
and all stood in awe.
"Do you understand?
God is the King!"
They cried, "We have sinned!
Please, Lord, don't sweep us away like the wind."
"If you follow God, then you'll know no fear.
But if you are evil, then you will pay dear."

I Samuel 13

Saul led a force of the Israelites
against the large Philistine army to fight.
They were outnumbered, so Saul did not wait
to make the Lord's offering. Samuel, irate
that Saul was so foolish, said, "You have presumed
that you knew the Lord. Your rule is now doomed.
If you had just waited for me, I'd have made
the offering for you, but you have betrayed

the law that the Lord set. You are impure.
Truly, your kingdom and rule won't endure.
The Lord seeks a man who will know the Lord's heart,
and He shall anoint him as you fall apart."
Then Saul went to battle, but none of his men
had their spears or swords. Instead, for Saul's sin,
on their day of battle, with scythes and plowshares
they went out to battle the Philistines there.

I Samuel 14

Saul's son, Jonathan, went with a friend
to check on the Philistine lines.
"We will send
for help if we need it, but I don't want you
to go tell my father what we plan to do."
They saw a small group of Philistines and
Jonathan said, "We are in the Lord's hand.
If we're to succeed, they'll invite us to fight,
but if they attack, then we're meant to take flight."
The Philistine men said, "Come up here, boys!
We'll teach you a lesson that we will enjoy!"
Jonathan said to his friend, "The good Lord
has given them to us by His own accord!"
They climbed up the hill and started to slay
the Philistines. Twenty men died on that day.
A panic broke out in their camp, and they turned
their swords on each other, for God's anger burned
against Philistia. Then Saul's troops attacked
and quickly their army and camp were both sacked.
Then Saul vowed, "No man shall eat before night
or he shall be cursed. We won't stop this fight
till I have revenge."
But Jonathan had
not heard of these things that were said by his dad.
As he and the men marched into the wood,
he tasted some honey and found it was good.
A man told him all that his father had said,
and he told the man, "Our army's near dead,

because they have not been allowed to eat yet.
Think how much greater their fighting would get
if my father let all of the men eat their fill.
How many more Philistines would be killed?"
When battle was done for the day all the men,
ate meat with blood in it, though this was a sin.
So Saul sacrificed to follow God's law,
for he was concerned with the actions he saw.
Then he said to God, "Should we go tonight
in pursuit of our foe and continue to fight?"
But God did not answer, so he said, "What sin
has turned God against His good servant and men?
Whoever has sinned against God must be killed.
Even if it is my own son, it's God's will."
The Lord showed to Saul that Jonathan had
betrayed Him, and this made Saul angry and sad.
"Jonathan, tell me now what have you done?"
"I ate some honey."
"Although you're my son,
the Lord will be angry with me if I don't
do as I've said."
The men cried, "Why won't
you spare him, for he brought us victory. Stay
your sword, for it's Jonathan who won this day."
And so he was spared, but Saul's army retreated,
for though they were winning, they would be defeated
if they went ahead, for Jonathan's sin
would have brought death to all of Saul's men.

I Samuel 15

Then Samuel told Saul, "The Lord says destroy
the Amalekites. When all your armies deploy,
do not spare one life. Wipe their nation away.
Even their cattle and sheep you must slay."
But Saul disobeyed. He said, "I shall keep
their king and the best of their cattle and sheep
as plunder."
Then God came to Samuel and said,

"It grieves me that Saul disobeyed Me. Instead
of doing My will, he now does his own.
He's the wrong person to sit on the throne."
Samuel went out to find Saul, but he learned
that Saul and the army had not yet returned.
Instead Saul had set up a monument to
honor himself. And so Samuel knew
that God had been right, so he went to Saul.
Saul said to Samuel, "Look, I've done all
that God has requested."
"Then why can I hear
the lowing of cattle and sheep in my ear?"
"That is the plunder we took, but the rest
was burned and destroyed. We just kept the best."
"Stop!" Samuel said. "The Lord spoke to me.
He said, 'I told Saul to kill all he would see.
Yet he disobeyed. Am I not the Lord?
Did I not put all of his foes on his sword?'"
"But I did obey Him," King Saul retorted.
"It seems that the Lord has His facts all distorted.
I killed everything except Agag, their king,
and these beasts, but I'll offer to God everything."
Samuel said, "God wanted you to obey.
Not sacrifice. Your actions led you astray."
"You're right. I have sinned. Now let's go before
it's night."
"That's all?! You would say nothing more
than that? You rejected the Lord! So in turn
He's rejected your kingship, for our Lord is stern."
With that Samuel turned, for Saul was condemned
but Saul in his anger, grabbed hold of the hem
of Samuel's robe, which tore in his hand.
Samuel said, "Saul, may you understand,
that God shall soon tear your kingdom in two.
A leader shall come who is purer than you."
Samuel put Agag to death, then withdrew
to his city. Then Samuel mourned, for he knew
that Saul, who was king, was destined to be
overthrown by someone much greater than he.

I Samuel 16:1 - 16:13

The Lord said to Samuel, "Do not mourn Saul.
I'm sending you one who will rule over all
of Israel. Go and anoint him, for he
is a son unto Jesse, chosen by Me."
Samuel went out to Jesse's home, and
he said, "One of your sons will lead the whole land.
Bring them to me."
As each one was brought,
Samuel thought, 'This is the one the Lord sought.'
But all seven sons filed past, and each time
God told him, "This isn't the one."
When the line
was done Samuel turned back to Jesse and asked,
"Are these all your sons? Have all of them passed?"
Jesse said, "No, the youngest has not.
He's tending the sheep."
So David was brought
to him, and when Samuel saw David he knew
that this was the son.
"The Lord is with you!
With oil, you are now anointed to be
King over Israel. Our God can see
that you keep Him holy to you in your heart.
Be true to the Lord and He'll never depart."

I Samuel 16:14 - 16:23

Saul was tormented because he had turned
his back on the Lord, and God's anger burned.
So Saul said, "Go find a harpist for I
am suffering. I must be calmed, lest I die."
A servant said, "I know a man who can play.
He is a good man who walks in the way
of the Lord. He is one of Jesse's fine sons."
They fetched David and when the music was done
it pleased Saul, so he gave a place in his court

to David. Then each time Saul gave a report
that God was tormenting him, David would play,
and the pain that God sent to Saul went away.

I Samuel 17

The Philistines gathered to battle against
the Hebrews, and King Saul set up his defense.
The Philistines had a giant whose name
was Goliath, and everyone feared him. His fame
had spread far and wide.
He yelled, "Why don't you
Israelites send a warrior who's true?
If I should beat him, then you shall submit
to us. If I lose, then we will commit
to serving your king."
All Israel shook,
because all it took was one simple look.
No warrior believed he could battle this man
who towered above everyone in the land.
But David, while taking his brothers some food,
heard all that Goliath had said.
"Who's so rude
to insult the people who follow the Lord?
His head should be placed on the end of our sword."
So David sought Saul, and said, "I will fight
this Philistine who taunts our camp every night."
"But you're just a boy," Saul said, "No offense,
but you cannot fight him. It doesn't make sense."
"I've fought the lions and bears when they came
to carry a sheep off. Now, in God's name,
let me go to battle, and I'll slay him just
as I've killed all those beasts."
Saul said, "If you must,
then go. God be with you."
Saul offered his shield,
but David said, "That is too heavy to yield."
He found a few stones and took out his sling
then yelled at Goliath, "You've cursed our good king

and insulted the Lord. I'll fight you!"
"Who? You?"
Goliath laughed. "You are the warrior who's true?
I'll teach you a lesson."
"You have brought shame
on yourself for disparaging God's holy name."
As Goliath came forth, David took out his sling,
then hurled a rock with his mightiest swing.
The rock struck Goliath on his forehead and
killed him, thus saving all Israel's land.
David ran over and picked up his sword
and cut off Goliath's head.
"Great is the Lord!"
The Philistines ran and the Hebrews pursued.
They caught them and there a bloodbath ensued.

I Samuel 18

So Saul loved David as he loved his son.
And Jonathan loved David, for they had won,
so they were like brothers. David soon rose
in rank because he destroyed all of Saul's foes.
The people cried, "Saul killed his thousands, and then
David killed his tens of thousands of men."
Saul became jealous.
"Do they all believe
that David is greater than me? Would he lead
these people?"
So Saul kept an eye on the boy.
These songs and chants, Saul did not enjoy.
King Saul even tried to kill David twice
but David eluded him. Then, to be nice,
Saul offered Merab, his daughter, to be
wife to young David, but David said, "She
is a princess. I am a servant. I should
not be son-in-law to the king. It's not good
for someone whose family's as low as mine is."
So Saul married Merab away but then his
daughter, Michal, wanted David to be

her husband. So Saul went to him and said, "See,
here is your chance to become son to me."
But again David said, "My own family
is so low."
Saul said, "All I ask of you
is one hundred Philistine foreskins, then you
shall marry my daughter."
At this David grinned.
He went forth and killed the Philistine men.
Then David brought two hundred foreskins to Saul,
double the number he'd asked for in all.
So Michal and David were married, but still
Saul became jealous. He knew the Lord's will
was always with David. God turned against Saul.
The king feared that David would be his downfall.

I Samuel 19 - 20

Saul said to Jonathan, "You must go kill
David, for if we do not, then he will
turn on us."
Jonathan said, "Father, he
is good to us. We can't kill him."
Saul agreed.
But Saul was afflicted. Again the king tried
to kill David. David escaped and his bride,
Michal, said "Flee, for my father will try
to kill you. Run now if you don't want to die."
So David fled during the night and the Lord
kept David from Saul, his spear and his sword.
The Lord was with David, so he could elude
the army of Saul when he was pursued.
So David sought Jonathan asking, "Why does
your father pursue me? Is it because
I've wronged him?"
"No, David. My father trusts me,
and we have agreed that you're to be free."
"He knows we are friends, so he won't tell you."
Jonathan asked David, "What should I do?"

"I am to dine with the king, but I'll hide.
Say to your father that I had to ride
to Bethlehem, where my people are from.
That's why I was not able to come.
If he is angry, then you will know he
is planning on hurting or murdering me."
So Jonathan made a pact with his friend,
that he would be loyal and that he would send
word if his father chose to pursue
such vengeance on David. Then he withdrew
and joined his father. When he was asked
where David was, he stated, "He had the task
of returning to Bethlehem to sacrifice
to God."
Saul said, "Son, here's some advice.
Don't lie to me! Do you think I do not know
that you side with David? Isn't it so?
I tell you as long as that jackal still lives,
this kingdom and all power I have to give
shall never be yours. You're a shame to my name
and a curse on your mother. You are to blame!"
"What's David done? I tell you, desist!"
Saul picked up and hurled a spear but he missed
in killing his son, so Jonathan knew
that David's concerns were all proven true.
So Jonathan told David, "Flee!" and they wept,
but Jonathan's word to his friend had been kept.

I Samuel 21 - 23

David set out and went to a priest
who gave him the bread of the Lord, without yeast,
and David asked him, "Do you have a sword?"
The priest replied, "Only the one that my lord
gained when he slaughtered Goliath."
"There's none
throughout the whole land that can equal that one."
So he took the sword of Goliath and fled.
If Saul were to catch him, he knew he'd be dead.

Now Saul, in pursuit, came to the same priest
and said to him, "Why do you love me the least?
Am I not your king, you treacherous fiend?"
The priest said, "My lord, what is it you mean?
David's your most loyal servant, so we
gave him bread and sword, for isn't it he
that serves you the best?"
But Saul in a rage
told his men to kill each priest and each sage.
So eighty-five priests were killed on that day
but a son of Ahimelech made it away.
He went and told David the things that occurred,
and David was saddened by all that he heard.
So David began to assemble some men
who sided with him, but he saw the sin
of the Philistines who were attacking a town,
so he asked the Lord, "God, shall I go down
and save Keilah's walls?"
The Lord said, "I'll give
the Philistines into your hands. Let none live."
So David went down. He battled and won,
and Saul was pleased when he heard what was done.
"David has trapped himself inside the walls
of Keilah. Besiege it and when the wall falls
then David is mine."
But David was told
Saul's plan, so he prayed, "Lord, will the walls hold?"
God said to David, "The town will hand you
over to Saul. You know what to do."
So David fled Keilah before Saul arrived,
and Saul was frustrated that David survived.
But Saul chased him into the wilderness till
he'd nearly caught David, but then the Lord's will
stopped Saul, for Philistines entered the land,
so Saul left before he had David in hand.

I Samuel 24

When Saul beat the Philistines, he went again
to find and kill David with three thousand men.
Saul didn't know he'd arrived just outside
the cave in which David had chosen to hide.
Saul looked around, but there wasn't a midden.
He went in the cave in which David was hidden.
David snuck up while Saul's back was turned,
but he was compassionate, so he returned
to his men with only a piece of Saul's cloak
that he had cut off, and when David spoke
he said to his men, "King Saul was anointed
by God. This man who the Lord has appointed
as king was my friend. Let's go and show we
know how to be merciful so Saul can see."
So prior to Saul's army leaving again,
David emerged and yelled, "Though within
my grasp, I allowed you to live. What you've said
are lies! Had I chosen, then you would be dead.
But look, here's a corner I took from your coat.
I'd rather take this than cut out your throat.
Why do you want to persist in this act
of vengeance when I have been honest in fact?"
Then Saul wept aloud, "You're more righteous than me.
No man would do this for his sworn enemy.
Just promise me this, and I will be done,
that you will not smite me or murder my son."
"Of course, Saul, I swear it."
At this Saul returned
to his palace, and Saul's anger no longer burned.

I Samuel 25

When Samuel passed on, the whole nation mourned.
Everyone wept for him. All were forlorn.
At this time David encountered a fool
named Nabal who cursed the king and his rule.
Through all of the battles, David's men kept

Nabal's flocks safe. His shepherds had slept,
secure in the knowledge that they'd be unharmed.
But Nabal insulted him. David was armed
and went to his house to talk to the man.
Nabal's wife, Abigail, heard this and ran
out with a gift, saying, "Please, lord, forgive
my husband. He is such a fool. Let us live."
"God be with you," David said, "I am glad
that you came to me, for I'd have been sad
to slay all the people in Nabal's house since
he'd cursed me. I will not accept such offense."
He accepted the gift and when she went home,
she found Nabal drunk in a feast all alone.
So on the next morning Abigail told
Nabal what happened. His heart became cold,
and just ten days later, the foolish man died.
When David heard this, he said, "The man's pride
has been taken care of by God up above."
So David sent Abigail word of his love,
asking if she would be wife to him, for
Saul took back Michal, his first wife, before
he'd fought with David. So Abigail went
to be wife to David with total consent.

I Samuel 26

Saul, not content to let matters just rest,
desired to kill David. He was obsessed.
He set out again with his army of men,
and when David heard this he feared Saul again.
So he and a friend snuck into the tent
of Saul and rather than kill him they went
away in the night with his jug and his spear.
Then David shouted to Saul, "Listen here!
Again I have spared you. Where is your jug
or spear? You say I am some common thug.
But I spared your life! No man can protect
the king except I, your humble subject."
"David?"

"I am your servant, my king."
Saul replied, "I have been wrong in all things.
Blessed are you for sparing me."
So
Saul returned home and let David go.

I Samuel 27 - 28

But David knew now that he couldn't trust Saul,
so he thought, "I'll leave here once and for all
and go live amongst the Philistine's land
and won't be within the king's vengeful hand."
The Philistine king said, "You may live here,
but you'll fight for me, so are we both clear?"
David agreed and the Philistine king
gathered his army and said, "We will bring
war upon Israel."
Saul was in fear
and said, "Fetch a medium and bring her here."
The witch met with Saul. He said, "Call for me
Samuel. Maybe his spirit can see
what is in store for my army and men."
The witch spoke for Samuel, and she said, "Your sin
has given your army and Israel to
the Philistines. This time tomorrow both you
and your sons will join me in death."
Then afraid,
Saul prostrated himself and he prayed.
In fear he returned to his army and thought,
"I shall be dead soon. What have I wrought?"

I Samuel 29

When the Philistines went into battle, they said,
"David's the reason so many are dead.
He has killed Philistine people, so might
he not turn against us in battle and fight?"
The king of the Philistines sought David out
saying, "I trust you, but some men now doubt

whether you're honest."
Then having been spurned,
to Philistia David returned.

I Samuel 30

When David returned, he found that his wives
had all been kidnapped and taken alive
by Amalekite raiders while he'd been away.
So he found his friends and without delay
David and his men all picked up their swords
and David bowed down and prayed to the Lord,
"If I pursue them will I overtake
their party?"
"You will," the Lord answered. "Make
an example of them."
His army set forth.
Out of their land, they came from the north,
and when they were shown the Amalekite site
they leapt upon them and they started to fight.
After they massacred all but the few
who escaped to the desert, the men went into
the tents and they found their families inside,
and gave praise to God because nobody died.

I Samuel 31

Just as Samuel's spirit had said,
many in Israel's army were dead
after they fought with the Philistine men,
for God was still angry because of Saul's sin.
The archers saw Saul and somebody shot
an arrow that hit him.
"I will not be caught,"
he said to his armor bearer. "Now draw
your sword. All these men who don't know the law,
these uncircumcised, shall never be my
captors. So stab me! Make sure that I die."
But his armor bearer would not, so he drew

and fell on his sword. His servant did too.
All of Saul's sons also died on that day.
The Israelites saw their leaders this way,
and ran for their lives. So the Philistines won,
and the first king of Israel died with his sons.

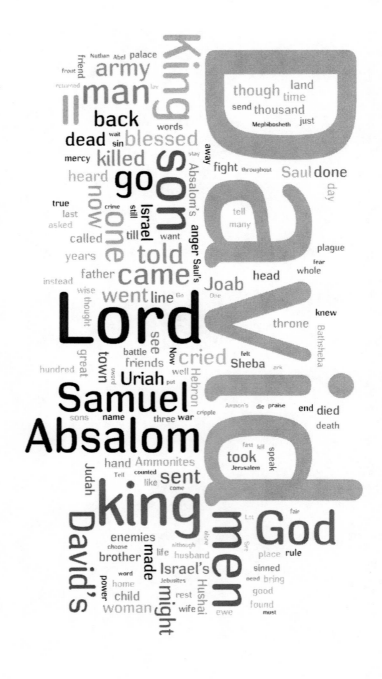

II Samuel 1 - 4

Seeing Saul dead, David mourned and he tore
his clothes, although Saul had caused David more
grief in his time than he'd ever deserved,
Saul was the king under whom David served.
David lamented Jonathan too
a friend like a brother. Then God said, "Now you
shall go up to Hebron and there be anointed
as king. Go forth, for you are appointed."
But the Israelites crowned one of Saul's sons,
even though David was set as the one
to rule over Israel and Judah too.
War raged between them, and as Judah grew
in power by David, Israel fell
and faltered, for that kingdom wasn't ruled well.
Its men went to David. Even the kin
of the king killed their brother and then went to him.
But David could not rejoice when he had heard
that Israel's king was deceased. He was stirred
to anger. Their king had been killed by the men
in his family, so David could not rest again
until he knew all his foe's killers were killed.
For David was humble, and so he fulfilled
the law of the Lord. Then he stood alone
as the man to rule Judah's and Israel's throne.

II Samuel 5 - 6

Then David was made the king over all,
and so he besieged Jerusalem's walls.

He conquered the Jebusites, going in through
a water shaft which took his army into
the city. They routed the Jebusites and
established that place as the throne of the land.
Then he put the Philistines under his sword,
because he was blessed by the grace of the Lord.
To celebrate, King David brought up the ark
of God, who'd made light where once there was dark.
Its power was great, and everyone voiced
excitement. The City of David rejoiced.
But Michal saw David, her husband, as he
was dancing half-naked.
"You fool! Don't you see?
You're disgracing yourself and the throne of the king!
Disrobing yourself among slaves? What a thing
for a great man to do. You should be ashamed."
"I just celebrated the Lord, who is famed
for lifting me up to rule in His land.
Your father has fallen, so I understand
that you are upset. But honor shall be
for those of us who love the Lord. He loves me."
Because she was not with the Lord, the Lord left
her childless until the day of her death.

II Samuel 7

Then David decided he wanted to build
a temple but God told him, "Have I fulfilled
My will through your hands? So if I required
a temple, I would have told you I desired
a place for My ark, and where I might rest.
I tell you a place will be built and be blessed,
but not by you, David, but by your own son.
This is the way that My will shall be done.
Your throne is established, and your son shall reign."
"You, Lord," cried David, "have spared me from pain.
You've given me victory and blessed my line.
On my head Your grace and Your mercy has shined."

II Samuel 8 - 9

David subdued all his enemies who
fought with him. Moab, the Philistines too,
Arameans and Edomites all felt the knife
of Israel's army throughout David's life.
But David was kind. He said, "Is there not
someone in Saul's line whom I have forgot?
Saul honored me before he became
my enemy. If I can, I'll do the same
for those of his line."
"Sire, there's one.
Mephibosheth, Jonathan's last living son.
But he is a cripple."
"Bring him to me."
And when he was brought, King David said, "See,
your father was one of my very good friends,
and I shall be good to you till the end.
All that was Saul's is yours. May you grow
and prosper. With you, the Lord God shall go."
Mephibosheth cried, "Why would you see me?
For I'm but a cripple."
"This I can see,
but it's my desire to care for your line
just as your grandfather Saul did for mine."

II Samuel 10

When the king of the Ammonites died, David sent
some men to the son of their king in lament.
But the Ammonites said, "You are spies," and they shaved
the messengers' beards. Through this they displayed
contempt for the Israelites. When the news
that the Ammonites had disrespected the Jews,
came back to King David he told his men, "Stay
in Jericho. When your beards grow we will pay
them back."
Then the Ammonites knew they would fight,
so they asked Aram to add their army's might

to theirs. When the Israelite army went
they routed the forces that both nations sent.

II Samuel 11

In spring, when David sent all of his men
to fight and to die in battle again,
he stayed in Jerusalem. While he was there,
he noticed a woman out bathing. So fair
was Bathsheba, that David called out to her and
she came and slept with him. In far distant lands
her husband was fighting with David's whole force.
As soon as the moon had made its full course,
she came back and said, "I am pregnant." In fear,
David told one of his servants, "Come near.
Go find Uriah the Hittite and bring
him back from the army."
Although it was spring
Uriah, her husband, was fetched and he came.
When he arrived home, David called him by name.
The king asked him how all the battles had gone,
then told him to go to his home until dawn.
He hoped that Uriah would lie with his wife,
and so avoid trouble, anger, and strife,
but Uriah instead slept down by the gate
of the palace. Then David said, "Why would you wait
to go to your home?"
"How could I go there
and lie with my wife? That would not be fair
to all of my friends who are fighting the war,
sleeping on rocks. They're hungry and sore."
So David sent word to his generals so
they would station Uriah where all of their foes
might kill him. And so by David's design,
Uriah was placed at the front of the line.
He was killed and Bathsheba mourned for her man
the requisite time, then took David's hand
and married him. Then she bore David a son,
but the Lord wasn't pleased with what David had done.

II Samuel 12

Nathan the prophet told King David, "There
was a poor man who raised a small ewe and he cared
for it like the ewe were his daughter, but then
nearby was a rich man who filled up his pens
with flocks. When a traveler came to their town,
the rich man decided that he would go down
and kill the small ewe of the poor man instead
of his own so the traveling man would be fed."
"No!" David cried, "That's a crime. Tell me who
this tyrant might be."
"That tyrant is you!
You have many wives. Have you not been blessed
by the Lord God Almighty above all the rest?
But you've done great evil in front of the Lord.
You took a man's wife and gave him the sword."
"I have!" David cried. "Oh God, please forgive
your servant."
"He will, but your son will not live."
And as Nathan said this, the babe became ill,
and though David fasted, it was the Lord's will
that the child should die. And when it was dead,
David stopped fasting and said, "I'll be fed."
His servants then asked, "Why'd you weep and fast
while the child still lived, but now eat at last
when the child is dead?"
"Why should I now weep?
When the child still lived, the Lord could still keep
His anger and wrath from the boy. But he's dead
so now I'll bow down to God's greatness instead."
And so David lay with Bathsheba again.
She bore him a son, but this time no sin
had clouded the union or birth and they gave
thanks to the Lord. The road was now paved
for David's successor, for God loved this son
and so the Lord blessed David's boy, Solomon.

II Samuel 13

Amnon, one of David's sons, was
lustful for his step-sister because
of Tamar's beauty. He even felt ill,
till one of his cousins said, "Is it your will
to go on like this? Tell David you need
your sister to bring you some food and then feed
you till you are well."
And that's what he did,
although he knew that the Law would forbid
his actions. When Tamar and he were alone,
he took her. She said, "The Lord won't condone
this incest."
But he raped her anyway, then
in anger he hated her now more than when
he'd wanted her.
She cried, "If you should send me
away now that I am defiled, you'll be
crueler than if you would wed me."
Instead
he pushed his step-sister away, so she fled
to her brother Absalom who took her in
though she was disgraced by Amnon's great sin.
Two years went by, and during this time
Absalom did not speak of Amnon's crime,
but then the day came when he got his revenge
and killed Amnon so Tamar could be avenged.
Absalom, fearing revenge, ran away,
though David hoped his son would come back some day.

II Samuel 14

Then Joab, who was one of David's friends, found
a wise woman who he sent into the town.
She spoke to King David, "One of my sons
has killed his own brother. It can't be undone.
But now the whole town cries out for his death.
I am a widow and with my last breath

I'll beg for his life, for there is no doubt
that if my son dies, my light will go out."
"Fear not," King David replied. "I will send
out a decree. This matter shall end."
Then the wise woman said, "See! You convict
yourself with these words. While you contradict
your very own actions, your son is outcast.
But God does not wait for a person to fast
before He allows them to find their way back
inside of His mercy."
"You do not lack
for words, but I think that they came from my friend,
Joab."
"It's true. He hopes you might end
this madness with Absalom."
"So it shall be.
Joab, fetch Absalom. Bring him to me."
Though Absalom came to the palace again,
for two years King David did not speak to him.
When King David finally called for his son,
he thought that the troubles between them were done.

II Samuel 15 - 17

But Absalom sought to be king of the land,
and so he went out taking every man's hand,
embracing them and winning over their hearts.
He thought to himself, 'This is how power starts.'
He said to King David, "I have made a vow,
to God if I ever returned here I'd bow
down at His altar in Hebron. Let me
go to our Lord."
"Then so shall it be."
But Absalom told many men, "When I come
to Hebron, then shout out and beat on the drum.
Yell 'King Absalom of Hebron' so all
will know I am king when they hear your call.
When David heard this, he said, "We must flee,
for we're undefended. My son threatens me."

Then David sent spies to learn of the plot
his son had against him, for King David thought,
'My friends will frustrate his plans.' So he sent
all he could trust, so they might prevent
Absalom's war on his father. Some men
blessed David, saying again and again,
"You are our king." But some cursed him too.
Meanwhile Absalom lay with the few
concubines David had left to maintain
the palace, in order to curse David's name.
Then Absalom's counselor said, "Let us go
and strike down King David, so Israel knows
that you are the true king."
Absalom called
for his father's friend Hushai.
"Should I take all
of the soldiers I have and go out to fight?"
"This is unwise," Hushai said, "for the might
of your father is known far and wide. If you fail,
then so will your kingship, while David prevails."
Hushai spoke wisely, so Absalom heeded
his words, but Hushai went out and proceeded
to send word to David of what his son planned,
so he would be saved from Absalom's hand.

II Samuel 18 - 20

King David assembled all his soldiers where
his son came to fight. He told the men there,
"Be gentle, for though we're at war, he's my son.
I don't want him dead when this day is done."
The battle was fierce. A thousand score died,
as Absalom's men fell to David's side.
When riding his mule, Absalom was caught in
a tree, but not one of the men would harm him
till Joab ran up and stuck in his spear,
chastising all those around him, "Don't fear
this man!"
When David heard his son was dead,

the king began weeping and cried out in dread,
"Oh Absalom! Son! It should have been me
who died."
Then Joab said, "Do you not see
you embarrass yourself, and humiliate all
of the men who have followed you. Why do you call
for the life of your enemies, but you despise
the ones who love you? Now dry out your eyes!
If you don't go out and thank all your men
before the moon rises, I tell you that when
the morning arrives, not one man shall stay
here by your side. Now cease this display!"
So David made peace with his men and returned
as king to Jerusalem. Those who had spurned
the king were forgiven. And Judah was true
to David, but Israel's men shouted, "You
aren't Israel's king!"
They followed a man
named Sheba. And David said, "We need a plan,
for Sheba will be more dangerous than
Absalom was."
And so they began
pursuing the army of Sheba until
they caught him at Abel. A woman said, "Will
you rain down your terror on this town? Please speak
and tell us what is it that your army seeks?"
Joab said, "We do not want to attack
your village. We don't want to plunder and sack
this town. Our mission is only to bring
Sheba's head back to David our king."
The wise woman said, "Be patient and we
will throw his head over the wall. Wait and see."
And so all the people of Abel went in,
killed Sheba and threw his head to the men
of King David's army. The battle was through,
and David was king over Israel too.

II Samuel 21 - 22

King David had prospered throughout all his days,
for God had been with him. He sang out in praise,
"The Lord is my Rock. My Fortress. For He
is Shield and Salvation. The Lord comforts me.
If death wraps me up in its grasp, it is through
the mercy of God that I stay here with you.
For He heard my cry and so split the sky
and came down from Heaven. As lightning bolts fly
destroying my enemies, I praise His name.
Creator of darkness; Inventor of rain!
He drew me out when I nearly had drowned.
I've kept the ways of the Lord, and I've found
that with Him before me, I turn from all sin.
The Lord God has blessed me again and again.
You are the lamp who lights up the dark.
You are our refuge and You are our spark."

II Samuel 23 - 24

David had men who were mightier than
the best fighters in any neighboring land.
One hundred men were not equal to one
of his mighty men, for they were second to none.
But King David sinned when he counted the whole
of his army. For once he had taken a toll,
he found there were eight hundred thousand who dwelled
in Israel. Judah was counted as well,
and five hundred thousand were there. But the Lord
told David, "This census was not My accord!
Because you have sinned, so now you must choose
three years of famine, or three years to lose
against all your enemies, or just three days
of plague?"
David said, "My Lord, as You say,
I've sinned. I choose plague, for let not a man
destroy us. I'll put us all into Your hand."

Seventy thousand were lost. David cried,
"Lord, why have so many good people died?"
Then David submitted to God, and He heard.
So God stopped the plague, for God is the Word.

I Kings 1 - 2

When David was elderly, one of his sons
sought to be king. Not his oldest one,
but one who was younger, boastful, and proud.
When Bathsheba heard this, she cried out aloud
to David, "My husband, why is this so?
You promised to me, and this you should know,
that Solomon was to be king. Here you lie
as others are hoping each day that you die.
When that day arrives, Solomon and
myself will be criminals in our own land,
and we shall be killed by your son who claims
he's king. You must do something, in the Lord's name."
So David proclaimed, "Adonijah, my son,
shall not be the king. Let God's will be done.
Nathan the prophet shall take Solomon.
Anoint him as king. Now let it be done."
And when it was so and David had died,
Solomon struck down each person who tried
to overthrow him, and so it was known
that Solomon truly established his throne.

I Kings 3:1 - 3:15

God, in a dream, came to Solomon and
said, "I am the Lord, so know that My hand
rests on your heart. Just ask and I'll give
whatever you want for as long as you live."
Then Solomon said, "I don't know Your will,
so give me the knowledge to know and fulfill

the things You desire."
And God said, "Because
you asked Me for knowledge to fulfill My laws,
you'll have it as well as long life and good health.
You'll also know victory, honor, and wealth."
And so it was done as the Lord said He would,
and Solomon lived a life that was good.

I Kings 3:16 - 3:28

Now two prostitutes, who lived side by side
came and said, "Solomon, won't you decide?"
The first woman said, "This baby is mine."
The second said, "This woman has some design
on gaining my child."
The first then replied,
"Yes, she had a baby, but her baby died!"
The other said, "No! The dead baby was
attached to your breast."
"That's only because
you put your own child by me in the dark."
"Sire, do not trust this woman's remark."
Then Solomon told them, "Silence! Be still.
Servant, now bring me a sword, if you will.
We'll cut through the child. Each woman will own
one half of the baby."
The first woman groaned,
"No! Give the child to her."
But the other
said, "Cut it. Then neither of us shall be mothers."
Then Solomon said, "Give the babe to the one
who would give him away."
And so it was done.
When Israel heard this, they were all awed,
for they knew such wisdom was given by God.

I Kings 4 - 9

The people of Judah and Israel ate,
drank, and were happy. Their life was a great
success under Solomon. All of the land
was peaceful so Solomon said, "Understand,
the Lord said that while my father still breathed
His temple would not stand. When I relieved
his rule, by my hand the Lord's temple should
rise from the ground, and it will be good."
And so it was built as the Lord had decreed,
a temple for God. And when this great deed
was done, Solomon built up a huge place
that would be his palace, and put in each space
furnishings that were appealing and fine;
fitting for kings from David's bloodline.
Then Solomon brought the covenant ark
to the temple and stood. There the monarch
said, "Great is the Lord who did as He told
my father He would. For in days of old,
the ark traveled with the women and men,
but God has desired a place to dwell in.
Now God, I ask You, great Peacemaker and
Lord of the heavens, the Lord of the land,
fulfill Your promise to keep David's own
bloodline to reign on Israel's throne.
I also pray You will dwell in this place,
showing Your servants mercy and grace.
Lord, be a bounty to foreigners who
hear of Your might, and native sons too.
Be with Your people, and let us be wise
so we may do that which is right in Your eyes."
God came to Solomon, in His response,
"You've done all I asked, in every nuance.
If you will uphold My laws and be true,
then I will be good and faithful to you.
But if you forget My laws or My name,
all within Israel shall be to blame.
Then even this temple will crumble and fall,

for you'll have forgotten that I am the Law."
With a warning God's temple was thus dedicated,
blessed by the Lord, and so consecrated.

I Kings 10

The Queen of Sheba then came and she saw
the temple and palace, built without flaw.
She saw Solomon was as wise as she'd heard.
This was the land where God truly stirred.
"I'm surprised," the queen said. "The rumors of you
are just as I heard. All of them true."
And thus many rulers knew that the Lord
was with Solomon; his greatest reward.

I Kings 11

Solomon's wives and all his concubines
numbered one thousand, but he did not find
them all amongst Israel. Many had been
plucked from idolatry. They brought this sin
and led him astray, so when he was old
he wandered from God, though he had been told
to follow the Lord alone as his own.
So God said, "I won't take you off of your throne.
But still I shall punish you, for from the hands
of your son, when he's king, he'll lose many lands
that once were one nation. But he will keep one
of the tribes so My promise shall not be undone."
During this time, Jeroboam rebelled.
The prophet Ahijah tore cloth that he held.
"Now, Jeroboam, ten pieces shall be
given to you, for God has decreed
ten tribes shall be yours, though David's line will
hold onto one, so the Lord's word is fulfilled."
On hearing this, Solomon sought to strike down
Jeroboam, for this news had threatened his crown
as well as the one that would someday be on
his son's head when Solomon was dead and gone.

But then Jeroboam fled and he stayed
in Egypt till Solomon went to his grave.

I Kings 12

When Solomon died, his son Rehoboam
succeeded his father. And when Jeroboam
heard this he went to the new king and said,
"Your father was harsh to the people. Instead
of continuing that, please give us some rest."
The king said, "Give me time to think on what's best.
Return in three days and then I will tell
my answer. Till then I bid you farewell."
The king then consulted the elders who gave
advice to his father. They said, "If you save
the people from toil, they'll always serve you."
But King Rehoboam's friends said, "Do not do
what those old men say. Aren't you the king now?
Tell the complainers that you'll show them how
hard they can work. If your father was tough,
then now they shall truly know work that is rough."
So when Jeroboam returned, the king said
what his friends had told him. With Solomon dead
and his son now king, the Israelites
abandoned Jerusalem, leaving the fight
to Judah alone to remain loyal to
David's house.
King Rehoboam said, "You
shall never abandon us!"
He went to fight
the whole house of Israel. But on one night
the Lord told His prophet, "Go forth and then say
'No one shall go into battle today.'"
When the king heard what the Lord had declared
he turned back the army that he had prepared.
With Israel separate from Judah, they then
worshipped false idols. Immersed in their sin,
Israel brought about their own damnation,
and God turned His face away from their nation.

I Kings 13

By the word of the Lord, a man of God stood
declaring, "Oh Israel, if only you would
stay true, but you won't. You will turn away
and the altar of God shall break on that day."
On hearing this, King Jeroboam reached out.
"Seize him," he shouted. His hand which was stout,
withered as if it were crippled and dead
and the altar was split as the man of God said.
Then the king begged the man, "Sir, please intercede
with the Lord. From this ailment let me be freed."
The man of God did, and so it was healed,
but the man of God's words were already sealed.
His curse on the land was set, and although
Jeroboam said, "Eat with me before you go."
The man would not yield, till a prophet spoke up
saying, "God wants you to share my plate and my cup."
But the prophet had lied, so when the man ate,
God said, "You were not to taste from the plate
of these wicked ones. Now you'll be buried afar,
and not where your kin or your ancestors are."
The man of God left, and as his donkey strode
a lion came out dragging him from the road
and killing him there in the foreigner's land.
Some saw him but they did not understand
why the donkey and lion stood next to him there.
They sought out the prophet and told the man where
his body as well as the beasts were all stationed.
The man was then buried in that foreign nation.

I Kings 14

Jeroboam did not change his ways, and his wife
sought out any prophet to foretell the life
of their son who'd be king once his father had died,
but when she went forth, she went in disguise.
The prophets of God were against the King and

she was told, "Woman, don't you understand
that God knows your mind? He knows your heart too.
You've come seeking hope, but I have bad news.
When you return home, your son will be dead.
You've worshipped false idols and so the Lord said
He'll strike down your line. You all bear the scorn
of the Lord, but your son, for him we shall mourn."
And when she returned, when she put her foot
in the house, her son died. Then ashes and soot
and sackcloth were worn as the people all cried
that a God-fearing boy should have tragically died.
And all through this time, the king, Rehoboam,
fought and made war with King Jeroboam.
They both went to fight with the hardest of hearts,
so Judah and Israel were torn apart.

I Kings 15 - 16

The kings who would follow all practiced the ways
of wickedness, except for Asa. His days
brought God back to Judah. But it did not last,
for Ahab, his son, made sins from the past
seem paltry. For he and his wife Jezebel
were the worst rulers ever inside Israel
and Judah. False idols were worshiped and God
was forgotten or worse, condemned as a fraud.

I Kings 17

Now Elijah, the Tishbite, came forth and proclaimed,
"The Lord says for years there shall be no rain."
Then God told Elijah, "Flee and I will
send ravens to feed you and you'll drink your fill."
But the brook soon dried up, and the Lord sent him to
Zarephath saying, "Waiting for you
is a widow who has been blessed by My hand."
Elijah found her when he fled to her land.
"Woman, will you fetch a drink and some bread?"
"But, sir, both my son and I soon will be dead.

The flour I own was to make our last meal."
"The Lord is with you, woman. Though you may feel
unsure, make a cake and bring it to me,
then bread for your son and you. Soon you will see.
The flour and oil will not run out till
the Lord brings us rain, for this is His will."
But not that much later, the widow's son died.
"Elijah, why does the Lord hate me?" she cried.
"Give me your son."
Then he stretched out his hand.
"Lord, heal this boy. Please, God, understand."
Three times he uttered this so God would hear,
as the woman stood by in her anguish and fear.
Then God put the breath back into the boy.
"The Lord is with you!" cried the widow with joy.

I Kings 18

In the third year, God said, "I'll soon bring you rain.
Elijah, now go forth to Ahab again."
He saw Obadiah and said, "Tell the king,
Elijah has come."
"If I do this thing,
surely I'll die. Those words will lead me
right to my death if then you should flee."
Elijah said, "Sure as the Lord God is one,
I will be here. Now see that it's done."
When Ahab was fetched, he came and he said,
"You troublesome fool. I wish you were dead."
"The trouble is you. Now call all the men
who prophesy, then come and meet me again."
When this had been done, Elijah called out,
"All of you men who stir up such doubt:
Go get two bulls, and sacrifice one,
but don't light the fire, for when you are done,
I'll take the other as my sacrifice.
I'll pray to the Lord, as you all entice
your gods and ask them to come down and burn
your offering up. And then I in turn

will do the same thing. Whoever's god hears,
shall light up their fire, and it shall be clear."
The men who worshiped the Baals danced around
their sacrificed bull. Despite all the sound
of their singing and cutting themselves, not a spark
was seen. Not one flicker cut through the dark.
Elijah told them, "Now, it is my turn.
Pour water on my altar, so it can't burn.
Pour more! Drench the wood! Oh, God hear my cry.
Send them a sign so they'll know that the sky
and earth are all yours"
Then a fire burst forth
that burned up the wood and the bull as it scorched
everything, even though it was all wet.
Elijah then ordered his servants to get
the prophets of Baal. He slaughtered them all.
Then he told King Ahab, "Rain will soon fall.
Get in your chariot before the storm
can come up the valley, before the clouds form."
Though Ahab was riding, Elijah ran faster
because of the power that flowed from his Master.

I Kings 19

Then Ahab told Jezebel all he had seen.
She said, "May the gods all punish this queen
if Elijah's not slain as he did to the men
who are priests of my gods, for this outrageous sin!"
So Elijah ran into the desert to hide.
While exiled, he spoke to God and he cried,
"I'm finished, O God! Kill me so that I
am done with this life and this pain. Let me die."
But the Lord sent an angel to feed him so he
had the strength to flee from the queenly decree.
Then God came to him and said, "Why are you
hiding, Elijah?"
"Lord, all that I do
is hated. Though I am still zealous, my cries
fall on deaf ears. The good prophets die!"

"Go out and stand on the mountain, for I
am coming to you. You'll feel Me pass by."
A powerful wind then tore through the air,
but Elijah could tell that the Lord was not there.
Then an earthquake. Again, the Lord was not in
the earthquake either. He waited, and then
a fire broke out, but the Lord did not dwell
in the fire. But after these three mighty swells
a whisper was heard, and Elijah bowed down,
"O God, it is You. The King and the Crown!"
"Elijah, go back. Anoint Hazael
king of Aram, and for Israel
make Jehu the king. Elisha you'll make
a prophet, for he is the one who will take
your place when you're gone.
"Yes, Lord, I shall yield."
He found Elisha at work in a field.
Elijah called to him, they sacrificed and
they both went and prophesied as the Lord planned.

I Kings 20

Ben-Hadad besieged Samaria and
told Ahab, "All you possess in this land
is mine. Your women, your silver and gold."
And Ahab relented, "I'll do as I'm told."
Ben-Hadad then sent a messenger who
said, "I also want what's important to you.
I'll come to the palace and take all I see."
But Ahab said, "This is insulting to me.
I gave all you wanted the first time, but now
I refuse."
Ben-Hadad said, "Then you'll see how
I can level your city." And so there was war.
But a prophet told Ahab what God had in store.
"The Lord says that He shall deliver this day
the army of Aram. Go forth and repay
this insult."
So Ahab went out and he won,

but the prophet said, "This war has only begun."
The officials who fought by Ben-Hadad's side
said, "We know the reason why so many died.
Their God is a god of the hills. Sir, we need
to fight on the plains if we want to succeed."
The next spring, he mustered his troops and he went
to the plains of Aphek and set up his tent.
Then the prophet told Ahab, "They think if they fight
us out on the plains, the Lord has no might.
Because of this, God gives them into your hands."
One hundred thousand were killed and the land
was covered in blood as Ben-Hadad fled.
When caught, he groveled to Ahab and said,
"I'll give you the cities that my father felled
and a place in Damascus' market as well."
"Then I'll spare your life," King Ahab replied.
But the son of a prophet heard this and cried,
"Stab me!" to one of his friends. He was cut.
He went to the king in disguise and said, "What
should be done to me? I let a man go
who should not have lived. Now should it be so
that I die for him?"
"This judgment is sound,"
said Ahab.
The prophet took his disguise down.
"Then so it shall be. Your life for the life
of the foreigner who should have died by the knife."

I Kings 21

Ahab was angered by what he had heard.
He didn't believe that it was God's word.
When he had returned to Samaria, he
approached a man, Naboth, and told him, "I see
your vineyard nearby. I'll pay a good price,
for I want a beautiful garden."
"That's nice,
but that is my birthright, which I cannot sell."
Ahab then sulked till his queen, Jezebel,

said, "What kind of king are you? Just wait and see.
I'll get you your garden."
And so it was she
who sent all the elders a message that read,
"Find me two scoundrels and when they have said
'This vintner cursed God,' then let him be stoned."
With that man now dead, Ahab could own
the vineyard. But God sent Elijah to meet
King Ahab.
"My enemy! You've come to greet
your king?"
"You have murdered a man for this land.
Where dogs licked his blood, the same dogs will stand,
and lick up yours too! God blots out your line.
On Jezebel's body the wolves shall all dine."
Then Ahab cried out, put on sackcloth, and asked
for forgiveness. God heard him.
"Judgment won't pass
on Ahab. Instead, it shall be on his son
that these troubles descend when the king's days are done."

I Kings 22:1 - 22:28

Jehoshaphat, king over Judah, went down
to Ahab and asked if he would lend his crown
to invading Ramoth Gilead.
"Let us go,"
Ahab replied.
"Don't you want to know
if God's on our side?" Jehoshaphat said.
"Surely the prophets of God aren't all dead."
"There's one," Ahab sulked, "but I hate him, for he
has always prophesied bad things for me."
"The king shouldn't speak so! Go, fetch the man."
Micaiah was summoned.
"I understand
you're a prophet of God. If we go to fight,
to whose army shall the Lord lend His might?"
"You'll triumph," Micaiah said.

"Wait! Swear that you
are truthful," said Ahab.
"I'll tell you what's true.
The Lord said, 'Will someone go lie to the king
so that he may die and in this way bring
the fall of his house?"
Then Ahab cried out,
"I knew you were lying! Good news made me doubt.
Put this man in prison until we have won."
"If you survive, God doesn't speak through my tongue."

I Kings 22:29 - 22:53

So Ahab entered the battle disguised.
Despite this Ramoth Gilead realized
that Jehoshaphat wasn't the one whom they sought.
Then out flew a random arrow that caught
between Ahab's armor. On that day he died.
And so in their quest, they were quickly denied.
King Ahab's body was taken and cleaned
in the prostitutes' bath, and as had been deemed
the dogs licked his blood as it fell on the earth,
for never was there such a king who lacked worth.
Ahaziah took up the crown of the king,
and, just like his father, sought out wicked things.

II Kings 1

Ahaziah fell and was injured so he
sent for the priests of Baal-zebub.
"See
if I will recover."
Elijah was sent
and said to the messengers, "Aren't you content
to follow the Lord? I say unto you
the king will not leave the bed he's bound to."
"Elijah?!" the king cried out. "Go arrest
that man."
Then fifty men went to request,
"Man of God, come with us now. Do you hear?"
"If I am of God, let fire appear
and burn you all up."
Then fire came down
from the sky. The fifty were burned to the ground.
Fifty more came, and fifty more died.
The captain came up.
"Please," the man cried,
"spare me and all of my men. For the king
has told us to come here. If we don't bring
you back he will kill us."
Elijah said, "Yay,
it will be as I said."
And the king passed away.
Ahaziah had no son of his own,
so Joram, his brother, took over the throne.

II Kings 2:1 - 2:18

Elijah said to Elisha, "Stay here,
for a whirlwind's coming, but do not have fear."
And Elisha said, "I'll go wherever you go."
So they went to Bethel and then Jericho.
When they came to the Jordan River they stood.
Elijah took off his cloak and his hood
and threw it against the water which parted.
Then in a fury the prophet departed
Fire and horses came down from the sky
and took him away, to Heaven on high.
Then Elisha gained some of the spirit that lived
in Elijah, because it was God's gift to give.

II Kings 2:19 - 2:25

When Elisha was walking, some men came and said,
"If something's not done, we'll all soon be dead
for our water is bad."
So Elisha said, "Get
a bowl and some salt."
And then he dumped it
down in their well.
"By the Lord's power I
make your water pure."
Then with a goodbye
he went up to Bethel, and there some boys came
and called him 'baldheaded' and other mean names.
So he cursed the boys and two bears came out
of the forest and threw the boys' bodies about.
They mauled forty-two of the youths on that day,
then the prophet Elisha went on his way.

II Kings 3

When Joram was king, Moab rebelled.
They didn't pay tribute because they'd been held
by Ahab so long, they sought to be free.

But Joram took up his army and he
convinced Jehoshaphat to come and fight
with his army so he could double his might.
They ran out of water, and said, "We must seek
a prophet of God to come here and speak.
We must find out if the Lord's on our side."
Elisha was there so they told him, "Provide
the word of the Lord."
He said, "You hate all
that is godly, so Joram, why is it you called?
I would not have come, except that I'll stand
with Jehoshaphat, but all the rest in this land
worship their idols, so I'd turn my back
on Joram and his army in this attack.
But God is with you, although I am not.
Water will come, and when you have fought,
you'll stand triumphantly over the men
of Moab."
So when it was morning again,
water appeared. They drank and were quenched.
When Moab attacked not one of them flinched,
for they knew that they were backed by the Lord,
and they put the Moabites all to the sword.

II Kings 4:1 - 4:7

A widow came to Elisha and said,
"As you know, great prophet, my husband is dead.
His creditor comes to collect on his debt.
He'll take my two sons. I have nothing left!"
"Tell me," he said, "what else do you own?"
"I have just a bit of fine oil at home."
"Go borrow some pots from your friends and then fill
each one up with oil, for by the Lord's will
you will not run out till you have enough
to pay off your debts. Although times are rough
the Lord is with you.
And when she had done
what the man of God said, she saved both her sons.

II Kings 4:8 - 4:37

A rich woman made a room at her home
for Elisha whenever he went out to roam.
To thank her, he said, "Please tell us how we
can repay you."
"Oh, sir, there's nothing I need."
But Elisha was told that the woman had no
children. Her husband was sickly and so
Elisha said, "You'll bear a son by next year.
You live in the Lord and the Lord knows your fear."
The woman then bore a son and he grew,
but the young boy became ill after a few
years. The woman embraced him and cried
when the gift God had given her exhaled and died.
She went to Elisha dismayed by his fate,
and he told her, "Come. It's not yet too late."
And so they set off, and when they arrived,
she said, "See! I told you he already died!"
But Elisha went in to where the corpse lay.
he stretched himself over it, to her dismay.
But then the boy breathed.
"See, your son lives.
You've followed your God, so this gift He gives."

II Kings 4:38- 6:23

Elisha performed other miracles too.
He fed many men with bread and with stew
that was poisonous or was too little to eat,
but he multiplied it and made it good meat.
He healed Aram's army commander who then
said, "Truly your God is the one God. My sins
are numerous, let me be cleansed."
So he took
the Lord as his God, and lived by His book.
When Aram attacked, Elisha helped too.
He told his king all of the things that he knew,

frustrating the army of Aram until
scouts were sent out to abduct or to kill
Elisha. But when they arrived they were blind,
for the Lord did not want them to know how to find
the prophet. Then he led them all to the king
of Israel saying, "See what I bring.
Do not kill these prisoners. Feed them instead.
Return them that they may go sleep in their beds.
When Aram's king sees your great mercy he'll go
away from our land."
And thus it was so.

II Kings 6:24 - 7:20

After some time passed, Aram returned,
besieging Samaria. Everyone yearned
for the Lord to release them. Famine was great.
A woman called out to the king, "Hear my fate."
"How can I help? I have nothing as well!
But I'll hear your story, if you will but tell."
"Yesterday, my neighbor said, 'Kill your son,
so that we may eat.' And so it was done.
Today I said, 'Now you must kill your son too,
so that we may eat.' But this she won't do."
Hearing this story, the king tore his cloak.
he wept, put on sackcloth, and then the king spoke.
"Elisha has brought us to this awful day!"
He sent for Elisha, but he hid away,
saying, "Tomorrow, the people won't want
for food. My king, now call off this hunt!"
The next day the armies of Aram had fled
for the Lord had put frightening thoughts in their head.
So the people came out, in great celebration,
for God heard their pleas and gave them salvation.

II Kings 8

Hazael went to Elisha and said,
"The great king of Aram is ill and in bed.

He sent me to find you for he wants to know
if he will survive or it's his time to go."
Elisha just stared at him, then he said, "When
you return you will tell him that he'll rule again.
But I have been shown that he'll die, Hazael."
Elisha wept, "How you shall harm Israel!"
Then Hazael left and returned to his king.
"Hazael, tell me the message you bring."
"You'll live," he replied, but the very next day
he smothered the king in the bed where he lay.
Now during this time, Jehoram began
his reign over Judah, and all in the land
of Edom rebelled and they broke away,
and so they have been that way till this day.
Jehoram passed on and Ahaziah's rule
started. Like his father, he too was cruel.
He continued the line of Ahab and all
the people knew this line did not heed God's call.

II Kings 9 - 10

Elisha summoned a prophet and said,
"Go to Jehu. Pour this on his head."
He handed the man some oil.
"Then say,
the Lord anoints you the king here today
over all Israel. Wipe out the line
of Ahab, and all of the false idol shrines."
Then Jehu set out to kill Joram and all
idolaters in Ramoth Gilead's walls.
As Jehu approached, Joram said, "Do
you come here in peace?"
"How can I when you
have tarnished the name of our Lord?"
Joram fled,
but with just one arrow, Joram was dead.
Then Jehu tracked down Ahaziah and
killed him as he tried to flee through the land.
Then Jehu went back to Jezreel, and found

Jezebel painted and dressed in a gown.
"There you are, murderer," she screamed at him.
He looked to her eunuchs and called out to them,
"Throw the witch down off of those castle walls."
They did and her body was smashed in the fall.
Dogs came and ate up her corpse in the street.
"Just as the Lord said they would!" he decreed.
"She's now torn apart. It's the edict God gave
so no man can worship at Jezebel's grave."
Then Jehu went forth to the people and said,
"Kill Ahab's sons and bring me their heads."
The word of the Lord was affirmed, for the line
of Ahab was ended, as God had designed.
Jehu then called for the blood of the men
who were Baal priests. All of them died for their sin.
This pleased the Lord, but Jehu sinned when
he was king, and the cycle began once again.

II Kings 11

Ahaziah's mother, Athaliah, then
took up the throne and killed all her kin
so she could be queen and not be betrayed.
But one prince, named Joash, was hidden away.
He was hidden six years, then a group came to raise
him up as the king. The people all praised
the new king. Athaliah rushed to the site
and screamed, "Treachery! This thing is not right."
"Seize her!" they shouted. "She is no queen."
She was then killed in a grizzly scene.
The usurper was vanquished. A crown made of gold
was placed on a boy, only seven years old.

II Kings 12

Joash did all that was right in the eyes
of the Lord. He was known as the king who complies
with what the Lord asked. He took money and
repaired the Lord's temple for all in the land.

Then Hazael brought Aram's armies to break
the walls of Jerusalem.
Joash said, "Take
the gold in our treasuries, but spare our lives."
So Hazael did and the Hebrews survived.
As for the rest of his reign, is it not
in the annals so that it will not be forgot?
His officials conspired and killed him. The men
installed Amaziah, his son, to rule then.

II Kings 13

Jehoahaz, son of Jehu, became
Israel's king and he was to blame
for the pain of the land. He turned from the way
of the Lord, so Aram oppressed them each day.
Jehoash was king when Jehoahaz died,
and sought out Elisha.
"Father!" he cried,
"Aram rules over us. What can I do?"
"Take up your arrows and grab your bow too.
Strike the ground with all your arrows!"
He pierced
the earth only three times.
"You are not fierce!"
Elisha proclaimed, "You'll beat Aram thrice,
but that will not be near enough to suffice."

II Kings 14

Amaziah, the son of Joash, did what
was right in the eyes of the Lord. First he cut
the heads off the men who had murdered the king,
his father, then challenged Jehoahaz.
"Bring
your armies and fight, for Judah shall best
your men!"
But Judah then failed in their quest.
Routed, they fled. Amaziah ruled till

they killed him, and his son then had to fill
the throne.
Jeroboam, the second by name,
was son to Joash, and he then became
the king when his father was dead. His own son,
Zechariah was king, when his reign was done.

II Kings 15 - 16

Judah was blessed by King Azariah,
while Israel's curse was King Zechariah,
then Shallum, then Menahem. Each king despised
the Lord and did evil in front of His eyes.
Pekahiah and Pekah continued the trend
of unholy kings of Israel. When
Jotham was king in Judah, he led
with the Lord in his heart and the Word in his head.
But Ahaz, his son, defied the Lord, and
he followed false idols from far foreign lands.
He sacrificed children, for he was a man
who did everything to oppose the Lord's plan.

II Kings 17 - 19

Hoshea became the last king to rule
in Israel, but all the people were fooled
and followed false idols. So the Lord sent
them into exile until they'd repent.
Taken away to Assyria, their
cities were settled by those from elsewhere.
Filled up with foreigners, not much remained
of the Lord in the land of the people He'd named.
But King Hezekiah of Judah still clung
to the ways of the Lord. He was not among
the evil kings who were so prevalent then.
But still Judah suffered for Israel's sin.
Sennacherib led the Assyrian forces,
their chariots, war machines, soldiers and horses
down to Jerusalem, saying, "You'll die

if you seek to oppose us. Why even try?
Egypt is crushed! You're a fraction their size.
Your god even sent us here. You are despised!"
"Use Aramaic. We're begging you, please,"
Judah's commanders said, "Do not speak these
words out in Hebrew."
"Ha!" said the man.
"I speak so that each of you will understand.
I offer you peace. Bow down and no pain
shall come to you. Otherwise you will be slain.
For we'll wipe you off of the Earth in one day."
But nobody answered him. They all obeyed
their king who demanded their silence when they
were addressed by the enemy.
Later that day,
the Lord said, "I've heard his blasphemous words.
My anger against Sennacherib's stirred."
By Isaiah, the Lord stated, "During this night
many shall die and the rest shall take flight."
One hundred and eighty-five thousand men died.
Sennacherib, seeing that much of his side
was dead, turned and fled back to Nineveh, where
he was killed by his sons as the Lord had declared.

II Kings 20

Hezekiah was ill, and Isaiah said, "You
must put your house now in order, for soon
you'll die."
Hezekiah cried out, "Lord, have I
been faithful?"
Isaiah said, "God heard your cry,
and knowing your faithfulness, he will provide
fifteen years more. Your fears may subside."
When Babylon heard about all of these things,
they sent several envoys, received by the king.
He showed them his treasures, and when they'd withdrawn,
Isaiah said, "Surely your wealth will be gone.
For you have been foolish, and Babylon will

take treasures and your sons as booty to fill
their treasuries."
King Hezekiah said, "Fine,
for I will not see it within my lifetime."
So fifteen years later, the king passed away,
remembered as one who had followed God's way.

II Kings 21:1 - 23:28

Manasseh then became king, and resumed
detestable worships.
God was consumed
with anger and said, "He is leading My nation
away from My will and into damnation."
When Manasseh died, his son Amon sought
the same evil path, and so the Lord brought
His will on the king. Conspirators rose
slaughtered the king and then they imposed
his son, Josiah, a king at just eight
years old. Then he reigned like all of the great
kings before him had done. He restored
the temple again, and honored the Lord.
When the Lord's temple had its restoration
a scroll was found hidden within the foundation,
and it was the Law of the Lord. It was read
to Josiah who threw his hands to his head.
"Lord, we have sinned, and we did not know!
Your word was forgotten, and we have been slow
to retrieve it."
He turned to a priest and cried out,
"The Lord is against us. We aren't devout.
Find me a prophet who will tell us how
the Lord will respond. Run! Find one now."
A prophetess was sought out and she said,
"It's true that the people should be full of dread,
but the Lord indeed heard our earthly king's cry,
so our punishment won't come till after he dies."
So during his life, Josiah sought to
destroy all the high places. He took and threw

the pagan gods down. He burned and he broke
the idols, so that they all went up in smoke.
He restored the tradition of Passover and
returned the Law of the Lord to the land.

II Kings 23:29 - 25:30

Josiah was good, but when he was gone
Jehoahaz, his son, undid all he'd done.
An evil king, he was imprisoned and then
replaced by his brother, who too lived in sin.
Jehoiakim and Jehoichin too
were beset by Nebuchadnezzar, who drew
his sword against Judah. He swept down and beat
the kingdom and made them all bow at his feet.
He took them away, as the Lord said he would.
The Lord did this, though it was not understood.
Then Zedekiah ruled and rebelled
against Babylon. So they came and felled
the gates of Jerusalem. Then they took all
who once lived in peace in Jerusalem's walls
to be slaves in Babylon. Only the sons
of King Zedekiah weren't taken. These ones
were killed so their father would see them all dead,
just before they cut the eyes from his head.
Then Nebuchadnezzar tore down every stone
from the temple, as he had torn down Judah's throne.

I Chronicles 1 - 3

The historical records name many men,
starting with Adam, descending from him
through Seth and to Noah, and all of his sons,
and all of the nations that out of them sprung.
The Cushites, the Amorites, Girgashites too,
the Canaanites, Hamites, to name just a few.
It chronicles Abraham, who is the man
upon whom three great religions all stand.
It goes on to Isaac and through Ishmael,
the sons of Esau and then Israel,
the sons of the twelve tribes and what their lines bring,
to Jesse, then David, the greatest of kings.
Then King David's sons, including the one
who ruled with great wisdom, King Solomon.
The line from Solomon, listed and filed,
before and then after the Jewish exile.

I Chronicles 4 - 9

The twelve tribes were listed, so all who came from
these lines would remember how far they had come.
The bloodline of Saul was given, as well
as the first of those who had returned from the hell
of exile within Babylonian lands.
This genealogy seeks to expand
on who came before, so Israel knows
the names of their forefathers, as their line grows.

I Chronicles 10

When Saul fought the Philistines and they had slain
his sons, an arrow struck him. Then in pain
he said to a servant, "Take out your sword
and kill me. Now do it! Or by God our Lord,
these fellows will take and abuse me so all
can mock me."
But his servant would not, so Saul
took his own sword and fell on it, dead.
Upon seeing this all of Israel fled.
The Philistines cut off his head and showed those
around them how they treated all of their foes.
Because Saul had not followed God he was killed,
and David took over, just as the Lord willed.

I Chronicles 11 - 12

One of the first things that King David did
was march on Jerusalem and make a bid
to take it and when David's army had won,
he made it God's kingdom under the sun.
David was joined by his warriors. One killed
three hundred men on his own with his skills.
And one killed a lion, and three fought their way
through a whole army all by themselves on that day
just to fetch water for David. Their swords
were stronger than those of a menacing horde.
David's great army and his mighty men
are recorded so all will remember again.
David ruled over an army of power.
With three hundred thousand men they'd devour
their foes, for their strength had never been seen.
God's holy army; a killing machine.

I Chronicles 13

David proclaimed, "Let us bring back
the ark of the covenant, and with this act

bring the Lord back to Jerusalem where
He may be with us in deed and in prayer."
Unanimously, all the people agreed.
They went to the city, the ark was retrieved,
but on their way back, a man put his hand
on to the ark. God struck down the man.
David was angry that this had occurred,
but now that it had, the king was concerned
that having the ark so close was a threat,
so it was not brought to Jerusalem yet.

I Chronicles 14 - 15

God said to David, "Now go forth and win
victory over the Philistine men."
They slaughtered the army and burned up the gods
that artisans chiseled or carpenters sawed.
When this had been done, David proclaimed,
"Hark! Now Jerusalem may be reclaimed
by God. We shall bring the ark and shall make
Jerusalem home. The Levites must take
it up, and don't let any other man touch
the ark, for the Lord has commanded as much."
With shouts and with joy, the men were elated.
David was dancing. As he celebrated
he danced there half-naked. And Michal, his wife
saw this and she said, "In all of my life,
I've never seen my husband be such a fool."
Her heart was against him, for she could be cruel.

I Chronicles 16 - 17

David gave thanks for the ark and the Lord
with song and with gifts, and for his reward,
God said to Nathan, the prophet, "Say to
David, I don't want a house built. For you
know I have long dwelled with My people in tents.
A house is not why King David was sent.
But tell him that this is what I shall now do.

I, your Lord, shall build a house made for you.
When your days are done, your son shall be raised
up on the throne for all of his days.
He'll build up My house and he will be loved
as I have loved you from here up above."
When David was told, he said, "Lord, You made
my line an exalted one. Your people prayed
that You would return. Let all You have said
come true, so the world sees Your greatness spread."

I Chronicles 18 - 20

David found victory in his campaigns.
His foes in the mountains as well as the plains
all fell by his sword; the Moabites and
Amalekites, and others found in his land.
The Ammonites who had been friends had betrayed
their truce with Israel and they had made
a pact with the army of Aram who fought
next to the Ammonites till they were caught.
The men of Aram surrendered and then
the Ammonites, who had lost so many men
were beaten as David laid waste to their land,
and Ammon surrendered down to a man.

I Chronicles 21

Then Satan incited David to count
Israel's people, to know the amount.
Though Joab warned him, David insisted
and learned that Israel's nation consisted
of one million one hundred thousand men, and
four hundred thousand who dwelt in the land
of Judah, but this number did not contain
the Levites or Benjamites. This was a stain
on David and Israel, for God did not
want to have His people numbered. He taught
David a lesson, by telling him, "Choose
your fate, 'cause your sin cannot be excused.

Three years of famine, or three months you'll stay
in your enemies' hands, or only three days
of My retribution - a plague."
"I will take
three days from you, for I know my mistake,
and my God is a merciful one."
In just three
rotations of Earth, the plague was set free
and seventy thousand men died there, until
the Lord told His angel, "Stop! Now My will
is done."
Many saw the great angel who
stood between Heaven and Earth. They all knew
that only the Lord stood between them and death,
so all of them fell and prayed with each breath.
Then David built up an altar that stood
as a testament that he now understood
the only respite saving them from the sword
of the angel was the holy word of the Lord.

I Chronicles 22 - 23:1

At the place of the altar, David said, "Here
the temple shall stand, where the Lord will draw near.
I shall make plans, though my son, Solomon,
shall build up the temple to worship the One."
So then he prepared and called to his son.
"When the Lord tells me my days here are done,
you shall be charged to build the house of
the Lord. You must swear this to me with your love.
Because I spilt blood across the whole land,
the Lord said I shall not build it with my hand.
Instead you're to do this and follow His law,
and you'll know a peace that I never saw."
So Solomon told David he understood,
and David was pleased by his son who was good.
Because he was old, he said, "It is well
that you shall be king over all Israel."

I Chronicles 23:2 - 27:34

The Levites were chosen to build and to care
for the temple, for they were the holy ones there.
Their line, back to Aaron, had always been priests,
and so it continued so no one would cease
to lift up the Lord in praise and in song.
Some Levites were left to judge right from wrong.
The Levites were given these jobs because they
were chosen to make sure that none went astray.
Now each of the rest of Israel's men
were required to serve in the army, so when
their month had arrived, they reported and stood
as soldiers, because their king said that they should.

I Chronicles 28 - 29

David called all of his men and proclaimed,
"My plan was to build up God's home and domain,
but God said because of the blood I have spilled,
His temple, in my time, shall not be fulfilled.
Instead, it is Solomon who'll build the throne
for the Ark of the Covenant's permanent home.
His kingdom shall reign forever if he
follows the Lord our God dutifully.
So now my son Solomon has been made king.
All the affairs of the state you shall bring
to him and he'll judge both wisely and fair."
And then to the masses he uttered this prayer,
"O Lord, everlasting and to everlasting,
You of our sacrifice, You of our fasting,
You are the power and You are the splendor.
You are our ruler and You're our defender.
We are the lowly, and we are to blame,
but thank You for mercy. Lord, we praise Your name.
All that we have has come from Your might.
We are but foreigners when in Your sight.
We offer all that we have so we may
build Your great temple for You on that day.

O God of our forefathers, stay in our hearts,
and be with us so that we don't drift apart.
Let my son, Solomon, keep Your commands,
so peace again flourishes throughout these lands."
And when David died, he was mourned by the nation,
for through his line Israel found its salvation.

II Chronicles 1

Solomon praised the Lord and God blessed
him saying, "Just ask and you'll have My best."
So Solomon said, "Lord, You have been good.
I ask only wisdom to lead as I should."
"You didn't ask Me for wealth or to live
a long life of power, and so I shall give
you wisdom, but during your life you will know
wealth, long life, and control of your foe."
So it was to be through Solomon's reign;
God was with him again and again.
Solomon's wealth and power were vast,
but wisdom is what he truly amassed.

II Chronicles 2 - 4

Solomon gathered the finest of wood,
silver, and gold. He saw it was good
and called for the best of all craftsmen to join
in building the temple. He spared not a coin
in making its greatness known to mankind.
During construction, it burned in his mind
that this was the house of the Lord. All in all,
two hundred thousand men worked on its walls.
The temple was massive and beautiful too.
Its greatness was there for the world to view.
Men stood in wonder, both inside and out.
That this was God's house, there was not a doubt.

II Chronicles 5 - 6

Then at the feast, Solomon brought
the Ark of the Covenant up, for he sought
to give it a place in the temple to stay.
The people who saw this remembered the day
that the ark found its home. The tablets remained
that Moses had brought for the ark to contain.
The people sang, "God is so good. He endures
forever. In Him, we're safe and secure."
Then Solomon stood saying, "God is at hand.
He promised my father this temple would stand.
He chose Jerusalem to be His home.
Let no man deny this. May God never roam.
O Lord, there is no one like You. You are One.
Through us on this day, Your will has been done.
Although it is earthly and You reign on high,
Lord bless this temple we pray. Hear our cry!
And if we should trespass against you, but we
turn back to Your ways in this place, hear our plea.
If a man swears an oath and it's done in this place,
let that man be bound by Your power and grace.
If foreigners come because they hear that You
are great, hear their pleas and honor them too.
Do not turn away from Your people, for we
have honored You here. We love and praise Thee."

II Chronicles 7

They gave sacrifices and thus consecrated
the temple that they and the Lord had created.
That night God appeared in Solomon's dream
and said, "All you've done in My name has been seen.
If you walk with Me, like your father when he
was earthly, then I shall maintain My decree
and make a great nation of you and your lot.
Be holy in both your heart and your thought.
If you turn away, My hand will be raised
against you and Israel. You'll rue the day

that you turned your heart. My temple, though fine,
shall topple, for I can destroy what is Mine."

II Chronicles 8 - 9

Solomon rebuilt the nation and brought
the daughter of Pharaoh to him, for he sought
to make her his bride, and so they were wed.
The nation adhered to all that God said.
The Queen of Sheba had heard of his fame.
She sought him out, and after she came
she saw that his wisdom in ruling was great.
"The Lord has blessed you and all your estate.
I had heard stories, but until this day,
I hadn't believed, but now I must say
what I heard was true. True and much more."
The two traded gifts before she left shore.
The greatness and wealth of Solomon grew
larger than any king's. He, wise and true,
ruled for forty years, over all things.
When he died his son replaced him as king.

II Chronicles 10 - 11

When Solomon's son, Rehoboam, became
the king, all the men said, "For the domain
of God and your father we've toiled, so now
won't you ease our work and our burden somehow?"
He said, "Give me time."
Then he sought advice
from elders who said, "Young king, if you're nice,
the people will follow you all of your days."
He asked the same question of his friends and they
said, "No! Tell them all you're a greater man than
your father was. Come, you're the king. Take a stand.
Tell them if they feared your father's whip then
you'll give to them scorpions."
And this pleased him.
So when all the workers returned he said, "Hear!

If you thought the workload was tough, then be clear,
that it shall be worse when my word is upheld."
The workers were angry and so they rebelled.
The king took his army to make war against
the people of Israel. He was incensed.
But God told His prophet, "Tell everyone to
go home. Do not fight. This I say to you."
So King Rehoboam went home, as did all,
and there were no sieges on Israel's walls.
The king's family grew as he fortified
his cities and his sons stood by his side.

II Chronicles 12 - 13

King Rehoboam abandoned the law.
As God looked on Israel, all that He saw
were idols and people abandoning Him,
so He sent an army to war against them.
Shishak of Egypt came up and attacked
Israel. Shishak pushed their army back
till they reached the walls of Jerusalem. Then
Rehoboam cried out to the Lord, "We have sinned.
Lord, you are great. So be with us, please."
God said, "I see that you're all on your knees,
so I shall not give you to Shishak, although,
you will serve him. In this way you'll know
that serving Me is not the same as to serve
foreign kings."
"Lord," they cried, "we deserve
much worse, but Your mercy is great and it's fair."
Though Shishak gained treasure, the people were spared.
But during his reign of seventeen years,
the king was against God, as it appears
in the annals. It also says King Rehoboam
was always at war against Jeroboam.
When King Rehoboam was dead, then his son
ruled Judah. He went out to war and he won
against Jeroboam. He prayed to the Lord,
and put the idolaters onto his sword.

II Chronicles 14 - 16

When Asa was king of Judah, he took
and destroyed the idols and lived by the book.
He sought to turn Judah back to God's land,
thus Judah knew peace by God's mighty hand.
The king was successful when enemies came,
for all that he did was in the Lord's name.
He built up his cities and made them all strong.
Till Asa was old, he never did wrong,
but he was attacked by Israel, and
he called to the kings in a neighboring land.
"Help me and we will crush them this day."
Although Asa won, his foe got away.
A seer said, "When you relied on the Lord,
did you not succeed and gain your reward?
But you turned from Him, and so ends your bliss."
The king threw the man into prison for this.
Asa's heart hardened, and then he oppressed
his people. This king, who once was so blessed,
was now filled with anger, hate, and conceit,
and died from disease that infected his feet.

II Chronicles 17 - 19

Jehoshaphat then became Judah's king and
sent prophets of God across the whole land.
They taught those in Judah the Book of the Law.
God was pleased with him and all that He saw.
But Jehoshaphat allied himself with the king
of Israel, Ahab, who asked him to bring
his army against a mutual foe.
Jehoshaphat said, "If the Lord says, we'll go.
Where is a prophet that I might consult?"
Ahab replied, "You won't like the result,
but Micaiah's near. I hate that man. He
has never said anything nice about me."
"A king should not say such a thing. Let him come."

Ahab's false prophets declared, as if one,
"You'll be victorious!"
Then they said to
Micaiah, "Tell them that what we say is true."
He said, "Only what the Lord tells me shall I
declare to be true. You prophets all lie.
A spirit's attempting to make Ahab come
and fight in a battle he won't return from."
"I told you he never says anything good!"
Ahab declared. "Now lock him up! Should
I return safely, then he'll be set free."
"If you return safely, God speaks not through me!"
Everything happened as Micaiah said.
At the end of the battle, Ahab was dead.
A seer then scolded Jehoshaphat for
going against the Lord in his war.

II Chronicles 20

Ammon and Moab both rose up to fight
with Judah. Jehoshaphat said, "Lord, Your might
is great. Why would You let us die at the hands
of these people whom we have not purged from the land?"
Then God told His prophet, "Tell them to go
and stand at the battlefield. There they shall know
that I am the Lord, for the battle is won.
No fighting by Judah shall need to be done."
Before the army of Judah arrived,
the enemy armies had already died.
The Lord made them fight each other, and He
destroyed them. He turned the plain to a sea
of bodies. The news spread throughout all the nations.
As Judah held feasts and great celebrations,
their enemies trembled, for they knew the Lord
was with Judah and this was of His accord.

II Chronicles 21

When Jehoshaphat died, Jehoram, his son,
was king over Judah. As his reign begun,
he slew all his brothers and then took a wife
from Ahab's line. He lived a most wicked life.
Elijah the prophet wrote and he said,
"You have done wrong. Your brothers are dead.
You've turned from the Lord, now without a doubt
your enemies come and your bowels will fall out."
The Philistines came and fought such a fight
that Jerusalem fell because of their might.
Jehoram, afflicted by illness, soon died,
and nobody mourned him, nobody cried.

II Chronicles 22 - 23

Jehoram's son ruled for only one year
before he was killed. The son had adhered
to the ways of his father. When he had been slain
his mother then governed through violence and pain.
A priest then brought forth the only true heir
of David, and made him the king, then and there.
And they put to death the evil queen who
had ruled in the place of a king who was true.

II Chronicles 24

Though Joash was only seven years old
when he began ruling, he sought to uphold
the ways of King David - the way of the Lord.
So what had been holy would now be restored.
Jehoiada was the high priest, and he
helped Joash do things the Lord God would see.
They built up the temple, restoring its walls.
But when the priest died, the Lord was appalled
by Joash who turned from the Lord and His ways.
Without the high priest, he was soon led astray.
He built up the Asherah poles and bowed down.

Jehoida's son reprimanded the crown
for turning away from the Lord who is One.
Ignoring the fact that it was his friend's son
Joash stoned him, the one who had spoken
to glorify God, till his bones were all broken.
The army of Aram attacked though depleted.
The army of Judah was quickly defeated.
King Joash was wounded, then killed by his own.
Amaziah, his son, succeeded the throne.

II Chronicles 25 - 26

Once Amaziah was king, he killed all
who had put his father to death, but the law
forbade him from killing their sons, for no men
shall be made to suffer for their father's sin.
He mustered an army made pure in the Lord,
and cut all of Seir's men down with his sword.
But he took their gods and made them his own,
and God's anger roared against him and his throne.
So when Amaziah set out to go fight
with Israel, then the Lord showed His true might.
Amaziah was captured. Jerusalem's walls
thus fell unto Israel. They plundered all
that Judah controlled. As for Amaziah,
when he had expired, then his son, Uzziah,
was king over Judah, and brought the land back
to God. Whenever his army attacked,
they won all their battles. But when he was old
Uzziah grew arrogant, prideful, and bold.
So God gave him leprosy and it remained
for all of the days that were left in his reign.

II Chronicles 27 - 28

Uzziah's son Jotham was honest, but when
Ahaz, his son was the king, then the sin
of Judah became so great the king shut
the temple completely. They molded or cut

their idols and then the people all bowed
down to false idols. Since this was allowed,
God was against him and handed him to
his foes. Still Ahaz's wickedness grew.

II Chronicles 29 - 31

When Hezekiah became king, he said,
"All that was wicked and evil is dead.
Levites! Make yourselves clean and then lead
us back to the Lord in thought and in deed.
Our forefathers turned their backs on the Lord,
and that is why they were all put to the sword.
Let all of our sins now be calculated,
so we may atone and be consecrated."
The temple was cleaned and purified. Then
the priests and the Levites were cleansed of their sin.
Then people arrived for the Passover feasts,
and they were cared for by all of the priests.
They gave their first fruits, and it was declared,
that it was the greatest Passover there
had been since the time of Solomon's reign.
Hezekiah had taken away Judah's stain.

II Chronicles 32

Sennacherib came to Jerusalem and
said, "What god can save your town from my hand?
Your God is nothing. Now I am the law.
I've taken each city and land that I saw."
Isaiah and King Hezekiah both prayed,
"Save us from this siege that Sennacherib laid."
God's angel came down and completely destroyed
the army Sennacherib led and deployed.

II Chronicles 33

Hezekiah, though proud, did all the Lord asked,
and when it was time that his soul should pass,

his son, Manasseh, ruled over the land
and ruled with an evil, idolatrous hand.
Manasseh worshipped the Baals by their names
and put his own infants into Molech's flames.
His wickedness was, in the eyes of the Lord,
more heinous than nations God put to His sword.
The Assyrians came and took him away.
This humbled Manasseh. He sought to pray
to the Lord of his fathers. When God heard these words
God saw he was honest, and so the Lord heard
his prayer and delivered him back to his land.
Manasseh then knew that it was God's hand
that saved him so he turned his heart to God by
destroying the idols. But when he had died,
Amon, his son, was as wicked as he
had been in his life. A Baal devotee,
Amon was not humble, and so his court
rose up and they slaughtered him. Then in retort,
others killed them, and placed Amon's son,
Josiah, as king. The bloodshed was done.
At just eight years old, Josiah was crowned.
He trusted the Lord, so his wisdom was sound.

II Chronicles 34

Josiah removed from the temple and land
all of the idols and Baal contraband.
In cleansing the temple, a priest found the Book
of Law and they said, "This text was found. Look."
And when it was read, the king tore his clothes,
"Our fathers were wicked. Only God knows
what He has in store for our nation. Go ask
a prophet what our Lord will have come to pass."
A prophetess told him, "The Lord God proclaims
that Judah shall suffer, for My Holy Name
was defiled, but I see the king's humble heart
is with Me, in no way shall he see one part
of My wrath."
At these words Josiah brought all

of Jerusalem's people out from the wall
and up to the hill, where all then confessed
their sins, then to God each person professed.

II Chronicles 35 - 36

After Josiah had passed away, all
the Lord had proclaimed occurred. Judah's fall
happened as Nebuchadnezzar came and
massacred and enslaved Judah's land.
He carted away all the valuable things,
enslaved all the people as well as the kings,
and took them all back to Babylon. Then
they struck down Jerusalem's temple. Her sin
created this exile. Seventy years
would pass as the Israelites shed their tears,
till Cyrus of Persia arrived and set free
the people of Israel at God's decree.

Ezra 1 - 3

In the first year of Cyrus, the great Persian king,
God moved his heart, so he wrote, "All the things
God's given to me shall be used to fulfill
the things God has told me. I must do His will.
He says we must build in Jerusalem's walls
His temple, *the* temple. The greatest of all.
Then Cyrus brought forth what had been taken from
the previous temple and said, "People, come!"
The people of Judah, and Benjamin too,
came forth as the people were freed. It is true
that all who'd been taken to Babylon gained
their freedom through God, who'd broken their chains.
Forty-two thousand were freed from the land,
when God gave King Cyrus His holy command.
As one group they rose up so they might rebuild
the altar so sacrifice could be fulfilled.
When that was completed, they laid down the base
of the temple, and everyone fell on their face.
They cried out with joy, "Let the Lord's temple be
an honor to Him that all nations may see."

Ezra 4 - 6

When their enemies heard that the Jews had come back,
rather than planning a massive attack,
they said, "Let us help you build and create
the temple."
But in this there was no debate.
"No!" they were told. "God set us all free.

We're to build His temple as He decreed."
Their enemies then sent a letter to King
Artaxerxes which said, 'Lord, please, you must bring
these Jews to a halt. They're a people who fought
with our tribes before this, and all that they brought
was suffering.'
King Artaxerxes agreed.
"Stop all their building at once," he decreed.
Several years passed and no building was done,
but many forgot what the king said, and some
started again. But their enemies frowned.
"Let's write to King Darius. He'll tear them down."
But Darius searched through the vaults and he found
a scroll where King Cyrus had said, "On my crown,
I'm freeing the Jews. Let them go and build
the temple to God."
So it was fulfilled,
and Darius said, "Do not stand in the way
of what's been proclaimed. I say on this day,
give money to help them construct. Let no man
interfere with their work, lest they die by my hand."
Israel heard this and they were elated,
for they had been helped by the people they'd hated.
The temple was built, and all celebrated
for this was the day that they all had awaited.

Ezra 7 - 8

Then Ezra, a teacher well versed in the law,
came down from Babylon. All that he saw
pleased him, and King Artaxerxes said, "Go,
and lead all your people with all that you know.
Let no one harm you or the people of God,
for my goodwill goes wherever you trod.
The hand of the Lord is upon me, and there
shall be none in Israel who know despair."
So the families returned to Jerusalem for
the first time in fifty long years, maybe more.

Before they could enter, they were consecrated
and cleansed. Through the Lord, they'd been reinstated.

Ezra 9 - 10

Word came to Ezra that though he had carried
thousands of people back home, they had married
people who worshipped false idols. So he
tore his cloak saying, "O Lord, be with me.
The people have sinned upon their return
I know that Your anger and jealousy burn.
You've placed us within Jerusalem's wall.
I did not believe it would crumble and fall
so quickly."
Then others joined with him and wept.
They knew the commandments, but they hadn't kept
them pure. So they said, "Let's swear we will send
away all the women and children of sin."
So Ezra rose up and appointed his priests
to send all the foreigners off to the east.
So every man who had a foreign wife sent
her out of the land and out of his tent.

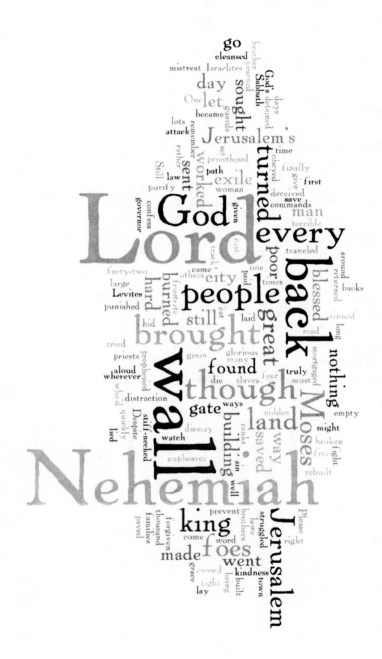

Nehemiah 1 - 2

A brother told me that those who'd returned
had found the wall broken, the city gate burned.
Jerusalem lay in a heap, so I prayed,
"Lord, the one God, to whom I've obeyed,
we Israelites have sinned, we confess.
Moses laid out the law and You blessed
our people until all we turned from You, then
the exile punished us all for our sin."
As cupbearer unto the king, when I went
he saw I was troubled. In kindness he sent
me back to my people and back to my land.
Artaxerxes is truly a fine king and man.
He granted me safety upon my return,
and offered me timber for that which had burned,
so we could replace our wall and our gate.
The Lord was with him. The Lord God is great!
I looked at Jerusalem's wall and was sad,
for its state was terrible. All that I had
I threw into fixing the wall, though our foes
tried to frustrate us wherever we'd go.

Nehemiah 3 - 4

The gates and the wall were rebuilt by our men,
though others insulted us to our chagrin.
Because there were plots to fight or attack
our builders, we had to look over our backs.
The Lord was with us when we stationed our guards.
But with this distraction, rebuilding was hard.

We kept a tight watch during every hour,
for we were not going to be overpowered.

Nehemiah 5

During this time, I heard a great cry
from all of the poor, "Would you rather we die?
We've mortgaged it all to pay taxes to
the king, and our interest must be paid to you.
We have nothing left! No grain we can eat."
I went to the nobles and said, "You mistreat
the poor! For so long we've struggled and yearned.
So quickly against your own brothers you've turned?"
All were ashamed. They had nothing to say.
I made them give everything back right away.
As governor, I could demand a reward,
but didn't because of my fear of the Lord.

Nehemiah 6

Still all of my foes sought hard to prevent
the building. No less than five times they all sent
a letter that said, "Let's meet far from where
you're building your wall."
I would not go there.
And so they deceived and then prophesied
against me. But with every word, my foes lied.
Despite all the people against me and mine,
the wall was completed as God had assigned.

Nehemiah 7 - 8

The city was large, but still it remained
empty because the many detained
in Babylon hadn't come back, and we found
forty-two thousand lived in the town.
All were brought out as Jerusalem's crowd.
The Law of Moses was then read aloud.

And all celebrated this beautiful day,
when Jerusalem finally escaped her dismay.

Nehemiah 9 - 10

"Lord," we confessed, "You are glorious. You
brought Abraham first and then Moses too,
so that he might save us from Egypt, but we
turned from Your mercy. O Lord, let us be
forgiven, for though we were stiff-necked, You still
saved us because of Your great grace and will.
You gave us our nation. You made our land strong.
But we became comfortable, and You were wronged.
Now we are slaves, though You brought us back
the same path we traveled on our exile track.
We all swear this oath to follow Your ways
and laws and commands for all of our days.
The Sabbath is Yours, and so it shall be.
To this every man and each woman agrees.
Your will is our way. Lord, let us be saved
through You, for that is the road You have paved."

Nehemiah 11 - 13

One out of every ten families were brought
to live in Jerusalem. They had cast lots.
The priests came as well. They cleansed themselves, then
they blessed the wall that was built up around them.
I ridded the priesthood of those who were not
Levites but hid in their ranks, and I caught
all of the people who worked on the day
set aside for God's rest. That is the way
I sought to purify all that the Lord
had given to us. We cannot afford
to anger Him. Please, God, remember me and
how I worked to bring You back into this land.

queen give done kill

request submission

bow today Come

must people

despair man

declared king's

replied bring gave

save Esther called

Haman's King

Jews day feast

Haman king

servant

asked fine

prepare guile gallows

Mordecai

die banquet saved brought went

least edict

Xerxes Now

love

told wipe even land

proclaim

anyone

sought

decree one

best tell Hagai time

beautiful go

slave thought

Esther 1 - 2:18

King Xerxes of Persia gave a great feast
inviting all people, from greatest to least.
With joy he called forth his wife. In reply,
his wife would not come. Feeling defied,
he asked of his counselors what he should do.
"The queen did not heed your order, so you
must banish her from your presence today,
unless you want wives who do not obey."
So it was done, and a search was begun
for a beautiful virgin who would be the one
the king would remarry. So many girls came,
brought to the king, with hopes to be named.
A Jewess called Esther brought by Mordecai,
her father, to King Xerxes' eunuch, Hagai,
was beautiful. Her family was brought to stay
in Babylon during the exile days.
Hagai liked Esther and thought her the best,
and she pleased King Xerxes above all the rest.
So Xerxes declared a holiday and
on that day made Esther the queen of his land.
Esther did not tell the king that she was
a Jew or in exile. That was because
Mordecai told her that if she confessed
it could put her queenship into distress.

Esther 2:19 - 3:15

Mordecai heard the guards launch a plot
to kill Xerxes, but he told Esther. They caught

the conspirators and Esther gave credit to
Mordecai, saying, "It's he that saved you."
About this time, Haman, a lord in the court
of Xerxes, received a disturbing report
that Mordecai would not bow down at his feet
because he was Jewish. To have incomplete
submission from all attacked Haman's pride,
so he sought a way to commit genocide
upon all the Jews. So he went to the king
and said, "There's a people amongst us who bring
disgrace on your name. Let me wipe all the Jews
out of our land."
"I will not refuse,"
King Xerxes replied. "You have my permission.
Kill them or beat them all into submission.
My royal decree shall fulfill your desire,
and wipe out this people, I say."
"Thank you, sire."
The edict went out, and the Jews were confused
why Haman's request had not been refused.

Esther 4 - 5

Mordecai sent word to Esther of all
that happened, but she said, "The king has not called.
I cannot approach him."
"Don't you see that you
were placed on the throne so that you could do
something to save your people today?
In this dire time, you can't turn away."
"Alright," she replied. "Be assured, I will try.
I'll give all I can, even if I must die."
She went to the king, and he said, "My queen!
You break through the boredom and through the routine.
What may I do for you?"
"Would you come to
a banquet, and would you bring Haman with you?"
The king thought that this was a fine plan, and so
he said he and Haman would both like to go.

Haman was pleased that he was invited,
but as he was feeling both proud and delighted
he passed Mordecai, who did not bow down.
This angered Haman, and so with a frown
he told his friends of this and they all declared,
"Build up a gallows and hang the man there.
Don't be so glum! You're going to eat
with the king and his queen. Don't ruin that treat!"
Haman replied, "On the morrow, that swine
shall die, but tonight you are right. I shall dine."

Esther 6

The king could not sleep, so he called to a slave
to list things he'd done. The statement he gave
reminded King Xerxes of Mordecai's deed,
and so he asked his servant, "Did we proceed
to award him for saving me?"
"No, we did not."
"Then what did we do when those traitors were caught?"
Before the slave answered him, Haman approached,
and so to his friend this question was broached.
"Haman, what should I do to honor the man
whom I favor?"
Haman did not understand.
Thinking the king was speaking of him,
he said, "I would bring out a robe with fine trim.
I'd give him a horse and proclaim all he'd done,
if he were the king's most favorite one."
"So it shall be!" King Xerxes declared.
"Mordecai saved me. So let us prepare
to go through the streets and proclaim Mordecai
as the king's favored servant. A man upon high!"
After this Haman rushed home in despair,
before he attended the banquet affair.

Esther 7 - 8

So Xerxes and Haman both dined with the queen.
King Xerxes said, "Now, my dear, you must come clean.
I asked you to tell me. Now, what's your request?
Tell me, for I would give you all the best."
"I ask you, my love, my husband, my king,
to save all my people from those who would bring
about our demise."
"Whom do you speak of?"
"Of Haman, who sits here. He'd kill me, my love!"
The king, understanding all that she had said,
ordered Haman to be hung until dead.
The gallows where he sought to hang Mordecai
ended up being the place Haman died.
Then Esther asked Xerxes, "Will you please prepare
an edict to save my whole race from despair?
This will erase what Haman asked of you,
which allowed him to persecute all of the Jews."
"This I can't do, for once I decree,
it can't be revoked. Not even by me,
nor anyone else. But I can give you
another that's favorable to all the Jews."
So it was declared that the Jews could defend
themselves from anyone who would intend
to kill them. Then Xerxes gave Mordecai and
Esther Haman's money and all his land.

Esther 9 - 10

The Jews struck their enemies down. Haman's sons
were killed, and when all of the carnage was done,
seventy-five thousand foes died at least,
and when it was over the Jews held a feast.
This new celebration, called Purim, began
when the Jews had been saved from their enemy's hand.
"This day's set aside," Queen Esther declared,
"so all shall remember the day we were spared.

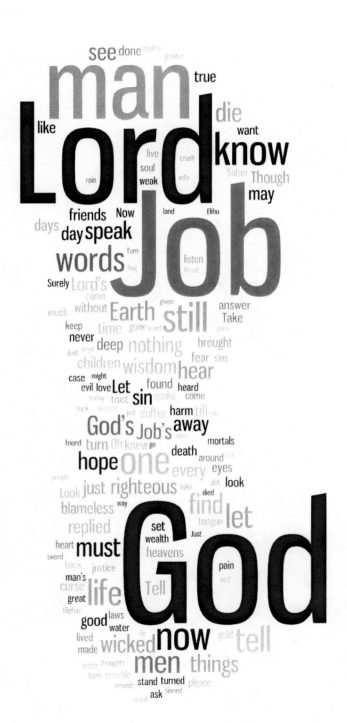

Job 1

Job lived in Uz. He was blameless and feared
the Lord. He was honest and always adhered
to the law of the Lord. He was wealthy and wise
and did everything that was right in God's eyes.
Satan came forth, and God said, "Where do
you come from?"
"From walking the Earth beneath You."
"And have you seen Job? What a servant is he!"
"You've made it too easy! All that the man sees
is blessed. Take his things and he'll turn away."
"He will not," the Lord said, "but go forth today.
Take all the man has, but Job you can't touch."
So Satan took everything, for Job had much.
The oxen and donkeys were stolen, and then
his flocks were burned up, and his serving men
were put to the sword. His children were killed.
Now he had nothing and his heart was filled
with woe. He fell down and cried, "I arrived
naked on Earth and so shall I die.
The Lord gives and also the Lord takes away."
But Job did not curse the Lord on that day.

Job 2

Then God said to Satan, "See! He maintains
his love for Me."
"This man has suffered no pains.
Strike a man's flesh, and then to Your face
he'll curse You. These mortals do not possess grace."

"Then harm him," God said, "but don't let him die."
So Satan went forth and first he applied
sores from Job's head clear down to his toes.
Job's wife said, "Curse God, then die, so that those
won't trouble you, Job."
"You are foolish and sad!
Should we accept good from the Lord, but not bad?"
Job's friends sat with him. They wept, but were awed,
for despite all his pain, Job refused to curse God.

Job 3

Job opened his mouth, and his words were forlorn.
"Curse the dark day upon which I was born.
Why didn't I die as I came from the womb?
Then I could be sleeping the peace of the tomb.
Why is life given to those who want death?
Like water, my groans pour out with each breath.
What I always dreaded has happened to me.
Now I have no peace. Swift death is my plea."

Job 4 - 5

Job's friend, Eliphaz, said, "Job, I know
you suffer, but tell me, for is it not so
that you've strengthened the feeble and lifted up men
with all that you know? You are blameless of sin.
Take strength in your piety. Let your hope swell.
Those who plow evil will reap it as well.
A spirit came to me and these things I heard,
'Can a mortal be greater than God? By His word,
if God charges angels to err, then how much
further are mortals away from His touch?'
Resentment and envy will slay the weak-hearted.
If you turn from God, your woes have just started.
Man is born into his trouble, my friend,
and if it were me, I would let my lips send
an appeal to the Lord. His miracles can
never be counted by any one man.

He lifts up the lowly. He strikes down the cruel.
The poorest find hope. Do not be a fool.
Blessed is he whom the Lord will correct.
He wounds, but he binds. He may harm, but protects."

Job 6 - 7

Then Job replied, "Oh, if my anguish were known
then it would reach up to the heavenly throne.
God's arrows are in me. He's marshaled against
my soul. Tell me why the Lord's so incensed.
Why won't the Lord hear my one lonely plea.
Lord, loose Your hand, I beg, and crush me.
Then I could die still having never denied
my God. Should I hope? I tell you, I've tried.
But where is my joy? Even friends turn away.
You've all proven you are no help here today.
Look at me. You are afraid and unjust!
There isn't one word that you spoke which I trust.
Is man's earthly service just trouble and toil?
Is he but a hired hand working the soil?
I have been given the poorest of terms,
to writhe as my body's infected with worms.
My festering wounds leave me empty of hope.
I never again shall know goodness. The scope
of my life has been set. Even deep in my sleep,
I am haunted by visions where cruel monsters creep.
Awake or asleep, my soul cannot rest.
Without any doubt I believe death is best.
How have I sinned, God? How have I turned
from a boon to a burden to You? I am burned
and broken. Will You not forgive me so I
may sleep without end? Dear God, let me die!
For a moment, I beg, let it be like before,
then I'll lie in the dirt, and I'll be no more."

Job 8

Then Bildad the Shuhite replied to Job's cries.
"How long will you bluster like this? I despise
anyone who declares that God might distort
justice. That nonsense I cannot support.
God took your children who sinned. But if you
are upright and pure, the good Lord will do
what you have requested, restoring your health.
Your humbleness will be the start of your wealth.
Our days here on Earth are but shadows that pass.
Without any marsh, how can there be grass?
Without any water, the reeds cannot grow.
So without the Lord, the desert wind blows
us all back to dust. But in God, you will find
you rely upon He who created mankind,
not something that's fragile. His roots all are deep.
Those who plant righteousness surely shall reap.
Again you'll know laughter. Again you'll find joy.
Just as you did when you were a boy.
Your enemies will be brought low, while you
are lifted on high, if your love for God's true."

Job 9 - 10

Job said, "I know that is true, but how can
a mortal be righteous? Compared to a man
God's wisdom is greater, His power is vast.
He can stop sunlight, and God can then cast
the mountains out into the sea. Just how far
can a man debate with Him who put up each star?
I cannot see Him when He passes me by.
All upon Earth is within the Lord's eye.
How can I dispute? What case can I plead?
And why should He hear me in my time of need?
Perhaps He would crush me for bothering Him.
I am one man. He must watch all of them.
I don't care for my life. Let my days just rush by.
God's will shall be till the day that I die.

Although I am blameless, my life is without
any value. And my complaints carry no clout.
If only somebody could arbitrate on
behalf of my case, but my hope is all gone.
I loathe my own life, and so I complain
to God. Speak my charges! Why all of this pain?
Is it pleasing to harm me and keep me oppressed?
My wounds will not heal, although they are dressed.
Is it funny to You? Do You see how I shake?
I am innocent, Lord. There must be some mistake.
You molded me out of the clay. Tell me, must
You crush me and break me till I am but dust?
I knew You would see if I sinned, so I tried
to be blameless, though now I wish I had died."

Job 11

Then Zophar the Naamathite said, "Should I not
rebuke you for all of your misdeeds and thoughts?
You mock the Lord saying you're flawless. God should
strike you for this. You have turned from what's good.
God has forgotten great numbers of sins
that you have committed. All women and men
must know He forgives. Yet you speak like you
know all of the secrets of God. If you do,
please share them. Can you measure all of His acts?
There's nothing He's not. There's nothing He lacks.
Stretch out to Him, Job, and lift up your face.
The Lord will receive you with infinite grace.
Your troubles will all be like waters gone by,
and life will be bright as the sun in the sky.
Then you will lie down at night without fear,
for the mercy of God will finally be clear."

Job 12 - 14

So Job said, "You act as if I've lost my mind.
Everyone knows this. Do you think I'm blind?
I'm now just a laughingstock. My life's a joke.

Though righteous, now I am afflicted and broke!
Marauders and thieves still frolic as I
curse every last minute that passes me by.
They carry their gods in their hands! Though I pray,
everyone knows God has made me this way.
Surely the Lord has great wisdom and power.
He proves this to mankind in every hour.
He overthrows priests and those who have done
no wrong. So beware noble men. Turn and run!
My eyes have seen this. He lets criminals free.
I know this, but I want the Lord to hear me.
You worthless physicians, what cure have you brought?
The words on your tongues? Your wisdom and thought?
Speak on behalf of the Lord! Take the case
and argue for God. Why have I been debased?
Your speeches are ashes. Keep silent! Let me
ask why should I put myself in jeopardy?
I hope, but the Lord still destroys me. Indeed,
death is the best reason I have to plead.
Grant me two things, God. First, please take back
Your hand from my throat. I am under attack.
Next, let me answer for all of my sins.
Show my offense. Tell me where it begins.
Why torment Your servant without giving cause?
I rot never knowing how I broke Your laws.
Life is so short and troublesome. Yay,
it springs like a flower, then withers away.
God sets the number of every man's days.
The man works them only to die and decay.
At least there is hope for a tree! It will sprout
once again if it's cut or if it's in drought.
But a man breathes his last, and then is no more.
There is no rebirth that man has in store.
Will a man who has died live again? No! You took
all of our hope. So, wherever you look,
the bodies of men don't rejoice in their sons.
They mourn for themselves, till their sad days are done."

Job 15

Then Eliphaz said, "Would a wise man reply
with such empty answers? You ask the Lord, 'Why?'
but your very own words testify against you.
Where is your wisdom? These cries are not new.
Why has your hard heart carried away
the man I once knew? I tell you this day,
if even the heavens aren't pure in God's eyes,
how much less is man? Though you may despise
God's justice, those who defy the Lord will
find their walls crumbled. Though good things once filled
their houses, all things shall be taken from them.
Don't provoke God. It's only through Him
that you'll find redemption. Don't trust what is false,
for lies cannot hold up within the Lord's walls.
The godless are barren of all things of worth.
They make and breed trouble, which covers the Earth."

Job 16 - 17

Then Job replied, "I have heard all this before!
You miserable counselors, please speak no more.
If our roles were switched, I might say such things.
But tell me, oh wise men, can one of you bring
some comfort to me? No! Still I'm beset
by all of these sores and I'm penniless. Yet,
you keep on persisting. The Lord's worn me out.
My gaunt, withered frame is proof a devout
life gets you nothing! Men strike me and jeer.
The Lord strikes me too. Have I been insincere?
Just look at this corpse that is me! Though I did
His will, God's mercy was strictly forbid.
The grave's all I have to look forward to now.
You wise men around me still can't tell me how
a righteous man is to be heard by the Lord
so I might find hope and thus be restored."

Job 18

Then Bildad replied, "Be sensible, man!
How are we stupid, but you understand?
The lamp of the wicked man shall be extinguished,
while God lifts the righteous man up as distinguished.
The evil man's trapped, ensnared, and entwined
by his sin. On his soul, calamity dined,
tearing him up. He shall burn in God's fire.
His name is erased while he's still on the pyre."

Job 19

"More foolishness!" Job cried out in despair.
"You exalt your own names as you tell me it's fair
that I am cast down. You've no sympathy for
my plight. Every time that you speak I hear more
foolishness from you. Although I was crowned,
God has delighted in knocking me down.
I am an alien in my own land.
My friends and my kinsman are gone. Understand
that now I am loathsome to even my wife!
The little boys scorn me. Oh yes, what a life!
My intimate friends detest me as well.
They sit here and mock me. Now, come brothers, tell
why I should listen to what you tell me.
I wish that my words were recorded. You see,
I know my Redeemer still lives. I will stand
and see Him when my bones are deep in the sand.
My heart yearns for God. I want to be near
the One who has turned from me. Let that be clear.
So if you have come here to shame me, the sword
will be brought down upon you, for I fear the Lord."

Job 20

Then Zophar said, "My thoughts are troubled, for I
have now been dishonored, so as my reply
you know it is true that the wicked man here

does not go to God, but instead disappears.
His earthly desires shall turn on his soul,
and only through God can a man be made whole.
The wicked are snared by their treasures and lust.
The Lord God is mighty. In Him we must trust."

Job 21

Job replied, "Listen to me now, my friend.
And then you may mock me to my bitter end.
Tell me why I should be patient? No man
can help me. I want God to tell me His plan.
Look at my body. It's broken! Can you
explain how the wicked are still allowed to
proceed with no punishment? Their children live
and flourish around them. How can God give
them all of the joy in their life, though they say,
'Leave us alone, God. Please go away.'
Why should we serve the Almighty if He
is in charge of how prosperous each man may be,
and He rewards those who are wicked, but I
am brushed aside as a man swats at a fly?
Truly, how often are evil men's lamps
extinguished? You said so, but look at their camps.
They're prosperous families. It's said that the sins
of the father are set on the son. Let's begin
to visit the sins of the man on the man,
so that they may end up where they all began!
Can anyone teach their knowledge to God?
Though one man is rich, and one man must plod,
when they both lie down side by side in the dirt,
what's different? Now that they both are inert,
one suffered life, and one, through his greed,
enjoyed it. Why suffer? I ask you what need
is there to be righteous, if God blesses he
who's wicked? So your words mean nothing to me."

Job 22

Then Eliphaz said, "Job, your wickedness speaks
against you. Have you not stood over the weak?
You've turned away widows and orphans. Your ways
of gaining your wealth are the reason these days
you suffer. And now you declare that the Lord
does not know His own mind. Can you afford
to speak in a way that's so callous, when He
is the one who rules over and punishes thee?
Submit to the Lord. Find mercy. You still
can thus be restored, for the Lord wants His will
to be understood. Let God be your gold.
And then you shall see your true wealth unfold."

Job 23 - 24

Ignoring these words, Job complained, "Even now
I suffer. Oh God, if I only knew how
to track You and find You, I'd utter my case.
But I cannot find You. I cannot chase
You into the east, the north or the south
or the west. Do You not hear the words of my mouth?
I am blameless. I fear You, but I shall not cease
my tongue till I find You and I speak my piece.
Why do You let all the poor be abused
by the wicked? They're beaten. The rich have refused
to feed them or clothe them. Their children are starved
as the fat of the lamb for the wealthy is carved.
The mighty gain power, but it won't last long,
for mortals are weak, and the Lord God is strong.
He may let them rest in security for
awhile, but God will keep track of their score."

Job 25

Then Bildad replied, "Dominion belongs
to God. All the heavens must line up along
His will. His force is the greatest indeed.

To the Lord, what's a man? We're no more than a seed.
How can we be righteous? How can man be pure
in the sight of the Lord? It seems to me sure
that we are just mortals! Throughout our short term
on Earth, we're as low as a maggot or worm."

Job 26 - 27

Then Job replied, "Oh, hear the wisdom you speak!
Who helped you utter these words? Have the weak
been lifted by you? The dead are in deep
anguish beneath the waters that keep
them held down below. God is the birth
of all that is wondrous. He hangs the Earth
out over nothing. We see but the fringe
of His deeds. If we knew His breadth, we would cringe.
As surely as God has punished me, still
my tongue shall not speak out against the Lord's will.
But I shall maintain my innocence till
it's my time to die or to be fulfilled.
The wicked and ruthless who scoff at the Lord,
shall know that their children shall die by the sword.
Whatever his treasures, they all turn to dust,
for God despises such evil and lust."

Job 28

"The mines where men seek both silver and gold
are deep in the ground where light can't take hold.
Man cuts the rock to find it, but where
can wisdom be found? It's not found in there.
It's not in the land of the living. It hides,
and when a man finds it and that man decides
to take it, he soon realizes that he
has found something better than jewels. It can't be
bought with his gold, and nothing compares
to the beauty of wisdom. Only God shares
this most precious gift with His people. To fear
the Lord - that is when great wisdom appears."

Job 29 - 31

And so Job continued, "How I long for days
gone by, when the Lord watched all of my ways.
He was with me and my children still lived.
There aren't many things that I would not give
to be there again, when I was still loved
by people I knew and the Lord God above.
I was a blessing to others. I stood
up for the poor, the righteous, and good.
I was respected and people would wait
to hear how I judged as I sat at the gate.
But now I am mocked. I'm detestable and
my name is disdained across the whole land.
God throws my body, naked and bruised,
into the mud. How I am abused!
Surely someone will lift up their voice,
but will the Lord listen? That is His choice.
Have I been deceitful? Weigh out my sin!
I've walked the Lord's path again and again.
If I have been lustful, let my wife be
given to other men. It was not me!
If I denied justice to those who had need,
or caused harm to widows or orphans, indeed,
curse me. If I suffered from love of gold,
then let me be judged for acting so bold.
If I have rejoiced at my enemy's loss,
then let me stand trial. I never have crossed
the lines that the Lord has drawn. I am free
of sin. Now I beg you, Lord, let me be!"

Job 32 - 34

So Job's friends stopped speaking, because he believed
he was right. But one man would not be deceived.
Elihu hearing Job's words became mad.
He chastised Job saying, "So now you have had
your say. I have waited, and though I am young,

now you must listen to me. Watch your tongue!
Wisdom is not bound by age. Hear me out.
You justify yourself and say you're devout,
but none of you men have proven Job wrong.
The words of the one have defeated the throng!
You three are dismayed. You have no more to say,
but I can tell you that on this very day,
none of you justified God or the acts
He has brought upon Job. The Spirit in fact
touches my lips with these words. You complain
that God is malicious, and shows you disdain.
You say you were blameless, but God cursed you still.
You whine that you cry out to God, but He will
not answer you. He answers us every day.
How? He will answer in various ways.
In a dream or a vision. Or maybe through pain.
The Lord will relieve the repentant. Don't feign
that God doesn't hear you! Do not believe it.
He's trying to tell you, "Turn back from the pit."
Be silent and listen, for I want you cleared
of all that now ails you. Open your ear
to the word of the Lord. Your argument's flawed.
You say no man profits who tries to please God.
He punishes men who decide they're above
His laws, and He blesses the ones who show love
to the needy. If God were to draw back His breath
from the Earth then I tell you, there'd be nothing left.
I ask you, can he who hates justice be called
a leader? Is God not the one who treats all
the same? Both the princes and peasants are one
and the same in His eyes. Let His will be done.
He sees every step. Nobody can hide
from His eyes. He sees what you do and decides
if you will be blessed or if you'll be cursed.
Repent, Job, for God could still make your pain worse!
Say you are guilty and you'll sin no more.
Hear what I say, and do it before
the Lord truly tests you. This is a taste
of God's wrath. I tell you, there's no time to waste."

Job 35 - 37

Then Elihu said, "Do you think it is just
to say you'll be cleared by the Lord, but not trust
that it profits you to live a life free of sin?
I hear contradictions again and again.
Look up at the heavens. How can you hurt
the Lord with your sin? But here in the dirt,
you see how the Lord can do harm to you!
Silence my tongue if it doesn't speak true.
Men will cry out for relief, but they won't
sing songs of His praise as they suffer. So don't
expect Him to answer each time you call out.
His answers come when you are truly devout.
Bear with me. There is still more to be said,
and all of my words and thoughts have been fed
by the Spirit of God. He enthrones righteous men
like kings, and He binds up the wicked with sin.
But if they obey, the Lord will forgive,
for what does God gain when a man does not live?
He delivers the suffering. Don't turn aside
for selfish desires, anger, or bribes.
Can man count the years of God? No, but we
can gaze at the heavens and His mystery.
The rain and the clouds, the lightning and thunder
are signs of His greatness, so stare up in wonder.
My heart pounds and leaps when He roars in the storm.
He sends down fresh water in every form.
The rain when it pours, and the snow and the ice
are His. Can you bring them? Of course not. Think twice
on all of your words. Look up at the sun.
Turn around, Job, see all He has done.
The Lord's work is awesome. In nature abounds
His glory. Where's God? Look around. He is found."

Job 38 - 41

Then out of the storm, the Lord spoke instead.
"Who darkens my counsel with what he has said?
Where were you, Job, when I laid the foundation
of Earth; all the water 'round every nation?
Who marked its dimensions and who set the line
as the angels rejoiced? Job, are you divine?
Have you made the morning? Have you brought the dawn?
Tell Me, have you ever set foot upon
the depths of the deep? And do you know where
the shadow of death is found? Take Me there.
And show Me the path to the way of true light.
Tell Me, great man, have you set your sight
on the storehouses full of lightning or snow?
Does rain have a father? Surely you know.
Can you loose the cords of Orion's belt? You
must know how the stars work. Tell me now. Do
you know all the laws of the heavens and Earth?
Are you with each babe at the time of its birth?
Are you by the side of each cub till it's grown?
Are you with each bird until it has flown?
Do the ox and the ostrich bow down at your feet?
Are you with each animal as they compete
for survival? Who wins? Surely you say
who eats and who starves. What happens today?
Let the one who contends with the Lord stand and speak!"
Job huddled in fear. His voice came out weak.
"I'm unworthy, my Lord! I must place both my hands
over my mouth. For I am but a man.
I'm unable to answer."
The Lord spoke again.
"Why do you seek to discredit Me then?
With the strength of an ox, still I can hide
in the lotus' shadow. Come now, confide.
Can you harness leviathan with just a hook?
Make a pet out of him and let little girls look?
One glance at the beast and you'll shake where you stand.
How much greater am I? I'm the mighty I AM!"

Job 42

Then Job spoke, "My God, I am but a man.
I've spoken of things I cannot understand.
I heard You and saw You. Oh Lord, I repent.
In ashes I grovel. My robes have been rent.."
God wasn't happy with Job's friends, for they
had not spoken as Elihu had on that day.
They were admonished and Job was restored
with double his previous wealth by the Lord.
Again he was blessed with daughters and sons,
and he lived a good life. And when it was done,
he died having lived a full life because
he repented, obeying the Lord and His laws.

Psalm 1

Blessed is he who delights in the Lord,
for sinners aren't part of the Lord God's accord.
He's like a tree whose leaves do not die,
he's pleasing and prosperous in the Lord's eye.
The wicked men bring destruction at hand,
and scatter the chaff across the whole land.
The righteous man's knowledge of God's to be cherished.
While those who are evil are judged and shall perish.

Psalm 2 - 7

God placed His king on His holy hill
and watched over me, when others would kill.
I sleep in peace, for I know that He stands
watch over me, with a shield in His hand.
He protects me from words. He protects me from deeds.
He's heard me cry out, and He fills all my needs.
Away from me, evil! For justice you'll know
by His rod and His staff at each mighty blow.

Psalm 8

O Lord how majestic Your name is in all
of the Earth and I sing it wherever I go.
Praise issues out from the children so small,
that clamps up the tongues of every foe.
The work of Your hands in the blackness of space
is seen in the moon and the stars set above.
Heavenly bodies that you put in place.

What is a man, that you should so love?
For You set us just a bit lower than Thee
and crowned us as rulers with glory and honor
over the birds and the beasts and the sea;
to rule over Earth and all that's upon her.
As governors over the great and the small
we are but servants who bow down so low.
O Lord, how majestic Your name is in all
of the Earth and I sing it wherever I go.

Psalm 9 - 13

Those who know You place their trust in You, God,
although we are faulted and though we are flawed.
We're never abandoned to our fate alone,
although You do not always make Yourself known.
Rise up and smite all the evil that walks!
In you I find peace, while others just talk.
They say, "Run and flee!" while I say, "Believe
in the Lord, for His glorious love never leaves."
But the hour is late, and the godly may change.
They'll honor themselves, saying God's word is strange.
They lie and they boast. How the faithful have vanished!
Cut out their tongues, Lord, let them be banished.
But don't forget me, and don't hide Your face.
I am Your servant and seek Your embrace.
I trust in Your unfailing love and salvation.
You've blessed me and so I sing without cessation.

Psalm 14 - 16

The fool rejects God,
and thinks he is clever.
To live blameless lives
the faithful endeavor.
Show me the way
to live like my God
forever and ever
and ever.

Psalm 17 - 22

Lord, hear my prayer that I lift to the air
Bring justice among us, for You know what's fair.
With You as my shield and my strength, I won't yield,
for You're the creator of sea, sky, and field.
Some boast of their swords and weaponry hordes
while our army boasts of our faith in the Lord.
And Your king rejoices! Although there are choices,
we worship our Lord with our multiplied voices.
For You will defend Your people and send
us into the battle and there we shall win.
You're great and I pray You will not turn away,
but be with Your servant for all of my days.

Psalm 23

The Lord is my shepherd, and I want for naught.
He leads me beside quiet waters in thought.
He leads me in ways in which my soul's restored.
He shows me the righteous way. He is my Lord.
I walk through the valley of the shadow of death,
and I fear no evil, as God's in each breath.
I am protected by His staff and rod,
for He is my savior as He is my God.
My table is set in the presence of foes.
I'm anointed by God. My cup overflows.
Goodness and love follow me where I roam.
Forever I'll dwell in the Lord's holy home.

Psalm 24 - 27

The Earth is the Lord's and all it possesses.
The world and its people are all His successes.
Be with me, Lord, and show me Your ways,
that I may be righteous for all of my days.
Test me and try me, that I may prove true,
for in all my actions I seek and love You.

The Lord is my light, and He's my salvation.
Why should I fear? I have His consecration.

Psalm 28 - 31

Praise God! He heard the cry from my heart.
I trust and I know that He'll never depart.
Worship His works and all He's created.
His voice thunders over the seas and I'm sated.
He's rescued me, turning my mourning to dance.
I worship my Father at every chance.
When I was distressed or uttered a wail,
He heard me and showed that His mercy prevails.

Psalm 32 - 35

Forgiveness brings joy when the Lord casts away
your sins, so praise Him and henceforth obey.
It is right to praise God. Sing a song, play the lyre.
Shout out your joy, for that's God's desire.
This poor man called out, and He heard me weep.
Be of His flock, as I am His sheep.
No servant of His is ever condemned.
He rescues us all, that we may come in.

Psalm 36 - 37

Sin whispers to the wicked man's heart.
There's no fear of God to keep them apart.
But God's love is faithful, mighty and vast.
His righteousness stands like a mountain, steadfast.
Be still in the Lord and patient for Him.
The wicked may snarl, but God scoffs at them.
Although they're defiant, they will succumb,
for God knows that their day of judgment will come.

Psalm 38 - 41

On the verge of collapse and in constant pain
I'm sorry for all of the sins I've committed.
Forgiveness resides in God's own domain
Lord, in Your mercy, let me be acquitted.
We are but shadows moving about;
we rush through our lives, but only in vain.
"What shall I put my hope in?" I shout.
My hope is in God. In Him I'm maintained.
Lord, I need You, I have to confess,
but I will wait patiently and not complain.
The Lord is with all of us in our distress.
He nurses with love and He eases our pain.

Psalm 42 - 44

A deer may pant for water,
as I shall long for God.
I thirst for Him, the living One,
though I know I am flawed.
Why am I so discouraged?
And why am I so sad?
My hope's in God. I praise again
the only God I've had.
Oh God take up my cause,
for lies are all I see.
Send out your light, send out your truth
and please let them guide me.
Why am I so discouraged?
And why am I so sad?
My hope's in God. I praise again
the only God I've had.
Only by your power
can we push back our foes.
What have we done to anger you
that we should be deposed?
Why am I so discouraged?
And why am I so sad?

My hope's in God. I praise again
the only God I've had.

Psalm 45

My heart overflows with a beautiful thought.
You are the greatest of all.
Put on your sword, oh glorious warrior
and know your foes will fall.
Ride out defending justice and truth.
The nations will fall to their knees.
God's throne endures forever and ever,
and he has anointed thee.
Your palace encrusted with ivory and gold.
Your robes are perfumed with myrrh.
Oh royal daughter forget your homeland!
Her husband delights in her.
Showered with gifts, the bride awaits,
robed in a gown of gold.
In a joyful procession, she's led to the king.
A beautiful sight to behold.
Your sons will be kings like their father
and rule over all they endeavor.
I'll honor your name in each generation
and praise you forever and ever.

Psalm 46 - 48

God is our refuge and we will not stumble
if earthquakes should rock or if mountains should crumble.
He is perfection! He is unflawed.
He whispers, "Be still and know I am God."
Then everyone shout; make a joyful noise!
He subdues the nations and then he destroys
our enemies, giving them into our hands.
We are the heirs to the Lord's promised land!
In Jerusalem, His holy city, we raise
our song to our God and offer Him praise.

God is her fortress; God is her lion.
Behold His great city on top of Mount Zion.

Psalm 49 - 50

Listen all people and you will have heard
the wisdom that lives in each of my words.
Our riches stay here when each of us dies.
The selfish are fools, though they are called wise.
The rich will all rot in their lofty estates
while the godly know heavenly treasure awaits.
God will proclaim, "Let the faithful draw near."
And all will know when His justice is here.
He will call out, "Sacrifice naught,
instead just be faithful in heart and in thought.
I don't need the blood from your doves or your bulls,
for the world is Mine, and My world is full."

Psalm 51

Have mercy, O Lord, and withhold disdain.
I pray that You'll come and You'll blot out my stain.
Cleanse me of guilt, for I stand in shame.
In evilness I have forgotten Your name.
Purify me and cleanse me as though
My heart were as white as a new fallen snow.
Create a clean heart in me, Lord, I ask.
Renew a right spirit in which I may bask.
I have shed blood, but O Lord who saves,
unseal my lips so Your name I may praise.
Although I could bring You a sacrificed prize,
still I am too broken, and I'd be despised.

Psalm 52 - 58

He who loves evil more than the truth,
shall be dragged down into the land of the dead.
God looks for any who have understanding,
but sees we all turned from His glory instead.

God hear my plea! It's my friend, not my foe,
who once I shared fellowship with in Your house,
who's turned on me. God, let the grave swallow up
that treacherous, dangerous, unpleasant louse.
But when I'm afraid, I turn to Your word.
For when I'm with You, what can mortals do?
Have mercy on me. Please give me protection
under Your wing till this storm is subdued.

Psalm 59 - 64

I shout out with joy at each morning sun
for You are my refuge each day I'm distressed.
Deliver my enemies into my hands.
Let those snarling dogs have no peace or rest.
No man can help me. I need You right now.
Do not reject us, but be with my men!
Hear this one prayer at the ends of the Earth.
Be with Your great King David again.
My God is my rock, and He's my salvation,
My fortress in which I can never be shaken.
My soul thirsts for you and I need your water.
I seek you so that I should not be forsaken.
My enemies sharpen their tongues just like swords.
Their words are their arrows aimed all at me.
But God is against them, and each man will fear
when they see the Lord's fierce response to my plea.

Psalm 65 - 67

You answer our prayers with Your perfect deeds,
our hope to the ends of the Earth and the seas.
The desert is bursting with flocks and with grain.
Abundance is everywhere in His domain.
Shout out your praise to God and His name!
All the Earth bows and I do the same.
God bless us and let Your face shine upon
Your people each evening, each day, and each dawn.

Psalm 68

May God arise and scatter his foes.
The wicked will perish as everyone knows.
Sing to the Lord who rides on a cloud.
Extol your praises, crying aloud.
A father to orphans, the widow's defender;
He honors believers and cuts down pretenders.
We marched through the desert with You as our guide
and gained our inheritance, though we were tried.
Great was the glory of those who announced
God and His name, but those who denounced
His honor were struck down, peasant and king.
But all who have seen His power now sing.
God sends one thousand chariots out
and crushes His enemies. Now who will doubt?!
The twelve tribes have come proclaiming a song.
Egypt and Cush will submit to the throng.
Announce His arrival across all the Earth.
All who know Him know what He is worth.
Wherever we tread and wherever we trod,
He will be with us. Praise be to God!

Psalm 69 - 70

Save me, O Lord! The flood's at my chin.
Pull me from waters which I'm sinking in.
My foes outnumber the hairs on my head.
I am insulted, and they want me dead.
Save me, my God, for I am in need.
Do not permit my foes succeed.
You're my deliverer, do not delay.
Hear me in need, and hear as I pray.

Psalm 71

In God I take refuge. He is my rock.
Deliver me God, for I'm of your flock.
You've been my hope since I was a youth.

You brought me forth and showed me the truth.
Your glory is known to all whom I've told.
Do not forsake me when I have grown old.
Those who conspire to kill me or seize me
fail, for Your strength will still me and ease me.
May they be scorned. May they be shamed.
Disgrace them, O Lord, and let them be named.
I'll sing your righteousness all the day long,
though it can't be measured in one little song.
Your deeds are marvelous. They touch the skies.
Though I have seen bitterness with my own eyes,
You do great things. Oh, who is like You?!
You have increased me with all that You do.

Psalm 72

Endow the king with justice, my Lord,
and righteousness for his son,
for he'll judge your people as You see fit.
Prosperity for everyone.
Defend the afflicted, the needy, and orphans.
Endure through all generations.
The righteous will flourish, and tribes will bow down
as he shakes the very foundations.
From the Euphrates and to the horizon
all will bow down to his will,
and he will deliver the needy who cry
as Your word he strives to fulfill.
Give us both grain and fruit in the land
and let Your great name endure.
Praise to the Lord, oh Israel's God,
in You we can truly be sure.

Psalm 73 - 76

Surely God is true to those
who have a faithful heart,
but, lo, I nearly stumbled
before I could even start.

I saw the carefree, wicked men
grow their wealth until
I thought of what awaits them once
their beating hearts are still.
I saw Your foes come in this house
where You had shown Your face.
They broke all things and then burned down
this righteous, holy place.
You are my God; my king of old.
You crushed Leviathan,
and let the beasts all eat his flesh
under the desert sun.
It's You who judge. You choose the time
in which Your verdict's shown.
The arrogant will boast no more,
for You protect Your own.
Surely You will burn against
those who curse Your worth,
then everyone will know my God
is King of all the Earth.

Psalm 77 - 78

When I was distressed, I sought out the Lord,
and He gave my soul its greatest reward.
For I thought of days - the years long ago -
where all of the people and even our foes
knew of the miracles our Lord had done.
His lightning lit up the Earth like the sun.
The thunder was heard and the earth shook about.
Moses then led all the Lord's people out
of Egypt. Let us tell the story again,
so our people do not slip back into sin.
Knowing our God, we all understand
we are to live and obey His commands.
You sent the manna, and parted the sea.
Without Him all Israel would cease to be.
Though in a pillar of fire, we still
cried and complained about the Lord's will.

God could destroy us, as was His right,
but He remained faithful by day and by night.
Then He lifted David, a shepherd of sheep,
to care for His flocks and commandments to keep.

Psalm 79 - 80

Oh God, they've invaded and torn down each stone.
The temple's destroyed. The flesh and the bone
of all of your servants are meat for the beasts.
We're scorned by our foes to the west and the east.
Help us, O Lord, to honor Your name.
Forgive us our sins, as we are to blame.
Restore us, oh God, may You shine upon
those who remain and those who are gone.
You brought a vine out of Egypt and made
a tree in this land and gave it some shade.
Now it has fallen, for that is Your choice,
but save us, restore us, that we may rejoice.

Psalm 81 - 85

Sing to the Lord, for He is our strength.
Strike a chord, bang the tambourine.
Sound the horn at our holy feast.
Our God is justice, fair, serene.
He keeps the weak and poor from harm,
though evil plots to foil Him.
Our foes are huddled up to plan
attacks on us. The future's grim.
But He's our Lord! My soul seeks peace.
How lovely, Lord, is Your dwelling place.
The blessed put their strength in you.
The Lord's a shield. Oh, show Your face!
O Lord, forgive Your children's sins.
Salvation nears His chosen land.
In Him, there's love and righteousness.
Indeed, all good comes from His hand.

Psalm 86

Guard my life! I'm devoted to You.
Be merciful, Lord, when I'm calling for You.
Bring joy to my soul, it is lifted to You.
Abounding in love, we believe in You.
In my day of need, I'll cry out for You.
There is no god to compare to You.
All of the nations come worshiping You.
Teach me to walk in the way of You.
I'll praise and I will glorify You.
In love I am delivered by You.
Compassion and grace are found in You.
I know that I will be saved by You.

Psalm 87-88

In Zion, His great foundation is found.
He loves those inside her walls.
He put all their names in the register
found in her hallowed halls.
Though I cry out, a prayer to God
as death is drawing near,
I wonder why those I call my friends
were taken away from here.

Psalm 89

With my mouth I'll make your faithfulness known.
You, God, placed David onto his throne.
Who in the world compares with my God?
In the council of holy ones, He is most awed.
You rule the seas, the heavens, and Earth.
Your justice and power are proof of Your worth.
Blessed are those who show You acclaim,
For they shall rejoice and walk in Your name.
As You turned a boy to a leader and man,
in David You laid out a beautiful plan.
You, Lord, sustain him and crush all his foes,

and he takes You with him wherever he goes.
The Lord blesses David and all of his line,
but if they ignore Him, then they'll be maligned.
Be certain that God's love will not go away.
God will make sure that His covenant stays.
But, lo, God is angry with His kingly servant.
We have been lax in our faith, not observant.
We have been shamed. Oh, Lord, do not hide!
Please, Lord, be with us. In You, we confide.

Psalm 90 - 91

Before the great mountains, You brought forth the Earth.
All that we see has come out of that birth.
You will return each man to the dust.
O how many years have You given to us?
Seventy? Eighty? Through so much we ache,
and soon all those years we will see in our wake.
But if we seek shelter inside of Your shade,
You'll walk beside us and we won't be afraid.
Through You, all disaster shall stay from my tent.
and I will not have to be sad or lament,
for when I'm in need, I'll be satisfied.
You're my salvation and You are my guide.

Psalm 92 - 100

It's good to give thanks to the Lord and sing praise,
to glorify You through all of my days.
The Lord is our king, sitting robed on His throne
above all the earth and the seas in His home.
The Lord is my fortress, a place I can hide.
Without His protection, I'd surely have died.
Come, let us sing to the rock of salvation!
Our forefathers wandered a whole generation.
They turned from the Lord and from His true way.
But now we shall sing and praise Him each day.
Declare to the nations His greatness and deeds,
In all He is righteous. In all He succeeds.

Light shines upon the godly and right.
At His word the Earth trembles, day becomes night.
The Lord has remembered Israel's house.
Let not your song or worship be doused.
Let the Earth shake, His justice remains.
Moses and Samuel have called out His name.
Honor Him with thanksgiving and praise.
May all generations in Him be amazed.

Psalm 101 - 102

I will be careful to live without blame,
I'll set my eyes upon Your holy name.
No vile thing will be set out before
my eyes. Let wickedness stay from my door.
Lord, hear my prayer. Lord, hear my plea.
In my great distress, do not turn from me.
In ages gone by, You laid the foundation.
God, You never fail! Watch over Your nation.

Psalm 103 - 104

The Lord is our Father, great in compassion,
and we are His children. We have been fashioned
from dust, and our days are so quickly spent.
The love of the Lord is heavenly sent.
You stretched out the vast, starry curtain above,
and created this mass of water and mud.
You gave it the beasts and birds of the air.
Great are Your works, with proof everywhere!

Psalm 105 - 106

Descendants from one thousand great generations
had faith that one day they would see confirmation.
That all that You promised would soon come to be,
and You made them whole; yes, You made them free.
But they were ungrateful, forgetting their gift.
Pride and false idols created a rift.

And though You put them in their enemy's hands,
You still gave to them this beautiful land.

Psalm 107

Give thanks to the Lord. Let me be redeemed.
My troubles and struggles are not what they seemed.
Those who have wandered cried out and were fed,
they were alone and very near dead.
Those in the darkness, suff'ring in chains
yelled out for Him, and felt no more pain.
Faith is salvation. He breaks down the gates
of iron and bronze for those who must wait.
Those who rebelled and suffered affliction,
found solace when they gave Him jurisdiction
over their lives. Let us give Him thanks,
for He puts His army back into our ranks.
Those who found tempests out there on the seas,
prayed to the Lord as they fell to their knees.
He stilled the storm to a whisper and hushed
the waves just before their vessel was crushed.
He turns the ground into flowing springs,
and when I'm in need, He does wondrous things.
He feeds the hungry. He makes the grain.
He shuts up the wicked. He rules His domain.

Psalm 108 - 109

He gives us victory over their lands;
Shechem and Succoth are placed in our hands.
Gilead, Manasseh, Ephraim, and Moab
conquered. No longer shall I be a nomad!
Others still lie and slander against
Your servant. Lord, shame them for their great offense.
Though they may curse You, we are still blessed.
Condemn all my foes for how they transgress.

Psalm 110

The Lord says to my lord, "Sit at the right,
and I'll put your enemies under your might.
Your troops will be willing to battle, arrayed
in holiness. Then you shall hear my Lord say,
"A priest like Melchizedek, that's what you are.
The Lord will crush kingdoms, both near and afar.
He'll tumble the nations, wherever you look,
then He'll be refreshed and drink from the brook.

Psalm 111 - 118

The fear of the Lord is the path of the wise.
Follow Him and you will know.
Happy is he who fears our God
as he triumphs over his foe.
Who would compare himself to our God,
the One who sits on high?
Even the sea is terrified
by the face of Adonai.
The idols of men are cast by them,
but cannot speak or see.
I love the Lord who hears my prayers
and counsels then with me.
Praise the Lord you nations. Men,
raise his flag and pennant.
This is the day the Lord has made.
Rejoice and be glad in it.

Psalm 119

Blessed are those who walk without blame.
If I were steadfast, I'd not know this shame.
But I still praise You, obey your decrees,
and pray that You, God, will not forsake me.
How can a young man remain true and pure?
I live in Your law, for that way is sure.
I think on Your ways, and love Your demands.

Though I am a stranger, don't hide Your commands.
I am laid low, dragged through the dust.
Though I am weary, I know You are just.
Teach me, O Lord, so that I will know
how to obey You wherever I go.
The wicked may bind me, but I will not waver.
In Your eyes I try to always find favor.
Your law makes me wise. My enemies fear,
for they know You're with me, because I adhere
to all You have shown and all You have told.
Your word is made new in Your law which is old.
Your word is a lamp to my feet and a light
for my path, and You guide me throughout the dark night.

Psalm 120 - 134

Woe, that I live in Meshech and Kedar.
These scoundrels who fight wherever they are.
When I look for peace, it's not to the hills.
Peace comes from God. It's He that fulfills
the needs of us all. Israel's fate
is His as we stand at Jerusalem's gate.
God, on Your throne in Heaven, You see.
I lift up my eyes and my singing to Thee.
We escaped like a bird from the trapper's lone snare.
God is our savior. His justice is fair.
His faith's as secure as Mount Zion is.
The Lord will surround all that which is His.
The Lord brought us back when we were destroyed.
Those who sow tears will soon harvest joy.
Without God's protection, a city's defense
is useless, so do not hang onto pretense.
The fruit of the Lord makes your wife like a vine.
Children burst forth! Gifts from the Divine.
Though I have been cut, and cried out aloud,
God has forgiven, but I am not proud.
I'm still and I'm quiet; a child, God's own.
As promised He'll place David's line on the throne.
One of his lineage will come to reign

over all that is under the Lord's great domain.
How pleasant it is when we live as one
in unity, brothers. All under the sun
is His. And although we have such little worth,
we're loved by the Maker of Heaven and Earth.

Psalm 135 - 136

The Lord's strength is great. He does what He will.
He's struck down the firstborn, and kings have been killed.
Their idols are meaningless silver and gold.
God's might is frightful and great to behold.
But our Lord is good, so give thanks, for He
created the heavens and laid down the sea.
His love brought us through each pain and endeavor,
and it shall endure forever and ever.

Psalm 137

At the rivers of Babylon we sat and wept,
remembering Zion, our home far away.
Our captors demanded we sing and play songs
from home. But there is no way we could play
a song of the Lord for these foreign ears.
But I won't forget Jerusalem's walls.
And Lord don't forget what Edom has done.
"Tear it down to its foundation!" they called.
O Daughter of Babylon, it won't be long
till God tends to us, the sheep of his flock.
And on that day, Babel, you'll know he is God
as all of your babes are dashed on the rock.

Psalm 138 - 139

In front of their gods, I still sing Your praise,
for it is in You that I have been raised.
Though I walk in strife, you comfort my life
and make all my foes fall onto the knife.
You've seen my heart and know all I believe.

You know when I stay and you know when I leave.
You stitched me together in my mother's womb.
Lead me, O Lord, till I go to my tomb.

Psalm 140 - 143

Rescue me, Lord, from these serpents of men,
for you keep the humble man sheltered from sin.
Let those who seek violence be hunted down.
May my heart find purchase in Your holy ground.
Set a guard on my mouth, that it may refrain
from wickedness that I might do in Your name.
When my spirit's faint, You still lead my way,
though no other person may care what I say.
Free me from prison. The righteous will kneel
and worship You Lord. O let me be healed.
My enemies come. Let me do Your will,
so that which You wish shall thus be fulfilled.

Psalm 144 - 145

O Lord, what are mortals, that you care for us?
We pass like a shadow; our days but a breath.
I pray for salvation! Reach down and destroy
my enemies. Lord, bring me out of death.
The Lord helps the fallen and lifts them back up
when they fall beneath their burdensome load.
He hears us cry out and sets us upon
His perfect and righteous and beautiful road.

Psalm 146 - 150

Don't put your faith in the power of men,
for every man's spirit departs in the end.
But blessed is he with God on his side,
in whom both the orphans and widows reside.
How absolute is the power of God?
He made everything! Not one thing is flawed.
The strength of a man or a horse is a joke

to Him, it's as if we are just wisps of smoke.
Let every created thing praise Him for this.
It's His word allowing us all to exist.
The beasts and the livestock, the lizards and birds
the kings and the people are all just His words.
Rejoice in a dance or a song. Make a sound!
Salvation is given, the humble are crowned.
With trumpet and lyre and harp strike a chord.
Let all who have breath praise the Lord. Praise the Lord!

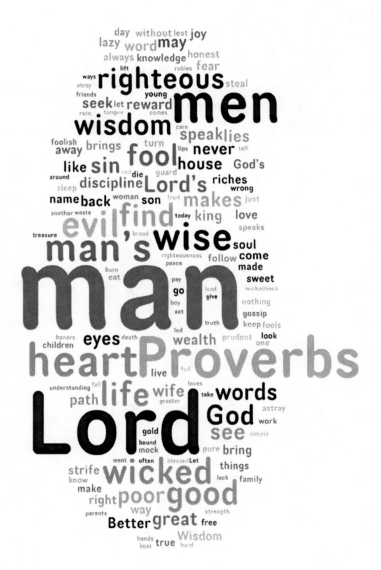

Proverbs 1

The proverbs of Solomon, written so you
may understand wisdom, knowledge, and through
these works become prudent. Let the wise hear,
and let the discerning find guidance that's clear.
Children, do not follow those who would say,
'Come let us steal, attack, or waylay
some stranger,' for surely their sins pave the road
to their own destruction. Don't bear the same load
as these fools. Wisdom will raise up her voice.
Don't turn from her words, but grab her! Rejoice!
The simple live lives that are simple, and those
who reject what is wise find all doors are closed.
The waywardness of the foolish man kills
his dreams and desires. But wisdom fulfills
the heart and the mind. Fear God and you'll find
His blessings and grace will find you in kind.

Proverbs 2 - 4

Listen for wisdom. Cry out that you may
have insight and great understanding this day.
For they are from God - they're treasure that's real
and they are a value that no man can steal.
Wisdom will save you from men who would turn
to the right or the left of the true path. You'll learn
to follow the footsteps of good men instead,
and never to stray from what our Lord has said.
Let loyalty be wrapped around your neck so
you never forget Him wherever you go.

Trust in the Lord with all of your heart,
for a man's understanding can tear him apart.
Only the Lord's will strengthens you and
brings wealth and abundance from out of the land.
Don't turn from His discipline, for He corrects
those whom He loves, not those He rejects.
Wisdom is greater than silver or gold.
And goodness is something you should not withhold.
Don't envy the violent; the wicked are cursed.
The wise man is honored; the humble made first.
Although it may cost you each thing that you own,
seek wisdom, for in understanding alone
is the light that shall keep you away from the path
that the wicked man walks into the Lord's wrath.
My words are like life to him who will find
and keep them inside of his heart and his mind.
Your heart is your life! The path is ahead.
Don't swerve to the right or the left as you tread.

Proverbs 5

The lips of adultery drip as if sweet.
Temptation's a blade. Her eyes are deceit.
Avoid her, lest you be known as a fool
who lets strangers into your pocket. She's cruel.
Would you look back over your life and say, "I
spurned discipline! I didn't listen to my
teachers." Rejoice in the wife of your youth,
so you avoid sin, as you embrace truth.

Proverbs 6:1 - 6:19

If you've struck a pledge, and are trapped by your words,
then you cannot sleep! Free yourself as a bird
is free. See the man you're bound to and plead.
Don't lie there just moaning. Go do what you need.
Like the ant who stores up what he needs for the cold,
work! Do not sleep. Get up and be bold!
The lazy man and the scoundrel shall be

overtaken by evil to die miserably.
Lying tongues, haughty eyes, a false witness who lies,
men who seek evil, and hearts that devise
wicked schemes, any hand that sheds innocent blood,
and a man who'll push his brothers down in the mud.
These are the things that the Lord God despises,
and those who seek evil of all sorts and sizes
shall find the Lord's fury upon them one day
because they've abandoned the Lord's holy way.

Proverbs 6:20 - 7:27

Heed your mother, my son, and bind up the things
she has told you, for her words are like angel wings.
They're a lamp that will light the right way in your life.
They'll keep you away from another man's wife.
Be aware of such lust. It will eat you, my boy.
For sin quickly follows what you might enjoy.
Steal another man's wife and your fate will be sealed,
for jealousy's wrath only grows once revealed.
I knew a young fool who was out after dark.
The adulteress came after him, saying, "Hark!
Beautiful boy, my bed smells of myrrh.
The fool was ensnared and he went after her.
Like an ox to the slaughter he went. Such a sin
cavorts and entices and prostitutes men.
Many will follow her. None will return;
her house is the grave, and in it you'll burn.

Proverbs 8 - 9

Wisdom calls out and raises her voice
saying, "Mankind, I will give you the choice.
Follow me and you shall soon understand.
My mouth holds the truth, so give me your hand.
Be discerning, so that you will find me and know
I'm more precious than rubies and greater than gold.
By me, a king reigns. The Lord made me shine.
Before there were oceans, He said I'd be thine.

Cursed is the man who ignores what I say
for my table is set, but mankind went astray.
The fear of the Lord is the key to the door.
But if folly you favor, seek knowledge no more."

Proverbs 10

The Proverbs of Solomon:
Wise children bring
joy to their parents.
Righteousness sings
to the Lord, and the righteous man always is fed.
But lazy hands find neither wisdom or bread.
The names of the wicked will rot on men's tongues,
but the names of the God-fearing fill up their lungs.
Hatred stirs up dissension, but love
covers all wrongs.
Those men who speak of
foolish things bring about ruin, but he
who heeds discipline finds God's mystery.
He who speaks much is often in sin.
Holding your tongue makes you wise among men.
The righteous man's words nourish many, but fools
are like fires that die because they lack in fuel.
A fool finds his pleasure in evil pursuits.
the storm sweeps him up, for the man has no roots.
Take strength in the Lord, for the righteous man forms
his faith in the Lord. He can weather all storms.
The fear of the Lord shall lengthen your life,
but the wicked man's days are littered with strife.

Proverbs 11

The Lord abhors cheaters. Be honest and true
so all trust your judgment.
Pride shall be viewed
as disgrace, but humility makes a man wise.
On the reckoning day, the righteous are prized.
The righteous man shall be delivered, but he

who is wicked shall be led astray.
You will see
a city sing out for a man who is pure.
An evil man's illness can never be cured.
Keep a friend's secret, for gossip will stain.
Advisers are needed in any man's reign.
A kindhearted woman deserves your respect,
but a cruel man is one you should hate and reject.
The wicked make money, but find no reward.
Perversions are foul.
If you walk in the Lord
you'll be free of your bondage.
The generous gain,
while misers have nothing to show but their grain.
Your family is precious. Don't harm them or you
will inherit the wind.
The righteous accrue
wisdom, so that they may follow the Lord,
but the sinner may just as well fall on his sword.

Proverbs 12

Seek discipline; you shall find knowledge.
But he
who dislikes correction is stupid indeed.
A man cannot be established by acts
of wickedness, but I shall tell you a fact.
A righteous man can't be uprooted by men,
for he is judged honest and lives without sin.
A wife who is noble is just like a crown
to her husband, but evil wives tear a man down.
Men are all judged as to whether they're wise,
and those with warped minds are always despised.
A good man will care for his animals, while
all can see through the wicked man's smile.
If you work the land, you will eat.
If you chase
fantasies, you will starve and be disgraced.
If you speak in lies or sins, you'll be caught.

The fruit of a man is in what he has taught.
Overlook insults.
Avoid lies.
Beware,
for reckless words harm, but loving tongues care
for the people around them.
Truth shall endure
a lifetime, but not he whose tongue is impure.
Promote peace, not evil!
Diligent hands
shall rule, but a slave shall be made of the man
who is lazy.
A kind word will lift up the heart
that is worried.
Be careful as new friendships start
that your friend is righteous.
If you go the way
that God set before us, and aren't led astray,
then you shall find life where a man never dies,
and on that good path, immortality lies.

Proverbs 13

A wise son accepts his father's advice,
but those sons who mock pay a terrible price.
To guard your own lips is to guard your own life,
but he who speaks rashly shall end up in strife.
The lazy crave nothing, which they shall receive.
The diligent man works hard and achieves.
Guard your integrity.
Hate what's untrue.
Avoid what's unholy in all that you do.
The man who pretends to be rich is a fool,
but the man who pretends to be poor is a jewel.
The lamp of the wicked will not burn for long.
The wise teacher turns men away from what's wrong.
A longing fulfilled is sweet to the soul.
It restores a man's heart, and makes the man whole.
A good man's inheritance lasts generations,

a sinner's wealth soon is dispersed through the nations.
Listen, you fathers! If you spare the rod,
then you hate your son, and do not honor God.
Carefully discipline him and he'll learn
how to be wise and how to discern.

Proverbs 14

A wise woman builds up her house with her hands.
The inept tears hers down.
A fool's talk can land
him into a beating.
Discerning men find
knowledge around them of all shapes and kinds.
Fools mock repentance, but wise men see they
will profit by doing the Lord's will today.
Each heart shall know bitterness and will know joy.
Faithlessness reaps the same gains it employs.
A simple man hears and believes anything,
but the prudent do research.
Quick tempers bring
unwanted results.
Evil shall bow
in the presence of holiness.
One who talks now
without action will find only poverty. When
treasures are found, it's by hard working men.
Witnesses who speak the truth will save lives,
but a liar's words are as deadly as knives.
The fear of the Lord is a fortress for all
of his family.
Without subjects, any king falls.
A heart that's at peace helps the body, but when
your soul's full of envy, you'll rot from within.
Oppressing the poor shall stoke the Lord's fury,
and such a man shall not escape judge and jury.
Even in death, the righteous have strength.
Wisdom is glory, as I've said at length.

Proverbs 15

A gentle word turns away wrath.
The Lord sees
everything; evil is never at ease.
A fool spurns his father and discipline, then
he tumbles right back into evil again.
The house of the righteous holds treasures.
If you
sacrifice, but in your heart are not true,
the Lord rejects you and your sacrifice too.
A happy heart brightens a man's face anew.
Better a life in the fear of the Lord,
than great wealth with turmoil as your reward.
Better no meat but a loving house, than
a fattened calf, hatred, and sin for a man.
A good son brings joy to his parents.
Delight
in the right course! The Lord leads us each through the night.
Timely advice is a joy.
The Lord tears
a prideful house down and strips such men bare.
He who hates bribes shall live honestly.
The Lord hears the prayerful and honors their plea.
A cheerful look's joyful to any man's heart.
Honor will come, but be humble to start.

Proverbs 16

The heart is the man's, but the word is the Lord's.
Commit to God's ways, and reap the rewards.
God uses everything for His own will.
Even the wicked have roles they'll fulfill.
The proud will be punished.
Sin is atoned
through love, for that is the path to God's throne.
Better a little with righteousness than
injustice that brings great wealth to a man.
A man plans his course, but the Lord chooses each

of his steps.
An honest king always should reach
for justice and honesty.
Wealth lies within
wisdom; it makes gold and silver look thin.
He who is prudent and guards his way does
indeed guard his life.
Each person who was
oppressed and beat down will share God's treasure when
the proud are brought down and trapped in their sin.
A pleasant word is so sweet to the soul;
it heals every person to whom it is told.
A scoundrel plots evil, enticing young men.
Dissension and gossip can separate friends.
Gray hair's a crown of splendor, attained
through righteousness.
Better a man who restrained
his temper, than warriors who gain great reward.
All our decisions shall come from the Lord.

Proverbs 17

Better a dry crust of bread brought in peace,
than strife in a house that is holding a feast.
The furnace shall test gold's purity, and
the Lord is the test for the heart of a man.
Someone who mocks the poor does the same
to the Lord, for he curses the Lord's holy name.
Ignoring offense will spread love everywhere,
but one's retribution makes close friends despair.
If a man pays back good with evil, then he
shall be haunted by evil and never be free.
Of what use is money to fools, for they won't
go seek wisdom out.
Discerning men don't
guarantee debts of their friends.
There's no joy
in a father's heart for his rebellious young boy.
Do not flog the godly.

Speak less, and act wise,
for the fool is despised in every man's eyes.

Proverbs 18

The mean and the selfish lash out and are not
respected.
Fools talk, but rarely are taught.
Wise words are deep waters, where men may drink.
Fools ask for a beating; they speak but don't think.
Laziness still is a form of destruction.
The name of the Lord is a fortress.
Instruction
and facts are the basis for wise men.
What man
can bear a dark soul?
Giving gifts can
open up doors.
The tongue's power brings
both life and death; those who love it will spring
to eat of its fruit.
A man with a wife
has found a great treasure that lasts his whole life.

Proverbs 19

Zeal is not good without knowledge.
Those who
testify falsely shall be punished too.
Everyone loves a good man who brings gifts.
He who gains wisdom shall see his soul lift.
Beloved is he who ignores petty crimes
that are done against him.
Each man in his time
inherits some wealth, but a good wife's a gift
from the Lord, for her words will comfort and lift.
A man who obeys instruction, in turn,
guards his own life, while stupid men burn.
The Lord will reward the men who help out

the poor, for those men are truly devout.
Please discipline children, lest you be a part
of their death and destruction and break your own heart.
A man makes his plans, but the Lord's will prevails.
A God-fearing man is kept safe during gales.

Proverbs 20 - 21

Wine is a mocker and beer is a brawler,
don't let them lead you astray lest you falter.
An honorable man will avoid strife, but those
who are foolish will quarrel and make many foes.
A sluggard won't plow, therefore he can't reap.
Inside your heart lies your purpose; look deep.
Blest are the children of righteous men; they
are shown the Lord's will and taught not to stray.
What man can say that his heart has been pure?
Your eyes and your ears will make you mature.
Gold coins and rubies are found everywhere,
but a mouth that speaks pearls of wisdom is rare.
Food gained through fraud tastes sweet to a man,
but he will end up full of gravel and sand.
A gossip betrays all your secrets - beware!
Wealth gained without any work leaves you bare.
Scales that aren't honest do not please the Lord.
Do not vow to do that which you can't afford.
The lamp of the Lord searches every man's soul.
Only through love is a kingdom kept whole.
Blows and wounds will cleanse evil away.
To do what is right is better than they
who sacrifice much.
A fortune made through
a lie is a vapor; it shall desert you.
The wicked crave evil, so they seek it out.
The Lord notes the man who brags and who flouts
his wickedness.
When you have closed your eyes to
the cries of the poor, I tell you, when you
cry out for God's help, you will be ignored.

Stray from what's good, and you stray from the Lord.
He who loves pleasure shall soon be made poor.
In the house of the wise are the choicest of stores,
but the fool will devour each thing that he owns.
If you guard your tongue, your wisdom is shown.
No wisdom or thought is as great as the Lord,
and victory comes through His mighty sword.

Proverbs 22-23

A good name is greater than riches by far
The humblest heart and the fear of God are
desirable traits.
The wicked men scorn
honor, so they walk a path full of thorns.
Train a young child to walk in the ways
of the Lord, never wavering all of his days.
The borrower serves his lender.
A man
is blessed when he shares with the poor what he can.
Drive out the mocker and out goes the strife.
The eyes of the Lord watch you all of your life.
Please heed these things I have written and said.
Place my words into your heart and your head.
All of these statements will counsel you when
you're asked for assistance or tempted by sin.
Don't harm the needy. The Lord's on their side.
Do not follow hot tempered men, or decide
to take out a loan that you can't repay.
Don't waste your life seeking riches.
Each day
is a gift, for your riches will not last for long.
Don't speak to a fool, for his words are all wrong.
If your heart is wise, then mine shall be glad.
Gluttons and drunkards will drive a man mad.
A drunk doesn't see his pain comes from his sin.
He just moans of his plight, then gets drunk again.

Proverbs 24

Don't envy the wicked.
A wise man has power.
Be strong and don't falter in your darkest hour.
Rescue those who have been led off to die.
Don't claim that you were not aware of their cry,
for doesn't God know what is true? He'll repay
each man for his actions - for each has their day.
Wisdom is sweeter than honey, my son.
Don't gloat when you find that your foe's been undone.
Fear the Lord and your king, for they rule over you.
Convict all the guilty and always speak true,
for honesty's like a kiss on the lips,
but false testimony will make a man trip.
Don't pay back injustice.
A little sleep and
a slumbering heart can ruin a man,
for poverty comes like a bandit to steal
a lazy man's wealth and trample his field.

Proverbs 25

As deep as the earth, so the heart of a king
is unsearchable.
Send out the wicked and bring
righteousness back to the kingdom.
Don't claim
you're great; it is better to be called by name.
Do not bring a suit on your neighbor in haste.
A wise word, like gold, does not go to waste.
Through patience even a king is persuaded.
Wear out your welcome and friendships are jaded.
Don't put your faith in the faithless when you
are in trouble.
If your foe is hungry, take food
to him. By doing so, he'll see the Lord
is with you and you shall have your reward.
Better to live on the roof than to share

your house with a quarrelsome wife.
If you bear
good news from afar, you're a spring to the soul.
Despised is the man who lacks self-control.

Proverbs 26

An undeserved curse does not come to rest.
A rod to the back of a fool would work best.
These proverbs are wasted on fools.
Do not hire
the stupid or lazy, the mocker or liar.
As a dog returns to his vomit, so too
does a fool to his folly.
A sluggard will do
no good for his town. Why, he struggles to bring
food to his mouth.
When you meddle in things
that are none of your business, you're bound to be bit.
Eliminate gossip, and quarrels will quit.
If a man digs a pit, he's bound to fall in.
Liars and flatterers do so in sin.

Proverbs 27

Don't boast of tomorrow. Live for today,
for you cannot guide the Lord or His way.
Let praise come from others, for if brags come out,
then each word you utter your neighbor will doubt.
Anger is cruel, but none can withstand
jealousy - it makes the harshest demands.
Better is open rebuke than restrained
love.
Hope and joy are often contained
in an honest man's counsel; as sweet as perfume
for it keeps a man righteous and saves him from doom.
The prudent see danger before it appears,
but a fool is too late and cannot steer clear.
As one piece of iron can sharpen another,

so we must all hone our sisters and brothers.
You'll eat of the fruit if you tend to the tree.
A man's eyes aren't satisfied with what they see.
Attend to your flocks, for riches will pass.
Even a crown and a kingship won't last
for all generations, but lambs will provide
both clothing and milk to fill you inside.

Proverbs 28

The wicked man flees, though no one pursues.
A king who oppresses the poor is refused
the mercy of God.
If you keep the law,
your Father will see that you live without flaw.
He who would lead the upright along
an evil path will be caught up by his wrong.
A rich man too often believes he is wise,
while others see clearly and with their own eyes.
When righteous men triumph, good people take pride,
but a wicked man's victory makes good men hide.
Tyrannical rulers lack judgment.
The blessed
don't look for great riches; they seek to live best.
Don't steal from your parents or stir up dissension.
Give to the poor with the purest intention,
and you'll lack for nothing. But God curses those
who injure the weakest. He makes them His foes.

Proverbs 29

If you mock instruction, woe to your health.
If you sleep with prostitutes, woe to your wealth.
An evil man shall be ensnared in his sin.
Mockers will stir up a city, but men
who are wise turn from anger.
A ruler who lies
makes wicked officials.
The Lord gave us eyes

so all men may see; oppressor as well
as oppressed.
It never is too hard to tell
a disciplined child. The rod leaves a mark
for life which is visible in light or dark.
Don't pamper your servants.
Don't speak out in haste.
Pride brings a man to ruin and waste.
Fear of men shall be a snare to a man,
but trust in the Lord and you'll find that He can
give to you safety and justice, for He
honors the righteous and sets good men free.

Proverbs 30

The sayings of Agur:
The skeptic said, "I
am an ignorant fool. Nobody supplied
any wisdom to me. Tell me God's name
and the name of His son."
The believer proclaimed,
"God is a shield if you hear and obey.
Do not mock His word lest you die here today.
Keep lies from me, Lord, and provide me with bread.
With riches, I fear I'll forget what You said,
but don't make me poor, or I may go steal,
dishonoring You. God, hear my appeal.
Don't slander a servant to his master. You
will pay for it.
Oh, the poor, foolish few
who think they are pure, but are not.
I'm amazed
by an eagle in flight, and the feminine ways
that a woman entices a man to her bed.
"I've done nothing wrong," the adulteress said.
If you played the fool, but plotted and schemed,
then all of the wickedness that you have dreamed
shall come back upon you, for trouble and strife
are an evil reward for an evil man's life.

Proverbs 31

The sayings of King Lemuel:
Do not spend
your strength upon women, and do not befriend
liquor or wine.
Remember the law
decrees we're to worship the Lord in pure awe.
Speak up for those who can't speak for themselves.
Do not set the needy away on the shelves.
A wife who is noble is worth more than all
of the rubies, for she won't let her husband fall.
She is caring, considerate, vigorous, and
she carries her family close in her hand.
Her family is warm and clothed when the snow
falls in the winter, and always she knows
her husband's respected because of the way
she's respectful and dignified. Throughout her days
she speaks with great wisdom and all the affairs
of her household are handled with grace and with care.
Her children are happy, and they call her blessed.
Beauty is fleeting. A woman is best
when she's faithful to God and honors the Lord,
so honor your wife with her due reward.

Ecclesiastes 1

The words of the teacher:
What does man gain
by his toil and labor and backbreaking strain?
Nothing! It's meaningless. Men come and go.
Generations will pass. How many? Who knows?
The wind blows from both the south and the north,
then switches around again on its course.
All that's been done, again shall be done.
There is nothing new that is under the sun.
If something looks new, it existed before.
When someone is dead, they're remembered no more.
I was Jerusalem's king. I was wise.
I've seen all there is in the earth and the skies.
It's meaningless. It is like chasing the wind.
I studied it all, and then in the end
I realized with wisdom comes sorrow. The more
knowledge you have, the more grief that's in store.

Ecclesiastes 2

Then I thought, 'Pleasure! Yes, that's what I'll seek.
But that too lacks meaning. The outlook is bleak.
For laughter is foolish, and folly as well.
My projects and treasures were just empty shells.
Though I have had wealth, and women, and jewels,
these things are possessions that make all men fools.
I lacked for nothing. Yet when I surveyed
all I had done, I was truly dismayed.
Meaningless! All of it. What can man do

that has not been done? It's maddening to
put yourself into something that you'll leave behind
for your family, your people, or all of mankind.
A man should just strive to work and to eat.
Whether down in the dust or on the high seat.
The highest and lowest of men are the same,
toiling at what is a meaningless game.

Ecclesiastes 3

There's a time to be born, and to pass away.
A time we should mourn, and a time we should play.
There's a time we should laugh, and a time we're to weep.
A time to plant seeds, and a time men should reap.
A time to tear down and a time to build up.
There's a time when you search and a time to give up.
There's a time to embrace and a time to refrain.
A time to speak out, and a time to abstain.
A time made for love, and that time is great,
but there is a time in which all men shall hate.
There's time made for peace. But there will be war,
when peace must depart, and can be no more.
The Lord shall make everything beautiful when
He decides so. It's not left to men
to choose such a time. And though we may see,
we'll never quite comprehend eternity.
All that God does shall endure. What we say
will not add to His deeds, and can't take away.
Under the sun, where there's justice, so too
is there wickedness. Only the Lord may undo
what is wrong. So if men know their work and their place,
that's all we can hope for. God in His grace
knows whether there's somewhere to go when we die.
Not one man among us can see through God's eye.

Ecclesiastes 4

I saw the oppressed. No comfort was found
for those who were mocked and those beaten down.

And those men who toil are also deceived,
for they found no peace and knew no reprieve.
But the man without friends is worse off by far.
For a friend will stay by you wherever you are.
If you should fall down, you'll be lifted again,
but not he who chooses a life without friends.
If two lie together then they shall be warm.
Two may defend themselves during the storm.
But better is three, for a cord with three strands
is not broken easily. That cord withstands.

Ecclesiastes 5 - 6

Guard your steps inside the great house of God,
for a wise man is humble and naturally awed.
And do not be quick with your mouth or your heart
for a vow to the Lord cannot be torn apart.
If you see oppression, do not be surprised,
for the poor and the weak are always chastised
by those who are rich. And those who have much
love money, and they are deep in the clutch
of greed. But they do not see that such things
are meaningless. Ask them what their great wealth brings.
More money? More goods? A laborer eats
and then sleeps a sleep that's honest and sweet.
But rich men are worried. The wealthy despair.
For everyone enters Earth naked and bare,
and so he departs, with nothing in hand.
If only the wealthy man could understand.
Men who have much don't take joy in all
that they have, and this is their greatest downfall.
Despite all the meaningless days a man's on
this Earth, he can't know what will be when he's gone.

Ecclesiastes 7

A good name is better than fragrant perfume,
and the day of death's better than leaving the womb.
Death is the destiny of every man.

The end will be better than how it began.
Don't be quick to anger. It's foolish to be
led by emotion. Can you not see?
What God has made crooked, no man may make straight.
A man who's too righteous may soon desecrate
his faith. Do not listen to what people say,
or no matter how wise you are, you will stray.
Do not be ensnared by the schemes of mankind,
for in them your downfall is all you will find.

Ecclesiastes 8 - 9

Obey your king always and keep your oath true,
for he rules the wicked, and righteous men too.
No man may have power over his death.
Be reverent and God-fearing with every breath.
The wicked don't fear God, and it won't go well
for them. But for you who honor and dwell
in the Lord, you will know His will and His way.
Until then appreciate every day.
The good man and sinner, the great and the small,
have one destiny. It's the same one for all!
The living have hope but know they shall die,
The dead have their peace. So shall you and I.
So eat food with gladness, and drink in your joy.
Treasure your wife and always employ
your full efforts during each day God allows.
Let all that life offers you stir and arouse.

Ecclesiastes 10

As sure as the sun, man's folly outweighs
wisdom and honor in every way.
Fools gain position and title, while men
of wisdom sink lower again and again.
Hold your tongue. Don't lay a curse on your king,
for a bird may carry your word on its wing.
The word of a fool is consumed by his lips,
but the word of the wise cannot be eclipsed.

Ecclesiastes 11 - 12

Cast your bread out, that it may return.
You can't harvest seeds you have kept in the urn.
A man who watches the skies does not reap.
A man won't gain interest on money he keeps.
The years you have left, enjoy them for they
are many, but they will fly pass like the day
as it turns into darkness. Be happy, young man,
and follow your heart in all that you can.
Be careful, though, for the Lord makes account
of all that you do, and He'll know the amount
you owe in the end. Take pleasure in youth,
although it is meaningless. This is the truth.
Think of your God before you are old
and your body is racked by the wind and the cold.
The strong man will stoop and his vision grows dim.
So young man, I tell you to think now of Him!
Before the cord's severed, before the bowl breaks,
so the dust may return to the ground where it bakes,
think of the Lord! Your spirit will be
returned to the Lord, the I AM who is He.
I'll end what I've said with how I began.
This life is meaningless! Every man
must fear God and keep His commandments until
the Lord calls us home and our bodies are stilled.

Song of Songs 1 - 8

Beloved
Let him kiss me with kisses, for his love is more
delightful than wine. Fragrances pour
out all around. Your name is perfume.
No wonder for you, this maiden's heart blooms.
Take me away to your chambers, I pray.
Let the king take me up in a hurry, I say.
I am as dark as the tents of Kedar
and lovely. Is that why you stare from afar?
I tended the vineyards and my skin was scorched,
so now I am browned as if I've been torched.
My vineyard's unkempt. Now come to my door.
Unveil me, my lord, for it's you I adore.

Lover
You're like a mare, bejeweled and tied to
the Pharaoh's great chariot. Gold covers you.

Beloved
My scent lures the king, though he's with his guests.
My lover's a sachet of myrrh 'tween my breasts.

Lover
My beautiful darling, your eyes are like doves.

Beloved
Our bed is so lush as you come to me, love.

Lover
Our house built with cedars, our rafters are firs -

Beloved
Come pluck the Rose of Sharon.

Lover
I'm yours.

Beloved
And you are the fruit tree, so sweet to my taste.
Give me your fruit, so I do not waste.
His left holds my head, as his right arm embraces.
Let nobody take me away from his graces.
Here comes my lover who leaps over mountains.
He looks to my door, his words are like fountains.
"Arise, lovely one," he says to my room,
"the winter is past. The rain and the gloom
have gone, so come out, for the flowers are here.
The season of singing and doves has appeared.
The fig tree forms fruit. The blossoms are sweet.
Arise! Come, my darling. My love, come to me."

Lover
My dove of the mountain. Show me your face.
Let me hear your voice, that lilts in its grace.

Beloved
My lover is mine. He browses the lilies.
Until the day breaks, run forth like the fillies
and like the gazelles on the steep rugged hills.
But all the night long, my bed is not filled.
I searched for my love, but wholly in vain.
I took to the streets, and still can't explain
what has happened to him. When the watchmen found me
I asked, "Have you seen my love? Where is he?"
Then just as I passed them, I found him and threw
my arms 'round his neck, for I never knew
how deep my love went. I would not let go,

until I was home. Only then did I know.
You girls of Jerusalem, let your love rest
until it desires, until it is blessed.
Now Solomon comes! It's the glorious king,
crowned as the ruler and for him I sing.

Lover
Your veil hides your eyes as pretty as doves.
Your hair falls cascading down shoulders I love.
Your lips are a ribbon of scarlet, and there
is your neck, like the Tower of David, so fair.
Your breasts are like fawns. Until the day breaks
I'll go to the mountain of myrrh and partake.
In you there's no flaw. So come now, my bride
from Lebanon, and take your place at my side.
You've stolen my heart with a look so divine.
Oh, how much more pleasing is your love than wine.
Your lips are like honey; a garden locked up.
You're a fountain that's sealed. Oh, fill up my cup!
The choicest of fruits and the finest of spices
flow from your garden. It lures and entices.
You're a well, rushing water from Lebanon to
the place where I live, and in all I see you.

Beloved
From the north and the south, let the wind spread my scent.
Let him taste from my garden. I give my consent.

Lover
I gathered the spices, ate honey and drank
your milk and your wine, and in you I sank.

Beloved
I was sleeping when my lover came, and he knocked.
"Open the door," he called, "It is locked."
From outside he thrust his hand through the latch.
My heart began pounding. I threw back the catch
so he could come in. My hands were all slick
with myrrh. I opened the door. What a trick!

For my lover was gone, so in search I went out,
but the night watchmen found me and threw me about.
They bruised me and tore the cloak off my back
in a brutal and hideous form of attack.
If anyone sees my lover, please say
I'm faint for his love, and send him my way.
My lover's a rugged and radiant man.
Of ten thousand men, only my love can stand
out from the throng. Oh, his hair is as black
as a raven's. In nothing does my lover lack.
His eyes are like jewels. His cheeks are like spice.
His lips are like lilies that thrill and entice.
His body's like ivory. His arms are like rods.
His legs are like pillars upon which he trod.
Like the cedars of Lebanon, my love is strong.
To be in his lordly presence I long.
My lover has gone to the gardens to browse
the lilies. We love with the strongest of vows.

Lover
You are beautiful, just like Jerusalem when
the banners unfurl as all of the men
stand at attention. O turn now your eyes,
for they overwhelm me. I cannot disguise
my desire. Though sixty queens there may be,
and the virgins and concubines. Love, unto me,
you are the finest, my only true one.
You who are blessed. My radiant sun.
I went to the grove to inspect and to see
the new growth, to view the fruit of the tree.
All was in bloom and I soon realized
my desire elicited passionate cries.
Oh sweet prince's daughter! Your feet and your legs
are crafted like jewels. It makes a man beg.
Your navel's a goblet that never lacks wine.
Your waist is like wheat, so supple and fine.
Your breasts and your neck are as smooth as fine jewels.
Your eyes are like Heshbon's beautiful pools.
Your nose is a tower. Your head and your hair

are the finest of tapestries found anywhere.
The king is held captive by you, one so pleasing.
My love, your delights are so tempting and teasing.
You are the palm tree. Your breasts are the fruit.
My most precious treasure, I come in pursuit.

Beloved
May my wine gently flow over his tongue.
I belong to my lover. His passion has sprung.
Let's go to the country and lie in the field,
and then to the vineyards and see what they yield.
Where blossoms are open and fruit is in bloom,
I give you my love. You'll again be my groom.
The mandrakes are fragrant. Such delicacies
I've stored up and offer to you on my knees.
I so want to kiss you, and let no one think
any worse of me for it. I'd offer you drink
and fruit in the house of my mother, and you
would embrace me. Yes, do it. Please do it. Please do.
Under the apple tree, there you were roused.
Make me a seal on your heart, where I'm housed.
It's true when they say that true love's strong as death,
and jealous of that which would take my love's breath.
Love is a fire that cannot be quenched.
It won't wash away, and cannot be drenched.
I am a wall and my breasts are like towers,
and I bring contentment to he who's in power.

Lover
You, whom I love, surrounded by all
your attendants, let me hear your voice and your call.

Beloved
Come to the spice-laden mountains and be
my stag and my lover. O love, come to me.

Isaiah 1

The Lord has spoken!
"My children have grown
to mock Me. Haven't I called them My own?
The ox knows his master, but in My own land
of Israel they ignore all My commands."
O you wretched nation! You pit of corruption.
You are the cause of this sinful eruption.
Your cities are burned and you are laid waste.
The daughter of Zion is sadly defaced.
Your sacrifices do not please the Lord.
Your hands are now bloody, and you can't afford
to upset your God.
"Come," He invites,
"let us use reason, and let us not fight.
Your sins have run crimson, but truly they can
be turned white as snow, for I am the I AM.
Return and obey, and I shall forgive
all that you've done against Me, and I'll give
you all that I have. Love Me as your Lord.
If not, then you all will soon die by My sword."
Your rulers are rebels and thieves. Only bribes
excite your high priests, your teachers and scribes.
Zion shall still be redeemed, but a price
is due, for the Lord will not forgive twice.
You'll be a mere timber, a twig in a drought.
Once God's fire starts, it can't be put out.

Isaiah 2

When the end of days comes, God shall humble the rest.
The people shall say, "If we're to be blessed,
we must go to the Lord as His congregation."
He'll settle disputes among all of the nations.
Plowshares and hooks will be made from the sword,
and people will not train for war anymore.
Let's walk in the light of the Lord, not the beasts
and false gods we've followed, brought here from the East.
Like Philistines, we have been pagans and slaved
for the idols and figures another man made.
Our arrogant pride shall be humbled as we
see our Lord exalted. The wicked shall flee.
Our idols shall be thrown away as we hide,
but the Lord knows the name of each man who denied
His word. What is man? Did not God make the Earth?
There's no death without God, but nor is there birth.

Isaiah 3 - 4

Judah! Jerusalem! God has left you.
Your heroes and warriors shall know it is true
when children...mere children...will govern your land.
God shall place you in your enemy's hand.
You've paraded your sin like a Sodomite would.
All that is wicked, you people call good.
"You've plundered My vineyard," the Lord says. "You grind
the poor under heel. You curse at the blind."
Instead of a fragrance, there will be a stench.
You'll thirst for what's holy, but you won't be quenched.
You'll fall by the sword and know only scorn
as Zion laments; as Jerusalem mourns.
Those who are left when the Lord's fury fades
shall all be recorded as holy. He stayed
His anger from them. The Lord shows His might
as smoke during daytime and fire by night.

Isaiah 5

My loved One built up a vineyard to sow
the choicest of vines. But only weeds grow.
He toppled the tower that once had been manned
and let it be trampled by beasts in the land.
The vineyard of God is Israel's house.
He loved Jerusalem just like a spouse.
He wants to see justice and know righteous men,
but finds only bloodshed and cries from within.
Woe to the proud, to the drunkards and fools.
You celebrate as you break all of His rules.
You'll go into exile, dying of thirst
and hunger, but you should have thought of that first!
The grave swallows you, but when should it cease?
God is the mighty, and you are the least.
Woe to you who want to see the Lord's deeds,
and those who spread lies as a farmer spreads seeds.
Woe to those people who think they are wise,
those who are drunkards, and those who take bribes.
Your roots will all shrivel and you'll blow away
like the dust in the wind. You are full of decay.
He calls to the nations, "Come forth and eat up
My people. Let Me pour their blood in your cup."
Their arrows are sharp and they'll roar like a lion.
They'll carry you off and make slaves out of Zion.

Isaiah 6

I saw the Lord seated up on His throne,
the seraphs encircled Him. His glory shone
as I cried aloud, "Woe! I have seen
the Lord, and I am a man who's unclean."
Then a seraph flew down with a coal in its hands,
and put it against my lips as a brand.
"Now," it said, "all of your sin is atoned."
Then the Lord spoke as He sat on His throne.
"Whom shall I send to My people?"
"Send me!"

I cried.
"You will go, but they will not see.
Nor shall they hear My message, until
their land is a wasteland. That is My will."

Isaiah 7 - 8:10

When Ahaz was king, Israel teamed
with Syria. While the two kingdoms schemed
to rule in Jerusalem. Isaiah then went
to Ahaz proclaiming, "The Lord God has sent
me to tell you not to fear these two men.
Their plot won't succeed, because of their sin.
If you remain righteous, then you shall avail,
but if your faith weakens, then surely you'll fail.
Test the Lord and he will show you it's true.
Ask, and I swear, it shall be shown to you."
"I will not dare test the Lord," Ahaz said.
"I told you to ask for a sign, but instead
you refuse. But a sign shall still be received.
Unto the virgin a child's conceived!
He shall be known as Immanuel and
when he is born things will have changed in this land.
But the Lord shall allow Assyria to
destroy Jerusalem. There shall be few
remaining in Judah when that day arrives.
Fear the Lord God and fear for your lives."
'Swift to go plunder and carry away'
is the name that I gave to my son on the day
that he was conceived, for before he would speak
the fate of Jerusalem would become bleak.
God said, "I love Judah, but she has scorned
My name, though repeatedly they have been warned."
Prepare all your strategies, but they will fail.
Your men will be crushed, your armies impaled.

Isaiah 8:11 - 8:22

"Don't think like the others," the Lord said to me.
"Fear Me, not Assyria, and be set free.
I'll keep you safe if you'll remain humble
for I am the Rock on which many men stumble.
Although they should look to God in their time
of need, their hearts have been darkened with grime.
They curse Me when they should approach Me in prayer,
so they will be thrown in the darkest despair."

Isaiah 9:1 - 9:7

The gloom shall be lifted. Believers shall see.
In the future God's glory comes from Galilee.
For those who have lived in the shadow of death,
the yoke shall be lifted. I shout with each breath,
unto the world a child is born!
A son shall be given. Great titles adorn:
Counselor, Mighty God, and Prince of Peace.
His greatness increases. His love shall not cease.
On David's throne he shall reign and uphold
a righteousness that is both honest and bold,
and justice that no man upon Earth may sever.
And so he shall reign forever and ever.

Isaiah 9:8 - 10:34

The Lord sent a message that fell on deaf ears.
Your foes all defeat you! Is it not made clear
that God's against Israel? Yet the Lord waits
for His favored people to fall and prostrate
in the dust as they beg for forgiveness, then He
shall stay other armies. Please listen to me!
And yet you refuse to do as I desire,
so each of you shall become fuel for His fire.
Woe to you who cheat the poor. Understand,
when enemies come from their far away lands,
no one shall house you for they know your deeds

are the reason they suffer, the reason they bleed.
Assyria, though you shall be the Lord's rod,
to punish us, your land is not loved by God.
Your king, in his pride, destroys many nations
and boasts as he topples kings down from their stations.
When the Lord is appeased by the punishment He
gives to us, beware, for then you shall see
His hand turn on you. A wasting disease
shall eat up your armies, your fields, and your trees.
On that day the remnant of Israel whom
the Lord has allowed to escape from your doom
will trust in the Lord. His anger subsides.
Then they shall embrace as a groom and his bride.
So people of Zion, fear not, though the pains
that you shall endure will be great, you'll regain
Jerusalem when God's anger has passed.
Fear God, not Assyria! Trust and hold fast!

Isaiah 11

A branch from the root of Jesse shall rise,
and the Spirit of God shall make this man wise.
His power won't come from the spear or the sword,
but instead from delight in the fear of the Lord.
He won't judge with his eyes or his ears, but instead
with righteousness all of the poor shall be fed.
He'll slay all the wicked with breath from his lips,
and faithfulness shall be the sash at his hips.
The wolf and the lamb shall live side by side.
The leopard and goat will lie down. Far and wide
the calf and the lion shall share the same stall,
and you'll see a child is leading them all.
Jesse's root shall be the banner that waves.
The nations will rally to him, for he saves,
and the Lord shall recover His remnant again
from their foreign invaders as well as their sin.
Ephraim and Judah shall sweep through the land
and God shall destroy all their foes by His hand

The Lord shall make paths so that His people may
come home to Jerusalem on that great day.

Isaiah 12

When you return, you will lift up in song
your praise to the Lord, for God's love is strong.
Although He was angry, He has turned away
His fury, and look! He has given this day!
Give thanks and proclaim to each nation that He
is exalted. Though exiled, now you are free.
Shout aloud and praise God, you most favored race
for the Lord is with you, and He dwells in this place.

Isaiah 13:1 - 14:23

An oracle spoken on Babylon. Hear!
Wail, for the day of the Lord's drawing near.
The armies of God are amassing from all
of the faraway lands. Do you hear the call
of their trumpets? They come to tear you apart.
They pound at your gates. It shall melt every heart.
Like a woman in labor, you'll writhe in your pain,
for they've come to punish the godless and vain.
Like a sheep with no shepherd, you'll panic and flee.
The Lord will not listen to your loudest plea.
You'll all be cut down, man, woman, and child!
In Babylon's walls, the Lord's been defiled.
Though jackals shall dwell within Babylon's walls,
God restores Israel. He hears their calls.
They shall return, making captives of those
who enslaved them. So each Babylonian knows,
your pride has brought this defeat to your land.
You thought you were mighty. Now you understand.
Your sons have been slain and then cast in the pit.
"Let Babylon fall!" So God declares it.

Isaiah 14:24 - 16:14

God says, "I've planned it, and so it shall come
that Assyria's empire shall be struck from
the land. And her greatness shall be like the dust.
Set My people free from her savage bloodlust."
Do not rejoice, Philistines, although the rod
that once was against you was struck down by God.
You too shall fall, like a lamb by the Lion,
for God loves, and therefore establishes, Zion.
Moab, your cities shall fall in one night.
The people cry out. Your armed men can't fight.
The refugees seek out Jerusalem's walls.
Shelter them, for the oppressor shall fall.
Then a throne will be raised in love, for a man
of David's house comes, for only he can
judge righteously for Me. You've all seen that pride
can level a nation. You'll hear Moab cry
when their men and their harvests are taken away.
The Lord can make great nations fall in one day.
In only three years, Moab will be despised
just as I've told you; as it's been described.

Isaiah 17 - 19

The power and fame of Damascus shall fade.
To waste all her fortified walls will be laid.
And the glory of Jacob will falter and wane,
but like grains at harvest a few will remain.
They'll turn all their eyes to the Lord, not the ones
made of wood or of metal; those idols God shuns.
Oh, the raging of nations! They roar like the sea.
At the breath of God, though, all the waves turn and flee.
So Cush too shall suffer. Their harvest will be
food for the beasts, but not people. You'll see
this strong foreign nation bring gifts to lift up
to the true God. They'll ask Him to fill up their cup.
Egypt, your suffering will be so fierce
that Egyptian shall battle Egyptian and pierce

the heart of your nation. Then God shall give you
to your enemies and to a king who is cruel.
The rivers will dry. Your canals will all stink.
the Nile shall turn to a bog where you sink.
The leaders at Memphis have all been deceived.
Judah shall come for you, and you'll believe
that they are the people of God, for they'll bring
terror by sword and arrows that sting.
But when Egypt cries out, God will send them
a savior, then Egypt will worship just Him.

Isaiah 20 - 21

The Lord said, "All you who have put your faith in
Egyptians and Cushites, that they'd save you when
Assyria came, your allies will be
led off in chains, just as I decree."
Concerning the desert that lies by the sea,
I tell you, the Lord gave a vision to me.
The lookout keeps watch as a horseman draws near.
"Babylon's fallen!" he cries out in fear.
And Edom? "Oh, watchman, what's left of the night?"
"Morning approaches, but soon shall take flight."
And what of Kedar? In only one year
her warriors and pomp will all disappear.

Isaiah 22

Oh, you troubled city, why are you afraid?
You tremble, though no one has lifted a blade.
When you heard their army, you built up your walls.
You stacked up and counted the arms in your halls.
You filled up the reservoir, but you did not
turn to the Lord, the One who has brought
this terror to pound on your doors. If you cried
out to the Lord, He would be by your side.
But you eat the finest and you drink the best.
Jerusalem, do you not know you are blessed?
You raise up your glasses as one and you cry,

"Let's eat and let's drink, for tomorrow we die!"
Until we're all dead, we cannot atone
for your sins. Without God, we're left here alone.
Oh, City of David, why are you so broken?
We'll falter and fail. The Lord God has spoken.

Isaiah 23

Tarshish, did you know that Tyre's destroyed?
You merchants of Sidon, how you have enjoyed
the bounty the banks of the Nile have brought.
But the Lord's fury burns. Now look what it's wrought.
For seventy years your harbors shall be
forgotten by merchants who travel the sea.
Though you'll rise again, all that which you make
shall be set aside for the godly to take.

Isaiah 24

The Lord shall create a great devastation
and lay waste the Earth and its population.
He'll scatter the people of all rank and class.
The Lord God has spoken and so it shall pass.
The Earth is defiled. Its people must bear
the guilt. Celebration shall cease everywhere.
The cities lie barren, allowing their gloom
to permeate them. Such is the doom.
I scream to the nation, "I'm wasting away!"
Oh, how the treacherous people betray.
Everyone shall be caught up in a snare.
The Earth's own foundations shall soon be laid bare.

Isaiah 25 - 26

Oh Lord, I exalt you. Though you make a heap
out of cities, in Your perfect faith I shall keep.
You are the refuge where people can flee,
a shelter from heat, a place to be free.
On this mountain God will prepare a great feast.

All shall be welcome, the great and the least.
If we trust in Him, He will be our wall,
and by His great hand, Moab shall fall.
On that day the song of the Lord shall be sung.
Peace be upon us! Bells will be rung!
The great Rock eternal has paved a smooth road.
He honors the humble and lightens their load.
Lord, lift Your hand. Let them see Your zeal
for righteousness. Show them and do not conceal
Your anger that burns and consumes all who seek
to do what's unholy. Then lift up the meek.
We can't save ourselves, but we all know that You
can lift up the dead. Your love is like dew
that brings about life. Now people, beware -
the Lord God is coming! Repent and repair!

Isaiah 27

The day that He comes, He will take up His sword
and slay the leviathan. Great is the Lord.
Raise up your song. Sing of vineyards that He
will watch over. Israel soon shall be free.
A great peace will reign, but first He must blast
out our oppressors. Oh come, Lord, come fast.
We'll yet be atoned, crushing altars of stone
and removing the Asherah poles from His home.
The people of Israel, from far and wide,
shall be gathered together. We no longer hide,
for God shows His face. The trumpet will sound
and all who were lost will finally be found.

Isaiah 28

Woe to you drunkards of Ephraim. You fade
like a beautiful flower. How you shall be laid
so low until you are the scorn of the land.
The Lord is our crown; a beautiful band
that shines, but you stagger, ignoring His glow.
You stumble and vomit. The wine makes you slow.

He sought to give you some rest, but you drank
your inheritance. Now you have no one to thank
but yourselves for your pain. The Lord has proclaimed
you'll be washed away and shackled in chains.
All comes from God, and you had a taste
of glory, but now it has all gone to waste.

Isaiah 29

Woe to you, Ariel, city where King
David once settled. You soon shall be ringed
and besieged, then brought down like dust on the ground.
Your voice will come, ghostlike, and whisper its sound.
But so shall your enemies turn into chaff,
blown by the wind. No enemy laughs
when they see your downfall, for theirs comes as well.
The Lord makes you stagger. You're caught in the swell
of His wrath. Even though I have said this, you hear
nothing. Don't you know that you are to fear
the Lord? Lebanon shall be but a field
where a new farmer plants and reaps a great yield.

Isaiah 30 - 31

Woe to the obstinate nation. You go
looking for Pharaoh's protection, although
the Lord is right here, before you! You shame
yourselves as you pray to God's holy name,
"Lord, show us visions that please us, not those
of plagues, holy things, or war with our foes."
The Lord is the Truth. So how dare you ask
for falseness from God and an easier task!
O, how the Lord waits to hear you cry out,
"God, we did not know what we spoke about."
He will forgive you and then He will slay
your foes on that glorious, God-fearing day.
Why do you not put your faith in God's hand?
Instead you seek help from idolatrous lands.

Egyptians are men. They're just flesh and bone.
The Lord is your refuge, as you should have known.

Isaiah 32

Let a kingdom of righteousness rise up and cease
the stammering tongues, and let there be peace.
You women, do not be complacent but turn
to the Lord. Let your husbands see how your faith burns.
This land's overgrown with briars. We must
sweep out all the sin with one mighty thrust
till the Spirit is given from God upon high.
The Lord soon approaches. I tell you, He's nigh.

Isaiah 33

Woe, you destroyers, you will be destroyed
to the same length and measure which you have employed.
In front of the Lord, the fearless cry out.
In His presence no man can be strong or stout.
"Now," says the Lord, "I will rise and conceive
a good land, not this one which schemes and deceives."
He who is holy shall stand on the heights,
while those who are evil shall slink through the nights.
Your eyes will behold the most beautiful King.
Resplendently, He has created all things.
So spread out your sail for the breath of the Lord.
Repent, be forgiven, and gain your reward.

Isaiah 34 - 35

Come, nations, listen. The slain shall be thrown
out into the streets. The Lord God has shown
His anger. Why is it you beg for His sword
to cut down your people? Cease! Heed the Lord.
You people are wicked with your persecution
of all who are holy. The Lord's retribution
will fall on your head. You will be replaced
by birds nesting in the place you've disgraced.

But the desert shall bloom like a crocus again!
The glory of God shall cleanse you from sin.
The blind will then see, the deaf shall then hear.
The sand will turn into a spring. Do not fear,
for a highway is built, and you'll know it by name:
The Way of His Holiness. Those who are lame
shall arise and return to Zion with praise
as the remnant returns from its darkest of days.

Isaiah 36

Sennacherib, king of Assyria, waged
a war on all nations, and when he had staged
an assault upon Judah, his men came to seize
Jerusalem. One of his men said, "To please
Sennacherib, you should bow down in respect.
For surely you've heard and thus should reflect
on the fact that no army nor god has yet stopped
Assyria. Surely the heads shall be lopped
off all of your men. Do you really base
your faith on a god? Is it not the case
that we have torn down many gods in our day?
None of them ever stopped us on our way.
And you beg for Egypt to aid your defense?
Egypt is weak! It does not make sense
to look to those cowards to bring spear and sword.
We're meant to destroy you...so says *your* Lord."
Judah's commanders said, "Please do not speak
in Hebrew, we beg."
"Why should I be meek?"
He laughed. Then he shouted so Judah would hear
the breadth of his insults. "Everyone fear
the wrath of Assyria. When we draw near,
our charioteers shall make the way clear.
But Sennacherib does not want Judah to die.
Make a treaty with us and you will survive."
But no man of Judah responded, for they
had been told that they weren't to speak on that day.

Then Hezekiah was told what was said,
and the people of Judah were filled up with dread.

Isaiah 37

Hezekiah and all of the priests tore their clothes,
for they knew that they were no match for their foes.
Isaiah said, "Don't fear, for they have blasphemed,
and you'll be victorious, though it may seem
that you are outnumbered. Praise the Lord's name,
and you will see Him respond just the same."
So then Hezekiah bowed down to the Lord
and just as Isaiah proclaimed, the Lord's sword
fell on Sennacherib's armies. The toll
was one hundred eighty-five thousand in whole.
The angel of death cut them down in the night,
so Sennacherib saw and knew the Lord's might.

Isaiah 38 - 39

Hezekiah grew ill, and Isaiah said, "You
must now put your house back in order." He grew
grave and said, "You won't recover, my king."
And so Hezekiah prayed, "In everything
I've honored You, God, and all of Your ways.
That's why You have blessed me throughout all my days."
The Lord then replied through Isaiah and said,
"I've heard you, and I have decided instead
of taking you now, you will gain fifteen years
of life. All your prayers and all of your tears
have moved Me. As proof, just look at the sun.
I'll move back its light."
And so it was done.
The sun was reversed! Hezekiah rejoiced,
for God proved He'd heard the prayer the king voiced.
God granted him life when there was but death.
As darkness approached, the Lord gave him breath.
At that time the king of Babylon heard
of the king's great recovery, so he sent word.

Hezekiah decided to greet the king's men
from Babylon. Then he invited them in
and showed them the wealth of Judah they'd stored
in the palace. Isaiah then came and implored,
"King, who were they, and what did they see?"
"They were from Babylon. They said to me
that their king was quite glad I'd recovered, then I
showed them our treasures."
Isaiah just sighed.
"I tell you one day, all the things you have shown
will be hauled away to Babylon's throne.
And even your own flesh and blood will go too.
They'll be turned into eunuchs. Yes, some born to you."
But King Hezekiah was not worried. He
was pleased to know during his life he'd be free.

<u>Isaiah 40</u>

"Comfort, My people," the Lord says. "Proclaim
to Jerusalem that I heard her call My name.
Her sin has been paid for. Her hard time is done."
A voice calls out, 'Make a straight path for the One
who is Lord. Make the rough places smooth for His way.
His glory shall soon be revealed on this day.'
Though mankind, like grass, can wither and fall,
the Word of the Lord shall always stand tall.
The Lord tends His flocks, and all are brought home
though many of His sheep are prone to go roam.
Who's held up the Earth? Who's measured the weight
of the mountains? No mortal has power to state
what is right and what's good. The Lord God alone
is eternal. Take up all your gods made of stone
and see if such things can bring life out of dust.
So why in these trinkets did you put your trust?
Even the young men get tired, but when
you put your hope into the Lord's word again,
you'll run without ceasing, you'll walk and not faint.
Praise the Lord without remorse or restraint.

Isaiah 41 - 43

"Be silent, you islands," sayeth the Lord.
"One who is chosen goes forth with his sword,
subduing the nations. Israel, I
have sent you My servant. I have heard your cry.
Do not be afraid, little Jacob, for through
My covenant I will be there beside you.
I am the Lord, and out of the sand,
I'll make you a lush and beautiful land.
I looked for a servant, but none were in sight,
so I chose someone in whom I delight.
He will not cry out or raise up his voice.
Justice won't falter. It won't have a choice!
The former things have taken place, but the new
shall now be declared, before they're shown to you.
Hear, though you're deaf. See, though you're blind.
The people were plundered and looted in kind.
My anger poured forth, enveloped in flames,
consuming them, though they did not know their shame."
The Lord says, "Oh Jacob, you have been redeemed.
You'll pass through the waters, and you will be cleaned.
Because you are precious and honored, I'll send
one who's a savior, so that in the end,
although you have sacrificed nothing for Me,
I shall forgive you, and you shall be free."

Isaiah 44 - 45

"Now listen, O Israel, I chose you for
My purpose and love. I knew you before
you knew your own selves. I'm first and I'm last.
Who then is like Me? Come, tell Me the past,
then tell Me the future. Bring forth your stone
and wood which you worship. What have they known?
I made them! Why then do you bow and lift praise
to things made by men? A carpenter strays
into the forest to pick up some wood.
Half he burns up, and that half is good.

But half he carves into a god. It's insane!
What heated his food and his god are the same?
I love and forgive you for all you have done,
but I am your God! Not a rock. Not the sun.
And Jerusalem shall be inhabited yet,
for I made a promise that I won't forget.
For do I not call out to Cyrus by name?
When Israel's cleansed of their guilt and their blame,
I'll send you back home and the temple shall be
rebuilt by you, then dedicated to Me.
I call out to Cyrus, 'Come forth and break down
Babylon's gates. Let your fury and sound
be unmatched, although you do not worship Me.
You serve Me by setting all Israel free.'
I am the Lord. There is no other one.
Let every man know who is under My sun,
I'm righteous and I love the people I chose,
and I shall deliver them out from their foes."

Isaiah 46 - 48

"The gods of Babylon bow down to Me.
Can they summon men to come set you free?
Babylon shall be torn down to the dust.
In what city's walls would you lay your trust
when compared with the might of the Lord? Let the shame
of Babylon follow and mix with her name.
No more shall the nations bow down to this harlot.
I tell you, her streets shall be colored scarlet.
Babylon's sins shall cause My disaster
to pour on her head. Her lovers run past her
and onto the next prostitute. She will burn
when My truth is acknowledged. Then you shall return.
O people of Jacob, though you have invoked
My name, you ignored Me when My prophet spoke.
I warned you of all that you're suffering now.
I told you the why and the when and the how!
You're saved for My sake, but I shall not be
mocked or defamed. I must set you free,

or I am a liar and false. I will show
the nations I'm God. So fear Me and know,
had you just obeyed My simple command,
your children would cover the Earth like the sand.
Freedom is yours, but not a reward.
No peace for the wicked!" So says the Lord.

Isaiah 49 - 51

The Lord shall call out to his servant, "Redeem
My people." Though they were in ruins, it seems
the Lord will forgive you, despite how you sin.
And you'll see the temple in Zion again.
The Lord says, "I'll send you the Gentiles who
will save you from Babylon. I'll send the few
remaining back home to Jerusalem's walls."
Watch, nations! You will see Babylon fall!
I've offered my ear and my tongue to be used
by God. And although I have oft been abused,
I've offered myself, for I know that I am
just a cog or a wheel in the Lord's larger plan.
Who amongst you fears the Lord?
God says, "I
made a nation of Abraham. Why should it die?
Salvation approaches. Hear Me and know
I can turn every mountain into a plateau.
So what is a city to Me? Though it fell,
I can heal Zion and make her feel well.
The cowering prisoners shall be let out.
Let all of my people return home devout."
You've drunk from God's wrath. Although you now stagger,
no longer shall you be kept under His dagger.
You never shall drink from this cup again,
and you shall be cleansed and freed from your sin.

Isaiah 52 - 53

Shake off your dust, and know your God reigns.
You've suffered as though you were in birthing pains.

To whom has the arm of the Lord been revealed?
God's servant will suffer, but he has appealed
upon your behalf that you might be saved.
Your iniquities and your transgressions were grave.
But he opened his mouth, was oppressed, and so died
as a guilt sacrifice for the whole nation's pride.
After he's suffered, again he'll know life.
He'll justify many and take on their strife.
Since he gives his life and shoulders the sin
of the many, he'll be loved above other men.

Isaiah 54 - 57

Sing out, O Zion, your husband has come.
The Lord has compassion on you, though the sum
of all your trespasses is countless indeed,
God's fury diminishes. Let it recede.
Come if you're thirsty and drink. Allow he
who does not have money to eat bread for free.
For what the Lord offers makes any king's fare
bitter to taste and as filling as air.
Look for the Lord and He's found! Do what's right,
for no one should hope that he sees the Lord's might
brought down upon him. Go forth and be good,
and follow His laws as you know that you should.
The men who have watched over Israel lie,
deceiving so that they might gain. Should they die,
not one can be judged having lived a good life,
like a man who chose prostitutes over his wife.
The righteous man perishes. None understands
that he has now entered into the Lord's lands,
and he shall be judged as a good worthy soul.
You think of just mortal life, not of the whole!
The lowly are saved as the lofty are brought
down to the depths, like thieves who are caught,
thrown in the dungeon and never released.
I tell you, the wicked will never know peace.

Isaiah 58

The Lord says, "My people are fasting, but they
do not know true fasting. They give Me one day,
but then they go back to their quarreling ways.
I tell you that fasting is stopping to raise
the chains of men's bondage. I want you to feed
the hungry. Your sackcloth and ash reek of greed!
Clothe the poor! Don't harm your own flesh and blood,
lest I cast you down to die in the mud.
If you humble yourself on the Sabbath that's Mine
and help your poor brothers, then your light will shine,
and I shall be greater because you will be
a beacon to all and a glory to Me."

Isaiah 59 - 62

Whenever you violate what God commanded,
do you not think you will be reprimanded?
You live as a pit of vipers, but still
He'll hear your confession. But you take your fill
from darkness, rebelling against what was set
in stone by the Lord. He's righteous and yet
all Israel turns from His good, holy ways.
And still He returns us to Zion. Give praise!
For the nations shall turn their eyes to our land,
and know we're redeemed by God's holy hand.
God sent me to bind the wounded and bless
the children of Jacob who truly confess.
The year of God's favor now has arrived!
Let the sins of the past be all set aside.
I delight in the Lord. My soul must rejoice!
Let us worship His glory and sing with one voice.
Jerusalem, you will not be called Despised
as you were before, but in the Lord's eyes
you shall be married to Him as His bride.
Pass through her gates, for the Lord is inside.

Isaiah 63 - 64

God tramples our enemies. He has been stained
with their blood, for the Lord holds only disdain
for those who oppress His bride. How I pray
that the Lord will come down and quickly repay
all those who mocked Him. Then they would see
their foolishness. God would ignore all their pleas.
We call on you Lord, for You are our Father.
We are the clay, and You are the potter.
We beg You, forgive and forget all our sins.
Have mercy, O Father, and draw us back in.
Your temple has fallen and now lies in dust.
But we shall rebuild it, for in You we trust.

Isaiah 65 - 66

The Lord says, "I showed Myself to a land
that chose not to seek Me. I held out My hand,
and said, 'Here I am.' But people withdrew
from all of My blessings, and so I took you
and threw you into a pit full of snakes,
for all of your priests were liars and fakes.
They showed you false idols. You ate the unclean.
I saw as you acted both lewd and obscene.
But still there is juice in these grapes. I will not
destroy you although in your deed and your thought
you've turned from My face. Your sins I'll forget,
if you will repent, obey, and submit.
Behold! I'll create a new Heaven and Earth!
The old is forgotten upon the new birth.
Be glad and rejoice, for the pains of the past
shall not come again. And you'll see at last
a new Zion born. I'll comfort My child,
and all who rebelled and all who were wild
shall not be forgotten, so all know that I
am Lord of the Earth and the heavens on high."

Jeremiah 1

In the thirteenth year of the reign of Josiah,
the Word of the Lord came to Jeremiah.
"The Lord said to me, 'I set you apart
before you were born. You must speak to the heart
of My people. Despite your age, you must go.
Although you are young, the people will know
that I have sent you.'
And the Lord put His word
into my mouth so that it would be heard.
A vision came, showing disaster would come
out of the north. And God said, 'Though some
of the wicked shall fall and die by the sword,
don't fear, Jeremiah, for I am the Lord.'"

Jeremiah 2 - 3

The Lord said to me, "Go forth and proclaim
that I still remember the honor My name
received in the desert. I saved them and took
them into the promised land. Then by My book
they followed My law. But why did they turn?
Haven't I loved them? Why now am I spurned
by those I adore? The priests turned their eyes
to Baals and the gods that I have despised.
When does a nation change gods? Here you are,
dismissing the Glory that comes from afar!
The heavens are shuddering as you bow down
to Egypt and to Assyria's crown!
You broke off the yoke of My will, and you slept

like a prostitute with other gods as I wept.
Your guilt is a stain. When a thief has been caught
he is disgraced. I know you all thought
you would not be seen, but I have seen all.
Show Me which gods will soften your fall!
You rebels! Am I worth nothing to you?
Your children shall suffer and you'll be subdued.
If a man leaves his wife and she marries another,
should he return to her? She has her lover,
and you have your idols."
And then the Lord said,
"Israel treats Me as if I'm as dead
as the stones they bow down to. Unfaithful one!
Return! I'll forgive and forget all you've done.
Acknowledge your guilt, and then, though we're two,
we'll be reunited, for I've chosen you.
I am your husband."
Then I cried out,
"You people, stop sinning and call with a shout
to the Lord in repentance and stand by His side,
so we're reunited with God as His bride."

Jeremiah 4 - 6

"Your hearts must be circumcised," sayeth the Lord,
"and flee to the cities, for here comes the horde.
The lion is angry and comes from his den.
He shall lay waste, and all your great men
will wail in despair, all covered with ash.
They'll tear at their garments and rip at their sash.
Your conduct has brought disaster your way.
Too prideful to ask for forgiveness, you'll pay
a terrible price. Look all through your streets.
Each heart in the crowd is filled up with deceit.
If you could find one…only one…you'd be saved,
but this is sin city and you are depraved.
You fat, lusty stallions who lust for the wives
of your neighbors, I tell you, you'll pay with your lives.
Your prophets are liars, your priests rule the land.

I'll spare some, but truly as few as I can.
I'll issue decrees that the trees all be downed.
Not for your ramparts, but storming your town!
Although I have loved you, I have been betrayed.
So all you have had shall be taken away.
My altar is thick with incense you burn
for your graven idols. Did you fools not learn
from all the mistakes that your forefathers made?
You were beautiful once, but beauty can fade."

Jeremiah 7 - 8

"Go, Jeremiah, and stand at the gate.
Tell all of the people that this awful fate
need not come to pass if they just heed My will.
I am not a God who desires to kill.
But their worthless idols have led them astray.
Their priests are adulterers. Tell them to stay
on the path of the righteous, but they will not heed,
and so their destruction will be great indeed.
The bones of their prophets and priests will all be
exposed to the sun and the moon, so they see
the spheres that they worshipped; those orbs in the air
that cannot speak back, can't hear, and don't care.
They do not have shame. The vine shall be stripped.
Your enemy comes, so ready the crypt.
I'll send out the vipers to slither and bite,
and you'll know My anger as well as My might."

Jeremiah 9 - 10

I weep day and night for my people, for they
have turned from the Lord. Shall I go away
to the desert so that I cannot be corrupted
by all of their sin? Deception erupted
out of their hearts. And so the Lord speaks.
"Call out the women, for times shall be bleak.
Let them all wail. My will shall be cruel,
until it is realized that I, the Lord, rule.

Lament! All your men shall be cut down to die
in the fields of their fathers. The wise man will cry
when his wisdom is lost. I desire to hear
from righteous men, those who have known Me and fear."
The Lord says, "The foreigners of other nations
will try to entice you with ornamentations.
Their gods made by hand are foolishness, for
they can't create storms or make the skies roar."
Gather your things and flee while you can,
for the Lord's vengeance comes. Destruction's at hand.
A man doesn't own his own life. So I pray
for the Lord to correct but not smite me today.

Jeremiah 11 - 13

The Lord said to me, "Tell all in My land,
I told them, 'Obey Me and all My commands!'
If this had been done, I'd love them much more
than all who come after and those from before.
But there's a conspiracy! They are against
the Lord, even though My wrath's been dispensed
on all of their enemies. Now I have no
alternative but to let My anger flow."
Then the Lord showed me that though I spoke true,
the men of the land sought to cut me down too.
But I was relieved when told by the Lord
that they and their offspring would fall by the sword.
O Lord, You have planted us so we take root,
grow tall and burst forth, abundant with fruit.
But though You're not far from their lips, You are kept
far from their hearts. I saw this and wept.
You know me, my God. I have always been true,
so separate me from the ones who hate You.
Drag them away to the pen for the slaughter,
but cleanse me, my God, with Your holy water.
Then God said, "Your family, even they sin
against me. I have had My fill of these men.
Although they shall sow, let them all reap thorns,
for their words of worship are filled full of scorn.

I'll make the men useless, and I'll make them drunk.
The great tree of Judah's a withering trunk.
She'll be chopped down and carried away,
because of her shameful and blasphemous ways."

Jeremiah 14 - 16

As Judah arrives at their cisterns, they find
not one drop of water. A drought is too kind
for this stubborn people. The donkey's eyes spin,
for he too is punished by all of our sin.
The Lord does not want me to pray for salvation
for His people, because of their desecration
of His sacred oath. Can the idols bring rain?
If so, tell me why they all choose to refrain.
And the Lord said, "I wouldn't help them if they brought
Moses and Samuel to beg for their lot.
The sword will come soon! The birds and the beasts
will see all your corpses and on you they'll feast.
The number of widows will be like the sand
of the desert, too numerous to count by hand.
Jeremiah, they'll seek you, but you will abstain
from turning to them, though you see their pain.
The sons and the daughters born here in this time,
will fall like the leaves of a tree for the crimes
of their parents. But there will be none who mourn, for
they'll be so used to death. What is one more?
I'll give them no reason to celebrate life
or mourn for the dead. My adulterous wife
has left me. Why should there be festivals when
the land is besieged and beset by their sin?"

Jeremiah 17 - 20

"Judah's sin shall be remembered by all.
Don't you see you have not heeded My call
to honor the Sabbath? Are you not clay
in the hands of the Potter? I mold you My way."
Though I was beset by my enemies, He

looked over my needs and heard all my pleas.
Then God said to me, "Go out. Buy a jar,
and take all the priests to the desert. Say, 'Are
you continuing to be a plague on the nation?
The Lord will soon bring you a great devastation!'
Then shatter the jar on the ground and say, 'There
is the fate of Jerusalem. All of your heirs
will be eaten as food. You'll taste of their meat.
I tell you destruction will be made complete."
But when I spoke thus, I was beaten and mocked.
Bloodied, they then put me into the stocks.
"O Lord!" I called out. "Why was I deceived?
You said to go forth, and because I believed
that You would protect me, I did so. But now
even my friends beat my body and brow.
Am I to be hated and cursed at each turn?
Am I not Your tongue to the ones who won't learn
of Your mighty power? I worship Your name.
Are my days to end in sorrow and shame?"

Jeremiah 21 - 22

The word of the Lord came to Jeremiah
when he was compelled by King Zedekiah,
"Plead and ask God to show His great hand,
for Nebuchadnezzar's invaded our land!"
But God said, "I'll join on Babylon's side.
With a plague I will make sure that many have died.
Those who survive won't know mercy when
Nebuchadnezzar has forced his way in."
And so the Lord told Jeremiah, "Go down
and speak to the king and those in the town
of Jerusalem. Many shall ask as they pass,
'Why would God kill off our city en masse?'
The answer is that you've forgotten your Lord
and worshipped your idols. And so God has roared!
Don't weep for the dead king. Weep for the man
who is banished and shall not return to this land!
As a donkey is buried, so shall your king

be thrown in the mud. All the offspring
of David are done ruling over this nation.
Prepare for exile!"
The Lord's proclamation.

Jeremiah 23 - 25

The Lord said, "The shepherds have scattered My sheep.
So I will go gather them, so I may keep
a remnant alive. One day I will name
a righteous branch, so that the throne is reclaimed."
After Jehoiachin, son of the king,
was carried away, God showed me this thing:
there were two baskets of figs. One was good,
but one was so bad not one person should
be forced to ingest them. Then God spoke to me,
"The bad figs are just like the ones who will be
destroyed, but the good will be exiled, and
I'll care for them till they return to their land.
But Nebuchadnezzar will take you from here
to Babylon. You will stay seventy years.
For the cup of My wrath is filled to the brim,
and for those who drink it, the future is grim."

Jeremiah 26

Jeremiah was preaching, "I tell you, repent,
for only in that way may you still prevent
destruction upon this city."
But then
the priests argued with him, "Your words are the sin!
Jerusalem cursed? You blaspheme! Now you
should be put to death."
"You know what to do,"
Jeremiah responded. "And as for my life?
Take it, for you'll still fall under God's knife."
The officials and people cried out, "Let him go!
He speaks for the Lord, for was it not so
that Micah spoke out to the king, Hezekiah?

He was not killed. Would you kill Jeremiah
for speaking God's word? We're a black mark
on Jerusalem. Soon we'll be cast in the dark."
And so he was spared, but the king killed Uriah,
a prophet who spoke just like Jeremiah.

Jeremiah 27 - 28

Then the Lord spoke saying, "Go to the kings
of Judah, and Sidon, and Edom, and bring
Tyre, and Ammon, and Moab as well.
Take up My word to the kings there and tell
them if they serve Nebuchadnezzar, they will
live in their own lands and none shall be killed.
But if they will not become slaves to him, they
will die by the plague and the sword on that day."
But then Hananiah, a false prophet said,
"The Lord says that Babylon's fall comes instead.
Nebuchadnezzar's harsh yoke will soon break."
And so Jeremiah cried out, "You're a fake!
You break wooden yokes to make a good speech,
but God sends an iron yoke no man can breach.
You liar, you'll die within the next year."
And so it was done to prove God was near.

Jeremiah 29 - 30

Jeremiah wrote to the exiles, "Make
Babylon home. Build houses and take
wives and have children. Pray to the Lord,
so that you may please Him and gain His reward.
And He shall come for you when seventy years
have passed. On that blessed day, all of your fears
shall disappear. All the false prophets shall die,
once they have suffered and paid for their lies.
Can men become pregnant? Then why do I see
them cry out as if giving birth? You will be
freed from your yoke, and you'll be restored
to Jerusalem, and you'll be blessed by the Lord."

Jeremiah 31

The Lord declared, "When this is done, those I save
from disaster shall be the good and the brave,
and I'll take them home to settle again,
the town of Jerusalem, cleansed of her sin.
I'll bring them all out of the north, overjoyed,
for they have returned. Though the town is destroyed,
it shall be rebuilt. The vineyards shall burst
with new wine as I, the Lord, quench their thirst.
I'll make a new covenant, not the one I
made with your ancestors. It was defied.
So this promise will be made for the ages,
written on hearts as it's written on pages.
All shall know Me, and I will forgive
man's sin and his wickedness, so he might live
in My grace and mercy. I tell you this day,
the city shall never fall if you obey."

Jeremiah 32 - 34

While Nebuchadnezzar besieged the whole town,
King Zedekiah could not stand the sound
of what Jeremiah was saying, so he
threw him in prison.
"The Lord came to me
and said, 'Buy the field that your cousin will sell.'
I wondered why. For we will soon bid farewell
to this land, but God said that we'd be restored.
When my cousin asked, I followed the Lord.
When we have atoned for our idols and sin,
the people will buy land and work it again.
Though you set your slaves and servants all free
on the seventh year and at the last Jubilee,
once it was over you took them all back!
You spit on His law, so you're under attack.
But God made His promise, which cannot be broken.
We shall be returned. The Lord God has spoken."

Then the Lord said, "This is all by design,
for one day I'll lift up a king from the line
of David, and he'll be the righteous one I
have chosen to rule over you from on high."

Jeremiah 35

Jeremiah was told by the Lord to go find
the Recabite men and pour them some wine,
but they said, "We're sorry, but we can't partake.
It is forbidden, and we can't forsake
our ancestors."
Then the Lord said, "People, see!
This is how I ask you to obey Me.
Because they've been loyal in word and in deed,
their line shall be prosperous. It is decreed."

Jeremiah 36

Jeremiah wrote all of God's words on a scroll,
but the king tore it up and burned it. The whole
thing was destroyed, but God said, "Now write
it all down again. The king will incite
My anger, so I will throw his body down
to rot without burial there on the ground."
And so the scroll grew from the first, as God's word
could not be destroyed, for the Lord must be heard.

Jeremiah 37 - 38

During the siege, Pharaoh's army approached,
and Babylon fled as the fighters encroached.
King Zedekiah rejoiced, but he heard
the prophet scoff, "What? Do you think the Lord's word
was a lie? I tell you that they will be back.
If you left ten alive, they still would attack
and burn this place down. Egypt won't save
Jerusalem. This place will soon be your grave."
Imprisoned, he still spoke the Lord's will to all

who would hear it, but all of the priests went to call
on the king, saying, "We must put this man to death."
Zedekiah said, "I will not waste any breath
trying to stop you. Do as you will."
They took Jeremiah, for they sought to kill
the prophet, but they didn't want to shed blood,
so they lowered him down in a well full of mud.
He sunk down so deep that he could not get free.
A palace official said to the king, "He
is going to starve. Sire, this can't prevail."
So he was pulled out and put back in the jail.
Then the king said, "Answer true, Jeremiah."
"If I do you'll kill me, King Zedekiah.
And if I advise you, you won't listen to
the things that I say as I try to help you."
The king promised secretly he would not kill
Jeremiah, if he would disclose the Lord's will.
"If you will surrender to Babylon, they
will not kill your family. The army will stay
their hand from burning the city down too."
The king said, "Tell no one that I spoke to you."
And so Jeremiah remained in his cell
till the walls of Jerusalem finally fell.

Jeremiah 39:1 - Jeremiah 40:6

The siege lasted two years, and finally the walls
of Jerusalem fell to cheers and applause
from the army of Babylon. Then they charged through
the gates of Jerusalem. Their soldiers drew
their swords and they chased Zedekiah who fled,
and when all his sons and nobles were dead,
they cut out his eyes. They bound him in chains,
and took him to Babylon where he'd remain.
But Nebuchadnezzar said, "Go forth and find
Jeremiah the prophet, and don't be unkind."
So he was released and was left there to stay
in Judah, while many were taken away.

Jeremiah 40:7 - 49:39

The governor of all who stayed in the land
of Judah was killed by a small rebel band.
The poor remnant left in Judah now feared
the day when Nebuchadnezzar would hear
his man had been killed. They went and they said,
"Jeremiah, we know that you have been led
by the Lord. Ask him what our fate will be, please.
And he told them, "Now let your hearts be at ease,
for the Lord says that if you stay here there will be
no war, and you'll live. But if you should flee
to Egypt because you fear famine or war,
then that is exactly what you'll have in store."
"You liar!" some shouted. "The Lord has not said
these things. You speak nonsense to fill us with dread."
They bound Jeremiah and others as well,
taking them with them as they bid farewell
to Judah. And so they went to Egypt's land.
And then Jeremiah was touched by God's hand
as he said, "On this spot God shall set the throne
of Nebuchadnezzar, for now I have grown
weary of telling you things you don't trust.
Babylon's army shall make a great thrust
in Egypt, consuming it. This very hour
has sealed your fate. Now you will see the Lord's power,
for you've baked your cakes for the one you call Queen
of Heaven…this idol is false and obscene.
For your actions, Pharaoh will be taken to
Babylon. This is God's sign unto you."
And just as he'd said, when the battle was fought,
Egypt was beaten and Pharaoh was caught
by Babylon's forces. The Philistines and
Moab were given to Babylon's hand.
Then Ammon and Edom, Damascus as well,
fought Nebuchadnezzar, and each of them fell.
Kedar and Hazor fell under the sword,
exactly as it had been said by the Lord.

Jeremiah 50 - 51

Then the Lord said, "Listen, people, for there
will come a time soon when you'll hear everywhere
a cry out of Babylon. She'll fall and all
of her gods will be toppled as well as her wall.
In those days the people of Judah will cry,
and I'll hear their wailing and weeping. Then I
will bring them back home. There's hope for them still,
if they speak My name and follow My will.
I'll bring the destroyer, My ax and My sword,
who unwittingly does the work of the Lord.
As I have used Babylon, so I will bring
a foreigner to fight and topple her king."
God's words were written down by Jeremiah
and then they were sent with a man named Seraiah
to be read in Babylon, so all would fear
the wrath of the Lord and know He was near.

Jeremiah 52

Because Zedekiah was wicked, he led
his people to suffer, although the Lord fed
Jeremiah the truth for all Judah. But they
would not heed the warning, so God gave the day
to Babylon. As God proclaimed, the king fled,
and was captured. When all of the king's sons were dead,
they cut out his eyes and took him to stay
in Babylon's prison till his dying day.
Then Nebuchadnezzar's army destroyed
the temple. Then all of the men he employed
took Judah's people to Babylon where
they were slaves, for the Lord had exiled them there.

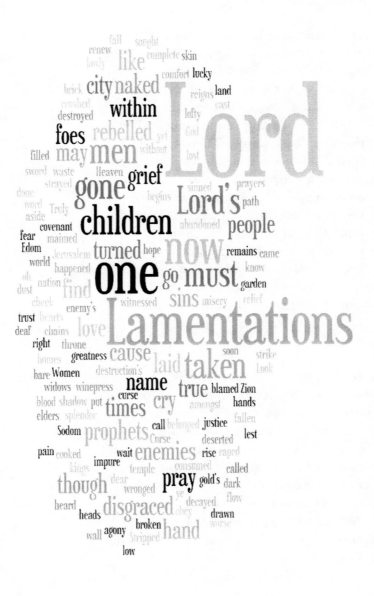

Lamentations 1

A city of widows; deserted she is.
Once she knew greatness, and once she was His.
All of her lovers are gone. She's betrayed
by all of her people. How far they have strayed.
Her foes are her masters. The Lord's brought her grief.
The splendor has left, and it's taken belief
right along with it. All that once was,
is gone like the treasures, and we are the cause.
Stripped naked and bare for the world to see.
Look on Jerusalem! Her agony
is known amongst nations. Her young men are crushed
as if through the winepress, so their blood has gushed.
We do not know comfort, for we have rebelled.
We turned from the sound of the prophets who yelled,
"Repent, now, oh Zion, lest ye be laid low."
We were not attentive, and now it is so.

Lamentations 2

The Lord swallowed up all of those who belonged
to Jacob's house for all the times He's been wronged.
He burned and consumed all the things we've held dear.
Don't quake at your foes. It's the Lord you must fear!
He laid waste His garden, so what might He do
to one who's as lowly as me or as you?
He abandoned His altar and tore down the wall
of the city and temple. We watched each brick fall.
So we put on sackcloth, threw dust on our heads
and wept for our children who must go unfed.

The false prophets misled our kings, and our sin
was the cause of the downfall that we're now within.
This was the word of the Lord, have no doubt.
As the night now begins, you should rise and cry out.
The Lord is not deaf to our pleas or our pain.
Through Him we must find our salvation again.

Lamentations 3

I've witnessed His anger. He drove me away.
His hand turned against me. My skin has decayed.
I've dwelled in the dark, ensnared by the chains.
I'm trampled upon. Now nothing remains.
I have been mocked, I've been beaten and maimed.
My bones have been broken, but I'm to be blamed.
And yet I have hope, for the Lord's love is true.
I cry out to Him, "Lord, only through You
shall I find Your path. I shall wait for Your call.
I'll bear any burden. You rule over all."
To one who would strike me, I offer my cheek.
If I am disgraced, I shall remain meek.
For men are not scorned by the Lord for all times.
If one yields to God, he'll be cleared of his crimes.
The Lord's justice reigns, so I shall obey.
Let's lift up our hands to Heaven and pray,
"O Lord, we have sinned and rebelled against You.
Our prayers were all selfish. Our hearts were not true.
My tears flow unceasingly without relief
for all of our sins are filled up with my grief.
My enemies sought me, and I called Your name.
You heard me, redeemed me, and that's when You came.
Destroy all my enemies. Curse them, for they
have slandered Your name. For this, Lord, I pray."

Lamentations 4

The gold's lost its luster; her sons cast aside.
My people are heartless. The good men have died.
The children go hungry. We live in a curse

like those within Sodom, though this may be worse.
Those killed by the sword are the lucky ones, for
we starve in the streets. We're naked and poor.
Women have cooked their own children to eat.
Truly, our total destruction's complete.
No one thought we'd be destroyed, but we were
and it was our sins, for we were impure.
We fell in His shadow, but soon He'll return
and for what they've done all of Edom shall burn.

Lamentations 5

Remember, O Lord, what has happened to us.
We have been disgraced. In You, though, we trust.
Our homes have been taken. We're orphans. Our land
was stolen from us by our enemy's hand.
We beg for our bread. Our women are raped.
From misery, not even one man's escaped.
The lofty have fallen. Our elders are gone.
Joy has been taken as darkness has drawn.
Your throne shall endure in each generation.
Why then forsake us, Your very own nation?
Restore us, O Lord, that we may renew
the love and the covenant we made with You.

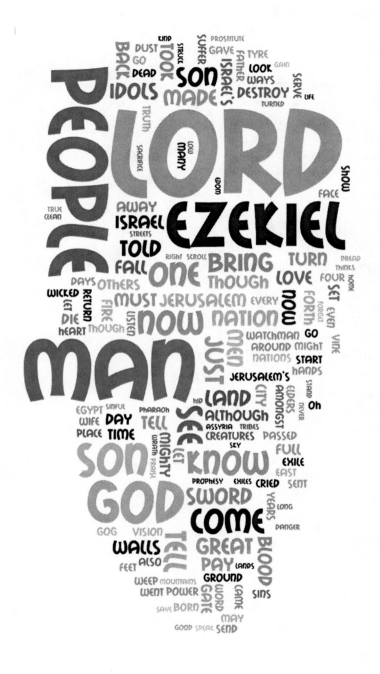

Ezekiel 1

As I was among the exiles by
the river Kebar, I watched as the sky
was opened. From out of a windstorm up north,
a cloud full of thunder and lightning broke forth.
The center appeared as fire, and in
the middle were creatures, but they were not men.
They had four wings and four faces that were
an eagle, ox, lion, and man. I am sure
that some won't believe, but I saw what conveyed
each creature: a bright, flashing wheel thus arrayed
with lights. When the creatures rose up from the ground,
the roar was an awesome and horrible sound.
Then came a voice and they lowered their wings,
and down came a sapphire throne for a king.
There sat a man, half metal, half fire,
and I knew it was God with His angelic choir.

Ezekiel 2 - 4

He said, "Son of man, get up on your feet.
Go to the Israelites and repeat
all that I say. Tell them that they
are an obstinate people. Although they may say
things against you, they'll know that again
I've sent them a prophet. My word amongst men."
And then He gave me a scroll full of woe,
and said, "Son of man, eat this scroll and then go."
It tasted so sweet. Then the Lord said, "Ingest
My word and go forth. Speak, and so test

My people. Tell them of the creatures you've seen.
Show them, through Me, how you've been made clean.
They are My people, but they will not hear!
Foreigners would have found My message clear."
And the Lord told me I was a watchman for all
of His people, that they should not stumble and fall.
The Lord sent me out to the plain, and He said,
"The people shall bind you with ropes, but don't dread.
For when I speak through you, whether they heed
or not, all your words will come from Me indeed.
Woe on Jerusalem! Lay on your side
and suffer for all the days that coincide
with all of the years that their backs have been turned
from Me. Through your actions forgiveness is earned.
Four hundred and thirty days shall be spent
for all of their sins, and you will repent
on behalf of a nation. But I am with thee,
for you serve all Israel as you serve Me."

Ezekiel 5 - 9

"Oh Jerusalem, they set more laws than the foes
who ruled over them. They've become slaves to all those!
Is it not My law that rules? I shall turn
and not pity her as her walls start to burn.
She'll be a warning to all as she cries
from plagues and from wars, locusts and flies.
Then to the mountains of Israel say,
'The Lord brings His sword against you this day.'
I'll smash all their idols, for My heart is grieved
by their hearts' adultery. Had they believed
in Me I would not have to raise up My sword.
But now I must, so that they know I am Lord.
Some shall survive and be placed among
their foes while in exile. Hands will be wrung
and tears will be shed, but all could have been
avoided, if they had but turned from their sin.
Son of man, hear! The end's come upon
the four corners. Soon a disaster shall dawn

like no one has seen in this life. It is doom
for all those who doubt and those who assume
that I cannot see them. Who thinks that I
am blind? Did I not place stars in the sky?"
Then God took me up, so I also could see
the acts of the people and His jealousy.
The Lord said, "Do you see how they don't comply?
Even their elders abominate by
worshipping idols in ways I abhor.
Now let Me show you what I have in store."
He called on His guards who went out and killed
the elders and people until the streets filled
with blood, and I cried and fell on my face.
God's wrath is as great as His mercy and grace.

Ezekiel 10 - 11

A sapphire throne descended and then
the Lord told a man in linen, "Begin
by taking hot coals and throwing them down
onto the city."
That's when I found
the Lord calling me to prophesy to
the elders. I said, "The Lord speaks to you.
Listen! The sword of the Lord has arrived.
You have defiled and you have defied
the Lord and His covenant, thus you shall pay.
Your leaders will die upon this very day."
Then one of their leaders died on the spot.
I kneeled and cried out, "Oh Lord, let me stop.
Am I to destroy all of Israel's nation?"
"Ezekiel, they are a proud population.
Son of man, they have defied the great name
of God, so their people shall be set aflame.
Though I scatter the people, yet shall there be
some who are spared and protected for Me.
Though exiled, they shall return to create
a new Zion that they shall not desecrate.
I shall be theirs, and they shall be Mine

just as I told Moses during his time."
Then God disappeared, and I went to share
my vision with all of the exiles there.

Ezekiel 12 - 14

I told them God sent me to tell them to pack
their belongings and leave, for God would attack
Jerusalem for all its pride and its lack
of faith, but eventually some would come back.
I told them and showed them, for I packed and bid
goodbye to the city. As I left, I hid
my eyes from its walls, for as God had said,
it was a city to fear and to dread.
Then the Lord said to me, "Did I not say
they're a hard-hearted people? Did they obey?
No, they just asked you, 'Why should we flee?'
Even now they will not listen to Me.
Tell them they'll know I'm the Lord when I chase
their prince and his followers out of this place.
They say that your vision has many years till
it shall come to pass, but I will fulfill
it now. Son of man, preach My word to the ones
who call themselves prophets, though they are undone
by their wickedness. Let them know their names will be
struck from the records for all history.
Those who seek magic have surely profaned
My will. Those contemptuous pigs shall be slain.
I'll show you true power, not fake divination
as I create havoc and great consternation.
I see the idols in every man's heart.
There's no time to lose. The people should start
repenting right now, for would I not do
all that I've told you if I am put to
the test? I tell you the day will soon come
when Israel's children shall all return from
their exile full of a love for My laws
and all will acknowledge I acted with cause."

Ezekiel 15 - 17

"Jerusalem, you useless vine. What's the worth
of you amongst all of the nations on Earth?
It once was your faith, and now it is scorn.
From an Ammonite and from a Hittite you're born.
Cast in the dust by your parents to die,
you all should be grateful that as I passed by,
I said to you, 'Live!' and helped you grow strong.
And I made a covenant with you, as long
as you walked with Me. Did I not make
all your days prosperous? Now you just take
the fine things I gave you for granted and sleep
with others, you prostitute! You could not keep
My simple commandment: the people shall not
place others before Me. Now you are caught,
you adulterous wife! Yet you do not earn
anything. You just pay! Where's the return
from your idols? You are the worst prostitute.
Though you lie with others, you are destitute.
As an eagle may carry a vine, I proclaim
Babylon will lead you all off in chains.
But a sprig of the vine shall come back to life
and she'll be a righteous and beautiful wife.
The others shall die and wither away.
All this shall be as I, the Lord, say."

Ezekiel 18 - 21

"You people quote proverbs and say that the sins
of the father are also the son's. Listen, men
of knowledge, I tell you, a son who is clean
won't suffer for what is unholy, obscene,
or otherwise sinful that his father did.
To that son My face will never be hid.
But his wicked father will pay for his own
obscenities. Let it be written and known.
So Israel, be as a son who is pure,
but I tell you this, your destruction is sure.

Your princes will fall as low as the man
who's poorest, for I've set My mighty right hand
against them and all of their line. I was there
when those fleeing Egypt cried out in despair.
Although I had promised a great land, they bowed
down at the feet of a small golden cow.
Even then they were rebellious. The Lord
will properly serve up your nation's reward.
Will you defile yourselves anymore?
If I bring a plague, a famine, or war,
you don't pay attention. Slavery then!
In Babylon's hands you will pay for your sin.
They'll come to Jerusalem's walls and attack.
I will not help, and you can't hold them back."

Ezekiel 22:1 - 24:14

"You'd pass your firstborn into the fire,
but not praise your Lord? My only desire?
This practice is wicked and foolish. Do you
not see that? Come tell Me now, what shall I do
with a nation of fools? You shed so much blood
that the dust of Jerusalem's streets turn to mud.
I looked for a man in your midst who might save
Jerusalem, but every one was depraved.
Like two lusting sisters, Samaria and
Jerusalem's lovers are faraway lands.
Inviting Assyria into her bed,
your sister was ravaged and left there for dead.
You choose the Chaldeans, and so it shall be.
They'll strip you for all of the nations to see.
The pot has been started. The meat is all in.
Look, sinful women, here come your men."

Ezekiel 24:15 - 24:27

The Word came to me, and God said, "Now I
will take from your home the delight of your eye.
Come, son of man, do not weep. Do not mourn,

for all mortals die, just as they are born."
That evening my wife passed away and I went
and said to the people, "You will not lament
when your family dies, as I have just done.
You will be fugitives out on the run.
When your child falls to the ground, you won't weep.
Nor when your loved one has died in her sleep.
The wrath and the fury of our Lord is such
that another dead body won't matter that much."

Ezekiel 25:1 - 28:19

Then God said to me, "Son of man, prophesy
against the Ammonites. Tell them that I
am angry at them, for they celebrated
when the Lord's temple had been desecrated.
I'll turn your nation into a great feast
of plunder for one of the lands in the east.
And when I destroy you with that foreign sword,
then you will know that I am the Lord.
And you, Moab, too shall fall to that nation,
because you joined Ammon's false celebration.
Edom, I'll topple your walls to the ground,
as the blood of your men and your beasts spread around.
Philistines, you have been hostile to Me,
so now My full vengeance and anger you'll see.
Tyre, you mocked all My people. Look fast,
you're cast in the sea with one mighty blast.
The armies I send shall tear your walls down.
Wail for your city that once was renowned.
The people shall weep at your story, distressed
because of your beauty and all you possessed.
All of it shall be carried away
on the shields of the Persians. Many shall say,
'I did business with Tyre, but where is she now?'
The Lord will destroy her. Wait and see how.
The king of your land thinks he is a god,
yet I see his footsteps wherever he trod.

Your wealth gave you power, but I've built a fire
that shall consume all of the people of Tyre."

Ezekiel 28:20 - 32:32

"Sidon shall suffer and Egypt will too,
for I made the Nile, but not one of you
worships My name. For forty years all
your land shall be desolate. Oh, how the fall
of Egypt will soon be completed and then
never shall you gain such power again.
The idols of Memphis are broken apart
and terror is struck into Egypt's black heart.
Son of man, ask Pharaoh, 'Who'll be compared
to you? Once a cedar in Lebanon dared
to outshine the forest around her. It was
Assyria. God cut her trunk down because
she was so prideful. Now she's a dead log.
So you will be brought down as low as the dogs.'
Lament for the Pharaoh. Though he was strong,
a man's time is short, but the Lord's time is long."

Ezekiel 33 - 34

The Lord then exclaimed, "Son of man, tell them all
that I'll send a watchman. If he should call
and say, 'There is danger!' but they do not flee,
their blood's on their own hands. But if he sees
the sword of the Lord is approaching and holds
his tongue and just watches as danger enfolds
My people, their blood is then on *his* hands.
I've made you the watchman for all, son of man.
Try to persuade the wicked to turn
from their evil ways, before they must burn.
For I would forget their sins if they would
ask for forgiveness and start doing good.
My people will come and sit at your feet
and listen to you. But they don't complete
their part by fulfilling all you have said.

Though they were brought manna, no one is fed.
Woe to the shepherds! Your flocks are all lost.
You clothe yourselves, but at what kind of cost?
So many have wandered away as you took
all you desired. Since you will not look
for all of your strays, so I reject praise
from you. I will find them, and I'll let them graze
on the finest of grass, but as for your kind,
I shall forget you. You have been blind
to their struggle. I'll make them a home that is good.
Something that not one of my shepherds could
say they would do. And they'll know My sword.
On that day the nation will know I am Lord."

Ezekiel 35 - 36

"Son of man, Edom shall fall as a waste
for though they have known Me, they have made haste
to turn and to run from My ways. So their towns
shall not be inhabited once they're torn down.
The mountains of Israel's towns have been scorned
by nations, but out of them love shall be born.
I will show favor to you, and you'll grow
fruit on your branches, and then you will know
that I am the Lord, and I love you still.
This is My promise to you, for I will
send out the many. Although they are cursed,
I'll bring back the remnant of those I dispersed."

Ezekiel 37

The Lord plucked me up, and He placed me down
into the desert with dry bones around.
"Son of man, tell Me, can these bones live?"
"Life is a gift only You, Lord, can give."
"Prophesy to them, so that they might stand,
gain tendons and breath, becoming a man."
So I prophesied and they lived again.
"Look upon Israel. These are the men

whom you must go save. Go forth and unite
the tribes of Israel. Show them My might
and truth. Let all of them know I bring peace.
Only through Me shall their numbers increase."

Ezekiel 38 - 39

"Son of man, now set your face against Gog.
Tell them My truth, for they live in a fog.
When they bring their army to fight against My
people, I'll listen to Israel's cry.
I'll bring an earthquake, sulfur, and hail
down upon Gog. Their conquest will fail.
Although they are mighty, none can compare
with Me. Their army shall be buried there.
The land must be cleansed with a blood sacrifice,
for though you will speak, son of man, your advice
is ignored. You bring the truth, but it dies
in the dust. So will Gog, the land I despise."

Ezekiel 40 - 48

God took me up in the twenty-fifth year
of our exile. I saw a vision so clear
of where the new temple would stand, and a man
who shone as if made out of bronze took my hand.
He showed me the measurements for every wall,
each gate, and the size of the great inner hall,
the altar, and also the rooms for the priests,
and then took me back to a gate facing east.
Then the Lord spoke, "Son of man, I shall bring
My glory to rest here. God shall be King.
Let all of My people destroy all the old
idols so that they may finally behold
My love and My glory. They'll sacrifice to
the true Lord Almighty and love Me anew.
But the gate on the east must always be shut.
For the Spirit of God passed through the gate. What

the Lord has demanded in law shall be done.
The Lord God is mighty. The Lord God is One.
The land is divided amongst all the tribes.
Go forth, son of man, and tell all the scribes."

Daniel 1

Nebuchadnezzar attacked and defeated
Jerusalem. Then he took and depleted
the wealth of the city, in men and in gold,
taking the booty to Babylon's holds.
He took all the royalty back with him too.
They served in his palace. Out of these few,
Daniel was one who would not defile
himself with the food of the king. All the while
the cook gave him vegetables rather than all
the rich, meaty food that was served in the hall.
Just Daniel and three of his friends ate apart
from everyone else, to stay pure of heart.
The Lord gave them visions and knowledge so they
were listened to when they had something to say.
And Nebuchadnezzar sought their wise advice,
because it was honest and always precise.

Daniel 2

The king had a dream. He called his magicians,
and said, "You are wise, use your intuitions
and tell me the dream I've had and then say
what this vision means. Do so right away."
"Tell us your dream," they said.
"You do not
understand what I've said. Read my mind and my thoughts,
then tell me my dream and interpret it too.
If not, then you're frauds, and I shall kill you."
"You won't tell us the dream?" they cried in dismay.

"Not a person on Earth can do what you say."
But Daniel went in, for he could reveal
the dream which Nebuchadnezzar concealed.
For God had told Daniel the dream so that he
might prove that there's nothing the Lord cannot see.
"Do you know my dream?" the king asked.
"No man
can say that he does, but the Almighty can.
You envisioned a statue of silver and gold.
Its feet were of clay. Your vision foretold
a rock that was not carved by men struck its feet.
The statue crashed down, its destruction complete.
The wind swept the gold and the silver away,
as the rock grew into a mountain that day.
Now let me interpret. Your kingdom is strong,
but it too shall fall as more come along.
But one day a kingdom that never can fall
shall come along, besting the best of them all."
Then Nebuchadnezzar bowed down and he said,
"Surely your God is the God who is head
over all other gods, for you knew what was true."
So Daniel was praised, and his power grew.
He appointed both Shadrach and Meshach, and then
Abednego all to be high ranking men.

Daniel 3

The king made a gold idol ninety feet tall
and said, "Everyone in the kingdom must fall
on your knees and worship this idol or I
will have you thrown into a furnace to die."
Abednego, Shadrach and Meshach refused.
The king asked, "Why is it that you three men choose
death over worship?"
They said, "Our God will
protect us."
"So be it. Then you shall be killed."
He said to the slaves, "Make the flames seven times
hotter, for these men will pay for their crimes.

As they were thrown in, the flames were so hot
the guards were all killed who held their cords taught.
But Nebuchadnezzar jumped up in surprise,
"We threw three men in, but with my own eyes
I see four in the flames, unhurt and unbound
and one is a son of the gods!"
The king found
the men were unharmed when they were withdrawn.
He looked at the three, for the fourth one had gone,
and said, "None shall blaspheme the name of their Lord,
for no other god has saved men from my sword."

Daniel 4

Nebuchadnezzar once dreamt of a tree
so huge that wherever he looked all he'd see
were the branches, and all of the men and the beasts
fed from it. It was such a glorious feast.
But a watchman came down from the heavens and said,
"Cut the tree down, and when it is dead,
turn the king's mind to an animal's till
seven years pass so he knows that the will
of the Lord is the greatest."
The king asked the wise
to tell him what this meant and what they'd advise.
Daniel was troubled and said, "If it were
your enemies who were cut down I'd prefer
to bring you such news, but this speaks of you.
For seven years you will not reign. It is true.
Like a beast you will live in the wild until
your kingdom returns, when it is God's will.
I advise you to beg for forgiveness and act
with kindness to keep your whole kingdom intact."
And it came to pass that the king lost his mind
and fled to the wild, away from mankind.
But seven years later, his reign was restored
and from that day forth he worshiped the Lord.
Those who are prideful will be humbled by
the might of the Lord who rules upon high.

Daniel 5

Belshazzar, Nebuchadnezzar's son, threw
a banquet with chalices that were taboo.
They drank from these cups, the loot that was brought
from the temple of God. Belshazzar sought
to discredit the Lord. But no man should test
His name, so in front of the king and his guests
the form of a hand appeared and it wrote
on the wall in huge letters; a warning or note.
Belshazzar called to his wise men, "Come and
tell me this message, and then by whose hand
this note has been written."
Daniel said, "I
can decipher these words. The one God on high
wrote, 'When your father was king, he was feared.
Although he was prideful, his sins were cleared.
He humbled himself to the Lord. But now you
aren't humble. I see all the things that you do.
You drank from the goblets that were consecrated
to God the Almighty. Now they're desecrated.
So you have been judged, and you are found wanting.
I tell you right now, your foes are out hunting.
Persia and Media come for your land,
and it shall be taken away from your hand."
On that very night, the king was found dead.
From Media, Darius rose in his stead.

Daniel 6

Darius saw that Daniel was good
at leading, so Darius thought that he would
give him more power, but all of the rest
were jealous of Daniel, and they thought it best
to have him arrested. They said, "King, proclaim
that any who do not lift up your great name
and say you're a god must be thrown to the lions."
For they knew that Daniel had come out of Zion

and he praised the Lord. And so it was done,
and all of the men said, "Daniel is one
who defies you're a god."
And nothing could be
done to negate the king's new decree.
Darius said, "May your God save you, friend."
And Daniel was thrown in a fierce lion's den.
But when the king came the next morning, he saw
Daniel alive.
"I follow God's law
and I did not wrong you, my king."
So they sent
for all of the men of evil intent.
All of these men were cast in for their sin
and killed before hitting the floor of the den.
And Darius, seeing the strength of the Lord
said, "There is no man who dares to ignore
your God. Let all men in my nation proclaim
that He is a mighty God. Honor His name."

Daniel 7

Daniel slept and had a vision where he
saw that the four winds had churned up the sea.
Four beasts came forth, the first had a head
like a lion but wings like an eagle. Instead
of flying, its wings were torn off and the heart
of a human was given to it. The next part
was a bear that had ribs stuck into its teeth.
Daniel heard some voice say, "Get up and eat
your fill of the flesh." Then a leopard was next
with four wings and four heads upon its four necks.
Last was a creature with iron teeth and
ten horns on its head. Thrones burst from the land.
The Ancient of Days sat there on His throne.
The great beast was slain and stripped to the bone.
The other beasts also were stripped of their power,
but their deaths were not meant to come at that hour.
The son of man came and was set up on high

to rule with dominion that never can die.
This is the meaning that Daniel ascribed,
"The vision was troubling, as I described.
The four beasts are kingdoms that shall come to pass.
But I was concerned by the beast that came last.
It is a kingdom that's different from all
that have come before it, but it too shall fall.
For the kingdom of saints shall rule the whole world,
when God lets His almighty banners unfurl.
And though I was troubled by what I had seen,
I did not speak of it, nor what it might mean."

Daniel 8

"I had a vision. A powerful ram
ruled over all other sheep in the land.
But a goat with a horn in its forehead came out,
attacking this one and thrashing about.
The goat became strong, but then his horn broke
and four new ones grew, all strong as an oak.
But a fifth that was greater, grew to the host
of the heavens, and it was the one that grew most.
The son of man came and told me these things.
He said, 'Both Media and Persia will bring
great power, for they are the ram with two horns.
Greece is the goat, and from it is born
four kingdoms…its horns. But one will be stronger
and his reign of terror will last so much longer.
He'll be destroyed, but not by a man.'
This vision was one I could not understand."

Daniel 9

"The scriptures foretold the exile would last
seventy years, but once that was past,
we would return. I prayed to the Lord,
asking, 'God, bless us, so we are restored.
Our sins have been grievous, and everyone knew
what would happen if we did not bow down to You.

Your mighty hand brought us all out of our graves
when we were in Egypt and just lowly slaves.
We are not worthy, but Your mercy can
save us and take us back home to our land.
Jerusalem's streets are now desolate. We
beg You to free us. O Lord, hear my plea.
Gabriel, that angel whom I had seen
in a previous vision, said, "In between
the time that you started and ended your prayer,
it was answered. I've come now to tell you that there
are just seventy weeks from the day the decree
is made till the time you will finally see
the temple rebuilt in Jerusalem. Then
an anointed one comes to release you from sin."

Daniel 10 - 12

In the third year of Cyrus, while Daniel was fasting,
a vision from God, the Lord Everlasting,
came to him. He saw a man cloaked in white
with a body like crystal, his face flashing light.
The men he was with couldn't see him but fled
because they were filled with a deep sense of dread.
The man said, "Don't fear me, for you are esteemed.
You who've deciphered what others have dreamed.
Soon all the kings in Persia will fight
against Greece's kingdom and all of its might.
The wars will go on and many will fall,
but one king will lift himself up above all,
declaring himself as a god. He will be
the ruler of all for a while, but he
will fall in the end. Then Michael, the prince
who protects all your people, will rise and come hence.
Some will awaken to life never-ending.
They'll shine with the light the great stars are sending.
But you must seal up the words of the scroll."
Daniel could not understand.
"By my soul,"

he cried, "what will be the outcome of this?"
"Many will be purified and know bliss.
Though wickedness still shall persist till the end,
when you die a treasure awaits you, my friend."

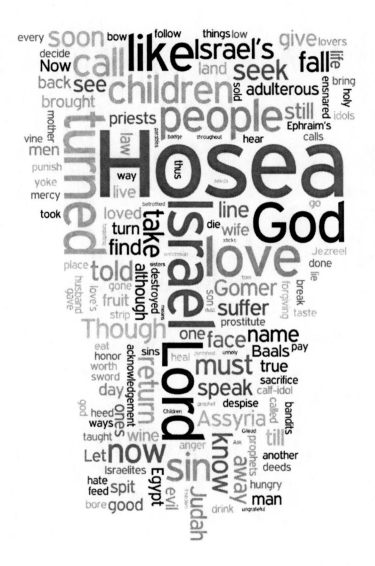

Hosea 1

The Lord told Hosea, "Go find a wife
who's adulterous. All of your children in life
will hate Me, for Israel's turned from My face.
They're ungrateful and an adulterous race."
So he married Gomer, and she bore a son.
"Name him Jezreel, for soon I'll be done
with Israel. I'll break their bow in the valley
of Jezreel, thus bringing about their finale."
Then Gomer conceived and bore him a daughter,
and God told him, "Israel soon shall be slaughtered,
so name her Lo-Ruhamah, which means 'unloved'
for Israel's turned from the one God above."
Then Gomer gave birth to a son and God told
Hosea, "You'll call him Lo-Ammi. They sold
their birthright, and so as the name will imply
they are 'not My people'. They've all gone awry.
Israel's turned. But Judah has not,
so I will love them. Though Israel brought
my anger, I will reunite them again
through a leader who'll save both the nations from sin."

Hosea 2

"Call all your brothers 'My people' and call
your sisters 'My loved ones.' Then you must all
rebuke your own mother, for she's not My wife.
She's been adulterous all of her life.
I'll strip her naked and she'll be as dry
as a desert, and so in her thirst she will die.

I won't love her children, for they have been born
of adultery. I look upon them in scorn.
She still believes other lovers will give
her all that she needs, so that she may live.
But I'll block her way. She'll seek, but not find
her lovers. Then watch as she changes her mind.
She'll say, 'I'll return to my husband. That's where
I was loved.' Why should I accept her or care?
For she's done Me wrong! The gifts she received
came not from the Baals, but were given by Me.
So I'll take them back, every gift that I gave.
None who have been with the harlot are saved.
I'll show you her lewdness. Let every man see.
I'll strip all her vines for turning from Me.
I'll punish her for all her time with the Baals,
but finally you'll see that My mercy prevails.
I shall speak tenderly to her and then
she'll call Me 'her husband', renouncing her sin.
And We'll be betrothed in faith and compassion
and all that is good will then be refashioned.
For those who were not My people or of
My heart, I'll forgive, so they know My love."

Hosea 3

The Lord said, "Hosea, go love your wife.
Though she loves another, give her your life."
Hosea told Gomer, "You must be true
to me. In return, I shall be true to you.
Do not lie down with another man, for
the Lord says you can't prostitute anymore."
The Israelites will return to God when
they know of their shortcomings and of their sin.

Hosea 4

"O Children of Israel, hear My command
and charges against you throughout the whole land.
There is no faithfulness, nor is there love

for the Lord, your Protector, your one God above.
You curse and you murder. You lie and you steal.
And so the land mourns. The beasts of the field,
the birds of the sky and the fish of the sea
are dying because you have all turned from Me.
You turned from My knowledge, so I turn from you.
You're not My priests. My law was lost too.
Your mother, called Israel, shall be destroyed,
for though I would favor you, you have enjoyed
the sins of the world, not that which I give.
You relish the wicked each day that you live.
You'll eat, but go hungry. You'll drink all the wine.
You'll prostitute, but you won't lengthen your line.
So turn to your idols, your small sticks of wood.
They're mute and they're deaf. You misunderstood
all that I told you. You spit in My face
with your offerings to them in My holy place.
I won't punish your daughters or daughters-in-law
for whoring themselves, for I know and saw
you men turned them to it. These low, shameful days
shall end as My whirlwind sweeps them away."

Hosea 5

"Priests, pay attention! This judgment's on you.
You can't hide from Me. Your debt has accrued.
Corruption and prostitution is all
I see in this land. How did Israel fall
so low as My people? Forgiveness? Denied!
Your arrogance testifies that you have lied.
You and your bastards all bow to the moon,
but take heed for I'll bring My vengeance, and soon!
Let the horn sound, for battle is certain.
Upon Ephraim's line, I'll soon draw the curtain.
I'll pour out My wrath on Judah and you.
Thieves, one and all. I am filth on your shoe.
I'm worth nothing in all of your hearts, so I'll send
a messenger showing the doom that impends.
Assyria! You will all turn in despair

to her, but I tell you, you'll not find help there.
And while you suffer, I'll wait in My place
until you decide to seek out My face.
It pains Me to do this, but I know I must,
for you won't seek Me till you're trampled like dust."

Hosea 6 - 7

"'Let us repent,' you will say, 'Let's return
to the Lord. He will heal us, although we have spurned
His love. He'll revive us and on the third day
we'll all be restored to follow His way.'
What do I do with you when you say this?
Your love's like the dew that dissolves in a mist.
I cut you to pieces with prophets and words,
but still you ignore Me. Have you not heard?
I want mercy, not sacrifice! Off'rings are dirt
when compared with acknowledgement. How you have hurt
Me with your contempt. Like Adam you broke
your covenant with Me. You'd choose the yoke
of sin rather than all the freedom I give.
In Gilead, priests and law teachers live
like bandits and murderers, loving their crimes.
And few men speak up in these evil times!
Judah, you too shall be reaping what's sown.
Do you not realize your evil is known?
You're thieves! You are bandits! Upon sin you feed.
I hate all your treachery and evil deeds.
You mock Me, and after you suffer and fall,
still you don't seek Me. Still you don't call.
Instead you call Egypt, Assyria too,
but as you flee I'll throw My net over you.
I long to redeem you, although you speak lies
against Me and seek out the things I despise.
Your leaders will fall on the sword for their act,
and it will be years before I take you back."

Hosea 8

"Though Israel calls out acknowledgement now,
they chose not to do so before I showed how
I am mighty. They turned and rejected My grace.
They set up false idols, and have been disgraced.
Their silver and gold are as worthless as that
calf-idol sitting there. Where's your god at?
They all sowed the wind, and reaped a tornado.
Israel's been swallowed up on this day, so
they've gone to Assyria, sold as a slave,
and in their oppression they'll soon waste away.
They've spit on My law, and torn My name down
so now I'll burn all of their cities and towns."

Hosea 9

"Israel, do not rejoice! You will find
your fields will not feed you. You'll not taste new wine.
Your sacrifice is so distasteful to Me,
for you are too late, and you are unclean.
Egypt will gather and Memphis will bury
the Israelites. All of My people carry
their sins like a badge. Now their punishment comes.
Did My prophet speak in some foreign tongue?!
He is the watchman and yet he's ensnared
in My house by people for whom he has cared.
Your fathers were like the fruits of the earth,
till they turned to Baal, and then they were worth
as little as that to which they have bowed down.
Woe unto Israel, you of renown,
who once were a people of honor and prayer
shall now bring your children out to the slayer.
In Gilgal I hated them, so for their deeds
I'll drive them all out and stomp on their seeds.
The root has been withered. Their tree bears no fruit.
Their children shall perish in ash and in soot."

Hosea 10

Israel's line is a vine spreading out.
As his fruit increased, so did the devout.
But now they bear guilt, demolishing altars,
ignoring their God, forgetting the Psalter.
Soon they will say, "Where is our nation?"
as they are ensnared in their own litigation,
for oaths have been made and their debts piled high.
The idolatrous priests have turned a blind eye
to the poison they preach. All shall be taken
off to Assyria. God is forsaken.
So shall you be! And your holy places
will fall to the brambles, for all your disgraces.
God sayeth, "Ephraim's a cow that can thresh,
so I will yoke her and tear at her flesh.
And Judah shall plow while Jacob must break
the ground. They will suffer, till I come to take
them back."
You shall eat the fruit of deception.
Though God was with man from our first inception,
we looked to our own strength instead of the Lord's,
so now our destruction shall be our reward.

Hosea 11

"I loved My children, and I brought them out
of Egypt, and I taught them what I'm about.
The more I called to them, the further they went.
They took their inheritance and it was spent
on Baals and on sin. Though it had been I
that taught them to walk, and I who supplied
all of the good things, I was denied.
I can be good, but I won't be defied!
Now if they call Me, I'll not heed the call.
How can I let My precious ones fall
under the sword of the ones I despise?
My love is aroused, and they shall arise.
They'll follow their Lord when I roar like a lion.

Trembling children will stumble to Zion,
and I'll settle them in their homes once again,
forgiving their trespass, forgiving their sin."

Hosea 12

Ephraim seeks treaties with all of his foes,
and Jacob's line searches for ways to oppose
the Father. And although he wrestled with God,
they love the unholy and listen to frauds.
You must return to love and to justice,
or all of our fraud and our boasting will thrust us
into the fire. The Lord says, "I brought
you out of your bondage, and so I have sought
to teach you with prophets and parables too.
But Gilead's wickedness still calls to you.
My anger has bitterly thus been provoked,
and so you'll be punished till all is revoked."

Hosea 13

"They kiss the calf-idol, so on his behalf,
I'll sweep you away like trash or like chaff.
There's no god but Me, and until you say
that I am the Lord, you people will pay.
When they were hungry I fed them, but then
they said to themselves, 'Look, are we not men?
We don't need the Lord.' They spit on My name.
They turned from My face. Now I'll do the same.
Israel, you've been destroyed. Where's your king?
I took him away, as I'll take everything.
Your children will suffer and then they will die,
until I decide to honor your cry."

Hosea 14

Return now, oh Israel, to our true King.
Fall down and beg! Rise up and sing!
Ask for forgiveness, or we'll be swept up

in chains by our enemies. Drink from His cup.
The Lord wants our love, and He says, "I'll heal
their wounds if I hear their heartfelt appeal."
His splendor will grow like the cedars we see
in Lebanon. His love's the greatest of trees.
We'll dwell in His shade. We'll taste of His vine.
There's no finer drink than drinking His wine.
Be wise and discerning, for His ways are right,
but if we rebel, then we'll know His might.

prayer well son
fortunes word
sun Prepare years
laid neighbors Rend
lots woman thunders scene
feasts throughout might
defiled Let every sought fall
Hashem
pour sackcloth back
house locusts weakest
thieves put
consume
people mountains soil
descending stripped took war
spirit
nations Joel witnessed cities
hear priests
rushes garments
men now darkness
Still ever girls
cast one
Get plague knees low fill ranks
done whole yield
stole fear yet breaking light
enjoy nothing grain pleasure
honest sin
else Mourn numbers heed
Call hearts see
trembled came Lord's may
nation time boys
waste blots
alarm come man's new
look spare resemble
Take crypt
child Judah Lord praise
fasting cavalry remains
army day
ravaged strength
sacrifice hand Return dream
heard husband's God man
noise uncountable
pale lamentations destroyed give
bowed know like restored
around Israel
seen old
plant incredible wine face
sold without declares flow
1:20 terrible Pethuel
bests Sound turned

Joel 1:1

To Joel, son of Pethuel, came the Lord's word
and here's the account of all that he heard.

Joel 1:2 - 1:20

Oh hear this, my people, throughout the whole nation
that you may pass on to more generations
all you have witnessed, for you have not seen
anything like this most terrible scene.
What still remains? Not one grain or grape.
The land has been ravaged. Our nation is raped.
Not by our neighbors, but locusts! What was,
is now just a dream of plenty, because
this plague has destroyed us. You drunkards, now wail!
Your wine and your vines disappeared in this gale.
In incredible numbers, our trees have been stripped.
Mourn like a woman at your husband's crypt!
Would you sacrifice now? I tell you, you can't!
For God has not left us one grain on the plant.
So put on your sackcloth and mourn, all you priests,
for it will be years until we see our feasts.
Call on the elders across the whole land,
for all men can now see the might of God's hand.
The pastures are empty as well as the fields,
and fires consume them. This is our yield.

Joel 2

Sound the alarm! Let every man tremble.
This darkness and gloom, does it not resemble
the army descending as all is laid waste?
It gallops like cavalry; nothing escapes.
It leaps over mountains, its noise like the sound
of chariots. Take heed and look all around.
Each face has gone pale. What man could give thanks?
It bests our defenses without breaking ranks?
It rushes through cities like thieves in the night.
It blots out the sun so day has no light.
The Lord's at the head of this army that thunders
and bears down on us with uncountable numbers.
"Still," says the Lord, "You may yet be saved.
Return to Me fasting and mourning the day
you turned. Rend your hearts, not your garments and then
to you I'll be gracious, forgiving your sin."
Let all of the men, every woman and child
seek to be cleansed, for we are defiled.
Beg! Get down now. On your knees, people. Plead!
And God will have pity in our time of need.
The Lord will reply, "I hear lamentations.
They're honest and true, so I'll spare this nation.
I'll drive back this army of insects and spare
this land for they fear me and fall down in prayer."
Then up, all you people! Get up then in praise.
For God spared the nation which He could have razed.
And we will have grain, new wine, and new oil
and He will replant all the wheat in the soil.
The Lord says, "On that day, I'll pour out for all
My spirit, and prophecy will make its call.
Young men will see visions, and old men will dream,
and you will see things that no man's ever seen."

Joel 3

The Lord declares, "When I have come and restored
the fortunes of Judah, you'll know I am Lord,

for I'll judge the nations who took you in hand,
scattered My people, divided My land.
They cast lots for people, they traded My boys
for whores. They sold girls, so they could enjoy
more wine, as they sought to have nothing but pleasure.
They took and they stole all the best of My treasure.
All that they've done shall be done to them."
Prepare for war, Israel. Follow Hashem!
Let the weakest find strength. Beat your plows into spears.
As we trembled at locusts, the nations shall fear.
"You will know I am God, when I reign on My hill.
A fountain shall flow out of My house and fill
the people of Judah, though all else shall be
brought low, laid waste, and bowed down to Me."

Amos 1 - 2

These are the words of Amos, two years
before the great earthquake. God's word appears,
declaring, "Damascus, you'll tremble and fall.
My fire consumes your great city wall.
Gaza, beware! Your king will be thrown
under My sword. My might shall be known.
Tyre, you too, shall know of My wrath.
Your kingdom will burn as I carve out a path
of death and destruction for all of the crimes
you've done to My people. Yet at the same time,
Edom and Ammon will wail and will gnash
their teeth. I shall set them ablaze. They are trash.
Moab will suffer and will be consumed,
and Judah, you too, must know you are doomed.
You turned from My laws and all My decrees.
You worshipped false gods. I won't hear your pleas.
Israel, you who were chosen now sell
the poor and the needy for trinkets. I tell
you your day has come. And all I have done
for you has been lost. You worship the sun?
I placed it! Did you make the birds or the beasts?
I took you from Egypt and carried you east.
I gave all your enemies into your hands,
and I placed you here in the finest of lands.
And now I'm found worthless in all of your eyes.
None shall escape their impending demise.
On foot or on horse, no one gets away.
Even the bravest will tremble that day."

Amos 3

"From all of the nations, I chose Israel.
But I did not do so with some kind of spell.
You had the choice to choose or reject
My path. I asked for your faith and respect.
I told you My ways through the prophets I sent.
Instead of repentance you showed Me dissent.
So now I shall send you an enemy who
will rule and oppress you in all that they do.
A shepherd may save but a leg of the whole
from the mouth of the lion. Such is the toll
of wandering off from the flock as you did.
When they heard My name, all Israel hid.
So I shall tear down every altar you built,
upon which is written the whole nation's guilt.
Your houses and mansions shall fall to the ground
until all of Israel's faith comes around."

Amos 4

You cows, you oppressors, you drunkards, hear now
the word of the Lord, as He makes His vow.
"The time will soon come when you're taken by hooks,
you idolatrous sinners, adulterous crooks.
So go sacrifice to your false gods till then!
And brag, fornicators. Preach on your sin.
Hard times have fallen as I willed them to.
Still I do not see repentance in you.
Your water is tainted, your food has gone bad.
I killed your young men and took all that you had.
I could have healed, but you preferred hell.
Prepare then to meet your God, Israel."

Amos 5

"Israel, you have deserted My law,
and for this most grievous and ungracious flaw,
when you send your armies and men out to fight,

just one out of ten shall return to your sight.
Seek Me and live! Betray Me and I
will exile you; far worse than to die.
I made the stars that you see up above.
I made your flesh, and asked only love.
But you hate the truth. You trample the poor.
Though you plant your vineyards, they will not mature.
Would you change your ways? Spurn evil for good?
I seek to love you. I ask that you would.
But still you have not. Instead you resist,
so you will all wail as I pass through your midst.
You each say you long for the day of the Lord.
How is it you don't know the might of My sword?
Few will rejoice when the judgment day's here,
and many will know the true name of fear.
I am disgusted by offerings brought
to My altars. You hate Me in deed and in thought."

Amos 6 - 7:9

Woe unto you, the complacent, who sit
in luxury thinking God's wrath is not fit
for you. Don't you know that no one is spared
from God's mighty hand? So thus be prepared.
Your comfortable homes, your meat, and your wine
will all fall away. You'll be first in line
for exile. All of your lounging will cease.
The dust and the dirt shall soon be your feasts.
The Lord hates the pride of our entire nation
and He's set His mind to our desolation.
He told me that He would send locusts, but I
cried, "Lord, how can Jacob's line hope to survive?
He is too small."
And so God relented,
but then the new plan of the Lord was presented.
He showed me how fire would burn us, but I
cried, "Lord, if You do this, how can we survive?
We are too small."
And so God relented,

but then the new plan of the Lord was presented.
He said that His judgment would be handed out
without mercy even for all the devout.
"I'll spare them no longer," He said. "All will fall.
And no cry of yours will cause Me to stall.
The high places and the fortresses will
be ruined so that My word is fulfilled."

Amos 7:10 - 7:17

Then Amaziah, the priest, sent a scroll
to King Jeroboam, stating his goal.
"Amos is raising a riot. You should
banish him now, for our greater good."
Amaziah replied, "Get out now, you seer!
Go back to Judah and just disappear.
Do not prophesy in Bethel. Don't you
know this is the king's sanctuary, you fool?"
Amos said, "I was no prophet, just some
poor shepherd's son in the land that I'm from.
But God took me out from the flock so that I
could go where He sent me and there prophesy.
So, hear now the Lord. Your daughters and sons
will die by the sword, and for the same ones
who killed them your wives will be prostitutes.
Israel's offspring shall be destitute."

Amos 8

The Lord said to Amos, "No time is riper
than now to wipe out this pit full of vipers.
Bodies will tumble, the sinners will pay
for cheating the poor. Today is the day.
The whole land shall rise, then sink like a stone.
Their feasts shall be days in which all will atone
in sackcloth, but it will be too late for prayers.
The Lord will not listen. I no longer care.
They'll stagger around, lost in the waste.
The lovely and strong will all be displaced.

They'll swear and they'll fall, adrift in their sin.
And what once existed shall not rise again."

Amos 9

The Lord said, "Crash each pillar down to the ground,
on the heads of the people who've gathered around.
And those who remain shall die by the sword,
so all who are left shall know I'm the Lord.
Wherever they hide, I will hunt them and seize
them each by their hair. Not one of their pleas
will be listened to. They're no better than Cush
and its sinners. Was I not the One from the bush
who spoke out to Moses? I gave him the Law.
And now Jacob's house ignores what they saw,
so disaster shall greet them at every turn
until the day comes when My love has been earned.
On that day, I shall repair all that I broke.
I'll bind up their wounds and give them a cloak.
I'll bring them up out of their exile then,
and then they will not be uprooted again."

fall wise held bloodline slaves Rise prophecy made
pride loftiness destroy fire like
destruction nation oppression seized slaughtered
Obadiah employ village wealth hand
Jerusalem's Let remembered Lord something
brought Judah's graves take
come scoffed left Tumbling used Esau's Edom's
Edomites outside generations vision brought
man rejoiced transgressions go aside completely declared children's burn
Esau sins igniting God Thus
violation Israelites battle
cause near lowly pariah houses consume pillaged news
even abduction land ground Joseph men remain
Edom Jacob day
blot stars to crashing one taking within
Go sick Thieves
nations brother

Obadiah 1

To Esau and Edom, his nation, I say,
a vision from God has come on this day.
Rise up in battle against the oppression
the Edomites cause, and for their transgressions,
their pride, and their loftiness, they'll be brought down.
Tumbling stars crashing into the ground.
Thieves even leave something left in the village,
but, lo, we will not, when Edom is pillaged.
The Lord has declared, "Will I not destroy
the wise men of Edom with all I employ?
All will be slaughtered, one after the other,
for what Esau did to Jacob his brother.
You scoffed at your brother, and then stood aside,
at Jerusalem's taking by those from outside.
You rejoiced at the news of Judah's destruction
her sick violation, her children's abduction.
You seized their wealth! *You* made them slaves!
For all of your sins you will go to your graves."
The day of the Lord is near for all nations.
It will be remembered by all generations.
The houses of Jacob and Joseph will fume,
igniting like fire to burn and consume
Edom completely. Let no man remain
of Esau's bloodline. Go blot out his name.
The Israelites will take all of the land
that used to be held within Edom's hand.
Edom will fall, that lowly pariah.
Thus is the prophecy of Obadiah.

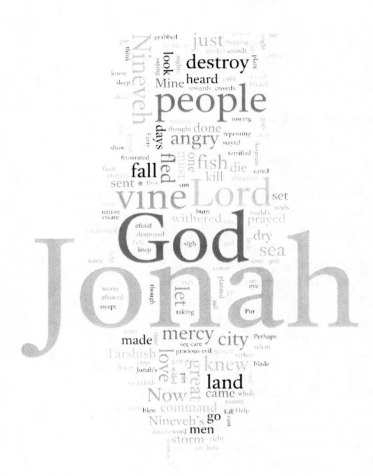

Jonah 1

God came to Jonah and said, "You must go
to Nineveh and let the people all know
I am angry with them. Speak out. Help them turn
from their wickedness, so that My anger won't burn."
But Jonah did not want to help them, so he
fled towards Tarshish, by taking to sea.
He paid for his fare on a boat set to sail
in the other direction. But soon a strong gale
blew up, then a storm. All the sailors were scared.
They prayed to their gods that they should be spared.
But Jonah was sleeping. They woke him and said,
"Pray to your God, or we shall be dead.
Let us cast lots to see who's at fault."
It pointed to Jonah. They said, "What assault
did you do to your God?"
"I am fleeing from Him."
This terrified them, and it angered the men.
"What should we do with you?" all of them asked.
"Kill me," said Jonah, "and this storm shall pass."
The men were afraid this would make matters worse,
and so they tried rowing to dry land at first.
But they made no headway, and so they agreed.
They grabbed Jonah and threw him into the sea.
Then Jonah was swallowed up by a great fish,
for he hadn't yet done all the things the Lord wished.

Jonah 2

Three days and nights in the fish Jonah stayed,
and while in the gut of the beast Jonah prayed.
"Lord, I was hurled out into the deep,
but You heard my prayers, and I'm in Your keep.
The currents and waves have swept over me,
but You've kept me safe out here in the sea.
Although I was banished, may I look again
at Your holy temple, for You knew my sin.
But You brought me up from Sheol's dark pit.
My prayer rose to You, and You have heard it."
At Jonah's repenting, God gave His command
for the fish to vomit him onto dry land.

Jonah 3

Then the word of the Lord came to Jonah. He said,
"I saved you though you disobeyed Me and fled.
Now go! Go to Nineveh. Preach to the crowds.
Tell them their evil deeds won't be allowed."
And so Jonah went to a city so great
that it ruled over all the Assyrian state,
saying, "Forty more days and the city will fall!"
The people believed him and so the king called,
"Put on your sackcloth and fall in the dust,
begging for mercy from God, for we must
all fast. If we don't, the Lord will destroy
each man and each woman, each girl and each boy.
Perhaps if God sees how the nation repents,
He'll have mercy upon us and He will relent."
And God saw how all had obeyed His command,
and Nineveh wasn't destroyed as He'd planned.

Jonah 4

But Jonah was angry. "I knew you would not
destroy Nineveh's people. It's just as I thought.
I fled to Tarshish, for I knew you'd let

the people survive and you wouldn't set
your wrath on this land. You're gracious. You love
to show mercy to us from Your throne up above.
Now kill me, O Lord. I'd rather just die."
"Why are you angry?" God said with a sigh.
But Jonah just sulked. He sat and he waited
for Nineveh's fall, but he was frustrated.
The Lord made a vine to give Jonah shade,
but then sent a worm to eat through the blade.
The vine quickly withered and God sent the sun
and a very fierce wind. Jonah said, "Now I'm done.
Just kill me now, God."
"Do you have the right
to curse the vine that only I have the might
to create?"
"Don't waste time. O God, let me die!"
"Jonah, the whole world's under My eye.
You did not tend the vine. It sprang up because
I willed it, and when the plant withered it was
My doing. If I care for one little vine
how much more do I love these people of Mine?
Nineveh has one hundred and twenty
thousand souls in it. Do you think that's plenty?
At least enough people that I should decide
to send you to save them? All those lives inside
are Mine to destroy or to look on in pity.
As I cared for the vine, I love this great city."

Micah 1

Micah was told by the Lord of the fate
of Jerusalem and the Samarian state.
Look! The Lord's coming! The Earth will submit.
The mountains all melt and the valleys all split,
for Israel's sin, Samaria!
"She
shall be destroyed and her foundations will be
laid bare. All her idols will be hacked apart.
I'll burn all her temples, her gifts, and her art.
The prostitutes' wages have built up her sin,
so all will be prostitutes' wages again."
And so I shall weep. And so I shall wail.
Her wound is incurable, winding its trail
to Judah. It's reached to Jerusalem's gate!
Everyone writhes, awaiting our fate.
Mourn for your children, you fools. Understand,
in exile your children won't know this land.

Micah 2

Woe to those men who plot evil and steal
the house of our fathers, the fruit of the field.
The Lord says, "Disaster shall fall on the proud.
Calamity shall be rained down on the crowd.
You will be ruined, your land thus divided
like spoils of war. It has been decided."
The false prophets say, "Do not say these things.
Disgrace is not coming."
But that's what God brings.

In all of our wickedness, I understand
that if a deceiver came into our land
and said, "I will prophesy of wine and beer,"
then that's just the prophet for these people here.
But the remnant of Israel will be preserved,
though this is a thing that we do not deserve.
We'll be gathered up, in the way that God said,
and we will march out with the Lord at the head.

Micah 3

Listen you leaders of Jacob who hate
all that is good. When you desecrate
my people, they'll cry out, but they won't be heard,
for they have not followed the Lord's holy word.
But all you false prophets, do not think you've won,
for you'll be disgraced for all that you've done.
The Spirit of God has filled me with power,
and though you're entrenched in Jerusalem's tower,
your money and bribes will not save your souls
when God comes to Zion collecting his tolls.
Like a plow does to earth, Jerusalem will
be flattened and thorns shall grow on Temple Hill.

Micah 4

In the end, God's temple will be recreated
on top of a mountain where He'll be awaited.
Nations will say, "Let us go to the Lord,
and walk in His paths, where He is adored."
He'll settle disputes and He will preside.
Then peace will replace man's murderous pride.
All will have land, and no one shall fear,
when all nations know Him and He has drawn near.
"Then," the Lord says, "I'll gather the lame.
They'll be a great nation. And I'll do the same
for all the exiles and those who know grief.
Jerusalem too shall find its relief.
But Daughter of Zion, I hear your cry.

For now, though, I only can turn a blind eye.
To Babylon you and your children must go,
but one day you will be redeemed from your foes.
For now many nations will gloat at your fall,
but they do not know the Lord's mind at all.
Now though, My children, your suffering increases,
but one day you'll rise and tear them to pieces."

Micah 5

Marshal your troops, for they're setting a siege,
and they'll strike a blow on the face of my liege.
But out of your clans, Judah, one will soon come.
A ruler for Israel. One who is from
the most ancient times, who'll shepherd his sheep.
He'll be their peace, and they'll cease to weep.
Assyria comes and shall rule by the sword.
Though Nimrod has taken you, stay with the Lord,
for He won't leave you, instead He'll command
that all of your foes be placed in your hand.
He'll uproot their idols and Asherah poles,
and they'll be delivered into your control.

Micah 6

Hear everyone, the Lord's accusation
against Israel.
"You once were My nation.
How have I burdened you? I brought you out
of Egypt through Moses, but still you all doubt.
Remember your journey and My righteous acts.
How can you argue against all the facts?"
There isn't an offering we have that could
appease the Lord. Judah seeks evil, not good.
The Lord calls to Israel, "Shall I forgive
the dishonest men or the sinners who live
amongst you? You're violent! You're liars! Therefore,
you all will be ruined by anguish and war.
You'll eat, but be hungry. You'll save, but not gain.

You'll plant, but not harvest. I'll crush all your grain.
You've practiced traditions of Ahab's damnation,
so you'll be the scorn of all foreign nations."

Micah 7

Israel's hunger will soon be at hand.
When all of the godly are swept from the land.
The powerful dictate as they have desired,
in bribes and in gifts. They love to conspire.
You can't trust a neighbor. Your friends all deceive.
Even your wife you cannot believe.
Amongst your own household you'll find enemies.
I wait for my savior. My God will hear me.
Though I am in darkness, God is my light.
I'll bear the Lord's wrath, till I'm in the right.
And all of my enemies that day will fall
under my feet, once and for all.
God, shepherd Your people, all of our number.
Just as in Egypt, You'll show us Your wonders.
Then all of the nations who scoffed at Your name
will fall in the dirt, covered in shame.
There's no other god who has such compassion.
Your anger with us will fade in the fashion
it did with our forefathers, and You'll be true
to the household of Jacob. We trust in You.

cease number protecting blood God carry knows slow
occur
heard till Oh people one desire
save slaves power peace
locusts Nahum strength storm
might
clap things allies deafening Thebes
consuming follows
go Lord fire festivals
lust day lies
army presence cruelty fly like
hearts walls appeased back
Nothing mountains
doors lift away chariots skirt
Soon quake sorceress way
grow
great charges destruction's turned reason
sword
grave shame angered fall jealous gates
holds cavalry dies roar defeat
anger explodes free
Fire's attack Nineveh Woe joy
cry coming
pale name city wrath hears
incur king
let cheer end ground treasure
land blame soon Jacob voice
felt actions covered men Judah gore
Brace longer preparing guilty dust sea
foes whore Assyria cut streets man
pours wounds destroyed greatest smites
shake guards disgust guard fiend
increase completely gather faces
still better everyone fortress Even
fast portend makes cuts
heal although melt nobles
splendor hills

Nahum 1

The Lord is a jealous God who smites His foe.
His power is great, although He is slow
to anger, He won't let the guilty go free.
His way is the storm. He can dry up the sea.
The hills melt away and He makes mountains quake.
In His presence, even the greatest men shake.
When angered, His wrath pours out like a fire,
but He is a refuge for those who desire.
But Nineveh! She is a fiend, and her end
is coming on fast as her actions portend.
Although she has allies, they'll all be cut down
and soon they'll become like the dust on the ground.
The Lord says, "No man will carry her name.
I'm preparing her grave, for she is to blame."
So lift up your festivals, Judah, with joy,
for Nineveh will be completely destroyed.

Nahum 2

Nineveh, guard both your fortress and roads.
Brace yourself before your city explodes!
The splendor of Jacob shall soon be restored
by the might of the army that follows the Lord.
The chariots soon will sweep all through your streets.
Nineveh's walls will fall in defeat.
"Stop!" they will cry, but no one holds back
for her treasure is ours, and in the attack
faces grow pale and hearts melt away.
"I am against you!" the Lord God will say.

He can't be appeased till destruction's occurred,
and the voice of her people no longer is heard.

Nahum 3

Woe to the city of blood and her lies!
The cavalry charges and everyone dies.
The lust of a harlot, that sorceress whore,
is the reason her walls will be covered with gore.
The Lord says, "I'll lift up her skirt so her shame
is synonymous with the disgust of her name."
Are you better than Thebes with her allies and walls?
Even that infamous city could fall.
Her nobles were turned into slaves. So will yours!
The gates of your land are like wide open doors.
Fire's consuming her walls. Soon they'll cease
protecting her people. No one will know peace
till the sword cuts you down. Who can save you that day?
Your guards are like locusts. They'll all fly away.
Oh, king of Assyria, while you still slumber
your foes gather strength as they increase in number.
Nothing will heal the wounds you'll incur,
and everyone who hears the things that occur
will clap and will cheer in a deafening roar.
For who has not felt your cruelty before?

Habakkuk 1

How long must I call to you, Lord, till you hear?
Injustice and wrong surround us in fear.
Destruction and violence and conflict abounds.
The wicked corrupt; the law has no grounds.
But the Lord says, "Now watch, and you'll be amazed.
The Babylon army I'm going to raise.
They'll sweep through the Earth, taking up land
like a law to themselves. This fierce, dreaded band
will swoop and devour their prey like the wind.
They'll scoff at the fortified cities. They'll bend
great kings to their knees. They'll steal and they'll kill.
And all this will happen because it's My will."
O Lord, You appoint them to carry this out.
Why do You give them the power to rout
our people? Your eyes are merciful. Why
are you silent while all of the righteous men die?
You've made men like fish, where the wicked ones hook
us out of the sea. Lord, how can You look
upon all those foes? Lord, would You forget
your people, and keep filling up our foe's net?

Habakkuk 2

Then the Lord told me, "Write down what I say.
This revelation will soon have its day.
And though some will doubt it, it soon will come true,
for though they are mighty, My love is for you.
The righteous man lives like each moment's a test,
but the arrogant foe is never at rest.

He's not satisfied as a king. He desires
to build up the strongest of all the empires.
But he built his city on blood, and they'll say,
'Woe to you, villain, for you'll have your day.'
One day your victims will rise up and wreak
havoc upon you. The ruins shall shriek.
Those you would crush down under your feet
will rise as an army that you can't defeat.
Drink from the cup that the Lord offers you,
for disgrace you'll imbibe. The cup that you drew
is filled with the violence that you brought to bear
all in the name of your god sitting there.
What good is a god carved by a man's hand?
It cannot hear. It cannot understand.
Woe to him who says, 'Wood, take a breath.'
It's mute mouth is metal. It's wood ears are deaf.
But I'm in My temple. I hate all I see
of your violence. The Earth shall be silent for Me."

Habakkuk 3

Lord, I have heard of Your fame and am awed
by all of Your deeds. I pray that my God
would use Your great might, that it may be known.
Your splendor is like the sunlight that's shone.
My God shook the Earth and made nations tremble.
His might made the mountains and seas disassemble.
The deep torrents swept and the waves all rose high
and He crushed the wicked kings whom He despised.
I quake at His might, but I wait here in peace,
for I know our suffering one day will cease.
For now there's no fruit, no harvest, no food,
but God is my savior. He's all that is good.

Zephaniah 1

The word of the Lord came to Zephaniah
while Judah was reigned over by King Josiah.
The Lord says, "I'll wipe the Earth clean until
there's nothing but rubble. This is My will.
I'll stretch out My hand against Judah and those
who destroy what is holy and seek to oppose
My name. Oh Jerusalem! That's where they are.
They worship false idols and bow to the stars.
You who love Molech, the Lord's day draws near.
The kings and their sons should tremble in fear.
They're a sacrifice offered for all of your sins.
Jerusalem, I shall hear wailing within
your walls and your gates. All your merchants shall be
ruined. I'll punish those who turned from Me.
Like those who shout out, as if they've gone mad,
'The Lord can do nothing. Not good and not bad.'
You, the complacent, you will be plundered,
when My fury's pounded and My anger's thundered.
The day of the Lord is near. On that day
you people shall anguish and moan in dismay.
The battle cry sounds, yet you walk around blind.
Your blood and the dust shall soon be combined.
Not silver nor gold shall save or defend
any of you from a terrible end."

Zephaniah 2

You nation of shame! O seek you the Lord!
For time is of value and you can't afford

to wait for forgiveness, so leave your sin's web
in hopes that His anger and fury will ebb.
Your cities shall fall to your greatest of foes.
Success will belong to all those who oppose
the great house of Judah, but it shall fall fast
and turn into pastures. The first shall be last.
The insults of Moab, the Ammonite taunts,
shall surely elicit a mighty response.
The Lord says, "Their land shall turn to a waste.
They'll know I am God, and I won't be disgraced.
The Philistines, Cushites, and Ammonites too
have rejected Me. No, I did not forget you.
You will fall by the sword, and your flocks shall fall down,
and neither of you shall get up from the ground.
Ah, Nineveh! You were a beautiful city.
What a lair of beasts you've become. What a pity,
that I shall knock all of your houses right off
their foundations, so all who pass by you shall scoff."

Zephaniah 3

Woe to the city defiled, and those
who don't heed the Lord. Stay away from such foes!
Her prophets are prideful, her rulers unjust;
her priests are profane, full of greed, full of lust.
Jerusalem, He brings you justice and is
not a wavering God. All that you see is His.
He asks only that we remember His gift
and His covenant. Take up an offering, lift
it up to the Lord.
"I have cut off all nations
who gave in to all the most sinful temptations.
At My indication, each stone and foundation
uprooted itself. And their sick populations
have all been wiped out. Though, surely I thought
they'd come to their senses, they could not be taught.
My jealousy raged, and My anger burned hot.
Without second thought, I destroyed the whole lot.
But I will show mercy to those who are humble.

I cannot speak lies. I won't beg or grumble.
I told you what I want, and still you all stumble.
You who are prideful and sinful shall tumble."
Sing, Israel! Shout aloud and be glad.
For the Lord chose to spare us, although He was mad
at all that we'd done. Bow down at His feet.
Delight in this day and rejoice in the street.
For He shall save us when He says the time's right.
Somehow we found favor in God's holy sight,
and He'll bring us back from our suff'ring one day.
When we deserve mercy, then we shall be saved.

Haggai 1

In the time of King Darius, Haggai was known
as a prophet who said, "This is what the Lord's shown.
The Lord says to those who would say, 'It's not time
to build up the temple,' is it not a crime
to leave the Lord's house a ruin while you
build up your own house? Now give God his due!
And give careful thought to all of your ways.
You plant but don't harvest all that which you raise.
You eat and you drink, but you are not full.
The Lord doesn't just want a lamb or a bull.
Go up, get supplies. Let us build the Lord's house!"
The people obeyed, and did not whine or grouse.
They knew that the prophet was sent by the Lord
and so they got stone and mortar and board
and built up the temple as they were to do.
And through Haggai, God said, "I am with you."

Haggai 2:1 - 2:9

Then God said through Haggai, "People, are there
not those in your numbers whose witness will bear
this temple's inferior? Look to the past.
For this shoddy thing you have built will not last.
Work! And take courage! For when it is done
it will shine as a beacon, just like the sun.
It will not be long until I shake the land
and the glory of this temple will be at hand.
I will bring treasures and I will bring peace
and they will pour into this place without cease.

My glory will be greater than in the past.
Behold, it approaches, so you must work fast."

Haggai 2:10 - 2:23

Then Haggai said, "Go forth and ask of the priests,
if their robe touched bread, is it then in the least
a little bit holy?"
But they replied, "No.
It hasn't been blessed. It is simply cooked dough."
Then Haggai asked them, "But does that then mean
if you touch the dead, that you are unclean?"
"Yes," said the priests.
Then Haggai said, "True!
Things are defiled by that which you do.
The temple does not make you holy, but when
you honor the Lord, you'll be free of your sin.
Now that the temple foundation is laid,
all is forgiven. Your debt has been paid.
All He's held back from you now will be gained.
Go forth and harvest the grapes and the grain.
Though God will soon shake the Earth and the air,
Judah, His precious gem, she will be spared."

Zechariah 1:1 - 1:6

The word of the Lord came to Zechariah,
a prophet of God, son of Berekiah.
"Return to Me," uttered the Lord, "and I will
return to you too, for there is time still.
Don't be like your forefathers. They turned away,
though I sent the prophets to them in their days.
They did not relent until punishment came.
I tell you, My children, do not do the same."

Zechariah 1:7 - 1:21

I had a vision and God was the source.
A man among myrtle trees on a red horse
with red, brown, and white horses standing behind.
"What does this mean?" I asked.
"All mankind
was resting at peace," the man in the trees
said to me. "Lord, please make your decree.
These seventy years, Jerusalem's known
only Your wrath."
The Lord's glory shone.
He spoke to an angel, who then spoke to me.
"The Lord says He's jealous for Zion, but He
will come back and rebuild His temple again.
Prosperity flows where poverty's been."
Four horns appeared, with four craftsmen at hand.
"These horns spread God's people across the whole land,
and these men are going to throw down the nations
whose horns caused the tribes such great lamentations."

Zechariah 2

I looked and a man with a measuring line,
said, "I'll measure Zion, home of God's shrine."
But an angel said, "Tell him those walls will not stand,
for the city is growing and it will expand.
I'll be the border, a wall made of fire,
encircling all as the Lord has required.
For God said, 'Escape from Babylon's land.
Against all who harmed you, I'll raise up My hand.'
Shout and rejoice! I'll live amongst you.
Let all nations know that My covenant's true.
Be still before God, mankind, for He's roused.
He seeks out His favorites, wherever they're housed."

Zechariah 3

And then I saw Joshua, high priest who stood
in front of the angel. Although he was good,
Satan stood next to him, set to accuse,
but God would not let him berate or abuse.
The angel changed Joshua's filthy clothes to
the richest of garments, and then he said, "You
have been purified. Go forth! Keep the ways
of the Lord and you'll govern His house all your days.
Listen, high priest, the stone the Lord set
shall now be inscribed, so none may forget.
The stone is set right in Joshua's way.
He'll cleanse the land's sin in one single day."

Zechariah 4

The Lord put a lamp stand in front of my eyes
with seven lights on it. I could not devise
what this symbolized. Two olive trees then
appeared at each side where the lamp stand had been.
"This," said the angel, "is what the Lord planned
as Israel's path to return to their land.

By the Spirit, not might, shall Israel roam
free through the desert and back to their home.
Zerubabbel has laid the foundation. His hands
will finish God's temple. Again it shall stand.
The olive trees symbolize two who will serve
the Lord so His holy name shall be preserved."

Zechariah 5 - 6

I saw a scroll flying.
"What is it you see?"
"A great flying scroll!"
Then the angel told me,
"That's a curse on the land, for the liars and thieves
shall be banished from here. No man who deceives
can live in Jerusalem."
Then in the air
was a basket, and I asked, "What is that up there?"
"Iniquity that has been spread through the land.
Let's open the basket, and you'll understand."
As he pulled back the cover, I could not believe
that a woman lay there, but I could not conceive
what the meaning might be.
"She is wickedness. She
shall be buried in Babylon."
Flying at me
were angels with powerful wings and they bore
the basket away and I saw it no more.
Four chariots came from two bronze mountain peaks.
And again I was shocked, and I could not speak.
One's horses were red, one's black, and one's white,
and the fourth set were dappled.
"The spirits alight.
These are the spirits God sent out to stand
at the corners of Earth."
Then they flew from the land.
Then the word of God said, "Take silver and gold
from the exiles. Melt it, then fashion and mold

a crown made for Joshua, branch of the tree.
He'll rebuild the temple, so all men may see."

Zechariah 7 - 8

In the fourth year of Darius, men asked the Lord,
"Shall we fast in the fifth month as we've done before?"
And the Lord said, "Did you really fast for My sake?
Or was all your pious behavior just fake?
Do you not listen? I've told you to seek
to show mercy to all of the ones who are weak.
But you hardened your hearts and you stopped up your ears,
which is why you were exiled so many years!
I am jealous for Zion. In her I shall dwell.
The streets shall be packed, and all shall be well.
Though you are amazed, I am not, for I sent
you into exile till you would repent.
Now I send you back, so build up again
My temple. So go and prepare yourselves, men.
For the vine shall yield fruit, and the people shall be
a blessing, as they are the root of My tree.
Let the feasts in My name be a time of great joy
for each man and woman, each girl and each boy.
Let My praises be sung, so on foreigners' shores,
they say, "Let us follow this God that is yours."

Zechariah 9

The word of the Lord's against Hadrach and Tyre.
And Hamath and Sidon will perish in fire.
They've gathered up treasures like dust in the streets,
but Ashdod and Gaza shall suffer defeats.
The Lord shall defend His house from their force,
and Israel's foes shall know that the source
of their suffering and their defeat is the Lord.
For all of their trespasses, death's their reward.
Rejoice, Israel, for your king and salvation
comes on a donkey with peace for the nations.

He'll rule to the ends of the Earth, and you'll be
secure in your hope, for you'll be set free.

Zechariah 10

The Lord brings the rain and the clouds in the spring.
The ruler-creator has made everything.
Diviners see visions that lie. People groan
and cry to their gods made of wood or of stone.
"My anger is fierce, for the leaders deceive,"
the Lord says, "for Judah has turned, so I grieve.
I'll punish her liars and then lift her up.
She'll be born anew. From Me she will sup.
Though I scattered My people, to Me they'll return.
On that day My anger will no longer burn.
They've passed through the surging sea of despair,
but when they seek Me, they'll find I am there."

Zechariah 11

The Lord told me, "Pasture the flock marked for slaughter.
For soon I will hand every son and each daughter
over to those who'll oppress everyone
for all the abuses My people have done."
So I took up two staffs named Union and Favor.
The flock hated me and their holiness wavered,
so the staff I called Favor I broke, and revoked
my covenant with them. My fury was stoked.
I said, "Pay my wages, if you should see fit.
For I was the shepherd." They paid me for it.
Thirty pieces of silver…the price of a slave!
The Lord said, "Go now and give all that they gave
to the Potter."
Then into the House of the Lord
to the Potter I threw my silver reward.
I broke my staff, Union, and God said, "They mock
the Lord, so the next shepherd shall eat the flock."

Zechariah 12

The Lord says, "When all of the nations rise up,
Jerusalem shall be a great shining cup.
And she shall be saved, and Judah as well,
so all know within her the Lord's glory dwells.
On David's house I'll send a spirit of grace.
They'll look to Me, and they shall all see the place
they pierced Me. They'll cry as if mourning a son.
Each clan and each house will regret what they've done."

Zechariah 13 - 14

"On that day a fountain shall flow forth and clean
the sin from the nation. All that is obscene,
the idols and prophets who lie, I'll destroy
and a new sense of holiness all shall employ."
A day is approaching when nations shall fight
Jerusalem, taking her off in the night.
But the Lord will then come to your aid and you'll know
that only through Him may peace be bestowed.
A unique day will come, without nighttime or day.
You'll be left in darkness and filled with dismay.
As evening arrives, then you'll see a light,
a beautiful radiance, burning and bright.
Then fresh living water, that all men love best,
shall flow to the east and flow to the west.
And the Lord will rule over the whole of the Earth,
for out of Him all that we see had its birth.
Then the nations who fought with Jerusalem will
rise up against one another and kill.
But those who survive shall bow down and pray
to the Lord for they'll know He is King on that day.

cast

cared great tree

tithes Jacob

faithful honor

ask made

may know left

little change led

fire

3:6 Malachi

bear cause

cheat first bring word bursts

honored offerings messenger rotted fruit

world poured man sun therefore laid

loved love broken

greatest see cleansing spoke dares

worthy men treat covenant God

law give blessings gods

bother serve vines

sick soon evil though

fall futile Judah curse

cursed root hate lift branch

weary

stain finger side

steal Though burn Esau 3:5 Father

Tween offer worship diseased mine

foe refresh nothing place life

Now 2:9

live day inside support

Israel's mate send incense

one approaches desert

still Elijah

priest naught spouse scythes beasts

kin foreign house name beast

husband peace prophet Lord's

gates prayed away utterly Edom

look Heaven's purify souls

forth pleased priests wind faith

frauds remain vanquish flesh

woman divorce

open offend hearts way

stand offense sinned

oracle swept

low

Lord

Malachi 1 - 2:9

As an oracle, Malachi spoke the Lord's word
for all of the world and this they all heard.
"I've loved you," the Lord said.
"How?" you retort.
"'Tween Esau and Jacob, did I not support
your side and curse Esau? I left his line naught
but the desert. Now look and see all that you've got.
Though Edom rebuilds, it shall all be laid low.
For Israel's mine and I'll vanquish her foe.
But where is the honor that's due to the Father?
I ask for so little, but still you won't bother
to lift up one finger to glorify Me.
Your sacrifice beasts are sick and can't see.
Would you offer a beast such as that to your kin?
Then why offend Me again and again?
Your offerings offer up only offense!
Do not cheat the Lord. Don't burn your incense.
"You priests, I have cursed all the blessings you give,
for in your hearts I know My name does not live.
I'm not just a word. I bring life. I bring peace.
If you cause men to stumble, then you are no priest."

Malachi 2:10 - 3:5

Judah, you've broken His faith and you've made
the great house of worship where we have all prayed
a detestable place as you've loved foreign gods.
You are led by the priests. They're the greatest of frauds.
As the Lord made a woman and man of one flesh,

your love should be faithful, your love should refresh
your spouse. But the Lord says, "I utterly hate
divorce and the husband who beats on his mate."
So why do you treat the Lord as a spouse
not worthy to be with you inside His house?
You weary the Lord when you say He is pleased
by the evil you do. Your hearts are diseased.
"I'll send you My messenger," God says, "You'll see
the one who prepares the way before Me.
He'll soon purify what has rotted away.
And which of you dares stand before him that day?"

Malachi 3:6 - 4

"I do not change, therefore you remain.
My covenant lives, though you are a stain.
You steal from Me! 'How?' you may ask. In your tithes!
You don't give the first off your vines or your scythes.
If you did, all the gates would be cast open wide
so that all Heaven's blessings poured forth from inside.
You say it is futile to serve Me at all.
The good shall be cared for; the evil shall fall.
The day soon approaches where those who have sinned
shall be swept away with the fire and wind.
The stubble shall burn. Not a branch or a root
of their tree shall remain; nothing left to bear fruit.
For those who have honored My name, the sun bursts
over you, cleansing you. You shall be first.
So remember My law, and know I shall send
the prophet Elijah so your souls may mend."

THE NEW TESTAMENT

Matthew 1

From Abraham's line, through David it wove,
from all the way back within Eden's grove
to a stable in Bethlehem where he was born,
Jesus the Christ; the Messiah adorned.
His mother, Mary, was pledged to a man
named Joseph. Before their marriage began
the Spirit came to her and blessed her with child,
for she was so faithful, honest, and mild.
When Joseph found out, he inwardly groaned,
then sought to dismiss her, for she would be stoned
if he brought a charge. But then in a dream
an angel said, "Joseph, things aren't as they seem.
Mary is blessed! Go and make her your wife,
for the Spirit has given her God's spark of life.
She is a virgin, still wonderfully pure.
This is the word of the Lord, so be sure
that all I will tell you is true. Yes, God's son,
Emmanuel, Jesus, sent for everyone."
He awoke and did all that the angel had said,
but until the birth, Mary stayed from his bed.

Matthew 2

Just after Jesus was born in the town
of Bethlehem, Herod who ruled as the crown
was visited by the Magi who came
asking him, "Where is the one of acclaim!"
"What do you mean?"
"The king of the Jews.

We saw his star shining, so we came to you."
Herod was king, and he was concerned.
He said in response, "Tell me all that you've learned."
"Judea will give us a savior, it's told,
in Israel. That's who we seek to behold."
So Herod said, "Travel and see if it's true,
so I may bow down and worship him too."
So they went along and followed the star.
They found him and said, "We have come from afar.
This is the Lord whom the prophets foretold."
Then they gave him gifts of frankincense, gold
and myrrh. In a dream, they learned Herod sought
to kill the boy king, and swore they would not
go back to report. So then they set out
to their home nations by a circuitous route.
After they left there, Joseph beheld
a dream where an angel said, "Go! Be compelled
to flee south to Egypt, so Herod can't find
the boy. Leave no sign of his birth behind."
When Herod had learned that the Magi had fled,
he cursed them and went to his soldiers and said,
"Let every boy under the age of two die."
Then out of Judea there came a great cry.
And so Joseph waited in Egypt with Mary
and Jesus until they heard Herod was buried.
An angel said, "Go, and return to the land
of Israel."
Joseph obeyed its command.
But Herod's son still was in power, so they
did not go to Judea. Instead they would stay
in Nazareth, just as the prophets had seen,
when they said, 'The Christ shall be called Nazarene.'

Matthew 3

A man, John the Baptist, told all who would hear,
"Repent, for the kingdom of Heaven is near!
Prepare the way! Make straight the path for the Lord."
He wore camel hair tied up with a cord.

The Pharisees and all the Sadducees came.
John cried, "You vipers! What will you claim?
That you were from Abraham? You should desire
an honest life lest you be cast in the fire.
I baptize, but one who is greater than I
will baptize with God's Holy Spirit. I cry
for the souls of all people, that you might be saved
by honoring him and his holy way."
Then Jesus came out to the Jordan where he
sought to be baptized, but John said, "By me?
I should be baptized by you, for I know
where you have come from and where you must go."
"Baptize me," Jesus said.
When it was done
the heavens were opened. "This is My son,"
a voice said from Heaven and flowed through the breeze.
"I love My son greatly. With him I am pleased."

Matthew 4:1 - 4:11

Jesus went into the desert to fast.
The Devil appeared and said, "You won't last.
You're hungry. If you are God's son," the Beast said,
"then turn all of these stones into loaves of bread."
Jesus said, "As it is written and known,
man needs God's word, and not bread alone."
Satan just laughed and in a great fire
they both flew and perched on Jerusalem's spire.
Satan told Jesus, "As you surely know,
God will send angels to catch you, so throw
yourself from this height. Your Father knows best."
"It's written," Christ said, "that no one's to test
the Lord."
"Where is He?!" the Devil screamed out.
"Why doesn't He just show His face? Don't you doubt?
But, lo, I have come here in person, you see.
All you need do is just bow down to me."
Then in a flash, they were up at a height
where all of the world was now in their sight.

"This can be yours. Just say you're *my* son."
"Away from me, Satan! The Lord God is one!
I worship Him only. And you are a fraud.
This Earth is not yours to give. It is God's!"
Quick as he came, the Devil was gone,
and angels attended to Christ in the dawn.

Matthew 4:12 - 4:25

Jesus returned, for John was in jail,
and so that the word of the Lord would prevail,
he shouted aloud, so it would be clear,
"Repent, for the kingdom of Heaven is near!"
While he was out, he happened to see
two men who were fishing. He said, "Follow me,
and I'll make you both into fishers of men."
They set down their nets, right there and right then.
The first was called Peter, and Andrew, his brother.
They hadn't gone far when they spied another
set of two brothers, and Christ called to them.
They too stopped their fishing to go follow him.
The first was named James. His brother was John,
and they followed him as Jesus led on.
They went to the synagogues preaching good news.
Many came to him and none were refused.
Those who were ill and those with disease
sought out this man who cured them with ease.
People from all of the Middle East came
to hear what this Nazarene man would proclaim.

Matthew 5:1 - 5:16

Jesus sat down on a mountainside where
he said, "Hear me, people, so you are aware.
Blessed are those whose spirit is poor,
for they hold the key to unlock Heaven's door.
Blessed are those who mourn, for they'll be
comforted. God will attend to their plea.
Blessed are all of the meek, who'll inherit

the Earth, not with gold, but on their own merit.
Blessed are those who hunger and thirst
for righteousness. They will be filled by God first.
Blessed are those who are merciful, for
they'll be show mercy if they should implore.
Blessed are those who are pure in their hearts,
for they will see God, and He won't depart.
Blessed are those who are peacemakers, they
are called sons of God and honored today.
Blessed are those persecuted for God,
for theirs is the kingdom, and Heaven shall laud.
And blessed are you when you are disgraced,
insulted, and people have spit on your face
for following me and all that I do.
In Heaven there's honor and glory for you.
You are the salt of the earth, are you not?
When salt loses saltiness, what have you got?
Salt cannot ever be salty again.
It's thrown on the ground and trampled by men.
You're the light of the world, placed on a hill.
It cannot be hidden, but must be fulfilled.
No one would place a lamp under a bowl.
It's placed on a stand, so all may behold
a light in their house. The same shall be so
with you. Be the light wherever you go!"

Matthew 5:17 - 5:48

Jesus continued, "I haven't been sent
to strike down the law. That's not my intent.
I'm fulfilling the law and prophecy too!
When I tell you things, you'll know that it's true.
Those who teach others to break His commands
insult what is holy and what God demands.
Surely no person will hold Heaven's keys
unless they're more righteous than our Pharisees.
They say, 'Do not murder,' but what about hate?
The hateful shall share in the murderer's fate.
Settle your issues as soon as you can

so you don't detest your own fellow man.
You're told that adultery's evil to do,
but lust in your thinking's adultery too.
Pluck out a lusty eye! You can afford
to lose body parts, but don't lose the Lord.
What of divorce? If she has been true,
divorce makes adulterers of both of you.
And they say each man should do as they swear,
but oaths are said carelessly. Men should beware!
Let 'yes' be yes, and let 'no' be no,
and don't swear on anything God has bestowed.
You have all heard, 'an eye for an eye.'
Fie on that rubbish! That foolishness, fie!
If a man strikes your cheek, then offer the other
in love to be struck, for he is your brother.
If someone would force you to travel one mile,
go two for your brother. Do so with a smile.
Don't love your friend, but then hate your foe.
Pray for your enemies, that they may know
the true love of God, and see it in you.
Seek to be loving in all that you do."

Matthew 6:1 - 6:15

"If charity's done so you can be seen,
then God sees your actions and finds them obscene.
Give to the needy in secret and quiet.
What your right hand does, let the left one deny it.
Don't be a hypocrite when you're at prayer,
do it for God, not men who are there.
Others may pray with numerous words,
but God knows what you need before you are heard.
Pray in this way, 'O Father above,
Your great name is holy, Your kingdom is love.
Help us do here what You'd do in Heaven,
and give us this bread regardless of leaven.
Forgive us our sins as we forgive those
who've sinned against us and whom we've called foes.
Lead us not into temptation, but then

keep us from evil. Amen, God, Amen!'
Stay true to this prayer, and you'll realize
that you must be cleansed before the Lord's eyes.
Before you can be forgiven, you must
forgive all your foes, for our Lord is just."

Matthew 6:16 - 6:34

"Listen, my friends, and let me be clear.
When you are fasting, don't grunt or sneer.
Be secret about it, false martyrs aren't true.
Your fasting's between God the Father and you.
Don't store up all of your treasures on Earth
where they may be stolen, where they have no worth.
Store up your treasures in Heaven above,
for where your heart is, so also there's love.
No one can serve two masters, so choose:
money or God, and do not confuse
one with the other, for that is despair.
The Lord sees your gold, but he does not care.
So, truly, don't worry! For God's always there.
The Lord watches over the birds of the air.
And God's love for you is so much more rife!
Worry won't add one more hour to life.

Matthew 7

"Do not judge others," Jesus said, "lest
you be judged as well. Do you know what's best?
Before you remove a speck from the eye
of your brother, perhaps you ought to have pried
the log out of yours. Hypocrites moan
on the faults of their brothers, but don't see their own.
If what is holy, to beasts you impart,
they'll trample them first, then tear you apart.
Ask and it's given. Seek and you'll find.
Knock and the door will be opened in kind.
Do unto others as you'd have them do
to you. This is law, and God's law is true."

Then Jesus told them, "Beware of the gate
that's wide, for that one will lead you to hate.
But enter the one where few men have been,
and you'll find what's rare and keeps you from sin.
Beware of false prophets. You'll know when you see
such fools, for good fruit is picked from good trees.
Bad trees are cut down and thrown in the fire.
Some who cry out to the Lord don't desire
to worship our God as they truly should.
They never knew me, for they did no good.
'We prophesied for you,' to me they will say,
but from Heaven's gate, they'll be cast away.
Lo, those who build their house on my rock
shall know that they've built on the most solid stock.
But build on the sand of those who have lied,
and your house will be swept away with the tide."
The crowds who had heard were amazed as they broke,
for he had authority each time he spoke.
Jesus had shamed all the priests with his words
and all were in awe at the things they had heard.

Matthew 8

As Jesus came down from the mountainside speech,
a leprous man fell down and knelt at his feet.
"Lord, if you're willing, I beg heal me now."
"Son, you are healed, but do not say how."
Once in Capernaum, a soldier of Rome
said, "Jesus, I have a good servant at home.
He's so deathly ill."
"Come, show me the way."
The soldier responded, "Jesus, just say
the word and he'll heal. I'm unworthy of you.
I'm a centurion. That's what I do.
I order my men about with commands,
but I have no power to issue demands
of you and your greatness."
"I tell you true,
throughout all of Israel, friend, only you

have faith such as this. In days yet to come,
men who are arrogant will be struck dumb.
They will not join at Abraham's feast.
There will be weeping and gnashing of teeth.
Go, faithful servant, for your servant's cured.
Your faith has been honest, and your heart is pure."
Then Jesus went in with Simon (that's Peter),
whose mother-in-law was ill with a fever.
He cured her, and then Jesus cured many more,
just as Isaiah had said long before,
'He cured the diseases of all the infirmed.'
And so the great prophecy now was confirmed.
The crowds gathered 'round to see what he'd show,
and one man said, "I'll follow you where you go."
"Foxes have holes as their home," Jesus said,
"But where can the Son of Man lay down his head?"
To escape all the crowds, they found him a boat.
The twelve then joined Jesus and started to float.
A storm blew the sea up around them. The swells
nearly capsized them. Not one felt too well,
except Jesus, sleeping, and so with a frown
they woke him up shouting, "We're all going to drown!"
"Such little faith!" he said. "Do you fear?"
He waved at the waves saying, "Get out of here."
The storm quickly calmed. The men said, "Yahweh
is with him! For even the winds must obey!"
When he had arrived at the sea's other side,
two men possessed by demons were spied
and they were so violent, that no one could pass.
They said, "Son of Man, would you now harass
us demons?"
"Be gone now from my friends and I!"
Then they were sent into a pigsty nearby.
The pigs then all ran and fell into the sea
and died so the demons could not be set free.
The men who'd been tending the pigs ran to town
and told them why all of the pigs had just drowned.
The people from town came to them then to plead
that Jesus leave now, with the greatest of speed.

Matthew 9:1 - 9:8

So Jesus went back to his town and some men
asked, "Lord, will you please see our paralyzed friend?"
The man on the mat just looked up and stared.
"Take heart. Be forgiven."
The teachers declared,
"It's blasphemy! Only the Lord may forgive."
Jesus asked, "Why don't you want him to live?
Forgiveness is easier than saying, 'Go.
Walk now, my son.' But so that you know
the Son of Man comes to forgive a man's sins,
get up, my son, and walk once again."
The man then stood up and started to walk
while all of the crowd stood silent, in shock.

Matthew 9:9 - 9:13

Jesus left and as he passed a tax booth,
he told the man there, "I tell you the truth,
follow me and you'll gain much more than here."
And so Matthew gave up his taxing career.
Then Matthew asked Jesus to come in and eat
with him so his friends could come there and meet
the Messiah. But when all the Pharisees saw,
they said, "Jesus scoffs and curses the law.
Look at this man who dines amongst sin."
On hearing this, Jesus said, "Doctors treat men
who are sick, not the healthy. So let me be clear.
I want mercy, not sacrifice. That's why I'm here."

Matthew 9:14 - 9:38

Disciples of John asked Jesus, "Why do
the Pharisees fast, but still we see you
eating?"
So Jesus said, "Should the guests mourn
while the groom's here? How they'll be forlorn

once the groom's taken. On that day they'll fast.
I have not come for the things that have passed.
If new wine is poured in old wineskins, they'll burst.
The new wine must go in the new wineskins first."
As Jesus confused John's disciples, a man
approached him and said, while taking his hand,
"Lord, my heart breaks. My daughter has died,
but if you will come, you can give her new life."
"Show me," he said. Away they both strode
when suddenly someone touched Jesus' robe
right on the hem. He turned and he peered
at a woman who'd suffered and bled for twelve years.
"If I touched your cloak, I knew I'd be healed,"
she muttered. The woman fell down and she kneeled.
"Take heart," Jesus said, "Your faith has ensured
your healing's complete, for your heart is pure."
Then Jesus went onward to where the man stayed,
and into the room where the dead daughter lay.
Jesus said, "What is this? Why was I brought?
This girl is asleep! Not dead, as you thought."
The crowd started laughing at him for they saw
the girl was a corpse. He made them withdraw,
and when the crowd left, he lifted her hand.
The girl then arose. News spread through the land.
"He healed her!" they murmured, "She's raised from the dead."
Two blind men found Jesus. "Please heal us," they said.
He took them indoors and asked, "Do you think
I can help the blind see? Let you gaze? Let you wink?"
"Of course," they replied.
"Then it shall be done.
But when they ask how, don't tell anyone."
The blind who now saw, told everyone, though.
Then more people came and they wanted to know
if they could be cured. A mute man was brought
to Jesus, who cured him, which made crowds distraught.
The Pharisees cried, "This man is a fiend!
A demon who does the unholy; unclean."
But still the crowds came, with hope bursting forth.
Sheep with no shepherd. A vagabond sort.

The disciples were gathered, and Jesus said, "You
see a harvest of plenty, but the workers are few.
Though we have compassion, the crowds are too large.
We must send out workers with this as their charge.
The Lord of the harvest has sent to His field
his workers, so all who have need may be healed."

Matthew 10

He gave the disciples the power to seize
and drive out a demon, and heal men's disease.
The twelve were called Peter, John, Matthew, and two
were called James, Philip, Simon, and also Andrew,
Bartholomew, Thaddeus, Thomas, then one
called Judas, who would turn his back on God's son.
He said, "Do not go to the Gentiles now,
for Israel needs you, and I've shown you how.
Tell them the kingdom of Heaven is near.
Heal, raise the dead, cleanse the lepers. Don't fear,
you've freely received, so now freely give.
Take nothing with you that you need to live.
For the worker will earn his keep as he goes.
You'll find hospitality's given to those
who do the Lord's work. But if in a town,
the people hate you, kick the dust of the ground
from your sandals and then take your leave from that place.
Gomorrah and Sodom will know greater grace
than that town when Judgment Day finally comes.
You're sheep among wolves! Be snakes among doves.
Be careful of men, for mistrust will mount.
They'll flog you and publicly curse my account,
but when you're arrested, you'll know what to say
for the Spirit will speak through your mouth on that day.
People rebel and brothers betray.
Stand firm in your faith as you go on your way.
I tell you the truth, you won't make it through
all of the cities I'm sending you to
before the day's here when the Son of Man comes
for time doesn't walk in our work, friends, it runs.

So don't be afraid. There's nothing concealed
that when the time comes will not be revealed.
What I whisper to you, shout out from on high,
and do not fear death, for the soul cannot die.
Rather fear God, who can send you to hell,
so that He may know you and think of you well.
Sparrows are bought for a penny a pair.
By God's will alone do they fly through the air.
Know this my friends, if God so loves them,
you're worth more than thousands of sparrows to Him.
In public, whoever acknowledges me,
so I will acknowledge in Heaven, but see
that those who deny me are also denied
by He who's my Father. They'll be swept aside.
Do not suppose I have come to bring peace!
I come with a sword, and I shall increase
division in families as it was foretold
in Micah's great text. The new is made old.
Fathers, if you love your children above
my name you're not worthy of my gracious love.
And anyone who doesn't take up their cross
and follow me shows me that their heart is lost.
Whoever finds his life, will lose it, you see.
To find life you must seek to lose it for me.
He who loves you, loves me and the Lord.
In serving you, that man will gain his reward.

Matthew 11

John the Baptist was locked up in prison,
and so his disciples set out on a mission.
When they found Jesus, they said, "Tell us true.
Are you the one or is there one after you?"
"Go back to John," Jesus said, "and then say,
the blind see, the deaf hear, the dead have been raised."
And as they were leaving, a crowd gathered round
and Jesus said, "Why did you seek to go down
to the desert? To visit a prophet? If so,
then you have seen me. It's written, you know,

that a messenger shall make the way for the one.
The Baptist has laid out the way for the Son.
It shall be said that in our generation
the festival came but without celebration.
Although there is food and wine, many call
us gluttons and drunks though the greatest of all
was amongst them. The invite has gone through the land.
But we shall be judged, for we understand
that collectors of taxes and sinners need more
assistance in finding the way of the Lord.
Those who judge us by our company kept
do not understand that the Lord will accept
all His lost children and welcome them home.
For He watches all, wherever they roam.
Woe to the cities who did not heed all
of my miracles. Pride will soon be your fall,
for Sodom would still stand if I had gone there.
Surely their days will end in despair.
Father, I thank You. You opened the eyes
of the children, but to all the men who are wise
You've hardened their hearts. They can't see Your ways.
Let all who are downtrodden offer You praise!
Only the Son knows the Father. Through him
the Lord's light shall overcome all that is dim.
Come to me, you who are weary. Take rest.
For my yoke is easy, and you shall be blessed."

Matthew 12:1 - 12:21

On the Sabbath, Jesus and his friends picked grain
from a flourishing field and ate. With disdain,
the Pharisees cried, "You have broken the law."
Jesus asked, "Why is your righteousness flawed?
Didn't King David eat bread that was blessed?
Yet God was not angry with him or distressed.
One greater than our holy temple is here!
You don't understand what I'm saying, I fear.
I do not seek justice, but mercy instead!
The Son of Man and the Lord's Sabbath are wed."

Leaving there, Jesus then came to a man
with a shriveled up limb.
"If you heal his hand,
you'll break Sabbath law."
"Now everyone hear!"
Jesus said, "Listen, so that I am clear.
If a lamb fell and was trapped in a pit
on the Sabbath day, would you not take hold of it
and lift it back out? How much more are you
loved by the Lord? It's okay to do
good things on the Sabbath. Now stretch out your arm."
He healed him, but all of the priests sought to harm
Jesus and have him arrested and killed,
but Jesus withdrew till all was fulfilled.
And Jesus kept healing all those whom he could,
showing the people that God's will was good.

Matthew 12:22 - 12:37

Jesus went forth and healed a blind mute
possessed by a demon. The priests were astute
and sought to accuse him.
"Do you not see?
This man is Beelzebub! That is how he
is able to cast demons out. He is one!"
The priests hadn't understood what he had done.
Jesus said, "If there's a kingdom divided
against itself, it cannot stand. I've provided
my services so the Lord's kingdom may find
its way to this Earth and work here in kind.
He who's not with me, is surely against
my ways. I tell you that every offense
will now be forgiven, except for the sins
that are done to the Spirit. I tell you again,
a tree with good fruit on its branches shall be
remembered as good, for that's how a tree
is judged, by its fruit. For a good man brings out
good things whenever he opens his mouth.

And by your own words, I tell all you men,
that you'll be acquitted or you'll be condemned."

Matthew 12:38 - 12:50

Some Pharisees said, "Jesus, give us a sign."
And Jesus replied, "By your wicked design,
none shall be given to you, except one.
The sign Jonah gave you shall now be outdone.
As Jonah spent three nights inside of the girth
of a whale, so the Son of Man shall in the earth
reside for three days. As Nineveh did,
will you now repent, and in doing so rid
yourselves of your sin? For a greater one than
Jonah has come; the true Son of Man."
Then Jesus was told that his family was waiting
outside as he sat inside still debating.
But Jesus said, "Who is of my family tree?
My disciples and friends who sit here with me.
For those who live lives for the Lord are my mother,
and those who are kind are my sister and brother."

Matthew 13

Later that day, Jesus went to the shore
of the Galilee. People came out to adore
and listen to him.
He said, "A man sows
some seed on the ground to watch the plants grow.
Some fell on the rocks where the soil was thin.
It sprouted, but its roots just couldn't sink in.
The sun scorched the plants until they were dead.
Some fell amongst thorns. They couldn't be fed.
But some fell on good soil. Those seeds grew tall
and flourished, producing a crop to feed all.
He who has ears, let him hear."
His friends said,
"Jesus, why can't you speak clearly instead?"
He said, "All the secrets are yours, but you still

do not hold the keys to His kingdom or will.
Though seeing, they're blind. Though hearing, they're deaf.
Their hearts are now calloused, and they are bereft.
If they would just turn, I'd heal them. You are
blessed, for you see, and your vision is far.
If you don't understand my parable, hear!
If one hears God's word, but still is not clear
on meaning, when trouble arrives his faith dies.
Seeds in the thorns will never survive.
So shall the faith of the man who's concerned
by the world and all of the pressures that burned
his soul. But all those who do understand
produce a crop greater than one single man.
The kingdom of Heaven's like one who sowed seeds,
but his enemy filled up his garden with weeds.
The servants asked him, 'Do you think that we should
pull up the weeds?'
'You'll pull up the good
crops right along with the weeds. It's too late.
When harvest arrives, then we'll separate
the wheat from the weeds. We'll keep the good crop,
but weeds we shall burn. Their fire won't stop."
Then Jesus told them, "A mustard seed's small,
but it grows to be the largest of all
the plants in the garden. So in this same way
is the kingdom of Heaven. Hear what I say.
Just one bit of yeast that's worked through the dough
will make the bread rise."
Thus it was so
as the prophet had said, 'Secrets are heard
in my parable tales. These most holy words.'
His friends said, "Explain."
And so he replied
in private, "The good seed, the Lord will provide.
The kingdom is just like a treasure that's found
by a man. He buries it deep in the ground.
He takes all he has and buys up that field,
knowing already what that land shall yield.
God's kingdom is just like a merchant who finds

a pearl that's beautiful, he doesn't mind
mortgaging all to own it. Do you
understand all that I tell you is true?
As a fisherman pulls up his net and casts back
all of the bad fish, seeing they lack
in richness, so too is the way that God will
throw back all the wicked who did not fulfill
His law."
Then he got up and went to the town
where he had grown up. The crowd gathered round,
but as they heard him, they said, "We all know
you, Jesus. You have nothing new you can show.
We know your whole family, for they all live here."
They acted insulted.
"Isn't it clear
that a prophet's not welcome when he returns home.
Though he speaks the truth, the truth won't be known."

Matthew 14

Herod had killed John the Baptist, but when
he heard about Jesus, he said to his friends,
"Is this John the Baptist come back from the dead?
He preaches, though I had men cut off his head."
When Jesus was told of his cousin's demise,
he tried to escape from the crowd's prying eyes.
They followed him, though. He took pity, so
he healed all the sick.
The disciples said, "Go!
We can't feed you people."
But Jesus said, "Wait.
There's enough for the people to fill up their plate."
"Jesus," they said, "we have five loaves of bread
and two fish in total."
"Do just as I said."
He broke the bread, giving his thanks to God, then
the disciples fed all of the five thousand men,
plus women and children. The people all passed it.
And when the disciples collected the basket

it held more than when they had started, so they
were amazed with what they had seen happen that day.
When each man was satisfied, Jesus dismissed
the crowd. Then he told all his friends, "I insist
that you take the boat. Do not wait for me.
I must pray, but soon I will come 'cross the sea
and join you."
When night fell, he still was on shore.
The disciples were worried about Jesus, for
a storm had whipped up and the waves were now quite
alarming. Then suddenly out of the night
came a specter that walked across all of the waves.
"Oh no, it's a ghost," they cried out. "The grave
approaches."
"Be calm, it is I," Jesus said.
"Then call to me, Lord," cried Peter.
The dread
had filled him, until Jesus said, "Come to me."
So Peter stepped out and onto the sea.
He took a few steps, his fear increased and
he started to sink.
"Lord, please take my hand!"
"Do you have no faith? Why did you doubt?"
He took Simon Peter, and pulled the man out.
They entered the boat, and the men cried aloud,
"You are the Son of the Lord!" as they bowed.
They all went ashore, and then they revealed
his glory. All who came to Jesus were healed.

Matthew 15

Some Pharisees asked Jesus, "Why don't your friends
all wash when they eat? Are they unclean men?"
Jesus responded, "Why do you tell
our children to violate God's law as well?
They dishonor their parents. Isaiah spoke true.
Your worship is vain. It's not God, it is you
whom you try to honor. A man commits sin
by what comes from his mouth, not what goes in."

The disciples said, "Jesus, you have offended
the Pharisees."
"Not one of them has defended
the Word of the Lord. If the blind lead the blind,
together they'll fall in the pit, thus entwined."
A Canaanite woman began to cry out.
Begging for help, she started to shout,
"My daughter's possessed by a demon."
"Move on,"
the disciples warned her. "Go woman, be gone!"
But Jesus told them, "I was sent here to be
a shepherd to those who are lost and need me."
Kneeling, he said, "It's not right to throw bread
that is meant for the children to canines instead."
"Yes, Lord," she said, "but dogs eat the crumbs
that fall when the master is eating."
"You come
with the greatest of faith, woman! Go now and find
your daughter restored to her right state of mind."
Having healed her, Jesus went to a field
on a mountainside. Hundreds had come to be healed.
Jesus told all his disciples, "Let's feed
these four thousand people, for they are in need.
They've traveled such distances, they are all weak."
The disciples said, "Jesus, of what do you speak?
We have seven loaves of bread and some fish.
Barely enough for one family's dish."
"Bring them to me," Jesus said. He gave thanks
to the Lord and then gave it to all on the banks
of Galilee. More than four thousand ate and
were satisfied. All of this came by God's hand.

Matthew 16

The Pharisees and all the Sadducees went
to Jesus and said, "Let us know you were sent
by God. Just show us a sign."
In disgust,
Jesus said, "You see the sky and you trust

that you can discern today's weather, but still
you don't see the signs of the times, but you will."
Then Jesus left them, for they were all blind
to the fact that he'd come to save all mankind.
He got in a boat that his friends had prepared
and said to them, "I tell you all to beware
of these hypocrites we call our teachers and priests.
Be on your guard when they offer their yeast."
His friends were confused, saying, "We have no bread."
"Did you not listen to what I just said?
I can feed hillsides. I speak of the way
that priests fool the people and lead them astray."
When they had arrived at their next destination,
Jesus asked, "If you asked those in this nation
'Who is the Son of Man?' what would they say?"
Peter replied, "If you asked them today,
they might say the Baptist, or others Elijah.
Or one of the prophets, perhaps Jeremiah."
Then Jesus said, "Who do you say that I am?"
"The Messiah," said Peter.
"This you understand
not because it has been said by a man
but instead by my Father in Heaven. You'll stand
as the rock upon which I shall build my church up.
The keys to the kingdom as well as my cup
are yours. Here on Earth, all you say shall be
affirmed up in Heaven. Tell no one of me.
Then he told them he would be killed at the hands
of the teachers of law, but all of the lands
would know of his death, for on the third day
he'd be raised from the dead to show them the way.
But Peter said, "Heaven forbid this, my Lord."
Then Jesus yelled, "Satan! You cannot afford
to look at such things like a mortal. God's plan
isn't selfish. His will is how all this began.
Let every man know you must take up your cross.
Come! If you cling to your life, it is lost.
But if you will give up your life for mine, then
your soul shall be saved and placed among men

whom the Lord loves, for He judges all deeds.
Only in that way can your soul be freed.
I tell you the truth, that some of you here
will witness the Son of Man come and appear.
His glory shall shine, for God's Kingdom will be
made clear so that every man may come and see."

Matthew 17:1 - 17:13

Following Jesus were Peter and James
and John, when suddenly, as if in flames,
Jesus' face shone as bright as the sun.
Then two men appeared. His friends were both stunned
to see that Elijah and Moses were there.
Peter said, "Master, let me now prepare
memorials for all that you three have done!"
A voice from the clouds said, "This is My son
whom I love and who brings Me joy. Listen to
the words and the message that he brings to you."
The disciples fell down in fear at the voice,
but Jesus said, "Rise up, my friends, and rejoice."
And when they arose, their friend was alone.
"Do not tell anyone what you were shone
till the Son of Man's raised up out of the grave."
"But is it not said that Elijah must pave
the way for the Christ?" the disciples asked him.
"Yes, this is true. But when he went to them
they abused him and turned him away, and so too
will the Son of Man suffer."
Then they all knew
that Jesus was speaking of his cousin John
the Baptist. And now that the visions now gone,
they followed their teacher back down the hill,
knowing the prophecy would be fulfilled.

Matthew 17:14 - 17:23

At the foot of the mountain a crowd had arrived.
A man said to Jesus, "O Lord, will you drive

the demon away from my son? For I brought
him to your disciples, but they said they're not
able to cure him."
Then Jesus cried out,
"You faithless disciples! Why do you doubt?!
How long must I deal with you? Bring the boy here."
From that moment forward the boy remained clear
of seizures, but when the disciples asked, "Why
were none of us able to cure him? We tried."
"Your faith is still lacking! You do not believe!
I promise you will when you're each made to grieve.
I tell you the truth, if your faith were the size
of a mustard seed, you'd tell this mountain to rise
and move over there, and it would be done.
You all lack in faith, though God gave you the Son."

Matthew 17:24 - 18:20

They arrived in Capernaum, and soon they were asked,
"Does Jesus, your teacher, pay his temple tax?"
"Of course," Peter said.
Then Jesus asked, "Do
kings tax their sons, or the people they rule?"
Peter said, "Kings tax their subjects."
"So we
as the sons are all free! But let's not disagree.
Take a line to the water and cast your hook in.
On the first fish you catch, check inside its mouth. Then
you shall find there a coin to pay for our tax.
The collectors shall have it so they may relax."
At about the same time, some disciples asked, "Who
is the greatest in Heaven?"
"This I can tell you."
Then Jesus walked up to a child nearby
and said, "Unless you each start over and try
to be like a child, you never will see
the kingdom of Heaven or stand there with me.
Be simple and loving, and when you are kind
to a child in my name, then truly you'll find

you've received me as well. But if you are cruel
to a child, you ought to be cast in a pool
a thousand feet deep with a millstone tied 'round
your neck, so you might be dragged down and drowned.
This world's not easy, but don't make it worse.
If your hand makes you sin, let it not be a curse.
Cut it off! For eternal life's better with just
one hand than to have two if then you are thrust
in the fire of hell. All my children must be
protected and loved, if you're to know me.
A man with a flock of one hundred sheep
will leave ninety-nine, to find and to keep
the lost one, and he will rejoice when it's found.
The Father's the same way when one turns around
and returns to His flock. You'll win someone back
if you privately point out their flaw, not attack
them publicly. That only turns them away.
But if they don't turn, go back the same day
with two or three friends and restate your case,
for I will be with you in that very place.
I tell you, wherever you gather with two
or three in my name, I am there beside you."

Matthew 18:21 - 18:35

Peter asked, "How many times, Lord, should we
forgive those who sin against us? Should we be
so gracious that we will forgive seven times?"
"Not seven, but seventy-seven! No crime
cannot be forgiven by God, so how can
it go unforgiven by woman or man?
A king had a debtor who owed him one ton
of silver, but when asked to pay, he had none,
so the king ordered that his whole family and he
be sold off as slaves to pay for the fee.
But the debtor fell down saying, 'Merciful king,
I need your forgiveness. I swear I will bring
the whole amount to you.'
The king's heart was moved,

so he let the man go and his debt was removed.
But later, the debtor went to a man who
owed him a few hundred coins and he threw
the man at his feet, saying, 'Pay your debt now!'
The man did not have it, but said, 'Please allow
a little more time. I swear I won't fail.'
But the debtor said, 'No,' and threw him in jail.
When the king heard of this, he brought the man back
and yelled at the man, 'How could you attack
and harm your own debtor, when I forgave you?
You owed so much more. Now you'll be made to
repay all you owe. To prison with him!
And let him be tortured by all those within.'
As the Father forgives you, so you must forgive
your brothers and sisters if you are to live."

Matthew 19:1 - 19:12

He went to the part of Judea that lay
to the east of the Jordan. The crowds came each day
and he healed their sick. But the Pharisees sought
to trap Jesus, so they asked him, "Is it not
a sin to divorce for no reason at all?"
"If you know the scriptures, then you will recall
when a man leaves his parents and joins with his wife,
the two become one in spirit and life.
Let no man split up what the Father made whole."
"But Moses allows men to cancel the role
of their wives by providing in writing that they
are divorcing their wives to send them away."
To this Jesus said, "That's because all your hearts
were hard. God doesn't want men torn apart
from their wives. If a man divorces and she
was never unfaithful, I tell you that he
is adulterous if he gets married again."
The disciples said, "If this is true, why would men
be married at all?!"
Jesus said, "There are men
who renounce marriage when the Lord calls out to them."

Matthew 19:13 - 19:14

Some parents brought forth their children to be
blessed by the hands of Jesus.
"Is he
not busy enough?" the disciples all scolded
the parents.
But Jesus took all and enfolded
them into his arms. He said, "Do not halt
my children! Be like them - pure, without fault -
if you are to enter God's kingdom."
Then he
blessed each little child, so all there could see.

Matthew 19:15 - 20:16

A rich young man came, asking Jesus, "What deed
can I do to enter God's kingdom?"
"You need
to fulfill the commandments," Jesus replied.
"I've done this," he said. "I have fully complied.
What else must I do?"
"To be perfect and dwell
with the Lord, take all that you own and go sell
it all. Then take what you've made and go give
it all to the poor. Then truly you'll live."
The young man was sad, for his wealth was so great.
Jesus told all his disciples, "The fate
of the rich is not easy. It's easier to
take a needle and then make a camel pass through
its eye than to help a rich man get in
to the kingdom of Heaven and give up their sin."
The disciples were shocked.
"Then who can be saved?"
"None," Jesus said, "We all are enslaved
by sin. But through God, we all are made new.
In the kingdom of Heaven, the Lord judges you.
Then the first will be last, and the last shall be first,

and the poor and the weak shall no longer thirst.
A man had a vineyard and hired some men
to work for him and he agreed to pay them
a denarius each, so they went to his field
and began to pick all of the grapes it could yield.
Then a few hours later the owner went in
to the town and he hired several more men
who were looking for work, and they went out too.
And a few hours later he hired a few
more from the town. At the end of the day
he said to his foreman, 'Go now and pay
each man a denarius.'
Some were incensed
who had worked the whole day.
'Did we not commence
in the morning and work through the heat? Pay us more
than you pay the others. We started before!'
But the owner said, 'I told you what I would pay,
when you got your job at the start of the day.
It's my money, friend, and it's my right to spend
it how I desire. Why does it offend
you all when you see I'm a generous man?'
So the last shall be first in the Lord's mighty plan."

Matthew 20:17 - 20:28

Jesus said to his disciples, "When we
go into Jerusalem, you will all see
the Son of Man taken and he'll be betrayed,
then killed, but he will return from the grave.
Then Jesus was asked by James and John's mother,
"Lord, you've been followed by both of the brothers
who are my two sons. In the kingdom allow
my boys to sit right by your side."
"Woman, how
can you ask such a thing? You don't know what you say.
To drink from my cup is a price they can't pay."
"Yes, we can, Jesus!" replied the two men.
"So it shall be, but the places have been

decided already, for God sets who will
sit at my side. Those places are filled."
When the other disciples found out what the two
brothers had asked, they said, "Who do you
think that you are? Are you greater than us?!"
But Jesus said, "All of you make such a fuss
of who shall be greatest. You act like the priests!
But the blessed are those you consider the least.
The Son of Man came here to go out and serve
and give his life so that mankind might deserve
the mercy of God. As a ransom he'll give
his life so that all of the people may live."

Matthew 20:29 - 20:34

As Jesus was leaving from Jericho, he
was asked by two blind men, "Lord, let us see!"
The crowd told the men, "Leave Jesus alone,"
but Jesus said, "Wait, let them speak on their own.
What did you ask?"
"Lord, give us our sight.
We've spent life in darkness. Please, show us the light."
Then Jesus replied, "Let your sight be restored."
So then the crowd knew that Jesus was Lord.

Matthew 21:1 - 21:17

As they neared Jerusalem, Jesus told two
disciples, "Go up to that village, where you
will find me a donkey. If anyone asks
tell them the Lord summons it for His task.
As the prophet proclaimed, "Oh Zion, your king
comes on a donkey - the gentlest thing."
When it had been fetched, he rode through the gates
of Jerusalem. There the crowds were in wait.
"Hosanna," they cried, "in the highest! Come save
us, Lord!" Holding palms they shouted and waved.
When he reached the temple, Jesus went in
and saw all the merchants who sold wares within.

In anger, he turned over all of their tables.
The merchants cried, "This man's completely unstable."
But Jesus said, "God looks upon you and grieves,
for you've turned His house into this den of thieves!"
He healed all the lame, and the children came out.
"Hosanna to our Son of David!" they'd shout.
The priests were indignant. "How dare children say
such things!"
"Let them all come to me on this day,"
Jesus proclaimed. "From out of the babes
and children shall come the Lord's highest praise."
Then he went to Bethany to spend the night,
but returned to Jerusalem at the first light.

Matthew 21:18 - 21:46

Returning he spotted a fig tree, and he
was hungry but he found no figs on the tree.
So Jesus said, "This tree won't bear fruit again."
It withered as soon as he said this. The men
with Jesus said, "Teacher, what did you do?
It withered so quickly!"
"I say unto you,
if you truly have faith and don't doubt, then say
to a mountain, 'Move, mountain! Get out of my way.'
Then it shall be done if you truly believe.
What you ask for in prayer, is what you'll receive."
On reaching the temple, some priests said, "Who gave
you authority to do these things and behave
as if you have power?"
So Jesus said, "I
will tell you if you give the proper reply
to this question. Who gave authority to
the Baptist to preach? If you tell me who
then I will tell you my authority."
But
they couldn't tell him by who or by what
John's authority came, so Jesus would not
tell them who sent him or for whom he taught.

But then Jesus said, "I'll tell you some things.
A man has two sons. The first one he brings
and says, 'Go into my fields.' But the son
says, 'No,' though he does and the work is all done.
Then the father gets his second son and says, 'Go
and work in the fields.' This son can't say no,
so he tells his father, 'I will,' but instead
when faced with the work, the second son fled.
So which of these two did as their father asked?"
The priests said, "The first. He completed the task."
And Jesus said, "So the corrupt ones who turn
shall be loved by God, but the priests who all spurn
the Lord in their actions, but said they would go
wherever he sent them shall be the Lord's foes."
He told them, "There once was a landowner who
leased out his vineyard to men that he knew.
At the end of the season he sent servants to
gather the rents, but the renting men slew
the landowner's slaves. Then he sent his son,
sure that they wouldn't repeat what they'd done.
But when his son arrived, they murdered him. So
what should the landowner do?"
"He should go
and kill all the sinners," the priests all replied.
And so Jesus told them, "The Lord will decide
to take His great kingdom away from you and
give it to others. Do you understand?"
The priests saw that Jesus spoke out against them,
but they knew they could not arrest him right then.

Matthew 22:1 - 22:14

Then Jesus said, "God's kingdom is like a king
who prepared his son's wedding feast. He said, 'Go bring
the guests I've invited.' But his servants found
that all those invited had turned the king down.
They would not attend, and the king was enraged.
He told all his army commanders, 'Engage
and cut them all down. Burn all that they own.

For who would turn down the king or his throne?'
The guests were all slaughtered, but still the king's son
was set to be married. 'Go find everyone
you can,' said the king, 'and bring them to feast.'
So the list of the guests was greatly increased.
The good and the bad were brought in to be
the wedding guests, just as the king had decreed.
But the king saw a man in the crowd who was not
dressed up. The king said to him, 'I had thought
you'd be more respectful. Bind him and throw
him into the darkness.' This you should know.
Many are called, but the chosen are few.
This is the truth that I speak unto you."

Matthew 22:15 - 22:33

The Pharisees sought to trap Jesus, so they
said, "Rabbi, do you think it's right that we pay
taxes to Caesar?"
"Hypocrites! Why
do you seek to trap me? I know that you try!
Here, give me that coin. Whose image is this?"
"It's Caesar's," they said.
"Then this coin is his.
Render to Caesar what's Caesar's, but give
to God what is God's and then you shall live."
His reply had amazed them so they went away,
but the Sadducees came to him that very day.
They said, "Rabbi, if there's a woman who's wed,
but as the law says when her husband is dead
she's passed to his brother and he dies as well,
whose wife will she be and with whom shall she dwell
on the day that the great resurrection occurs?"
And Jesus replied, "No one shall be hers
and she shall be no one's, for when the dead rise
marriage is gone. In the heavenly skies
they'll be like the angels, but I must remind
you of the scriptures. Look and you'll find
that our God's the same God of Abraham and

all his descendents and all of his land.
He's Lord of the living, not God of the dead."
And all were astonished by what Jesus said.

Matthew 22:34 - 23:39

The Pharisees, hearing this, went back to call.
"In the law, what's the greatest commandment of all?"
"To love God with all of your heart, soul, and mind,"
Jesus replied. "After that you will find
second to this is the love of one's neighbor
as you love yourself. All the effort and labor
men put in the law revolves around these.
Go forth and do this, and God will be pleased."
Then Jesus asked them, "The Messiah...whose son
is he?"
They replied, "He is David's."
"The one
who said the Messiah was his lord? If so,
it can't be his son."
But the priests did not know
how to answer this statement, so they did not dare
ask Jesus more questions with all gathered there.
But Jesus spoke, "These men interpret the law.
Hold all scripture sacred and treat it with awe.
Listen to them when they speak and teach,
but know they don't practice the things that they preach.
They love to be seen as wise, and to sit
in the places of honor. They will not admit
their vanity. Don't try to teach. Try to be
an equal with your brothers. Do you not see?
You just have one Teacher. One Father. Those who
exalt themselves soon shall be humbled. If you
knew all that awaited these blind men who lead
you away from the things that the people all need.
Do not trust these vipers. I tell you, seek out
mercy and justice and faith. Be devout!
Like fresh painted tombs, these priests all appear
austere, but inside they are dead. You should fear,

for you say that you love the prophets, but you
are just like the ones who killed them. Go through
with your plan and finish the thing that they started!
You'll be responsible. You, the hard-hearted,
shall kill all the saints. O Jerusalem, you
have slaughtered your prophets. When will you renew
your vows? Look around, you desolate nation.
Your house is abandoned. The great desecration
is nearly complete. You won't see me again
till you open your gates and let God's children in."

Matthew 24

As Jesus was leaving the temple, he stated,
"This temple shall topple and be desecrated.
Not one stone will stand."
His friends asked him, "When
will you come again, so we know it's the end
of the world?"
"So many shall come in my name.
Do not be misled, for they seek only fame.
Famines and earthquakes, nations at war;
these shall all happen, and even before
I come, every one of you will be arrested,
tortured and killed. Each man shall be tested.
Not one of you will live to see the true end.
The nations shall all become filled up with sin.
Love will grow cold, but the ones who endure
temptation are blessed for they remain pure.
But the day shall arrive when a great desolation
is made of the holiest place in our nation.
On that day, Judea must flee to the hills.
Don't pack or prepare, for this shall fulfill
what Daniel proclaimed. In that time you'll see
false prophets and those who shall claim to be me.
They're liars! The Son of Man shall come upon
the clouds of the heavens. The trumpets of dawn
shall break forth and all of the angels shall find
and gather the chosen ones. They shall be mine.

But nobody knows when the judgment shall come;
not the angels in Heaven, not even the Son.
But the Father knows when, so watch for His time!
Be ever alert. Avoid sin and crime.
A good servant's given the charge over all
of his master's possessions, but if he should fall
into drunkenness, sin, or debauchery, he
shall be cut into pieces for all men to see."

Matthew 25

Then Jesus continued, "Ten bridesmaids sought
to go to the bridegroom, and five of them thought
to bring extra oil so their lights would shine.
But five did not bring enough, so when the time
arrived that their lamps were extinguished they went
to buy more, but that's when the bridegroom was sent.
He took the five wise women with him, and when
the others returned, he would not let them in.
'I don't know you women,' he told them, for they
had not been there waiting. And that's why I say,
keep a good watch, for the Lord honors those
who keep watch for Him, whose lamp always glows.
A master took three of his servants aside,
and said, 'I must leave, so I will divide
my money between you until I return.'
He gathered up eight bags of silver he'd earned.
To his most trusted servant he gave five bags, and
he gave two to the second, and one to the man
who was third, then he left. So the first servant went
and invested the money his master had lent.
The second did too, but the third was afraid,
for the master was cruel. He took up a spade
and buried the money, so that when the man
returned, it would still be right there in the land.
When the master returned, the first servant said,
'I invested your five bags of silver instead
of holding it, and I have made you five more.'
'Well done, my servant! You've done this small chore

so well I shall give you a greater place in
my home.'
He turned to the next servant then.
'I invested the two bags and made you two more.'
'Well done, my servant! You've done this small chore
so well I shall give you a greater place in
my home.'
He turned to his third servant then.
'Master, I know you're a cruel man who reaps
what you didn't sow, so I thought I would keep
it buried so that it would be there when you
returned from your trip.'
'But why would you do
such a foolish thing? You could have gone to a bank
so I had some interest. These two men I thank
for they honored me, but you're useless to me!
Throw him into darkness!'
God's gifts are not free.
To those who use what they are given, then they
are given much more. But those who betray
the Lord shall be stripped of such gifts and thrown out
into darkness and fear where they'll stumble about.
But the Son of Man comes. And the nations will be
gathered for him. And the Lord shall decree,
'You fed Me when I was impoverished, and when
I was naked you clothed Me.'
But He'll be asked then,
'When did we feed You or clothe You?'
'When you
helped the weakest or poorest, you helped the Lord too.'
The wicked who did not help lift up the weak
shall fear the Lord.
'You did not care for the meek,
so you shall be cast into fire and strife,
while those who loved others gain eternal life.'"

Matthew 26:1 - 26:16

He told his disciples these things, and he said,
"In two days, at Passover, blood will be shed.
The Son of Man comes, but is taken aside,
arrested, condemned, and then crucified."
Then a woman came forth with a jar of perfume
and poured it on Jesus.
"How dare you consume
such expense!" the disciples all shouted. "We could
have sold it, and used all that money for good!"
But Jesus said, "Friends, why do you criticize
this woman who came to cleanse and baptize
my body for burial? Don't you know you
will have the poor always, but my time is through.
I tell you the truth, where the good news is heard
what she's done today will be part of the word.
On hearing this, Judas Iscariot went
to the priests, saying, "I know that it's your intent
to arrest Jesus. How much will you pay me to
betray and then hand Jesus over to you?"
For just thirty pieces of silver they bought
Judas' service in their wicked plot.

Matthew 26:17 - 26:30

On the day of the Passover feast, Jesus said,
"I tell you the truth," after all had been fed,
"that one of you here will betray me.
They yelled,
"Never, Lord!"
"That man will surely be held
in contempt for the ages."
Then Judas replied,
"It isn't me, Lord."
"You sit by my side
and lie to my face."
Then Jesus took bread
and broke it. To all his disciples he said,

"This is my body, that's broken for you.
Take it and eat it."
And when they were through,
he took up the wine, saying, "Here in this cup
is my blood of the covenant. Drink it all up.
It's poured out so all are forgiven of sin,
and I tell you I won't get to drink wine again
till I drink it with you up in Heaven."
Then they
went to a garden to end that last day.

Matthew 26:31 - 26:35

On the way to the Mount, Jesus said, "All of you
will desert me, but once I have been born anew
after death, I will join you out in Galilee."
But Peter said, "I won't desert you! Not me!"
Jesus responded, "Before the cock crows,
you'll deny me three times."
But Peter said, "No!
I'd die before I would deny your great name."
And all the disciples vowed they'd do the same.

Matthew 26:36 - 26:56

They went to Gethsemane. Jesus took three,
Peter and both the sons of Zebedee,
John and James. They followed Jesus, who said,
"My soul's crushed as if I am already dead!
Stay with me."
Then Jesus bowed down to pray,
"Father, take this cup of suff'ring away!
Yet I know it's Your will, not mine that shall be.
Despite my fear, no one will stay up with me
on this night."
In anger he called out to them,
"Is there not one man amongst all you men
who will stay up this night? Rise up! It is time.
My betrayer comes though I've committed no crime."

Then Judas arrived with a crowd armed with swords.
And Judas approached, saying, "Jesus, my lord!"
He kissed him, and Jesus said to him, "Now do
this act that I know is required of you."
Then soldiers moved forward arresting him, till
a disciple jumped forward, ready to kill.
He slashed at a man and cut off his ear,
but Jesus said, "Put your sword down, my friend. Hear!
If you live by the sword, you will die by the sword.
Do you not know I can call on the Lord
and the angels would come without hesitation?
God's will must be filled in proper formation."
He turned to the soldiers and said, "I sat in
the temple for days, but you brought your men
in the night for you fear. As the prophets have said,
so it shall be." The disciples then fled.

Matthew 26:57 - 26:68

They took Jesus to the Sanhedrin and sought
to find some false witnesses. Two men were brought
to the front where they said, "He claims he could tear
the temple walls down, and in three days repair
and build it back up."
But Jesus would not
refute this.
The priests said, "We've heard that you taught
that you are the Christ. Do you claim this is true?"
"It is as you say, and I say unto you,
the Son of Man shall sit by God up on high."
"Blasphemy! Kill him!" the Sanhedrin cried.
They spat upon Jesus and some men struck him,
saying, "Prophesy, Christ! Who hit you just then?"

Matthew 26:69 - 26:75

Peter sat out in the courtyard. He waited
for word of his teacher, but then a girl stated,
"You are with him, the one who's inside."

"No, you're mistaken," Peter replied.
"She's right," someone said. "You were there with that man."
"No, you are wrong. I don't know him."
"How can
you say that? We saw you!"
"You didn't, I say!"
The cock crowed that moment to start the new day.
Peter recalled what Jesus had spoken,
"Three times you'll deny me before dawn has broken."
So Peter cried out and wept bitter tears,
for though he loved Jesus his heart filled with fear.

Matthew 27:1 - 27:10

The priests quickly sentenced Jesus to die.
But Judas went to them and let out a cry,
"Take back your money! For I have betrayed
an innocent man!"
"But you have been paid.
Go feed the poor."
He took the coins then
and threw them, for they were the proof of his sin.
He fled, found a rope, and then a strong tree.
He hanged himself, knowing he'd never be free.

Matthew 27:11 - 27:31

Meanwhile, Jesus was taken to stand
before Pilate of Rome who ruled in the land.
Pilate told Jesus, "The priests want you dead.
Are you king of the Jews?"
"It is as you said."
But Pilate replied, "Jesus, hear what I say.
If you don't change your story, they'll kill you today."
But Jesus would not. Pilate still had a plan.
"You Jews! As you know, I will give you a man
who has been locked in prison to mark your great feast.
I do this to show you that I am no beast.
So who shall it be? Barabbas, the foe

whose nefarious deeds everyone knows?
Or Jesus, who seems to have done nothing wrong?"
But the priests got the crowd to all go along
with their plot. So Barabbas was let go, and then
the crowd shouted, "Crucify Jesus!"
"What sin
has this man committed?" Pilate cried out.
"Crucify him!" they replied with a shout.
Then he washed his hands. "Then so it shall be.
But the blood of this man shall not be on me."
Jesus was flogged, then taken by men
to soldiers who threw purple robes about him.
They spit on his face as they crowned him with thorns
and they mocked the king of the Jews with their scorn.

Matthew 27:32 - 27:66

They found a man, Simon, and they made him bear
Jesus' cross up to Golgotha where
they set up the cross. They took Jesus and
they pounded nails into his feet and his hands.
Then they placed a sign up over his head.
'Jesus, the King of the Jews,' the sign read.
Two robbers were crucified with him and all
of the people yelled, "Save yourself now! Don't you call
yourself Son of God?" They mocked him as he
hung there on the cross; nailed to the tree.
In the ninth hour, he cried out, "God, why
is it You've forsaken me?" With that he died.
At that very moment the curtain that hid
the holy of holies where men are forbid
was shredded. The earth started shaking and then
from graves rose the holiest women and men.
Then those at the cross saw what they had done.
"It's true!" they exclaimed. "We killed the Lord's son."
Pilate then ordered the body to be
given to Jesus' friends. They would see
that Jesus received a good burial when
the Sabbath had passed. But up until then

they placed him inside of a tomb and they rolled
a large boulder over to cover the hole.
But the Pharisees knew that Jesus had said,
"I'll arise on the third day after I'm dead."
So they placed some guards at the tomb who would stop
any disciple from opening up
the tomb and removing the body so they
could tell everyone he'd arisen or say
he was the Messiah. For that, they agreed
would be a deception far worse than their deed.

Matthew 28

Mary Magdalene came when the Sabbath was done,
Mother Mary was with her and just as the sun
arose a great earthquake occurred and the stone
was rolled back, and standing atop the rock shone
an angel. The guards were terrified and
became like the dead, but he reached out his hand
saying, "Women, don't fear. Your purpose is clear,
but Jesus is risen! He's no longer here.
He's alive!"
They were joyous as they left that place.
A few minutes later they came face to face
with Jesus. They fell at his feet and he said,
"Tell my disciples I'm no longer dead.
Tell them I'm traveling to Galilee.
And when they arrive there, they will see me."
The women rushed off, then the guards did as well.
The guards found the priests and started to tell
their story. The priests paid them great sums to say
the disciples had stolen the body away.
But all the disciples met Jesus and saw
he'd beaten the grave. They worshipped in awe.
Then Jesus said, "Hear now this one proclamation.
Go! Make disciples of every nation.
Baptize and teach them what I taught you, friends,
and know I'll be with you from now till the end."

Mark 1:1 - 1:28

The prophet Isaiah wrote in his day,
'I send forth the one who's preparing the way
for God. Make straight paths for Him.' And so John
the Baptist was out in the desert, withdrawn.
A wild man who told the people, "Be sure
that one is approaching whose word will endure.
I baptize with water, but he will cleanse you
with the great Holy Spirit. He's coming! It's true!"
Then Jesus of Nazareth came to be blessed
by John, and the sky with a frightening unrest
was ripped open wide, and out came a dove.
God spoke, "I'm pleased with My son, whom I love."
Sent to the desert and facing down Satan,
for forty days Jesus withstood all temptation.
Then Jesus went back to Galilee to
tell all the people, "I come with good news."
As he was out walking by Galilee's sea,
he said to two fishermen, "Come. Follow me.
Be fishers of men." So they both got out
and followed Jesus, for they did not doubt.
Simon and Andrew were now by his side,
and when he saw James and John, Jesus cried,
"Come!" and they left without any fuss.
They said, "We will follow you, lord, so lead us."
They went to Capernaum on Sabbath to teach,
and people were shocked by the way Jesus preached.
He spoke in a knowing way they'd not expected,
till one man possessed by a demon objected.
"Jesus of Nazareth, what do you want?

To destroy us? Aren't you from the Lord? Let's be blunt."
Then Jesus said, "Silence! Come out of that man!"
And that demon had to obey his command.

Mark 1:29 - 1:45

When Jesus had done this, he left and went to
see Simon's Mother-in-law for he knew
that she was too sick to walk. At his touch,
her fever departed and she could get up.
Those who heard this brought all of the ill
and demon-possessed who were hopeless until
Jesus had come, and they were all cured.
All who had needs were thus reassured.
Then Jesus told all of his friends, "Let us leave
and go to the other towns. They must believe
in the greatness of God, for that's why I'm here."
Wherever he went the crowds would appear.
A leper came to him and dropped to his knees,
"If you are willing, please cure my disease."
Jesus said, "Yes, I am willing. Be clean.
But do what I say and hear what I mean.
Don't tell the people what I have just done."
But the man went to town and told everyone.
So Jesus could not stay inside of the towns
for people would travel from miles around
hoping he'd heal them and do things so they
could say, "I saw Jesus do great things today."
Jesus and his friends would stay away from
the towns, but the people continued to come.

Mark 2:1 - 2:12

Jesus returned to Capernaum where he
was surrounded by crowds who all came to see
and hear him. While preaching, though, he was surprised
when four people lowered a man paralyzed
down through the roof. Jesus was moved,
"Your sins are forgiven."

But some disapproved.
"Who is this man," they whispered, "who states
such things that only the Lord can dictate?"
Then Jesus stood up and scolded this talk.
"Should I say instead, 'Get up, man, and walk?'
You do not believe. The sin's on your hearts.
Without seeing signs, your faith will not start.
But so that you know my power is true
to forgive and much more, then this I shall do.
Take up your mat, friend. Walk from this place."
He did, and surprise was on everyone's face.

Mark 2:13 - 2:17

Levi was there at his tax booth one day
when Jesus passed by. He heard Jesus say,
"Follow me."
So he got up and he went.
That night Levi held a large dinner event.
He introduced Jesus to all of his friends.
The Pharisees said, "These people all sin.
Why would you eat with the taxers and sinners?"
"Why are you priests criticizing this dinner?
Are you so blind?" Jesus scolded, "Don't you
know what a doctor is sought out to do?
Does he heal the healthy? He cares for the ill!
I've come so these people may know of God's will.

Mark 2:18 - 2:28

The Pharisees fasted when Jesus did not.
They said, "You are eating. Have you, sir, forgot
to honor the Lord through sacrifice?"
He
replied, "They have only so much time with me.
Are all at the wedding to fast with the groom?
No! They must celebrate! They know that soon
the groom will be gone, and soon so will I.
On that day they'll fast and look to the sky."

The Pharisees, though, did not want to yield,
and later they saw Jesus out in a field
where all his disciples picked grain they could gnaw.
"Look," cried the Pharisees, "they break the law.
For they are now working on this Sabbath day."
Then Jesus said, "Do you not know what you say?
Don't you remember that David, in need,
took sanctified bread, so his men could feed?
The Sabbath is here for the good of all man,
not man for the Sabbath. Do you understand?
You should remember, the Son of Man reigns
over even the Sabbath. Now we'll eat our grains."

Mark 3

Jesus went into a synagogue where
a man with a shriveled hand was standing there.
Many were watching to see what he'd do
for it was the Sabbath and this was a true
test of the law in many men's eyes.
Jesus saw him and said, "Sir, arise."
He said, "Someone tell me, what's the Lord's will?
To do good or evil? To save life or kill?
Isn't the Sabbath a day to do good?"
But all just observed from the places they stood.
His anger burned deeply at their stubborn hearts.
"Stretch out your hand." And he healed that part.
Immediately, all the Pharisees went
to obtain the Herodian leaders' consent.
They said, "He has broken the law God fulfilled.
We must determine how he can be killed."
Jesus withdrew while he was allowed,
but not far behind was a gathering crowd.
Seeing such need, he gathered twelve men
to be his apostles and stay with him. Then
the teachers of law came out and they said,
"Beelzebub has invaded his head.
He is the devil!"
But Jesus said, "Nay.

The devil does not cast the devil away.
A house that's divided simply can't stand,
and Satan cannot cast himself from a man.
I tell you the truth, our sins can be cleaned,
but not when the Holy Spirit's blasphemed."
Then Jesus' mother and brothers arrived,
and had to send someone to fetch him inside.
The person said, "Jesus, your family's out there."
And he replied, "My family lives everywhere."
He looked at the people who sat all around
and said, "In your hearts, the Lord's love abounds.
Whoever does God's will, that is my brother,
my sister, my uncle, my father, my mother."

Mark 4:1 - 4:9

Jesus got into a boat while the crowd
sat on the hillside. Then just as loud
as he could, Jesus shouted, "Now listen to me.
A farmer went out and he scattered some seed.
What fell on the road, the birds came to eat.
What fell on the rocks, grew up at his feet
but the soil was shallow and didn't take root.
It perished unable to bear any fruit.
Other seed fell by the bushes of thorns,
but it was choked out and nothing was born.
But some seed fell into the good dirt to grow
up into the crops that the farmer had sowed.

Mark 4:10 - 4:34

When they were alone again, Jesus said, "You
twelve have been chosen. If only you knew.
The secret of Heaven is already yours
but it will be missed by he who ignores.
They will be seeing but never perceiving.
They hear my words, but their hearts are deceiving.
Did you understand my story today?
I spoke about people, and how they will stray.

My word is the seed, so take it and sow,
for there will be people who take it and grow.
But some will not hear, and some won't take root,
and some will be choked out and never bear fruit.
The word must be scattered to find the good soil.
Each day of your lives, my friends, you will toil
to search out those people. In this work, be bold!
For you will yield harvests of one-hundred fold.
At night you don't put a lamp under a bowl.
You place it on stands for all to behold,
for light overcomes what darkness concealed,
so all that was hidden may now be revealed.
Scatter the word as a farmer would sow,
for whether he wakes or he sleeps, the seed grows.
All by itself the soil creates
a harvest, for which the Father awaits.
The mustard seed held in your hand is so small,
but planted it grows to be biggest of all.
So is the kingdom of God. It all starts
with the smallest of words planted into a heart."

Mark 4:35 - 4:41

They left in a boat to cross Galilee,
but a storm blew in quickly and churned up the sea.
The disciples were scared, but Jesus just slept,
They woke him and said, "We will sink to the depths.
Do you not care if we go to our graves?"
"Be still," Jesus said to the wind and the waves.
The storm disappeared.
"You see? You are safe,"
Jesus said. "Why do you still lack in faith?"
And all the disciples who'd seen and who'd heard
were shocked that their teacher, with two little words,
could silence the winds. And they asked each other,
"Who is this man that we're following, brother?"

Mark 5:1 - 5:20

Jesus was out by the sea with his friends
when out of the tombs came the largest of men;
a man who was known by all in the town
as demonic and living in caves underground.
He had been chained, but always broke out.
The man came toward them and started to shout,
"What do you want of me, Jesus, God's son?
To torture me, like all the others have done?"
Jesus asked, "What is your name? Have you any?"
"I am called Legion," he said, "for we're many.
Please do not cast me to lands far from here."
Jesus saw there were some pigs that were near;
two thousand hogs, if you counted them all.
"Into those pigs, all you demons! Don't stall!"
The spirits did just as Jesus decreed,
then all of the pigs drowned themselves in the sea.
The man who had just been possessed was now free
and all who had witnessed this uttered a plea,
"Leave here now, Jesus. Get up and go.
Your powers are frightening. This kind of show
is wrong." But the man who'd been cured asked to go
with Jesus and his friends, but Jesus said, "No.
Go to your family with gladness and say
how much the Lord's done for you here on this day."

Mark 5:21 - 5:43

Jesus moved on to a different town,
and there a man came and fell to the ground.
"My daughter's near death. She'll soon pass away.
But tell her to live, and she'll do what you say."
So Jesus agreed, and as he followed him,
the crowds followed closely and pushed around them.
Suddenly Jesus knew someone had clutched
the tassels on his robe. When he had been touched,
the power drained out of him, so Jesus turned
and saw a poor woman who said, "Lord, I yearned

to meet you, for I have been bleeding twelve years.
I thought I'd be healed if I touched you." Her tears
moved Jesus. He told her, "By faith now you are."
And all of the crowd thought this was bizarre,
for not even those who were closest to him
could tell how he'd known when her hand brushed his hem.
But as this was happening, men came to tell
the man who'd been leading this gathering swell,
"Your daughter is dead. There's no need to lead
the teacher to her."
"Don't fear, just believe,"
Jesus told them. "But now we must leave
all except John, James and Peter. Proceed."
The man led the four of them on to his home,
where they found his daughter as still as a stone.
"Why do you moan?" Jesus said to the mother,
"She's sleeping."
They laughed, "You must be drunk, brother."
He took the girl's hand saying, "Child, arise."
The little girl rose and opened her eyes.

Mark 6:1 - 6:13

Jesus went back to his hometown to preach
on the Sabbath. In temple, when he stood to teach,
people said, "He is a carpenter. Who
does he think he is to teach me and you?
Isn't this Mary's son? Aren't those his brothers?
Joseph and Judas. And there are the others.
Simon and James with his sisters as well."
They took offense at what he'd come to tell.
"At home," Jesus said, "a prophet's abused,
his teachings discounted and honor refused."
And he was amazed at their lack of faith,
so he left them all to their foolish debate.
Then Jesus sent out the twelve two-by-two,
and told all of them what they were to do.
"Take just yourself - no money, nor sack,
nor bread, just the shirt that you have on your back.

You'll receive shelter and something to eat.
If not, leave that town. Shake the dust from your feet."
And so they went out with one guiding goal;
to cast demons out, and heal bodies and souls.

Mark 6:14 - 6:29

Jesus' name had spread far and wide.
King Herod was told, "It is John, who had died.
This is the Baptist come back from the dead."
"It can't be," said Herod, "I cut off his head!"
He'd given the order when John was arrested,
imprisoned, and killed as his wife had requested.
For Herod's wife had held a grudge from when John
said, "Herod and his wife have sinned. It is wrong
that Herod should marry his own brother's wife."
But she had succeeded in taking John's life.
Herod had not wanted him to be killed
for he feared the holiness John had fulfilled.
But at a large party, he said to his spouse,
"Name anything, and it's yours, for this house
is great and I'll get anything for my mate."
"I want John the Baptist's head on a plate."
He worried, but Herod did not want to seem
weak to his guests, so he said, "It shall be."
He gave the command, so his guests wouldn't scoff,
and that's why the Baptist's head was cut off.

Mark 6:30 - 6:56

The apostles returned to tell Jesus about
what they had been doing, but people came out.
The crowd was so large, they could not withdraw.
Jesus felt pity for them for he saw
that this group of people was just like a herd
of sheep with no shepherd, and his heart was stirred.
He said to his friends, "Give them something to eat."
"That's five thousand people! We've no bread or meat."
He said, "Tell me, friends, what we have to share."

"Two fish and five loaves," they said with despair.
He looked up to Heaven, gave thanks and then broke
the bread. "Hand it out to the people," he spoke.
The disciples saw then that their teacher was great,
for they handed the food out and everyone ate.
And when they were done, enough bread remained
to fill up twelve baskets, which none could explain.
Later that night, his friends all sailed on
to Bethsaida after their teacher had gone
to pray. That same night he looked out and found
the twelve in a storm, not yet to dry ground.
So Jesus went out and walked on the lake.
They saw him, but thought it a ghost or a fake
until he called to them and said, "Do not fear.
It is I." Then Jesus approached. Drawing near,
he climbed in the boat. They all were amazed
for they hadn't understood how he had raised
enough bread and fish for all to consume
till they saw this miracle under the moon.

Mark 7:1 - 7:23

The Pharisees came to Jesus' meal
to ask, "If you're holy, then how do you feel
that your friends don't properly cleanse their own hands?"
"Isaiah was right. You don't understand
for you honor me with your lips, but your hearts
aren't with me or God. You hypocrites start
your worship in vain with a typical sin,
exchanging God's word for traditions of men."
He called to the crowd, "All, listen and glean,
that nothing outside of us makes us unclean.
Instead it's what comes from the mouth of a man
that soils him and violates God's command."
When Jesus retired that night, he said, "Friends,
impurity's not in our food, it's in sin.
Theft, immorality, murder, deceit.
These are our sins, not that which we eat."

Mark 7:24 - 7:30

Jesus moved on. While he was in Tyre
a Greek woman found him and said, "My desire
is that you should heal my daughter who's cursed
by a demon."
"Should not all the children eat first?"
Jesus said, "Good parents don't give the bread
to the dogs."
To Jesus the Greek woman said,
"Yes, Lord, but even the dogs on the ground
may eat up the crumbs as they fall all around."
Jesus then smiled, "For such a decree,
go and you'll find that your daughter is free."
Though Jesus' message was first for the Jews,
the Gentiles too could share the good news.

Mark 7:31 - 7:37

Some brought to Jesus a man deaf and mute,
for everyone knew of his healing repute.
He said, "Now be opened," and those present saw
the mute speak to them. The crowd was in awe.
"Go," Jesus said to them, "But do not say
what you have witnessed at this place today."
The more that he asked, the more they all talked,
and so he was followed wherever he walked.

Mark 8:1 - 8:10

During those days, another large crowd
gathered to hear Jesus preaching aloud.
They'd traveled to see him, and so Jesus said,
"Let's feed all these people. Have we any bread?"
"Just seven loaves," the disciples replied.
"Go hand them out. The Lord will provide."
At this place again, Jesus fed all
of the four thousand who'd followed his call.
When all of the people had eaten their fill,

Jesus said, "Gather what's left, if you will."
They did, and their utter amazement was plain,
for seven full baskets of bread still remained.

Mark 8:11 - 8:21

Then Jesus crossed over the sea to a town
and a group of the Pharisees came running down
shouting, "If you are divine, show us proof.
Show us a miracle under this roof."
"Why must I show you a sign to believe?
I tell you the truth, you will not receive
a sign if your faith is so truly bereft."
He returned to the boat and all of them left.
As they were all out on the sea and afloat,
the twelve realized that they had only one loaf.
Jesus said, "Careful. Beware of the yeast
of Herod and that of the Pharisee priests."
All the disciples were very confused.
"It must be because we've no bread," they all mused.
"Are you so dense? Am I that unclear?
You have eyes and ears, but don't see or hear!
When I fed five thousand, how much remained?"
"Twelve baskets," they said.
"And I did the same
and fed the four thousand. What was left then?"
"Seven," they said.
"Don't you understand, men?"

Mark 8:22 - 9:1

They went to Bethsaida. There a blind man
begged Jesus, "Lord, can I be healed by your hand?"
So Jesus then spit upon both of his eyes.
"What do you see?"
"Some people the size
of trees walking round." And so Jesus took
his hands to the man's eyes. Then he said, "Look.
Now do you see?"

"It's as clear as the day."
Jesus said, "Tell no one else on your way."
As they moved along through the villages and
the towns, Jesus asked, "Who do they say I am?"
"Some say Elijah," his friends all replied,
"and some say that you're John the Baptist who died."
"What do you say?" he asked.
"The Messiah,"
said Peter, "The Christ. The one we desire."
"Tell no one yet, for they would accuse
you all of blasphemy. You'd be abused.
The Son of Man suffers and must be rejected
by many, and when the time comes he's subjected
to torture and death, but on the third day
he'll rise once again."
"What is this you say?"
asked Peter, for all the disciples were spooked.
"Get back from me, Satan!" Jesus rebuked,
"You think like a man, not God." Then he called
the crowds to come near him. "Hear me, you all.
If you want to follow me, you must deny
yourself, and then take up your cross. If you try
to save your own life it is lost, but I say
if you lose your life for me, it will be saved.
What good is it if a man gains the whole
of the world, if then he must forfeit his soul?
I tell you the truth. Some standing here
will not die before God's kingdom appears."

Mark 9:2 - 9:13

Just six days later, Jesus took John
and Peter and James, and they went up on
a mountain and when they were standing alone,
Jesus transfigured and his glory shone.
His robe became blindingly white and it seared
their eyes. Elijah and Moses appeared
and they spoke with Jesus. Although Peter feared,
he said, "Let us set up three shelters right here."

But then a great cloud enveloped them all
and Peter and James and John heard a call
from nowhere and everywhere; all around them.
"This is My son whom I love. Trust in him."
Then, just as suddenly, they were alone
and Jesus said, "Friends, you all must postpone
speaking of what you have seen, and instead
tell of this when I come back from the dead."
They were confused by what Jesus had meant
in saying this, but they all gave their consent.
They asked Jesus, "Doesn't Elijah come first?"
"Of course," he replied, "It's all been rehearsed.
Elijah will come and set things in play.
The Son of Man suffers and must be betrayed.
But truly, Elijah has already come,
and as it is written, it shall be done."

Mark 9:14 - 9:32

When they had returned, they saw a large crowd
arguing with the disciples aloud.
When Jesus was noticed, a man went and said,
"I've brought my son. Jesus, please heal him, I beg.
I brought him to all your disciples, but they
could not heal my boy."
"How long shall I stay
with this generation that does not believe?!"
cried Jesus. "Go get him and bring him to me."
The man brought the boy and said, "He is cursed
with a demon that shakes him."
"Tell me this first.
How long has it been that he's suffered this way?"
"Forever! If you can, please help him today."
"*If* you can?" Jesus repeated and grieved.
"Everything's possible when one believes."
"I want to believe! Help me!"
"I will."
When he touched the boy, the writhing was stilled.
"Now your boy's well." Then he left the place,

quickly, before all the crowds could give chase.
When they were alone, the disciples all said,
"We tried to, but you had to cure him instead.
Why couldn't we do what you just did back there?"
Jesus said, "That demon only fears prayer.
The Son of Man comes and he'll be betrayed.
They'll kill him, but he will arise the third day."
They all looked at Jesus, unsure of just why
he was telling them this or how it applied.
But he looked so sad and serious when
he told them this, they were afraid to ask him.

Mark 9:33 - 9:50

They went to Capernaum, but quietly fought
amongst themselves over which one Jesus thought
was the greatest among them for Jesus' task.
"What are you talking about?" Jesus asked.
The twelve were ashamed and said nothing, so
Jesus said, "There is a thing you must know.
If you want to be first, then you must be last.
A servant to all." He stopped and he asked
a child close by to join them and said
"Each time you welcome a child, instead
you welcome me in. In welcoming me,
you welcome the One who sent me to thee."
A disciple said, "Teacher, we all stopped the shame
of a man who cast demons out, using your name."
"Do not stop this man! He's for us if he
is not against us. This man *does* believe!
The smallest of kindness in my name shall bring
the greatest reward when you do that thing.
But he who would cause my children to sin
would be better served if he were cast in
the sea with a millstone tied up around
his neck so that this evil human may drown.
If your hand should sin, cut it off. If your eye
should sin, pluck it out. It is better to die
and enter the kingdom of Heaven with one

of your eyes than to be completely undone
and end up in hell where the worm never dies
and the fire's not quenched by the loudest of cries."

Mark 10:1 - 10:16

While Jesus was teaching, the Pharisees saw
a chance to trap him.
"Is it in the law
that a husband may leave his wife in divorce?"
"What's Moses say here?"
"He says, 'Of course'."
Jesus sighed, "It is because you have hardened
your hearts that he wrote that. No man is pardoned,
nor woman, if they seek divorce from their spouse,
for they are adulterers in the Lord's house
if then they remarry. For in His creation
God made a male and a female formation.
So men leave their parents in great celebration
to be with their wife in the true consecration
of love, adoration, and unification.
What God joins together in His combination
let no man divide, regardless of station."
The Pharisees lost in this confrontation.
Some people wanted their children to see
Jesus, but all the disciples said he
was too busy, so they kept the children away.
When Jesus heard this, he stood up to say,
"Let them come here! For the kingdom is theirs.
I tell you the truth, in all your affairs
be just like a child, tender and mild,
to enter God's house." And then Jesus smiled.
The children came forth and gathered around
his feet, and Jesus then slowly knelt down,
touching each child and blessing them. He
said, "Only my children may come unto me."

Mark 10:17 - 10:31

As Jesus was starting to walk on his way
a rich man ran up, calling, "Teacher! Please say -
how can eternal life be understood?"
"Friend, God alone is the One who is good.
Know your commandments."
"I do, and I've kept
them all."
"There's one more that you must accept.
Sell your possessions and give to the poor,
then follow me, for I have great things in store."
The rich man was sad and left in a huff,
because he did not want to sell all his stuff.
"How hard," Jesus said, "is it to enter in
to the kingdom of Heaven for all the rich men.
A camel may pass through a small needle's eye
far easier than a rich man should find
the kingdom of God."
A disciple said, "Who
can find the Lord? We gave our lives up for you."
"In God, everything is possible, and
all who leave home setting out to expand
God's kingdom may know they will be quenched of thirst.
For the first will be last, and the last will be first."

Mark 10:32 - 10:52

On the way to Jerusalem, Jesus said, "Know
that the Son of Man will be betrayed where we go.
They'll condemn him, mock him, flog him, then kill.
In three days he'll rise, for this is God's will."
All the disciples but two were in thought.
James and John told him, "Jesus, you ought
to seat us upon your left and right side."
"You ask, but I tell you, you must be denied,
for you cannot drink from the cup I'm to drink."
"But teacher," they said, "we can."
"So you think.

But I know you'll drink from my cup and you'll be
baptized the same as they'll soon baptize me.
But my left and right are not to be shared
for they've been reserved and they've been prepared."
Then Jesus called over the rest of them and
said, "You who'd be first, must first understand
that you must be slaves. For the Son of Man came
to serve as a ransom for man, not to reign."
In Jericho, they passed a man who was blind
who called, "Jesus, is there a way you can find
any mercy for me?"
"Shut up!" others cried.
But Jesus asked, "Friend, what may I provide?"
"Rabbi, I so want to see!"
"It is so.
Your faith healed you. Come. Follow me on this road."

Mark 11:1 - 11:19

At Jerusalem's outskirts, Jesus said, "You
will find a young colt tied up just a few
miles from here. Go, fetch it and bring
it back. If you're asked why you're doing this thing,
tell them the Lord is in need of it and
it will then be returned as soon as it can."
And so it was done. When people asked, they
said all of the words Jesus told them to say.
And so Jesus rode the young colt down the hill
so that the prophecy would be fulfilled.
And people spread cloaks and reeds on the ground
shouting, "Hosanna!" as he came to town.
He went to the temple, but it was too late
so he and his friends decided to wait.
Hungry for food, Jesus found a fig tree,
but there was no fruit.
He said, "Let there be
no fruit on your branches ever again."
His friends were confused, but forgot his words when
the temple was opened and all could go in.

They saw that the temple was packed full of men
buying and selling their wares. Jesus flew
into a rage, shouting out, "Why have you
made my great temple a den full of thieves?
Get out of here! Out of here! All of you leave!"
The priests watched him overturn tables and said,
"We cannot allow this man's message to spread.
He threatens our power with all he implies.
We must find a reason that Jesus should die."

Mark 11:20 - 11:26

The next day as all of them walked into town,
the Twelve saw the fig tree was withered and brown.
"Jesus," said Peter, "You cursed this tree. Now
it's dead! How'd you do it? Please tell us how."
"Have faith," Jesus said. "If you truly believe,
and say to a mountain, 'Sink into the sea,'
then it shall be done. For that which you ask
in prayer, if you trust, shall then come to pass.
But you must remember in every prayer to
ask for forgiveness. God asks that you
forgive those who harm you so that He may give
forgiveness to you, so that you may live."

Mark 11:27 - 12:12

When they had returned to the temple they saw
that all of the elders and teachers of law
were waiting for them, and as they approached
the elders said, "How do you dare to encroach
on God's law? Upon whose authority do
you do all these things?"
"I'll tell this to you,
if you will tell me if John's baptism came
from Heaven or men."
"If we make the claim
that it was from Heaven, he'll ask us why we
don't have the faith to believe what we see.

But John was a prophet, so can we say men?"
They turned back to Jesus, and answering him
said, "We do not know."
"Then neither shall I
tell you from where all of my power's derived."
He then began speaking to them in the way
of parables, so they might learn what he'd say.
"A man made a vineyard and built up a wall.
He then had a winepress and tower installed.
He rented it out to some farmers and then
went on a journey, but he sent some men
back for some fruit, but they were abused,
beaten till they were all broken and bruised.
Some of his men were killed by the ones
who'd rented. So finally, the man sent his son.
'Surely,' he said, 'they'll show some respect
to him.' When his flesh and blood went to collect
the rent, all the farmers killed him because
they said, 'The heir's dead, so now the land's ours!'
What will the land owner do? He will kill
those tenants and find better people to fill
his land."
The elders knew they had been tested,
but they had to wait to have him arrested.

Mark 12:13 - 12:34

The Herodians and all the Pharisees then
were sent to see Jesus and ambush him when
he spoke in a way that a case could be made
for lawlessness. Jesus knew this trap was laid.
"Teacher," they said, "you aren't swayed by men,
so is paying taxes to Caesar a sin?"
"Why are you trying to trap me?" he asked.
"Bring me a coin. Who set up the tax?
The same man whose face and also whose name
is inscribed here - Caesar's. God has no claim.
So render to Caesar what's his. But give God
what's His."

The whole crowd looked on and was awed.
The Sadducees, who say there's no resurrection,
said, "Jesus, before you go, we have a question.
Moses wrote that if a man's brother dies
leaving a childless widow behind
the man must then marry her, but if he too
dies without children, then tell us who
will be called her husband when God comes to raise
the dead on His day?"
"Don't you know His ways?
Or don't you know scripture? No one will be
married when God comes for you and for me.
We'll be like the angels when he comes, but you
have misread your scripture. I'll tell you what's true.
When Moses fell down at the bush, God declared
'I'm Abraham, Isaac, and Jacob's God' there.
He is the God of the living, not dead!
You're badly mistaken, my friends," Jesus said.
Then one of the teachers said, "That answer's good.
I'd still like to ask you one more, if I could.
Which of the Lord God's commandments is best,
set as the greatest, above all the rest?"
"One," Jesus said, "cannot be undone.
Hear O Israel, our God is one!
Love Him with all of your heart, soul, and mind.
Second to this, show love and be kind
to your neighbors as you wish they'd be to you.
No other surpasses these greatest, these two."
"Well said," the teacher replied. "It is true!
There's only one God and we are to do
just what you said. Love our Lord above
all others. Second to that, we're to love
our neighbors, for that is a greater deed than
a sacrifice - caring for our fellow man."
Jesus saw this man was wise in the way
he had answered, and he had not sought to betray.
Jesus just smiled and said with a nod,
"You are not far from the kingdom of God."

Mark 12:35 - 12:44

While Jesus was teaching, he said, "How is it
that all of the teachers of law would permit
you to believe that David's the Christ -
our long sought Messiah, for it should suffice
to read David's words where he says, 'My Lord
says I will put all of your foes to the sword.'
If David calls him 'my Lord' it is done!
How then could David be called the Lord's son?
These teachers of law, they like to be seen
in great flowing robes, all primped and pristine.
Out in the market, they like to be greeted.
At synagogue they always like to be seated
in places of power, but they will devour
the houses of widows, for their hearts are sour.
They will be punished, for they know what's right!"
The large crowd all listened to him with delight.
Jesus sat near to the place where they gave
their offerings, and he watched how they'd behave.
Rich people came with the large sums that they
gave to the temple in public display.
Then came a widow, just one in the many,
with only two coins worth less than a penny.
She dropped them both in and Jesus said, "See!
No one among us can equal what she
has given. I tell you the truth, she exceeded
all other giving here. This is what's needed!
She gave out of poverty, all she could bring.
While others gave some, she gave everything."

Mark 13

When they had left, a disciple said, "Wow!
Look at these buildings. I do not know how
they all could be built."
But then Jesus spoke,
"Each building will topple, each stone will be broke."
"When will this happen and how will we know?"

they asked him.
"Be careful for there will be foes
who come in my name. And there will be war.
There will be earthquakes and famines and more.
These are the birth pains. Be on your guard.
I tell you, my friends, your lives will be hard.
Your path will be clear, but the world's a fog.
You'll be stripped and flogged inside synagogues.
You'll offer the gospel to all of the nations,
and you'll be arrested for my accusations.
And when you're to speak, fear not, for it's true
that the Spirit will utter the Lord's word through you.
Brother hates brother. Man is enslaved,
many will hate you, but you will be saved.
When you see the one that enjoys desolation -
he who degrades and creates desecrations -
standing in places he's not meant to be
at that very moment Judea should flee.
Don't take a thing, just make for the hills
for this is a beast that's longing to kill.
These will be days of anguish and pain
not seen since the Father first started His reign.
If any should say "It's the Christ!", don't believe.
For many will come with the hope to deceive
the truest believers. But then all the crowds
will see that the Son of Man comes from the clouds
with power and glory and he'll gather all
of his chosen who've heeded and followed his call.
From the ends of the Earth, throughout the four winds,
he'll gather his women and children and men.
So learn from the fig tree: its leaves will appear,
and that's how you know that the summertime's near.
I tell you the truth, our race will not pass
away until all of these things come at last.
But no one will know of the day nor the hour
except for the Father who has all the power.
Not His son, nor angels, nor holy devout
can know when it comes, so keep the watch out.

Don't be caught sleeping. His clock never stops.
I say unto you, and everyone - Watch!"

Mark 14:1 - 14:11

Though Passover was only two days away,
the chief priests were trying to find any way
to have Jesus killed.
"But we must stay quiet,
till after the feast, or the people may riot."
During this time, Jesus was spending
time with his friends, when a woman came tending
to him with perfume that was costly and fine.
"Woman!" some said, "What is your design?
That perfume you poured was worth a year's wage.
We could have sold it so we could assuage
the poor. They could eat! How wasteful of you!"
Jesus said, "Tell me, friends, what's she to do?
Feed everyone? You will always have poor,
but truthfully it will not be long before
you will not have me. Only she in this room
has done what she could. I'm prepared for the tomb.
I tell you wherever the gospel is heard
so shall her kindness be known in that word."
Then Judas Iscariot went to the priests,
and was paid to deliver him after the feasts.

Mark 14:12 - 14:31

On the first day of feasts, when the lamb is to be
slaughtered, they said to him, "Jesus, let's see
if we can find somewhere that we may go eat."
He said, "Go to town, and there you shall meet
a man with a water jar. Follow him to
the house and his master will take care of you.
Tell him the Teacher will soon come to call.
He has a room where I'll eat with you all."
They went into town, and everything there
was just as he told them, and so they prepared.

Later that evening, while they were eating,
Jesus said, "Truly, my time here is fleeting.
One of you sitting here soon will betray
and give me to them before the next day."
"Surely not I!" each man said in turn.
"It's one of you twelve," he replied. "He will burn.
For woe to that man, who should be forlorn.
Better for him if he'd never been born!"
While they were in shock, Jesus broke bread.
"Take it; this is my body," he said.
Then he poured wine and said, "In this cup
is my blood of the new covenant. Drink it up.
It's poured out for many. I'll tell you what's true,
I'll not taste the vine till I drink it anew
in the kingdom of God."
In silence they ate,
while one man amongst them sat brimming with hate.
And when they had finished they went to the Mount
of Olives, and there Jesus gave this account.
"You'll all fall away from me, for it is said
the sheep shall be scattered, but I'll go ahead
of all of you."
Peter said, "Jesus, not I!"
"I tell you the truth, Peter, you will deny
me three times tonight before the cock crows!"
"Jesus, I'd rather I die than disown
your name or your teaching."
The others agreed.
"You'll be the first, Peter. Just wait and see."

Mark 14:32 - 14:52

They went to Gethsemane. Jesus said, "Stay
with me for a while so that I might pray.
Peter and James and John walked with him
until he stopped, turned, and confided in them.
"My soul's overwhelmed with sorrow. Would you
stay with me, friends, my precious, my few?"
He stepped off a ways and said, "Father, please!

You can do all. Take this cup from me!
But it is not my will, but Yours to be done."
Returning he saw his friends sleeping. "Not one
of you could stay up?"
But no one would speak.
"The spirit is willing. The body is weak.
Come!" Jesus said, "The decision is made.
Rise, friends. They're coming, for I am betrayed."
Just at that moment, Judas appeared
with soldiers well armed, and as they all neared
Judas kissed Jesus, for that was the sign.
The armed men then seized him, though he was resigned.
But one of his followers hacked off the ear
of the priest's servant, and Jesus said to them, "Hear!
Is this a rebellion? Why do you need swords?
I came here to teach all of you of the Lord.
You could have arrested me or had me killed,
but all of the scriptures must now be fulfilled."

Mark 14:53 - 14:72

The high priests heard charges of his insurrection
while Peter stayed outside, avoiding detection.
He waited in fear while Jesus was tried,
as all the false witnesses came forth and lied.
The high priest said, "What do you say to these men
who've come to accuse you of blasphemous sins?"
But Jesus was silent, so they said, "Are you
the son of the Lord as you've claimed? Is it true?"
"I am," Jesus said to the muttering crowd.
"You'll soon see the Son of Man come on a cloud."
The priest said, "That's it! We need nothing more.
He's blasphemed our God, and he shames the Lord."
"Death!" they all shouted, and he was condemned.
They beat and they battered and blindfolded him.
"Prophesy!" all of them shouted as they
spit on his face while they took him away.
Now Peter was still waiting out in the yard.
A servant girl came and looked at him hard.

She said, "I know you! You were with that man too."
He said, "I don't know him and I don't know you."
She cried, "He was with them."
"I wasn't, now please
go back to your work and just leave me be."
Another said, "Surely you were. I can tell
that you're Galilean."
"Oh, not you as well!
I'm telling you all that I never have known
this man, so why don't you leave me alone!"
The cock crowed that moment and Peter knew he'd
denied Jesus thrice, as Jesus decreed.

Mark 15:1 - 15:20

Only through Rome could a death sentence be
handed down, so they took Jesus to see
Pilate who asked, "Are you king of the Jews?"
Jesus said, "Yes," and the priests all accused
this blasphemy.
"Will you not answer their cries?"
But still Jesus did not give any replies.
Though Pilate was shocked, he had an idea.
"At Passover every year, here in Judea,
we Romans set one of our prisoners free.
Jesus seems like a good prospect to me."
"No!" the crowd yelled, "This Jesus should die.
Set free Barabbas. This one, crucify!"
"Barabbas, the murderer? Why not this man?
What crime has he done that he should now stand
in the place of Barabbas?"
"Crucify him!"
"Fine," Pilate said, giving Jesus to them.
First he was flogged, and then led away
by soldiers who mocked him, then later that day
they gave him a robe of purple and crowned
his head with some thorns and beat him around.
"The king of the Jews!" they laughed and derided,
for soon came the time which had been decided.

They led Jesus out where he'd be crucified
on a cross; to be tortured, to suffer and die.

Mark 15:21 - 15:47

The troops forced a man to carry the beam
of the cross to the place where the entire scene
would play out, called Golgotha. They placed a sign
"THE KING OF THE JEWS" and offered him wine.
This he refused, as they nailed him up high
with a robber on Jesus' left and right side.
The crowds laughed at him.
"You say you can build
the temple when it is destroyed? Where's your guild?
Come down and be saved!"
The priests also scoffed,
"He saved all the others, but he can't get off
this cross? It is obvious he is a fraud.
This is no savior. He's no son of God."
Six hours passed since his torture began
and darkness enveloped the entire land.
Then Jesus cried out, "My God, why have You
forsaken me here?"
Then a man ran up to
the cross with a sponge of vinegar wine
as everyone watched to see the divine
occur, but just then with a horrible cry
Jesus let out his last breath and he died.
Inside the temple, the curtain that hung
at the holy of holies was ripped from its rung
and torn right in half. A soldier who'd stood
by the cross, who had watched Jesus die understood
saying, "Surely this man was the son of God."
Near
to him stood the women whom Jesus held dear.
As they'd always followed and cared for his needs,
they stayed there with Jesus and watched their friend bleed.
That evening Joseph of Arimathea
told Pilate, "Tomorrow through all of Judea,

the Sabbath will keep us from burying him."
So Pilate gave Jesus' body to them.
Jesus' body was wrapped and prepared
and placed in a tomb with the greatest of care.
They rolled a great stone at the entrance so none
could pilfer the corpse of the Lord's only son.

Mark 16

When the Sabbath was over, the women returned
with spices, but they saw the stone had been turned
back from the grave. They hurried to where
they saw a young man in white sitting there.
"Don't be alarmed," he said, "as you look
for Jesus of Nazareth. Nobody took
his body. He's risen! Tell all of his friends
that they'll see him soon. This is not the end!"

Luke 1:1 - 1:4

Many have tried to account for the things
that Jesus fulfilled, so now I will bring
the message to you that was passed down to me
by those who were with him, that you might believe.
In all of my studies, I never have found
any doubt in the word that I now hand down.
This account's written so you, my friend, may
know all about what you've been taught of the Way.

Luke 1:5 - 1:25

In King Herod's day, there lived a priest who
had no children. When the man entered into
the temple to light the incense he found
an angel of God stood there on the ground.
"Zechariah," it said, "fear not, for you soon
shall find a son dwelling inside your wife's womb.
His name shall be John. He's a blessing to all,
and he'll be filled up by the Lord's holy call.
He's come to prepare the way for the Lord.
For soon shall be sent the greatest reward."
Zechariah was shocked, "But I am so old!"
"I'm Gabriel! Shall it not be as I've told?
You did not believe, and so for your sin
I'll close up your mouth until the day when
your son is born."
Then Zechariah found he
could not speak or tell the great vision he'd seen.
Elizabeth, his wife, felt her stomach swell

with child.
"The Lord and His glory will dwell
in the life of this child. You've taken away
my disgrace. Let him follow and do as you say."

Luke 1:26 - 1:55

In the sixth month, God sent his angel to go
to the small town of Nazareth, and so bestow
a child to Mary, a virgin, though she
was pledged to a man as his young bride to be.
The angel went to her and said, "Greetings to
the one who is favored. I come unto you
for the Lord loves you truly, and so He has sent
a gift unto you with the greatest intent.
A child...*the* child!...will fill up your womb!"
"But I am a virgin, sir. What of my groom?"
"Don't fear," said the angel, "for soon you shall bear
the Son of God, who shall be known everywhere.
Name the boy Jesus. He'll reign on the throne.
They'll call him Emmanuel. You're not alone.
Your cousin, Elizabeth, is pregnant too.
There is not a limit to what God can do.
Though fearful, she said, "I'm the Lord's servant. May
I be used by His hand to pave the Lord's way."
Then Mary set out for her cousin's to be
with family nearby during this pregnancy.
She called out, "Hello!" and Elizabeth heard
and the child inside of her leaped at the word.
"Mary!" she called, "O blessed are you
among women! How is it that I am blessed to
stand with the mother of our Lord, for I
felt my baby leap at the sound of your cry!"
Then Mary replied, "My soul glorifies
the Lord. How my soul rejoices and sighs
for He has been mindful of this humble girl.
Generations shall bless me across the whole world.
The Mighty One, He has done great things through me!
He scatters the proud. Take notice, and see

Him lift up the humble and strike down great kings.
The hungriest bellies fill with great things.
He's merciful. Israel, his servant, cries
out and He hears her, for she is His prize."

Luke 1:56 - 1:80

Elizabeth's child was born and the name
they gave him was John. The tongue that was lame
was healed up, and then Zechariah cried out
his praises to God as some stood about.
They said, "This is strange. The Lord's hand is on
their son."
Zechariah said, "Silence is gone!
Replaced by the love that I have for my Lord.
He cut out my tongue, but it has been restored!
God's raised His horn of salvation for all.
Remember the covenant, and do not fall
into the temptations this world provides.
We each must serve righteously as He decides.
My child...my son...will be called the one
who readies the way so God's will may be done.
The rising sun comes and shines without cease
through the shadow of death so that we may find peace."

Luke 2:1 - 2:20

In those days Caesar Augustus decreed
that a census be taken, so men went to be
counted in their town. Joseph went to
Bethlehem with Mary, though she was due.
And while they were there the baby was born.
They swaddled him tightly to keep the boy warm.
In a small stable manger the savior of men
lay sleeping, for there was no room in the inn.
The shepherds who tended their sheep in the fields
nearby were alarmed when God's glory revealed.
A chorus of angels shone round them and said,
"Do not be afraid. We bring good news instead!

The Messiah is born! He lies now within
a manger and stable behind a small inn."
The chorus broke forth, "O glory above!
And peace to all men who seek God in love!"
So the shepherds went forth and found the new babe,
in the manger the angels had said he was laid.
They praised Jesus, and Mary treasured their words.
They left to tell everyone what had occurred.

Luke 2:21 - 2:40

Then Jesus was brought to Jerusalem where
he'd be blessed in the temple, and while he was there
a man who was touched by the Spirit was told
that he would not die till his eyes could behold
the Messiah. When Jesus was brought in he said,
"Lord, as you promised, before I was dead
I'd see the salvation which You have prepared
for the Jews and the Gentiles as You declared."

Luke 2:41 - 2:52

When Jesus was twelve his parents went down
to Jerusalem. They always went to the town
for the Passover Feast, and when it was done
Joseph and Mary left. Somehow their son
slipped away. Thinking him still with them, they
did not realize he wasn't there for a day.
Returning, they searched for three days till they found
him there in the temple courts sitting around
with teachers who all were amazed at his words.
Each answer he gave amazed all who heard.
His mother said, "Don't you know how scared we were?!
Why did you hide from us?"
He looked at her.
"Mother," he said, "did you not know I
would be in my Father's house when you arrived?"
His parents did not understand his words, though.
His wisdom and stature continued to grow.

Luke 3

John, the cousin of Jesus, became
a preacher who sought to teach and proclaim
repentance and of the forgiveness of sins.
Isaiah had written of John's preaching when
he wrote of "A voice of one man calling out
in the desert. 'Prepare for the Lord. Be devout
and make straight His path.'"
John said to the crowd,
"Repent and be baptized. The haughty and proud
shall all be cut down and thrown in the fire."
The crowd asked him, "What does the Lord God desire?"
So John said, "If you have two robes, then take one
and give it to someone who's poor and has none."
Collectors of taxes came too and asked, "How
can we all be purified?"
"Take what's allowed,
but don't collect more."
Some soldiers said, "And
what shall we do?"
"Do not plague the land
with extortion and lies. Be good to those who
you protect and the grace of God shall be with you."
Many thought John was the Christ, but he said,
"I baptize with water, for I go ahead
of one who comes after me. I heed his call.
With Spirit and fire, he'll baptize you all!"
And when the day came that Jesus came to
John to be baptized, John said, "It's you!"
The heavens were opened and just like a dove
the Spirit came down and a voice said, "I love
My Son, and I'm pleased by him."
And so began,
at thirty, Christ's ministry to all of man.

Luke 4:1 - 4:13

Jesus went into the desert and stayed
for forty days where he was tempted and plagued
by Satan who said, "You are fasting? Be fed!
Turn one of these stones lying here into bread."
But Jesus replied, "Bread alone will not feed
a man. The Lord's glory is what the soul needs."
The devil then said, "You can rule everything
if you'll worship me as your lord and your king."
"Man worships one God, ignoring the rest
and no man should put the Lord to the test."
Bested, the devil retired again
to wait for his chance to tempt Jesus with sin.

Luke 4:14 - 4:30

Then Jesus returned to Nazareth, and
went to the synagogue, taking in hand
the scroll of Isaiah. He started to read.
"The Spirit of God is now upon me.
I'm sent to give sight to the blind and proclaim
the Lord's favor to the oppressed and the lame."
He rolled up the scroll saying, "All you God-fearing,
today this scripture's fulfilled in your hearing."
The crowd had all heard but did not understand.
As they started to speak, Jesus lifted his hand.
"Surely you'll ask for miraculous signs.
No prophet's accepted in his town, and mine
is surely no different."
They all gathered 'round.
They shouted at him and drove him from town.
They tried to throw him off a cliff on that day,
but he parted the crowd and went on his way.

Luke 4:31 - 4:44

In Capernaum a man possessed said, "What do
you want with us, Jesus of Nazareth? You

have come to destroy us. I know where you're from!
You're God's Holy One!"
"Be silent and come
out of this man, demon!"
Then the man fell
as the spirit possessing the man was expelled.
News of this spread as Jesus kept healing
all the possessed and those who were feeling
feverish, ill, and those who were dying.
Many came to him, because he was trying
to heal all he could, but finally he said,
"I must leave because the good news must be spread."

Luke 5:1 - 5:11

As Jesus walked by the Galilee, he
saw fishermen's boats all beached by the sea.
He launched Simon's boat away from the beach
and then from the sea he started to teach.
When Jesus was done, he said, "Simon, go
to sea in this boat and I want you to throw
your nets out again."
"But Master, we sought
to catch fish all night and nothing was caught.
But since you have asked, we'll try it again."
So they threw their nets out and then they hauled in
a catch so enormous the boat could not hold
them all.
"I am sinful!" Peter extolled.
"I did not believe!"
But Jesus said, "Now
you'll catch men, not fish. And I'll show you how."
They pulled up their boats and left them on shore
and went off with Jesus so they could learn more.

Luke 5:12 - 5:26

In town a man came who had leprosy and
he cried out to Jesus, who took the man's hand.

The man said, "Lord, heal me."
So Jesus replied,
"Be clean!" Thus he healed him and said, "Now confide
in no one that I was the one who healed you."
But when people saw that his skin was like new,
they questioned him, and many heard how he came
to be healed, but Jesus did not want the fame.
He often withdrew from the crowds, but then he
would go back to teach so the many could see
the path of the Lord.
As he taught one day
a crowd gathered round and impeded the way
to get in the house where Jesus was teaching.
One group had come there, but not for his preaching.
Instead they had carried their paralyzed friend,
that Jesus might touch him so that he would mend.
Because of the crowd they climbed on the roof
and lowered him down. When he saw the proof
of faith, Jesus reached out and said to the man,
"Your sins are forgiven."
But some men on hand
were Pharisees and they said, "Blasphemy! Who
forgives but the Lord?"
But Jesus said, "You
should not think such things. It's easier to
forgive this man's sins than say to him, 'You!
Get up now and walk.' But so you'll believe;
get up now, my friend. Take your mat and leave."
The paralyzed man stood up and received
the joy of the Lord, and many believed.

Luke 5:27 - 5:39

Then Jesus went out and saw a man who
collected the tax. He said, "I tell you,
get up now and follow." The man, Levi, left
his booth and his life of sin and of theft.
He threw a great party, inviting his friends,
all of them sinners who came to attend

and meet this man Jesus.
The Pharisees scoffed,
"You eat with these people?"
"Why would you cut off
these people from God? I ask you who needs
a doctor? The healthy? Of course not. Indeed,
I wasn't sent here for the righteous at all.
I'm here for the sinners. Let them hear my call."
But Jesus was questioned, "Why do you not fast?
The law says you must."
"My time has not passed.
Do guests of the groom fast when he is there?
Rejoice while I'm here. The time for despair
is not yet upon us. I tell you new wine
can't go in old wineskins. For after a time
the skins can't accept what is new, so they burst.
The wine I give will not quench everyone's thirst."

Luke 6:1 - 6:11

On the Sabbath, Jesus was out in the fields.
His disciples took handfuls and ate of the yield,
but the Pharisees said, "Why do you break the law?"
"Have you been offended by what you just saw?"
asked Jesus. "Remember that David's own men
ate holy bread. Would you declare that a sin?
Yet you rebuke me! I tell you, the Son
of Man is the Lord of the Sabbath. What's done
on that day is his. No one else's."
When they
were waiting to see if he would disobey
the Sabbath by healing, he said to the crowd,
"What on the Sabbath has our Lord allowed?
Would God rather have us go heal or go hate?
Is it good to just leave all the poor to their fate?"
So he healed a man and the Pharisees then
said, "Now we have witnessed this man and his sin."

Luke 6:12 - 6:49

Jesus took his twelve disciples and he
went to a place and a crowd came to see.
"Blessed," said Jesus, "are all of the poor,
for the kingdom of God is theirs. Furthermore,
Blessed are those who are hungry for they
will be satisfied. Blessed are those on this day
who are weeping, for they will find comfort. And you
who are hated because of all that which I do
are blessed in my name. Rejoice and proclaim,
for all of the prophets were treated the same.
But woe to the rich, for their comfort has come.
The well fed and laughing forget where they're from.
But those who have hated you, you have to love.
Bless those who curse you, for you are not of
this Earth if you're mine. If one strikes your cheek,
offer the other to him and be meek.
Give when they ask and do not demand
that they give it back. My greatest command
is do unto others as you'd have them do
to you. This above all I ask out of you.
Any man loves those who love him, so why
should that bring you credit? In sacrifice I
am with you. So do not judge your fellow man.
Forgive and you will be forgiven. How can
the blind lead the blind? If you should perceive
a speck in another man's eyes, first relieve
yourself of the log that's in your own eye.
Only a good tree brings good fruit. You cry,
'Lord!' when you see me, but all that I say
is ignored. A house built on sand sweeps away
when the water comes in. But a house built on rock
is safe. So in righteousness put all your stock."

Luke 7:1 - 7:10

In Capernaum a Roman centurion's slave
was ill, and some elderly Jews came and gave

testament to all the good he had done.
"Jesus, please help him. His slave's like a son,
and he even paid for our synagogue, so
would you please go see him?"
"Yes, I will go."
But the Roman said, "Why should you help me, for I
am unworthy of you. Just say so and my
servant will heal, for authority's yours."
Surprised, Jesus said, "Even on my own shores
in Israel I have not seen faith so strong.
Your servant is healed and to me you belong."

Luke 7:11 - 7:35

Later a woman came out and she cried,
for she was a widow and her son had died.
"Don't cry," Jesus said. He touched the boy and
the boy sat up, having been healed by his hand.
The people were shocked, and word spread around
that a prophet fulfilling God's will had been found.
The Baptist sent men. They asked, "Are you he
who we have been waiting for?"
"You've come to me
for now the blind see and now the dead live.
Go and tell John of the one who can give
the life everlasting. Go tell him that he
was the messenger sent to proclaim before me."

Luke 7:36 - 7:50

A man had invited Jesus to come
dine at his home with some friends who were from
the Pharisee class. When a sinner approached
she knelt down at Jesus' feet. Though she broached
etiquette, Jesus did not stop her when
she poured out expensive perfume on his skin.
She used her own hair as she cleansed his feet. She
cried, "Mercy, Lord Jesus. Have mercy on me."
The Pharisee thought that a prophet should know

to cast off this sinner and that he should show
her out. But Jesus said to him, "Let me
tell you a story. Two debtors could see
that they couldn't pay, so the lender forgave
their debts, rather than turn them both into slaves.
One owed five hundred, and fifty the other.
Which of these two was more grateful, my brother?"
"The one who owed more," said the Pharisee.
"Yes!
And she needs forgiveness much more than your guests."
Then Jesus told her, "You're forgiven."
But men
said, "No one but God can forgive someone's sin."

Luke 8:1 - 8:21

When many were gathered, Jesus said, "There
was a farmer who scattered his seeds everywhere.
Some fell on the path and were eaten by crows.
Some fell on the rocks with no moisture to grow.
Some fell in the thorns, and were choked from the field.
Some fell in good earth and they gave a yield
a hundred times more than what had been sown.
From seeds of the godly, great numbers are grown.
What man lights a lamp, then hides it? And so
those who have light are expected to grow
the faith amongst others. So when you receive
these gifts you must share them so more may believe!
Then someone said, "Jesus, your family is here."
But Jesus said, "You are mistaken it's clear.
My family are those who hear the Lord's word
and follow His will and all they have heard."

Luke 8:22 - 8:39

Jesus and his twelve disciples were in
a boat on the Sea of Galilee when
a storm arose blowing the boat around and
the apostles weren't sure they would make it to land.

Still Jesus was sleeping. They woke him and cried,
"We're going to die in the waves and the tide!"
But Jesus said, "Quiet now, storm!" And the waves
subsided. "If you just have faith, you'll be saved."
The disciples were shocked.
"Who is he?" they gaped.
"He silenced the winds so we could escape."
They sailed on in awe, amazed by the one
they followed; they didn't know he was God's son.
They reached the far side and encountered a man
who lived in the tombs and was touched by the hand
of a demon.
He saw Jesus and he said, "You!
Son of the Lord! What have you come to do?"
"What's your name, demon?"
"Legion. For I
am many."
A large herd of pigs stood nearby.
So Jesus cast those demons into the swine,
they ran from their pen and to the ridgeline.
They all tumbled over the ledge to the sea
and drowned. The witnesses all turned to flee.
They told all the townspeople what had occurred,
and many came out after what they had heard.
They saw the man who'd been possessed at the feet
of Jesus. His change had been so complete,
the people feared Jesus, and seeing this he
returned to his boat and the Galilee Sea.

Luke 8:40 - 8:56

He sailed to the other shore, where he was met
with cheers by the people, and he was beset
by those who declared, "The daughter of our
rabbi is ill. She's in her final hour."
So Jesus went with them as they swarmed about,
and a woman who suffered from bleeding reached out
and touched just the hem of his robe.
"Who is there?"

His friends told him, "Jesus, the crowd's everywhere."
"No, someone just touched me for healing. For I
felt the power go out of me."
"I did," she cried.
"Forgive me."
"Oh woman, your faith is so strong.
For that you are healed."
Then they went along,
but a man rushed up crying, "O rabbi, she's dead."
The crowd started weeping, but then Jesus said,
"Have faith."
So they went to the home and they saw
the little girl's body.
"Let us all withdraw.
It's true, she is dead," said the rabbi.
"She's not,"
said Jesus, "she's sleeping."
Then everyone thought
he was crazy, but he took the little girl's hand
and life returned to her upon his command.

Luke 9:1 - 9:27

Jesus told all his disciples, "You've seen
my miracles. Now you must be the machine.
I give you the power to do in my name
great miracles, and to go forth and proclaim
the good news to all. You never shall lack
for food or for shelter. Take what's on your back
and go."
The disciples began speaking of
the things Jesus taught them; of hope and of love.
Herod was wary of Jesus, you see,
he'd heard Jesus was John the Baptist, whom he
had beheaded, returned from the grave. So he sought
to meet Jesus and hear the things that he taught.
During this time, the apostles returned
to tell Jesus all they had done and had learned.
So they were with Jesus when he preached the word

to five thousand people.
"Tell all those who heard
you speak that they now must go into the town,"
the disciples told him. "The crowd must go down
and find their own meals."
But Jesus said, "We
should feed them."
"There's only two fish from the sea
and five loaves of bread," they told him. "How can
we feed all five thousand? We might feed a man
and his family."
"Give me what you have," Jesus said.
He gave thanks to God and passed out the bread
and fish. When the people had eaten their fill,
the baskets came back. Each one of them still
was full of food; even more than they contained
when started, which none of Christ's friends could explain.
Then they all realized the message was true.
"He's the Messiah. Look what he can do!"
they said to themselves.
But he said, "Do not
tell others who I am. Just teach what I taught."
He preached to the crowds, "If you are in love
with this earthly life, you'll lose it. What of
the eternal? If you hate your life, you will gain
true joy, and you'll escape worldly pain."

Luke 9:28 - 9:62

On a mountaintop, Jesus was visited by
Elijah and Moses. A voice in the sky
said, "This is My son, whom I love. So obey
the things that he's taught and all he will say."
Some apostles saw this. In fear they did not
tell others what they had seen, for they all thought
no one would believe them. In fear they left and
went back down with Jesus, then into the land.
A man came to Jesus and said, "Please come fast.
My son is possessed. For in the months past,

your disciples could not cure him."
"People, how long
must I preach to you? Your faith is not strong!"
Jesus said. "Take me to him."
Together they found
the boy. Jesus cured him.
"Surely the sound
of my voice is not understood by you, for still
you don't listen nor do you know the Lord's will.
Betrayal approaches. Hear me while I
am here. For later you surely will cry."
But rather than hearing his words, all his friends
argued which one was the closest to him.
Then Jesus pulled forward a child and said,
"Welcome a child to your side instead
of arguing. You who bring my children in
welcome the Father and shun what is sin."
"But what about those using your name to save
others, Lord? We know that you never gave
them authority."
"Fools! Those who are not against
you and your mission are for you. But since
you don't understand the price that it takes
to follow me, friends, then soon I shall make
you abandon your lives and preach what is true.
A difficult path will be given to you."

Luke 10:1 - 10:24

He took his disciples and sent them in pairs.
"Take nothing with you, for much will be shared,"
he told them. "If you are not greeted, don't scoff
or shun anybody. Just brush the dust off
your shoes and continue, for there will be those
who love you, but you shall encounter some foes.
The kingdom of God is now drawing near.
Spread hope to the people, for hope destroys fear."
They found that by using his name then they could
destroy wickedness and enhance what was good.

"We can drive demons away!" they exclaimed.
"All things, with faith, can be done in my name."

Luke 10:25 - 10:42

An expert asked Jesus, "Out of the ten
commandments, which one is the greatest of them?"
"What do you think?" Jesus asked.
So the man
replied, "To love God with all that you can.
And after that, to love your neighbor as you
love yourself."
"Exactly! If you can go do
these things you will please the Father. Hear me!
As a Jewish man walked on the road alone, he
was attacked and left on the road there to die.
A priest who walked by ignored the man's cry.
So did the temple assistant, but then
the despised, a Samaritan, stopped to help him!
So who here showed mercy?"
The man who had asked
said, "The Samaritan."
"This is your task!
I won't be here long, so hear all I say
so you can do God's will when I've gone away."

Luke 11

Jesus then spoke to his friends about prayer.
"The Lord listens to all you ask for. He cares,
but you must keep asking. For if you persist
the Lord will deliver, for He can't resist.
Just knock on the door, it is opened for you."
Despite what he said, there still were a few
who believed that the devil had given him power.
"I cast out the demons because it's the hour
that God came to man so His word is taught."
A man cried out, "Blessed is she who has brought
you into this world."

"More blessed are they,"
said Jesus, "who heard the Lord's word on this day.
The world seeks signs, but Jonah was shown
what would happen to Nineveh. He was not known
in that place. The same way, the Son of Man's signs
are sent for the people in these troubled times.
You don't light a lamp, then hide it away.
The light overcomes the darkness till day
has come to the world. You Pharisees shun
what's righteous! Why do you want God's will undone?"
"How dare you insult us!" a Pharisee said.
"Should I not correct you before you are dead?
Such sorrow awaits those who turn men from light.
You study the law, but don't know what's right!"

Luke 12

Jesus then spoke to the crowd, "Fear the yeast
of hypocrisy that has been spread by the priests.
My friends, do not fear if they seek to kill you.
Fear God! Your faith will truly accrue
in the eyes of the Lord. But money does not.
Guard against greed. The man who has bought
many things on this Earth is a fool. So I tell
you all not to worry if you buy or sell.
What's that to the Lord? Does God not provide
the food for the birds? But you are His pride.
So why should you fear? Can your worries add one
moment to life? When your life is done
the Father shall greet those who built up their stores
in Heaven, not those who were here and earned more.
So always be ready, for no man will know
when the Lord shall arrive. Wherever you go
prepare yourself, people. The Master returns!
I'll set the whole world on fire. It yearns
for my terrible baptism. I don't bring peace!
I've come to divide people. I will not cease
till families are split; when daughter and mother
divide, and till brother is set against brother.

Some are my children, but some are against.
Let no man say my words have ever been minced.
Many men know how the weather will be,
but few know what's right. So come, follow me.
For the Judge shall come soon, and the jailer awaits,
but still there is time to avoid such a fate."

Luke 13:1 - 13:9

Then Jesus told all his disciples, "Repent,
for there is still time. That's why I was sent.
A man had a fig tree that didn't bear fruit.
He said to the gardener, 'Cut out the root.
It's taking up space.' But the gardener said, 'Give
me time. If it bears fruit, then we'll let it live.
But if it does not, cut it down.' Don't you hear
the words that I share? Will you all adhere?"

Luke 13:10 - 13:35

On the Sabbath day, Jesus saw one woman who
was stooped in her back. He said to her, "You
are cured of your sickness."
But then the priest said,
"Don't heal on the Sabbath! Why don't you instead
heal on the other six days? Don't you know
that this day is holy?"
"You hypocrites show
that you know the law, but still you don't see
what God really wants! Now listen to me.
God's kingdom is like the yeast in the bread.
With one tiny pinch the yeast will be spread
throughout all the dough. A little love brings
His kingdom to Earth and into all things.
Work for God, or He won't open the door
to His kingdom."
"Do you not know what is in store
for you?" said the priests. "Herod has said
that he will not stop until you are dead!"

Then Jesus replied, "Go tell him that I
will continue today and whatever he tries,
I'll continue tomorrow, but on the third day
I'll accomplish my purpose. The only good way
to martyr a prophet is when he's within
Jerusalem's walls. That's the time when
the death of a prophet can be made complete.
Oh Jerusalem, how near you are to defeat."

Luke 14:1 - 14:24

Jesus was out at a dinner one night
and noticed how everyone wanted to fight
to sit in the seats of honor, so they
would be given respect. But Jesus said, "Stay
away from the head of the table, for when
a distinguished guest enters, the host will come in
and ask you to move. How embarrassing! Though,
if you take the lowliest seat then you'll know
that your host will see you and ask you to move
to a place of more honor, and you'll be approved
by all who are there. And if you should throw
a banquet, do not invite those whom you know.
Instead invite all of the poor and the lame.
Then you'll be blessed, for the Lord does the same
by inviting those in who have comforted those
who are lowly, for they are the ones that He knows."
A man at the party said, "How fun to be
at a banquet in Heaven! I can't wait to see
how it is."
Jesus said, "A feast was prepared,
and the man asked his friends to come and to share
in the meal, but they made excuses, so he
said to his servant, 'Bring unto me
the weak and the lame. Invite them. Make haste!
Those I called first won't have even a taste.'"

Luke 14:25 - 14:35

A crowd was with Jesus when he turned to say,
"My path, you will find, is a difficult way.
For those who come with me must give up the ones
they love. You must carry your cross. As I've done,
you must give up all things, all possessions, for you
can have nothing if you are to do as I do.
But count the cost carefully. One does not start
a great building if he cannot pay for the parts.
Salt seasons all. If it loses its taste,
you can't make it salty again. It is waste.
So if you have ears, you must listen today
so you understand all these things that I say."

Luke 15

The tax collectors and sinners would come
to hear Jesus speak. He would not shy from
being around them, despite what some said.
He spent time with them and often broke bread
in their homes. He told them, "If one sheep is lost,
the good shepherd searches for it, though the cost
is to leave the whole flock until it is found.
The joy when he finds that one sheep is profound.
How great is the joy God feels when He finds
one who was lost, though He leaves some behind
who have known Him. There once was a man with two sons.
One son was steadfast and faithful, but one
was headstrong, so he told his father, 'Give me
my inheritance now. I want to go see
the world.' He left then, with money in hand.
The son set his sights on faraway lands.
He wasted his money and soon he was so
destitute he didn't know where to go.
He took a poor job feeding pigs, and he found
that he envied the things that they ate off the ground.
'My father's slaves even live better than me,'
he thought, so he said, 'I shall go back and see

if my father will take me as one of his slaves.'
Embarrassed and shamed by how he'd behaved
he returned to his home. When his father saw him,
he shouted and ran out, filled to the brim
with compassion and love for his son.
'Father, please,
let me be your servant. Set my heart at ease
and make me the lowliest for I have sinned.'
But his father cried, 'My son's home again!
Slaughter the fat calf and call all around.
Though my son was lost, he now has been found.'
The older son said, 'He has squandered away
the money you gave to him, but all of my days
I have been by your side, being faithful and true.'
The father said, 'I shall give all things to you,
but do not be angry, for I'm full of joy.
For though he was lost I've recovered my boy!
I love both of you, so forgive my elation,
but today is a time for great celebration!'"

Luke 16

His disciples were gathered, so Jesus said, "There
was a man who had managed a rich man's affairs.
But the rich man decided to fire him, so
he said, 'Get the books all in order. I know
you've wasted my money, so at the day's end
you're fired.'
The man knew he couldn't depend
on others to help him, so he thought, 'I know
how I can make friends.' He set out to go
see all those who owed the rich man. He asked
the first, 'What's your debt?'
'It's 800 casks
of oil.'
'Now we'll make it 400.' So
he went to the next. 'Tell me what you owe.'
'1,000 bushels of wheat.'
'Let us make

your debt now 800.'
In this way he'd take
every man's debt and reduce it so he
built up many friends. The rich man could see
that this man was shrewd. My point is that you
are shrewd in this world, but God asks you to
take all that you have in this world and use
your efforts to help, not harm or abuse.
Your time here is short! If you're trustworthy when
you have worldly treasures, the Lord sees and then
He'll give to you treasures in Heaven reserved
for righteous men. Truly, no man can serve
two masters. This message was written and said
by prophets. If they all returned from the dead,
the rich would not heed them, and they would not save
the poor, and so they won't be saved from the grave."

Luke 17:1 - 17:10

Jesus said to them, "Temptation awaits
every man, but there is truly no fate
worse than the one that the tempter shall face.
For he who leads little ones into disgrace
ought to be cast out into the sea
and dragged to the bottom, for his fate shall be
his hell. But the sinners you all must forgive
if they should repent, for then they shall live."
Then one of his friends said, "Master, how can
we improve our own faith?"
"You don't understand.
With faith just as large as a mustard seed, then
you can say to this tree, 'Go cast yourself in
to the sea,' and it would! Do your duty and you
will find you're not thanked for the things that you do.
Though a servant's not thanked by his master, still he
does what he's told, as you must do for me."

Luke 17:11 - 17:37

On Samaria's border, ten lepers cried, "Lord,
please save us!"
So Jesus said, "Find your reward
of healing. Go now to the priests."
So the men
went into the temple and saw that their skin
was healed. One ran back and said, "Jesus, you
are the glory of God! All honor is due
to you and the Lord!" Then he fell at the feet
of Jesus and bowed down to him in the street.
"I thought I healed ten?" Jesus said, "Where are they?
Only you, a Samaritan, knows to obey
and honor the Lord. Your faith is much stronger
than that of my kinsmen. It won't be much longer
until you all see God's Kingdom arrive,
but for that the Son of Man cannot survive.
He'll suffer and then be cut down by this nation;
rejected completely by this generation.
Your parties and feasts will be swept away.
The good shall be honored, and evil shall pay
a terrible price. How the mighty shall fear.
For the signs indicate that the end has drawn near."

Luke 18:1 - 18:14

Jesus said, "There was a judge without care
for his people or God. To him, in despair,
a widow would come every day with her plea,
'Judge, give me justice.'
He wouldn't, but she
persisted, so finally he said, 'I cannot
bear this any longer. Give her what she's sought.'
So even this wicked man gave her what she
had asked for. God loves you! Won't He hear your plea
if you are persistent and cry for what's right?
Be ready by day and steadfast at night.
Two men went to pray. A Pharisee and

a tax man. They two of them both went to stand
in prayer. The Pharisee said, 'I know I
don't sin, I don't cheat, I don't steal, I don't lie.'
But the other man beat on his chest and he said,
'Be merciful, God! I sin and I dread
Your greatness.'
This man received honor for he
had humbled himself, but the proud Pharisee
had exalted himself. Their places will switch
in the kingdom of God where the poor man is rich."

Luke 18:15 - 19:10

Some parents brought their little children to see
Jesus, but all the disciples said, "He
is too busy for children."
"Let them come to me,"
said Jesus. "I tell you the truth, you must be
like a child receiving God's word, for to them
the kingdom is given." So they went to him.
A priest said, "Good Teacher, what's needed to
inherit eternal life?"
"Friend, you must do
what's commanded. Abstain from all evil."
"I've done
these things all my life."
"Then there is still one
commandment I give. Sell all you own and
follow me, friend. That's the final command."
But this man was rich, so he slipped away,
disliking what Jesus had told him.
"I say,
it is easier to thread a camel right through
the eye of a needle than for the rich to
enter God's kingdom."
"Then who can get in?"
a man asked.
"We all can, for though we have sin,
the Lord can forgive us. When we are alone

we are nothing, but we can inherit the throne
through Him. The Son of Man soon goes to die
so all men may enter and sit by his side."
Then Jesus continued his ministry and
his miracles. He came to save the whole land.
He cured a blind man who believed in him, then
he went down to Jericho. There with the men
was a tax man...a sinner. To him Jesus said,
"Zacchaeus, why don't you and I go break bread?"
The priests were disgusted, and they said, "That man
is a sinner."
But Jesus ignored the priests and
broke bread with Zacchaeus, who told Jesus, "I
will give half of my wealth to the poor. If I lied
or cheated a man, I'll return what I owe."
"You were lost," Jesus said, "but you're found, and you know
the way into Heaven. The Son of Man came
to find and to bless all the lost in God's name."

Luke 19:11 - 19:27

When the crowd gathered 'round, Jesus said, "There
was a man who told his servants, 'You must each care
for my wealth while I'm gone.' And when he returned
he went to his servants to see what they'd earned.
The first said, 'I took what you gave me and I
made ten times your money.'
'Good job!' he replied.
The second said, 'I have made five times what you
entrusted to me.'
'You're good and you're true!'
The third man said, 'Master, I know you are cruel.
I hid what you gave me. It's still here.'
'You fool!
Your own words condemn you! Why did you not take
the coins to a bank? At least I could make
some interest upon it. Give it to the man
who increased my wealth tenfold, for all those who can
do well with what's given to them shall receive

more blessings. But to those who lie and deceive,
the little they have shall be taken away.'
All those who have ears, hear what I say.
With talents you're given, you must understand,
God expects you to use them to do His command."

Luke 19:28 - 19:44

Jesus went on, and as he drew near
to Jerusalem he said, "Before I appear
in the City of David, go just up ahead
and there you will find tied up in a shed,
a donkey. Go fetch it, and if someone asks,
say the Lord needs it, then finish your task."
He rode on the donkey as they started down
to Jerusalem. When they came into the town,
people were shouting, "All blessings to he
who comes in the name of the Lord. Peace shall be
his crown and his glory."
"Stop saying such things!"
the Pharisees said.
"Then voices would ring
right out of the rocks," Jesus said, "because none
can silence their praise for the Lord and His son."
But as he came near, he wept for he knew
that none truly wanted such peace.
"Oh, the few
who still shall remain when your walls are destroyed!
You don't seek salvation, though you have enjoyed
the Lord as your own. If you understood
what peace truly means, you'd do as you should!"

Luke 19:45 - 20:19

Jesus entered the temple and saw
the merchants, their money, and all of their stalls.
"My Father's house now is a den full of sin!"
yelled Jesus.
They could not arrest him right then,

so Jesus taught there in the temple till they
shouted at him, "These things that you say.
Upon whose authority is it you teach?"
Jesus asked, "Who told the Baptist to preach?"
The Pharisees said, "We know if we say
it was Heaven he'll ask why we did not obey.
But if we say man, we'll be stoned today,
for the crowd thinks that he was a prophet." So they
replied, "We don't know."
"Then I will not say
who tells me to speak." Then he went on his way.
He spoke to the people, "There once was a man
who planted a vineyard, and leased out his land
to farmers.
When it was the time to collect
the rent he instructed his servant, 'Inspect
my land and bring back my rent.' So he went
but they beat up the servant. The landowner sent
two men after that, but both were run off.
The landowner said, they surely won't scoff
or attack my own son, so he sent him, but he
was killed by the farmers.
'So it shall be,'
the landowner said. He killed each evil man.
He found righteous men and leased them his land."
The priests knew that Jesus had just chastened them,
so they looked for reasons to go arrest him.

Luke 20:20 - 20:47

The leaders sent spies who asked, "Jesus, should
we pay tax to Caesar? It does not seem good."
So Jesus said, "Show me a coin. Tell me who
is shown on the coin?"
"It is Caesar."
"Then you,
should give unto Caesar what's his. But then give
to God what is God's, so that you might live."
Some Sadducees came, asking Jesus to speak

on marriage.
"I tell you that this is unique
to Earth, for in Heaven you don't marry. You
shall live again there when your life here is through.
He's Lord of the living, and not of the dead,
for all are alive in His eyes." Then he said
to all in the crowd, "I tell you, beware
of the teachers of law, for they only care
for honors. Watch them cheat widows as they
pretend to be pious as you watch them pray."

Luke 21

While Jesus was there in the temple, he saw
the rich people tithing to uphold the law.
A widow then entered and dropped two coins in
the offering box. Jesus said, "There have been
many others who gave more money than she
but she offered everything, so she shall be
credited that in Heaven. Soon none
of this temple will stand. It shall all be undone.
Many shall come in my name, but the end
is not at our doorstep. You've known me, my friends,
but others will not. Do all that you can
to spread the good news to your fellow man.
A great persecution is coming, and you
will be hated because of my actions. So do
everything to help my faithful to be
strong in the face of adversity. See
the signs everywhere as the leaves of a tree
come out for the seasons. Say to them, 'We
are the people of God. So let us watch out!
Ignore what is worldly. You are devout.'
Though Heaven and Earth may disappear, my
words shall not falter, and you shall not die,
for in me there's hope."
He taught anyone
who would listen to him, and turned away none.

Luke 22:1 - 22:46

Judas Iscariot left and betrayed
Jesus. Then when all the plans had been made
for the Passover meal, he waited as he
looked for the perfect time Jesus could be
arrested.
When all the disciples came to
a room to break bread, Jesus said, "You
are friends. I am glad to spend time here before
my suffering starts."
And then Jesus tore
the bread saying, "This is my body. It's broken
for you. Remember me." Once he had spoken
he passed it around, and then took the wine
and told the disciples, "This blood is mine.
It's poured out in sacrifice. This is the new
covenant. My blood is given for you.
But one at this table betrays me."
But none
could believe it was true, except for the one.
All the disciples were arguing who
was considered the greatest amongst them.
"How do
you think it will be? I tell you that he
who's the lowest of servants, that one shall be
the greatest of all."
He told Peter, "I
have prayed that your faith won't falter."
"But why?
I'd happily die for you, Lord."
"Before dawn,
you'll deny me three times."
"I won't! You are wrong!"
"You say that you won't, but you will," Jesus said.
Then after the whole of the group had been fed
they went to the Mount of Olives and there
Jesus stood off by himself deep in prayer.
"Father, take this cup of suffering from

my lips. But I know that this deed must be done."
He woke all his friends, saying, "Pray for this nation,
and pray that you're saved from the coming temptation."

Luke 22:47 - 22:65

At this time a group of soldiers came near
and Judas was with them.
"So, finally you're here,"
said Jesus. And then Judas kissed him.
"Is this
how the son is betrayed on this night? With a kiss?"
But then the disciples came out of the night.
One picked up a sword and started to fight.
He sliced off the ear of a servant.
"Now cease!"
yelled Jesus. "Don't you know that I long for peace?"
He healed the man's ear.
"You came to arrest
once night had descended and you're hidden best.
Have I not been there in the temple where you
could find me? But this is what you chose to do?"
They took him away. Some disciples then came
to see what would happen. They feared that the same
fate would befall them if anyone knew,
so Peter came quietly.
"Hey, I know you,"
a servant girl said. "You're with Jesus."
"I'm not,"
Peter retorted.
"But I also thought
that I saw you with him," another man said.
"No, you're mistaken."
"I thought you were led
by Jesus," said someone.
"No! I don't know
that man!"
Right then, he heard the cock crow.

And Peter remembered the words Jesus said,
as he wept at his weakness, his fear and his dread.

Luke 22:66 - 22:71

At daybreak the priests asked Jesus, "Are you
the Messiah?"
"No matter what I say or do,
you will not believe me. The Son of Man will
soon sit by the Lord, and you will fulfill
the words of the prophets."
"Are you saying you
are the son of the Lord?"
"Your words."
"My friends, do
we need to hear more? He blasphemes!"
So they
took Jesus to Pilate to kill him that day.

Luke 23:1 - 23:25

The priests accused Jesus, so Pilate said, "Do
you really call yourself the king of the Jews?"
"You say so," he answered.
So Pilate said, "He
has done nothing wrong. He's from Galilee.
Send him to Herod."
So Jesus was brought
to Herod who wanted to hear this man's thoughts.
But Jesus would not answer Herod, so he
ridiculed Jesus, but said, "I can't see
any guilt on this man. Send Jesus back to
Pilate. We'll let him decide what to do."
Pilate was going to let Jesus go,
but all the priests said, "Crucify him!"
"You know
I pardon one prisoner each year," Pilate said.
"Kill Jesus! Give us Barabbas instead!"
the crowd yelled at him.

"Very well," he said, "take
this man and go kill him. It's now your mistake."

Luke 23:26 - 23:56

In a place named Golgotha, they crucified him.
They placed him with criminals since he'd defied them.
Jesus said, "Father, forgive them for they
don't know what they do," as he suffered away.
They mocked him and cried, "Oh, Messiah, come down!
You're King of the Jews, so *now* wear your crown!"
One of the criminals said, "If you're great,
save yourself and us as well from this fate!"
But the other said, "Quiet, you fool! We should die
for we're guilty, but this man is not. Jesus, try
to remember me when you're in Heaven."
"Today
you will join me in paradise."
Though it was day,
a darkness fell over the entire land
and the holy shroud ripped, though no human hand
tore it.
And then Jesus said, "Father, I
give over my spirit to You," as he died.
A righteous man, Joseph, who owned a new grave,
asked for the body and went to the cave.
They laid down the corpse of Jesus inside.
The Sabbath was coming, so though he had died
they could not prepare the body so they
knew that they would have to wait for the day
after the Sabbath. In order to block
the body, they covered the tomb with a rock.

Luke 24

On Sunday two women went back to the tomb.
The stone was rolled back. A feeling of doom
encompassed them both. Then two men appeared.
"Don't fear, for the Christ, the one you revered

is not dead! He is risen! And just as he said,
upon the third day he would rise from the dead."
The women ran to the apostles and told
them all that had happened, but none were so bold
to believe what they said, except Peter who ran
to the tomb. Though he saw, he did not understand.
That same day two men were walking along
the road to Emmaus.
A man asked, "What's wrong?"
The two men were sad and said, "You don't know
of Jesus' death? This great prophet showed
us so many miracles. Our priests have killed
our friend. We had hoped that he had fulfilled
the prophecies saying the Christ would arrive.
And even this morning, we heard he's alive.
His body is missing, and no one knows why."
"You fools! Even scripture has said he must die
and suffer for man," the stranger told them.
And so the two men both listened to him.
They sat down to eat. When this stranger broke
the bread and he blessed it, then both men awoke.
It was Jesus with them! When they'd realized,
he disappeared from right in front of their eyes.
They ran to Jerusalem and went to tell
their friends. He'd appeared to Peter as well.
This was amazing, for how could he be
two places at once? Then suddenly he
appeared in their midst just as they began
to tell the disciples their story. All ran
to him as he cried, "Peace be unto you!
Don't fear, for everything you saw is true."
Then Jesus held out his hands and they saw
the holes in his hands. All were in awe.
He ate with them, saying, "It all was fulfilled
as the prophets have written. And though I was killed,
it had to be done. But forgiveness for all
is within each man's grasp. You must give the call
so all people hear. Now the Spirit will be
given to you, so when you follow me

you'll do as I've done. To this city it comes,
and you shall know this is a gift that is from
the Lord."
Then he rose up to Heaven above,
having ended their fear and replaced it with love.
So his followers joyously spoke about him,
till the Spirit came just as Christ promised to them.

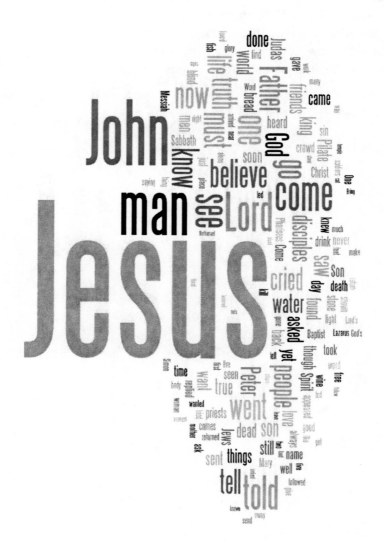

John 1

In the beginning the Lord's Word existed.
The Word was with God. It was God. It resisted
the dark, for the darkness cannot best the flame.
It can't overpower the Word or His name.
God sent a man, John the Baptist, to tell
that the light was approaching so all might be well.
God entered the world that He had created,
but nobody knew Him, though all had awaited
His coming. The people He'd claimed as His own
did not recognize Him, rejecting His throne.
But those who believed were given the right
to be called His children and known in His sight.
The Word became flesh and dwelled here among
us mortals, and out of His glory truth sprung.
The Baptist cried out, saying, "This is the one
I said would come soon. Let God's will be done."
But many asked, "Aren't you the Christ?"
John replied,
"I am the voice in the desert that cried,
'Make straight the path for the Lord!'"
But some asked,
"Why do you baptize? That is a task
the Messiah fulfills."
"I use water," John said,
"but he'll pour the Spirit out over each head.
I am unworthy to touch the Christ's feet.
His grace is amazing. His mercy is sweet."
The next day when John saw Jesus approach,
he cried, "As I said, one above all reproach

is here now amongst us!" Then John said, "I saw
the Spirit come down, more pure than the law,
and it rested on him. This is our reward!
The Messiah has come; the Son of the Lord!
And two of John's followers heard what he said,
so they followed Jesus wherever he led.
One was named Andrew who went out and found
his brother.
"Come, Simon! Great glories abound!
The Messiah has come. Come meet him and see."
And when they arrived, Jesus said, "Before me
stands one who shall be called Peter."
Then they
went out and found more to join the next day.
First Philip, who went to Nathanael and said,
"The Messiah is here. The one men have read
about every Sabbath has come. It's a son
of Nazareth."
"Nazareth? What good can come
from that town?"
"Come on and I'll introduce you."
As they approached, Jesus said, "Here's a true
Israelite. In him I don't see
any falseness."
"How is it that you can know me?"
Nathanael asked him.
"I saw you, as you
sat under the fig tree when Philip came to
invite you to me."
Nathanael was stunned.
"Truly," he said, "you are the Lord's Son!"
"Do you now believe me because I said I
saw you by a tree? How will you reply
when you see the heavens torn open and all
of the angels of God as they rise and fall?
I tell you the truth: if you come with me,
you'll never forget all the things you will see."

John 2:1 - 2:11

At a wedding in Cana, the wine all ran out.
So Jesus' mother went searching about,
and when she found Jesus she told him, "The wine
is gone."
"Dear woman, it's not yet my time."
She turned to the servants and told them, "Just do
whatever it is that my son asks of you."
Then Jesus said, "Fill up the water jars and
take a full ladle. Give it to the man
who's in charge of this feast."
And when this was done,
the man told the groom, "This wine is like none
that I've ever tasted. Most serve the best first,
but this is the good wine. It quenches my thirst."
This was the first of all Jesus' signs.
By turning the water into a fine wine,
the glory of Jesus was shown to the men
who'd be his disciples and call Jesus, "Friend."

John 2:12 - 2:25

Then Jesus went down to Capernaum to spend
the Passover with his whole family, but when
he went to the temple he saw all the stalls
where the vendors changed money and sold things to all
of the visitors there.
So Jesus, enraged,
yelled at the men, saying, "Are you engaged
in turning my Father's house into no more
than a market?"
And he drove them out of the door.
But they began yelling, "What sign can you send
that proves your authority? Show us now, friend!"
Then Jesus responded, "Tear this temple down.
In three days I'll build it back up from the ground."
They laughed, "Don't you know it took forty-six years
to build up these walls!"

But they had deaf ears.
He spoke not of buildings, but all he had said
referred to his body he'd raise up instead.
On the day Jesus returned from the grave,
his friends would remember this speech that he gave,
for though they were with him, they did not yet know
the plan Jesus laid out or where they would go.

John 3

Nicodemus, a Pharisee, sought Jesus out
and said, "Rabbi, we know that you are devout.
The Lord is with you, for in all of your signs
we see all the mysteries of the divine."
And Jesus replied, "I tell you the truth,
you must be reborn. Faith like a youth
is required to enter God's kingdom."
"How can
I be born again once I'm a grown man?"
"Be born out of water and Spirit. Then you
can enter God's kingdom."
"Can this be true?"
Then Jesus replied, "Don't you understand?
You teach and yet still what I say is too grand
for your comprehension, so why would I speak
of godly ideas or Heaven's mystique?
For God so loved the world that He
gave His only son, so those who believe
would find everlasting life. He did not
send His son to Earth to condemn the whole lot.
The light has come into the world, but men
who love evil hide. They seek after sin.
But if they seek goodness, they'll dwell in the light.
The Lord sees their actions, proclaiming they're right."
Then Jesus moved on to see his cousin John
the Baptist and all of the people he'd drawn
for baptism.
As Jesus went to him there,
the disciples of John said,

"John, be aware!
The man whom you baptized is doing the same
with others! How dare he!"
"But it's in his name
that I baptize people for I have told you
that I'm no messiah. But one will renew
our hope in the Lord. I make a straight path.
Believe in the Son, or know the Lord's wrath."

John 4:1 - 4:42

Jesus then traveled to Galilee and
the path took him into Samaria's land.
He sat down to rest and a woman came near.
Jesus said, "Woman, I just arrived here.
Would you draw some water for me?"
"You're a Jew,
and I a Samaritan. I ask why you
would ask this of me, for Jews shun such things."
Jesus said, "If you knew that which I bring
you'd ask for the true living water from me."
"Where is this water?" she asked.
"When you see
a man drink some water, his thirst will return.
But those who drink that which I bring shall not yearn
for water again."
"Let me drink it then, sir."
"Bring back your husband to me," he told her.
"I have none," she stated
"That's true," Jesus said,
"though five times you have been and now share your bed
with a man who is not yet your husband."
"Indeed,
you've seen in my heart, prophet. What do I need
to do to be cleansed?"
"The Lord shall arrive."
"I've heard the Messiah shall soon be alive."
"I'm he. Woman, go. Bring your friends all to me."
His disciples arrived, and Jesus said, "See!

All Samaria comes. Reap the benefits of
my work. Go receive all these people in love."

John 4:43 - 4:54

In Cana, a man came to Jesus and said,
"Please save my son, or he soon will be dead."
"You all demand signs!"
"I beg you," he cried.
"Very well. Go. Your son has not died."
Believing these words, the man left to go
back to his homeland. While travelling, though,
his servant found him and said, "Be relieved!
Your son's well again!"
And that man believed.

John 5

At the pool of Bethesda an invalid lay,
and Jesus walked up to the man on that day.
"Do you want to heal?"
"I can't get to the pool
whenever it's stirred. My life has been cruel.
For thirty-eight years in this spot I have lain."
So Jesus said, "Walk now and live without pain."
He'd healed on the Sabbath - a trespass - so when
the priests heard of this they were angry with him.
But Jesus said, "My Father's work's never done.
I tell you the truth, there's nothing the son
can do on his own. The son can just do
what the Father has shown him, and so I show you.
All judgment's entrusted unto the son.
Honor the Father. His will shall be done.
Whoever believes in my word and the One
who sent me gains life and shall not be shunned
or condemned by the Father. If I testify
for myself it's not valid, but one before I
spoke of these things. John the Baptist is known
and trusted by all. Through him truth was shown.

But you did not listen. To scripture you turn,
but if you were faithful then you would have learned
the scriptures have testified of me as well.
If false prophets came to you, you could not tell.
I'm not your accuser. For you have all set
your faith upon Moses. You read law, and yet
you don't believe it and push God away.
So how would you ever believe what I say?"

John 6

Jesus returned to the Galilee where
a great crowd of people had followed him there.
Jesus said, "Let's give them something to eat."
But Philip said, "We cannot buy bread or meat
for five thousand people!"
Then Peter said, "Here
are five loaves of bread and two fish."
"Come near."
Jesus gave thanks and they passed the food out.
Then baskets were found and carried about.
The food that came back after thousands were fed
was more than just two fish and five loaves of bread.
The people there saw this miraculous thing
and so they all wanted to make him their king.
But Jesus withdrew and the twelve all went down
and climbed in their boat rather than walk around
the lake. A strong storm blew up and they saw
Jesus out walking on water. In awe,
they watched him approach. He greeted them, and
with him in the boat they safely reached land.
Seeing he'd left, the crowd left as well
to watch what he'd do and hear what he'd tell.
When they found him, he said, "You followed me when
I fed you, but you can be fed without end.
For I am the true bread of life. If you will
believe in me, you'll never lack for your fill."
But when he professed he had come from above,
they grumbled and said, "Is he not the son of

Joseph the Carpenter?"
"All that you do
is complain! The life everlasting goes to
all those who believe. The bread of life lives!
For all of the world, my flesh I shall give.
You must eat my flesh and drink of my blood
if you are to live in the Lord's holy love."
This teaching was hard and many returned
to their homes. They didn't like what they had learned.
The twelve still remained, for Jesus chose them
although he knew Judas would soon betray him.

John 7

At the Feast, Jesus went to the temple and he
said, "My teaching comes from the One who sent me.
You're angry when I do the things God would do!
Seek to find God, and He will find you.
You circumcise boys on the Sabbath, but when
I heal someone you all declare it a sin.
Don't judge on appearance. Judge what is right."
The crowd tried to seize him and wanted to fight.
His time had not come, so he said, "I shall be
with you yet awhile, then I go to see
the One who has sent me, and there you can't go."
Some said, "The Christ! How else could he know
so much of the truth?"
And others said, "He
is a charlatan."
Much of the crowd disagreed.
When the Pharisees heard what he'd done they said, "No.
That prophet from Galilee; he has to go."

John 8:1 - 8:11

A woman was caught and then taken to
see Jesus. The people said, "What should we do?
She's an adulteress. Now she's been caught.
Shall we now stone her as Moses has taught?"

He picked up a rock and said to the men,
"You cast the first stone if you're without sin."
The crowd dispersed quickly and Jesus said, "I
do not judge you, woman, but leave sin behind."

John 8:12 - 8:59

Jesus spoke out saying, "I am the light
of the world. Walk with me and drive off the night."
The Pharisees cried, "You can't speak on your own
behalf."
"I tell you, I'm never alone.
My Father speaks for me as well."
"Bring him out."
"You do not know Him, nor what He's about.
I'm not of this world and you won't receive
freedom from sin if you don't believe.
If you know the truth, the truth sets you free."
"We are not slaves!"
"To sin you shall be.
God sent me to you, but you want me dead.
If God was your Father, you'd love me instead.
But you're of the devil, you murderous beings.
Who amongst you has seen what I've seen?"
"You demon! You've claimed you can overcome death!"
"You curse what is holy with each of your breaths.
I tell you the truth, before Abraham's birth,
I am and have been, before even the Earth."
They wanted to stone him. He had to hide from
their eyes, for his time was still yet to come.

John 9

While Jesus was walking he passed a blind man.
The disciples said, "Rabbi, help us understand.
Which of his parents have sinned to make him
a blind man?"
"Neither," he said unto them.
"This man was born blind so that you might see

the work of the Lord, so you will believe."
So he healed the man and word spread around
that Jesus had cured the blind man in town.
Jesus had healed on the Sabbath and so
the Pharisees hated him. "Jesus must go."
They questioned the man who'd been cured and they sent
for his parents.
"This Jesus has evil intent,"
they told him.
But he replied, "How could he do
these things if he wasn't from God?"
So they threw
him out of the courts.
Jesus said to the man,
"The Son of Man comes, for judgment's at hand."
"I believe in you, Lord," the man said to him.
"The blind shall soon see that I've come here for them.
But those who can see shall be blind to my name,
and so on their shoulders their guilt shall remain."

John 10

Jesus said, "Listen! The sheep will not go
with a stranger. They follow the shepherd they know
who calls them by name. So enter the gate.
Be saved from the thief and a horrible fate.
The good shepherd lays down his life for his sheep.
I'm the good shepherd and I shall not sleep
till I lay it down and raise it again."
But Jesus' words confused all the men.
The Jews asked him, "Are you the Christ? Tell us now!"
"I've told you before, but no matter how
I tell you or show you, I'll never be done.
Don't you know I and the Father are One?"
At this then men wanted to stone him.
He said,
"For what miracle do you all want me dead?"
"You blaspheme! For you are a man, but you claim
that you are the Lord!"

"How have I profaned
the Lord, that you'd seek to harm me?"
But they
would not listen to him, so he slipped away.
He returned to the place where the Baptist had been,
and there many people came forth to see him.

John 11:1 - 11:44

Now word had been sent that Jesus' friend,
Lazarus, had become ill.
"This won't end
in death," Jesus said. "God's glory will shine."
He waited two days, then said, "It is time
to go see my friend. He's asleep, but I will
awaken him."
But his friends said, "If he's ill,
sleep will revive him."
"Friends, he is dead.
But we shall go see where he's laid," Jesus said.
The sister of Lazarus, Martha, said, "Were
you here, he'd have lived."
Then Jesus told her,
"For I am the resurrection and I
am the life. Believe in me; you will not die.
Do you believe me?"
"Yes I do, Lord."
"Then truly, I tell you, you'll have your reward."
Then Mary, her sister, saw Jesus and said,
"If you'd have come, our brother wouldn't be dead."
Jesus was moved. He said, "Where's he kept?"
"Come," they all said. As they led, Jesus wept.
When they came to the tomb where the body was laid,
they rolled the stone back and then Jesus prayed.
"Father, I know You have heard me. Allow
Your power and mercy to be revealed now."
Then Jesus cried, "Lazarus, come!" At his call
the dead man walked out, astonishing all.

John 11:45 - 11:57

The Pharisees heard this and they said, "How can
he do all these things?"
"We must stop this man,"
the high priest, Caiaphas said. "Revolution
is next, then we will see Rome's dissolution
of all of our powers, positions, and such.
None of you fools seem to realize how much
damage he'll do. We must kill Jesus now."
So they followed the high priest in plotting out how.

John 12:1 - 12:11

Jesus was taking a meal with his friends.
Martha, the sister of Lazarus, then
entered the group with her finest perfume
to wash the Christ's feet. The smell filled the room.
But Judas Iscariot stood and declared,
"If you'd sold that oil the wealth could be shared
with the poor!"
But he was the one who took care
of the money, and he always took out a share
for himself.
But Jesus said, "Leave her alone!
She is the only one here who has shown
such care for my burial. Friends, there will be
poor always, but you won't always have me."

John 12:12 - 12:50

"Hosanna!" the crowd cried as Jesus rode in
to the streets of Jerusalem. All who praised him
swung palms, for they thought they were greeting the man
who would lead them in battle and free the whole land.
"It's time for the Son of Man's glory to rise.
Don't love your life, for every man dies.
The one who hates his earthly life shall find he
has eternal life waiting, for he comes to me.

Though my heart is troubled, I won't stay this hour.
This is the reason why God gave me power."
A voice came from Heaven, "I have glorified
it once, I shall do it again," the voice cried.
The people were shocked, but Jesus said, "He
has spoken for your benefit, not for me.
For I know the truth. But the light shall soon leave.
But it can return if you only believe."

John 13:1 - 13:30

That night at their meal, Jesus got down
and washed his friends' feet as he kneeled on the ground
like a servant.
But Peter said, "Jesus, don't do
this thing."
Jesus said, "If I don't wash you
then you can't be with me."
"O Lord, then I pray
that you wash my feet *and* my hands so I stay
always beside you."
"I clean, but not all
are cleansed," he told them. He knew his downfall
was in Judas Iscariot who had betrayed
him to the high priest.
"Today I have made
an example for you," Jesus said. "You must be
servants to all if you are to serve me.
But I tell you the truth that one of you here
betrays me tonight. My death has drawn near.
It's the one whom I hand the bread to."
And then
he gave it to Judas and Satan went in
to Judas' heart.
"Do it quickly," he said
to Judas, who left them still holding the bread.
He went to the Jewish courts and told the priests
how they could arrest Jesus during the feasts.

John 13:31 - 13:38

While Judas was gone, Jesus said, "Where
I go, none of you can follow me there.
So now I command: as I have loved you,
so love one another. When they see you do
this others will know you are mine."
"But we need
to be with you," said Simon Peter. "Indeed,
I'd perish for you."
"Before the cock crows
you'll deny me three times!"
"That's not true, Jesus! No!"

John 14

Jesus told his twelve disciples, "Put all
of your faith in the Lord, and you shall not fall.
In my Father's house there are many rooms, and
I go to prepare a place for you as planned.
Someday I'll take you there."
"But Lord, how can
we get to that place? We don't understand."
"I am the life and the truth and the way.
None comes to my Father except those I say.
I'm in the Father and He is in me.
Whatever you ask for in my name shall be.
Love and obey my commands and He'll send
the Spirit of Holiness to dwell within
each one of your hearts. In that way I will
forever stay with you and you'll have me still.
I go to the Father, so celebrate, for
you've known me, but my Father offers you more."

John 15 - 16

"I am the vine, and each branch that won't bear
good fruit must be severed. And so you must share
this message. So love one another as I

have loved you. A branch that's cut off will soon die.
So life shall be had if you live on the vine.
If you remain fruitful, then you shall be mine.
You are my friends, and whatever you ask
shall be given to you to help in your task.
If people hate you, they hated me first.
But those who drink my water never shall thirst.
They've seen all the miracles. You have seen me.
Through these and your witness, mankind can be free.
I've told you all this so you don't go astray.
The time shall soon come when you're each turned away
from synagogue. People will want to kill you.
But I'm with you still, so do as I do.
I go to the Father, and though you may grieve,
the Spirit shall come to all those who believe.
I have more to say. More than you can bear.
So the Spirit shall come so that all may be shared.
In a while I'll leave, but I'll return,
for there is so much that you still have to learn.
The Father loves you, and though I'll be gone,
through you and your work, His will shall live on."

John 17

Once Jesus said this, he prayed, "Father, I
am ready to follow You and glorify
Your name. I have honored You. Please come and be
with me as I do all that You've asked of me.
I've shown my disciples. Protect them now, Lord,
as I submit to You of my own accord.
I gave them Your word and the world now hates
them all, so I pray that in all that awaits
You're with them. Please sanctify all that they do,
and be with those whom they shall bring unto You.
Though they've turned from You, let this world find
Your word through my friends. Bless all of mankind."

John 18:1 - 18:27

Then Jesus went out to a place where he'd be
alone, but Judas already knew he
would be there, so he sent some soldiers. They found
Jesus there with his disciples around.
At this, Simon Peter grabbed hold of a sword
and cut off the ear of a man.
"Stop! The Lord
does not need more blood," Jesus told them. "The cup
the Lord has presented me, I must drink up."
So Jesus was bound and taken in front
of all of the priests.
"You have who you want,"
he said as they questioned him. He told them, "You
know all I have said. Do what you must do."
Meanwhile, Peter was outside where he
was approached by a girl. "Hey, didn't I see
you there with the man who is inside?"
"Who? I?"
asked Peter. "You must be mistaken."
"You lie,"
a man said, "I saw you."
"You're wrong!"
"But last night,
I thought you were there. Didn't you start a fight?"
"No, I wasn't there, people! I do not know
that man!" shouted Peter, and then the cock crowed.

John 18:28 - 19:16

The priests went to Pilate, Rome's governor, who
said, "What do you want me to do? He's a Jew!
Judge him yourselves."
"But we have no right
to execute him! It's your oversight
that is now required."
So Pilate asked, "Why
have you been brought to me? Are you not, as I

have heard, the one they call the king of the Jews?"
"My kingdom's not here. I have nothing to lose
in this earthly world," said Jesus.
"So you
say you are a king?"
"I'm the king of what's true.
All truth sides with what I say," Jesus replied.
Pilate looked at him. "What is truth?" he sighed.
Then Pilate yelled, "Jews! I always give one
of my prisoners to you, as it has been done
for the Passover. Would you take Jesus?"
"No, we
want Barabbas the rebel!"
So that man was freed,
while Jesus was flogged, insulted and crowned
with thorns. All the soldiers knocked him to the ground
saying, "Hail to the king! The king of the Jews!"
But the Pharisees said, "Do not just abuse
this man. Crucify him!"
"But there are no grounds
to kill him," said Pilate.
"But he has been found
guilty of breaking our laws. He must die,"
said the priests.
But Pilate told Jesus, "Have I
not the power to free you or kill you?"
"All you
can do is that which you were placed here to do."
Although Pilate tried to free Jesus, they said,
"If you do not kill Jesus, you are not led
by Caesar. For anyone who makes the claim
of kingship hates Caesar, so you must proclaim
his death sentence."
"Shall your king be crucified?"
"We have no king but Caesar."
"So be it," he sighed.

John 19:17 - 19:42

The soldiers took Jesus and then made him bear
his cross up to Golgotha. When they were there
they crucified him with a man on each side
of his cross, and placed a sign up to deride
the Christ. It read, 'Jesus, the king of the Jews.'
The priests said, "Don't write such a thing and abuse
our faith."
Pilate answered, "Whatever I've done
is done."
And the people looked up at the Son.
As soldiers drew lots for his garments he hung,
suffering there, breath torn from his lungs.
His mother stood near; Mary Magdalene too.
He told the disciple he loved, "I give you
my mother as your mother now." Then he cried,
"It is finished!"
And there on the cross the Christ died.
They took down the body and had to work fast
to entomb it, then wait till the Sabbath had passed.

John 20:1 - 20:18

Mary Magdalene went to the tomb and she saw
that the stone was rolled back. She knew that the law
forbade Jews from working or toiling on
the Sabbath. She looked and the body was gone.
The disciples saw too, but then they went home.
Mary Magdalene stayed there, crying alone.
Two angels appeared in the tomb, and they said,
"Why are you crying?"
"My Lord, who's now dead,
has been taken away."
Then Jesus appeared.
"Why are you crying?" he asked.
"'Cause I feared
that this thing would happen," she said, thinking he
was a gardener.

"Mary, don't cry. It is me."
"Teacher!" she cried. "You were dead!"
"I have yet
to return to the Father. You must go and get
my disciples and tell them I'll come."
So she ran
and told them while praising the true Son of Man.

John 20:19 - 20:31

The disciples were gathered, and Jesus appeared.
"Peace, I've come back to you, friends. Do not fear."
In joy they surrounded him, and with a breath
he breathed on them, "See, I have overcome death.
I send you the Spirit. When you forgive sins
of a man, they're forgiven. Do so to all men."
Now Thomas, who wasn't there when this occurred
arrived later.
Seeing his friends were all stirred
he said, "What's the matter?"
"The Lord was just here!"
"Come now! Don't lie. When the Lord can appear
and show me his wounds, I'll believe you all then."
A week later, Jesus appeared amongst them.
"Thomas," he said, "come, touch and believe."
"My Lord!" Thomas cried, "I have been so naïve!"
"You've seen and believed, but blessed are they
who can't see me but still believe in my way."

John 21

The disciples were fishing together though they
did not catch a single fish during that day.
Then Jesus appeared on the shore and he cried,
"Have you caught some fish?"
"No, but we've tried."
"Try throwing your nets on the other side then."
They did, unsure why they should listen to him,
but then in surprise the nets were filled till

they couldn't haul in all the fish.
"How'd he fill
these nets?"
"It is Jesus!" someone cried out.
Then the fishermen all began rushing about
to get to the shore. They reached it and then
they sat down, so pleased to see him again.
"Simon Peter," he said, "do you love me?"
"Of course."
"To all of my lambs, you must be a source
of goodness, so feed and care for them."
Three
times he told Peter this.
"Lord, it is me!"
"Then make sure my children are all clothed and fed
for when you are old, one day you'll be led
to somewhere you don't want to go."
In this way,
Jesus told Peter of his death that day.
I tell you these things so you might believe.
My words are all true. Do not be deceived
by suspicion. There's so much to tell you, but I
could not write down all that Christ did if I tried.

Acts 1

In my previous book, you'll see my selection
of deeds Jesus did through his resurrection,
and during the forty days he spent on Earth.
But his greatest miracle was his rebirth!
But just as he said, we all were baptized
in the great Holy Spirit, and we were advised
to not sit and wait for him to return,
but instead to go forth and share what we'd learned.
So all then returned to Jerusalem and
Peter said, "I tell you, it was all planned.
Judas had his role to play, but we must
now choose someone new, a man we can trust.
Two men came forth. We prayed, sitting there,
"Lord, choose the man who can shoulder and bear
to be an apostle."
Then both lots were cast,
and Matthias was added to our Twelve at last.

Acts 2:1 - 2:41

When the day of Pentecost came, they were all
together. Then there was a fiery squall,
and each man began speaking languages they
had not known or learned till that very day.
Many Jews heard them and wondered at how
these men had just learned all these languages now.
Some said, "This work is the Lord's. It's divine."
But others said, "These men just drank too much wine."
Then Peter said, "We are not drunk! Don't you see?

The Lord poured His Spirit on my friends and me.
People of Israel, Jesus has died,
but he rose again, and his Spirit's inside
each one of us. It can be in you as well!
Death could not hold him, for he was compelled
to come to your rescue. And David, the king
of old, even knew this. He wrote of the thing,
"The Holiest One won't rot in the grave."
The Messiah he spoke of has come now and saved
us all."
"But what should we do?" the crowd cried.
"Repent and be baptized, for though Jesus died,
he was reborn and you shall be too."
So many stepped forth so that they might do
what Peter had said. Three thousand in all
were baptized that day, upon hearing God's call.

Acts 2:42 - 3:26

The believers all gathered together to share
in meals and in fellowship. They were all there
performing great wonders. With each passing day,
many were added to those who were saved.
One day as Peter and John passed a man
who was lame and was begging, he stretched out his hand.
Peter said, "Silver and gold I can't give,
but I'll give you something to help you to live.
In Jesus' name, arise. Walk again!"
The lame man sprang up and walked with the men.
When others saw this, they were shocked, for he'd been
begging for years at the gate they'd come in.
Seeing that they were amazed, Peter stood
and said, "You all stare, for you know it is good
when lame men can walk. But it wasn't me
that made this man stand. It's God's majesty!
You've all seen this man as he stretched out his hands.
By faith in the good name of Jesus, he stands.
Your leaders conspired to kill him, but they
were part of God's plan. If they did not slay

the Messiah, how would he come back from the dead?
Repent now, my brothers and sisters," he said.
"In Jesus, God blessed us. You've seen, so now act!
For Jesus was sent as a sign of God's pact."

Acts 4

The priests were upset by Peter and John.
They had them arrested and held until dawn.
But the people were listening to every word,
and the numbers were growing as more people heard.
Five thousand men were believers, plus there
were women and children who now also shared
in the faith. And when John and Peter were brought
before the high council, they said, "We were caught
and arrested for curing a man? Do you know
that he was cured because you made a great show
of killing our friend? But Jesus was real!
He rose from the dead. Can you mortals steal
the will of the Lord and make it your own?
You rejected the one who's the true cornerstone
of salvation. There is no one else! He has come,
but you do not know it, for you're deaf and dumb."
The council was shocked by such boldness, and they
conferred saying, "How can we stop them today?
Their proof stands there next to them."
So they said, "Go,
but don't speak of Jesus from now on."
"We know
what the Lord wants of us, so why would we do
these things you command? We'll share the good news."
Though the council was threatened, the men were released.
Their tongues did not stop and no actions were ceased.
The faithful ones prayed for great courage, for they
were opposed by the masses. With boldness they'd say,
"He died, but he rose! The Messiah has come."
Not everyone followed, but their words brought some.

Acts 5

The faithful sold all that they had, to give to
the apostles to use for good and to do
the will of the Lord. One woman and man
took only a small part received for their land
to give to the group. The rest they had hid.
But Peter said, "Why did you do what you did?
It isn't the money. It's that you both lied
to God."
In that instant, the two of them died.
Fear gripped the church when they saw this occur,
but that didn't stop them, nor did it deter
their ministry. They cured so many, but they
were thrown back in prison. Then without delay
an angel broke their prison door saying, "Go,
teach all of the people so that they may know."
The apostles went out to the temple courts where
they taught till the soldiers arrested them there.
The soldiers then took the apostles to stand
in front of the council.
"Can't you understand?
We told all you people. Don't speak of this man!
But you tell the people we killed Jesus and
he rose from the grave!"
Then Peter said, "Yes!
We shall obey the Lord who has blessed
us all by sending our savior to reign.
If we heeded you, it would all be in vain."
The council was angry and wanted to kill
the apostles, but one Pharisee said,
"Be still.
We've seen the false prophets. And when they are killed,
their people all scatter, for naught was fulfilled
in their teachings. So I tell you, let these men go.
If they break apart, then we will soon know
that Jesus was merely a fake and a fraud.
But if they keep going, then this is of God."
So all the apostles were flogged and then freed,

and each man was grateful to suffer and bleed
in Jesus' name. They proceeded to speak,
"The Messiah is Jesus. It's him that you seek."

Acts 6 - 7

The believers grew quickly, but soon discontent
spread all through their ranks.
"Have we just been sent,"
the apostles cried out, "to manage the fate
of believers? Or are we to go consecrate
the masses who have not yet heard the good news?
Let us find more men; there must be a few
who administrate well."
And when they were done,
seven were chosen. Amongst the men, one
named Stephen performed many signs among men.
But many came forth to destroy him. To them,
Stephen was dangerous, so the crowds lied,
"He blasphemes the Lord!"
Before the crowd's eyes,
Stephen's face lit up as bright as the sun,
like an angel of God, the Lord who is One.
But the council of priests said, "Is this claim true?"
So Stephen said, "Must I explain to you too
our history? It all began when our God,
the most holy One, the One without flaw,
made Abraham father of all of our race
and said He would give his descendents this place
where you sit today. Through Jacob's twelve sons,
the Lord's will and way has always been done.
Like Moses who led us from bondage, and then
the prophets who each tried to turn us from sin.
Is there one prophet you've not persecuted?
You kill them, but that cannot keep the Lord muted.
The Righteous One came. You killed him as well!
Your eyes look to Heaven; your hearts look to hell."
On hearing this they shouted insults at him,
but he looked to Heaven, ignoring all them,

where he saw a vision.
He said, "Son of Man,
I see you and know you. You are the right hand
of God the Almighty."
The council arose
and said, "Stone the blasphemer!"
Some took their clothes
and laid them all down at the feet of a man
named Saul.
Stephen said, "They don't understand.
Forgive them, O Lord," as the stones fell upon
his body. And then, before he was gone,
he said, "Jesus, please, I pray that you take
my spirit."
He slept, and did not awake.

<u>Acts 8</u>

Saul was a witness to this. He approved
of the stoning of Stephen, for he wasn't moved
by Stephen's impassioned speech or his cry.
He felt it was right that Christ's followers die.
Saul hunted believers as if he was crazed!
For those who believed, these were terrible days.
The apostles were scattered, and Philip went down
to Samaria, preaching to all in one town.
A magician called Simon lived there. He'd made
a name for himself with the tricks he had played.
But the good news was powerful. Many, including
Simon, heard Philip. They started concluding
that this was the truth, and they were converted.
With such success, Peter and John were alerted.
They went to Samaria, laying hands on
the people. Into them the Spirit was drawn.
Then Simon brought money and said, "Let me buy
this Spirit from you."
"How dare you! You try
to purchase God's gift?" Peter spat. "Is your heart
so blackened? Look, I can see sin in each part

of your being. Repent!"
Then Simon cried out,
"Pray with me, friends! God, make me devout!"
They prayed for the man, then Peter and John
returned to Jerusalem. Philip had gone
to Gaza, and there he encountered a man,
a treasurer from Ethiopia's land.
This man was a eunuch who worked for the queen.
He asked, "This Isaiah book...what does it mean?"
So Philip then shared how the good news was told
by Isaiah, through Jesus.
"Philip, behold!
There's some water right there," the eunuch advised.
"Philip, please wash me. Let me be baptized!"
And when it was done, the Spirit then came
and told Philip to teach the weak and the lame,
the sinners in need of the good news so they
could be saved from their sin and escape their decay.

Acts 9

Saul was still threatening every believer,
calling them blasphemers, devils, deceivers.
As he neared the walls of Damascus a light
shone bright upon him. Saul's face became white.
"Why do you persecute me?" said a voice
from the heavens. "Saul, you've made a terrible choice."
"Who are you?" cried Saul.
"I am Jesus. The one
you despise. Go on to Damascus. Don't shun
the help I will send."
Saul's friends were all scared.
They heard the voice too, yet no one was there.
Saul stood up, but he had been stricken blind.
He let his friends lead him so that he would find
his way to the city. A man lived there who
was named Ananias.
The Lord told him, "You
will go out to Saul and place your hands on

this man so his blindness can thus be withdrawn."
"But Lord," Ananias complained, "it's this man
who has thrown Your believers in jail. By his hand
many have died!"
"You will go to him, so
that My word will go out so the Gentiles know
I am God."
Ananias got up and he went,
saying, "Saul, Jesus came to you, and the Lord sent
me here to your side. May your blindness be healed."
With joy Saul was cured. By baptism sealed.
Saul went to the synagogues saying, "It's true!
Jesus is God's son, sent here for you,
for me, and our sins."
People said, "Is he not
the one who arrested believers?"
They thought
that Saul had gone crazy, but he was debating
those who had followed him, those who were hating
everyone following Jesus. In fact,
he was so persuasive, that some men attacked
and drove him away. He fled in the night,
preferring to spread the word than to fight.
The same thing occurred in Jerusalem too,
but through Saul's persuasion, the followers grew.
Meanwhile, Peter had been many places.
He went down to Lydda. In one of these cases
he spoke to a paralyzed man and he said,
"Lift up your mat. Your infirmity's shed."
The man stood and started off walking around.
When everyone saw this, not one in the town
refuted the miracle. All of them turned
their hearts to the Lord. But then Peter learned
that a faithful believer named Tabitha died.
He went to her town.
The mourners all cried,

"Raise her back up."
Peter prayed, for he grieved,
and said, "Get up."
When she did, all men believed.

Acts 10

Within Caesarea, there lived a man who
was a Roman Centurion. Everyone knew
that this was a God-fearing man who gave to
the poor. In a dream, a great angel flew
up to him, saying, "Cornelius, you
have given such gifts to the poorest, so through
your actions you've given these gifts to your Lord.
Now do as God asks, and reap your reward.
When you wake up, send messengers out
to find Simon Peter, for he is devout."
Cornelius woke and sent men away
to fetch him. As they approached Peter that day,
he too had a vision of animals, and
God held them all out within His great hand.
"Eat them now, Peter," God told him.
"But I
have not eaten meat that's unclean, Lord, so why
would You ask me to do such a thing?" Peter said.
"Nothing I've made is unclean. Go ahead."
Three times this occurred, then the vision was gone,
but the Spirit told Peter, "Three men have now drawn
close to the gates of this town. You must go
along with them."
Peter saw them and said, "So,
you have come to see me?"
"Our master has sent
us here to fetch you."
"Let's go."
So they went.
When Peter arrived, Cornelius fell
at his feet.
"Don't bow to a man. It is well

understood that a Jew and a Gentile don't
associate. It is the law, but this won't
stop us, for God told me all that he's made
are sanctified. How can I lend you my aid?"
"The Lord came to me, and told me to send
for you, Simon Peter. You come as a friend.
I'm glad you are here, for this very day
God's given to us. Let us hear what you say."
"I now understand," Peter said to the man,
"that God has no favorites, for here we two stand.
A Jew and a Gentile, sharing the news
God sent us through Jesus. No person can lose
if he knows what's happened. They pierced and they killed
our Lord, but that was just part of God's will,
for he rose on the third day and came to proclaim
to his followers, "Go forth and preach in my name."
We all are forgiven our sins if we turn
to Jesus and God. The fires that burn
are quenched by His water."
And all who heard were
amazed by his words.
The Spirit then stirred
them all to convert. They were baptized and they
asked Peter to stay and to teach a few days.

Acts 11:1 - 11:18

When Peter returned to Jerusalem, he
was criticized for he had lived with and seen
the Gentiles baptized.
"You ate with ones
who aren't circumcised. Don't you know what you've done."
Then Peter said, "God, in a vision told me,
to eat unclean animals. I made a plea,
asking him why I could not remain pure.
'Nothing I've made is unclean. So be sure
that you're doing My will.' he replied to me. Still,
I opposed him three times. But it was God's will.
So God sent me forth to the Gentiles and

I remember when Jesus told us, 'Understand,
John baptized with water, but I tell you soon
the Spirit shall come and baptize you too.'
When I saw the Spirit had baptized these men,
I knew they'd received the forgiveness of sin.
So even the Gentiles share the good news.
The Lord came for all, not just for us few.
Through Jesus, the many shall find God and know
that He's always with us wherever we go."

Acts 11:19 - 12:25

In Antioch, many believers were made
of the people. Then Barnabas came and he bade
Saul to come with him, and they led those who
had come to find Jesus, and so the church grew.
During this time King Herod arrested
some of the church. Many were tested,
and some of the people who called Jesus Lord,
like James, son of Zebedee, fell by the sword.
Seeing the people had cheered when a man
who had been an apostle was killed, Herod's plan
was to capture apostles like Peter as well.
An angel came to Peter while in his cell,
and said, "Come with me." He led Peter out
of the prison and into the streets.
"There's no doubt,
that the Lord rescued me," Peter said as he stood
in the streets, a free man. He did what he could
to alert all his friends before leaving to hide.
When Herod found out that he wasn't inside
his cell, he had all of his guards put to death.
It wasn't long till Herod breathed his last breath.
The Lord struck him down, and afflicted the king
with worms, then he died. Despite everything
he had done to restrict the spread of God's word,
more came to Christ by the teachings they heard.

Acts 13

While Saul and Barnabas both preached and taught
in Antioch, God said to them, "You will not
stay here any longer."
So then they were sent
to Cyprus. God willed it, and both of them went.
There they encountered a sorcerer who
perverted God's word.
Saul said to him, "You
are an enemy. Thus, for a time, you'll be blind."
And the man's eyes were misted, so he could not find
his way through the streets, even though the sun shone.
All were amazed. And Saul, who was known
as Paul, made believers of many. When he
went into the synagogue, he said, "You see
the Lord has been with us since Moses retrieved
our people from Egypt. They did not believe.
They wandered the desert until they went in
to Canaan and took it. But still they all sinned.
They wanted a king, though the Lord reigned above
the Jews. He was angry, for all of His love
was ignored. But He still gave us David to rule.
A wise king was David, but we were all fools.
So He sent us Jesus, that we might be saved,
and so we might see how to conquer the grave.
In killing His son on the cross, they fulfilled
the scripture that you read each Sabbath. They killed
a man, but God didn't let his Son decay.
Even King David was done on the day
of his death. You are freed. Let the scoffers all scoff,
for they ignore God. Take your blinders off."
The Jews were not happy with all the things Paul
had said to the Gentiles.
"I came so all
could hear about Jesus and know the good news.
It is for each person, not just for the Jews."

Acts 14:1 - 14:20

Some heard the good news, while others refused.
Not always the Gentiles, nor always the Jews
who hated the words the disciples had used.
Some were enlightened, the rest were confused.
In Lystra, a lame man sought out the Lord's word,
and Paul said, "Stand up, for now you have heard
what's possible."
So the man stood, but the men
in the crowd said, "They're gods! Let us all go in
to the temples of Zeus and Hermes, for they
must all be immortal."
So they went to lay
flowers and garlands as sacrifice, but
Paul heard about this and yelled at them, "What
are you doing? We're humans! Just as you are.
We speak of the Lord, but look at how far
you stand from His will."
The crowd was displeased.
So some of the Jews riled them up and seized
the disciple, then they took him outside the walls.
They stoned him, then thinking him dead, they left Paul.
But as the disciples all gathered around,
Paul stood up, disgusted by all in that town.

Acts 14:21 - 15:35

They went back to Antioch, only to find
men preaching the word of a fraudulent kind.
"Men must be circumcised," they all proclaimed.
Then Peter came forth, saying, "This is the same
sort of thing we've been told and believed for too long.
The Spirit God gave us is what makes us strong,
not a cut to the flesh. Brothers, you're saved
by the grace Jesus showed us, the love that he gave."
Then James, son of Alphaeus, said, "We must take
measures to keep all our brethren from fake
idols and prostitutes. Open the door

so all the believers can grow to be more."
They wrote a long letter addressing these things,
selected both Silas and Judas to bring
the letter to Antioch to clarify
the right way of living, which none could deny.

Acts 15:36 - 16:40

Both Paul and Barnabas fought over who
should accompany them. The argument grew
till they parted ways, and Paul took a man
named Timothy with him. This man helped to plan
and grow many churches, for he was a Greek,
and people would listen to him when he'd speak.
Many were saved; the rich and the poor.
The slaves and the free. The young, the mature.
In one city, both Paul and Silas were thrown
in prison. As they prayed to God on His throne
an earthquake occurred. The prison guard ran
to see what had happened. He knew that no man
would stay in his cell, and if there were none
in the prison, the guard's life would surely be done.
So he readied himself to fall on his sword,
when Paul cried out, "Wait! We're still here, my lord.
Not one of us fled."
The guard replied, "Now
I know you are truly from God. Tell me how
I might be saved too."
Paul said, "Just believe.
Jesus shall bring you the rest and reprieve
that each man desires. Your household shall be
one with the Lord, and you shall be free."
When Silas and Paul were released, the men went
to other towns doing God's holy intent.

Acts 17 - 19

Wherever they went, trouble was found.
Sometimes they were hassled or kicked to the ground,

but some would believe, so Paul did not cease
his ministry, and so the numbers increased.
When Paul was in Athens, he felt quite distressed
by all of their idols, so he did not rest
until he was heard. The Athenians said,
"Tell us of this god you worship instead."
"I speak of the One God," he stated, "for He
does not live in temples. Whatever you see
was created by Him. And He shall forgive
your sins, for His son died, then once again lived."
He told them of Jesus, and some changed their ways.
He taught them to follow the Lord and to pray.
He went on to Corinth, and preached to the Jews,
but all the crowds mocked him and he was abused.
"Your blood is on your heads," he cried. "I will not
be treated so by my own people. I thought
you'd seek the good news. If not, then I'll go
to the Gentiles so the whole world will know."
Then God spoke to Paul, saying, "Don't be afraid.
Keep speaking to them. I am with you."
Paul stayed
and brought many into the light of God's grace.
For eighteen months, Paul remained there in that place.
Paul traveled to Ephesus, where he found men
who hadn't heard how Christ released them from sin.
He told them of Jesus, and laid his hands on
these twelve. Into them the Spirit was drawn.
He went through the land preaching. Many men knew
of Paul and his preaching. The Holy Word grew
as those who were sorcerers ended their ways,
and Paul preached to new people each of his days.
In Ephesus there was a riot because
Paul was converting so many. The laws
did not forbid this, but the men who were paid
from the sale of false idols were very dismayed.
They captured Paul's friends and had them all tried,
but all were found innocent. Nobody died,
so all idol vendors were left with frustration,
while Paul remained free to preach to the nation.

Acts 20:1 - 20:12

While preaching one night to a crowd, there were some
who were sitting in windows, for when Paul would come
the crowds would be great. A youth who was there
fell from a window and onto the square.
Those in attendance yelled in alarm,
rushing to see if the boy had been harmed.
The body was dead, but Paul jumped on the boy,
and said, "It's alright. He's alive."
Then the joy
as all saw the young man arise and then stand
was wonderful. They could all see the Lord's hand
was with Paul, and many came to Jesus then,
the one who could overcome both death and sin.

Acts 20:13 - 20:38

Paul went to Ephesus, telling the men
who led the church there, "You won't see me again.
I sail for Jerusalem. You must ensure
that the church you have started remains true and pure.
Wherever I've gone, I've faced down the mob,
but that is just what I must do, for my job
is spreading the word about Jesus, so those
who seek him can find him, and so the faith grows.
Watch over your flocks, for they'll wander off,
and there will be some who lie or who scoff.
So be on your guard! As Jesus believed,
it's better to give than to have received.
I've given the good news to you. Be elated
to share it with others. You're all consecrated
to glorify God."
They knelt down to pray,
then went to the shore to watch Paul sail away.

Acts 21 - 22

On the way to Jerusalem, many told Paul,
"You shouldn't go into the city. We all
believe you will be thrown in prison."
One man
came and bound up both his feet and his hands
saying, "I tell you that if you persist,
you'll surely be bound by your ankles and wrists."
Then Paul said to them, "Stop worrying so.
For Jesus, I tell you, I'd happily go
to death! What is prison?!"
And so he went down
to Jerusalem, preaching to those in the town.
He met with his brothers who tried to protect
Paul from the Jews whom they knew would object
to Paul's work with Gentiles. It wasn't too long
till Paul was attacked by a large, angry throng.
They beat him and they would have killed him if not
for a Roman commander who ran down and brought
his soldiers. The crowd was dispersed but they yelled
for Paul to be killed, so the Roman man held
him under arrest.
As he took him to jail,
Paul asked, "Might I speak to the crowd at our tail?"
Given permission, he stood up and said,
"Brothers and fathers who call for my head,
hear me. I once was as zealous as you
for the law of our fathers. I jailed people who
spoke about Jesus. Some I put to death.
A lightning bolt struck me, and then like a breath
Jesus' voice washed over me, saying,
'Don't persecute all of my people. The slaying
of innocent lives, who have preached in my name
is a sin. Stop now, lest all of the blame
be placed on your shoulders.' And I was struck blind,
then cured by a follower. All of mankind
can be saved through Jesus. Though I am a Jew,
this message is meant for the Gentiles too."

At this the crowd yelled, for they wanted him dead.
As the Romans were ready to flog him, Paul said,
"Is it legal to punish a citizen who
is of Rome?"
The Romans were shocked, "How are you
a citizen?"
"I was born one."
So they
did not strike him, but he could not go away.

Acts 23 - 24

The commander then took him to meet the Sanhedrin,
saying, "If not for the crowds we'd have freed him."
Then Paul cried aloud, "I've done the Lord's will,
for through Jesus, prophecy has been fulfilled."
Then Paul was abused by the priests, but he said,
"I am a Pharisee too. But the dead
have been resurrected, and that's why I stand
on trial. For I spoke of Jesus, the man
who overcame death."
A ruckus broke out,
and Paul was accosted and thrown all about.
The Romans rushed him from the room and then back
to the barracks.
Once there, God told him, "Now pack.
For as you have spoken to those in your home,
now you must go speak to the people of Rome."
But a plot to kill Paul was discovered, so then
he was snuck out of town.
The commander said, "When
he is taken on to Caesarea, then there
his case shall be heard. May it be found fair."
His accusers soon followed, and once in the court,
they said, "Gracious governor, let us report
how Paul incites all of the people to riot
with talks of this Jesus. Don't let him deny it.
For he is a ringleader of this foul sect,
and all of his blasphemy seeks to infect

us God-fearing Jews."
Then in his defense,
Paul said, "I've committed no act of offense.
It's true that I follow the Way that was laid
by my Lord, the Messiah, for Jesus has paid
the ultimate price for the sins of all men.
But I made no trouble when I was within
the walls of Jerusalem. No man can name
the law that I've broken as they have all claimed.
It's because of my Lord's resurrection that I
now stand here on trial. My teachings defy
that of their own, so they long for my blood
as a lamb longs for grass or a pig longs for mud."
The governor wasn't swayed by either side.
In fact, he hoped Paul would give him a bribe,
but Paul did not do this, and so he remained
for two years imprisoned in shackles and chains.

Acts 25 - 26

At this time the governors changed, and again
Paul was on trial before all the men
who accused him. But none could prove claims against
the actions of Paul. So in his defense
Paul then appealed to Caesar!"
"Then to
Caesar you'll go," said the governor. "You
will not be my problem."
Before Paul could leave,
King Agrippa said, "Let me see Paul, who believes
in this Jesus who lived, although he was dead."
So Paul was brought forth. To Agrippa he said,
"I'm accused of no crime, yet I am imprisoned,
and men want me dead because Jesus has risen.
Why do we Jews not believe our Lord can
yet raise up the dead? We have prayed for the man
who would be our Messiah. He's come, and yet still
we wait. Not just that, we went out and killed
the one who came for us! I did the same to

his followers when I was still a blind fool."
Then Agrippa asked, "Do you think you can make me
a Christian in such a short time with this plea?"
"I pray," replied Paul, "that my words might still change
each person, so all have a faith that's unchained."
Then Agrippa said, "This man could be freed had he
not appealed to Rome's rule, but now he can't be."

Acts 27

So Paul was then placed on a ship set to sail
for Rome, but on this trip a furious gale
blew up and the entire crew was afraid.
But Paul stood before them and said, "I have prayed.
An angel of God said that all of our lives
will be spared, for I was told I must arrive
before Caesar in Rome. The ship will be lost,
but none of us will pay the ultimate cost."
And just as he said, after two weeks at sea
they neared a small island where they would all be
rescued. Two hundred and seventy men
made it to shore, and not one of them
perished at sea. They found they had landed
on Malta. The Lord had never abandoned
Paul in his mission. When Paul went aground,
a viper bit him, but the people there found
that Paul did not swell up nor die, so they thought,
'Is this man a god?' So Paul was then brought
to the chief of the island, whose father was ill.
Paul prayed with the chief and remained there until
the man had been cured. Then many came for
a cure from this stranger who'd washed up on shore.
After three months, a boat found them and
took all men to Rome. When Paul reached the land,
he sought all the Jews within Rome and then he
explained the false charges.
They said, "Let us see
what we think of this. Tell us of the Way

and what you believe in. We'll hear what you say."
Some were convinced while others were not.
But many were troubled by what Paul had taught
about how salvation could be shared with all
of the Gentiles. Because of this some hated Paul.
But these Jews had listened, and though not all turned
to follow the Way, Paul's fire still burned
to spread the good news, and so for two years
Paul spoke to the Romans and all who would hear.

Romans 1 - 2

I, Paul, write to those in Rome who are loved
by God. His grace comes to you from above.
It seems that the Father has sought to provide
a chance so that I can come stand by your side.
I long to see you, for I hear you are strong
in your faith. I shall come and will not be long.
God's wrath for those who have shunned Him is plain,
for although they knew Him, they turned from His name.
They traded His truth for a lie, and God let
them go down that path, where they would forget
His power and peace, but because they knew
the truth at one point, the Lord's anger grew.
But please do not judge, for if you condemn
and do the same things you have scorned, then like them
you'll be judged by God. So do what is good,
and do not judge others, for only God should.
Take up the law, whether Gentile or Jew,
and hearken to it in all that you do.
You Jews of the law, remember, you men!
You preach against wrongdoing, but then you sin.
When you are dishonest, God's name is dragged through
the mud by the Gentiles because of you!
You're circumcised, yes, but that doesn't relieve
you from your trespasses. God's not naïve.
If the uncircumcised live in purity, then
he's lived in the law, as you've lived in sin.
For true circumcision takes place in the heart,
and they are the ones that the Lord sets apart.

Romans 3

What advantage then is there in being a Jew?
Much! The Lord's words were entrusted to few,
and we are that few! Our Lord, God, is true.
When you lack in faith, God is faithful to you!
We all sin, for no man is perfect. Not one!
Name one who is pure that is under the sun.
The law doesn't save us! It shows us our sin,
so we may remember the Lord's path again.
The Lord's holy righteousness now is made known,
for our faith in Christ Jesus leads us to God's throne.
God sacrificed him so all were atoned,
for God loves his children. Not one is disowned.
God is one God, not just God of the Jews.
He's the God of the Gentiles. God does not choose.
So we must choose Him and live in His law,
but to think He belongs just to you is a flaw.

Romans 4

Think of our forefather, Abraham, who
believed in God. His faith's a great credit to
his righteousness. Look closer There is still more...
not after he was circumcised, but before!
So if he was blessed before he gave flesh,
and then gained the seal of his true righteousness,
it's faith that's important, not cutting his skin.
The Lord doesn't look at what's outside, but in!
It's not through the law that his offspring were born,
so don't treat your Gentile brothers with scorn.
Jesus died for every person and nation,
and rose back to life for our justification.

Romans 5

Since we're redeemed, in peace let's rejoice.
There's hope in the glory of God. Every voice
be faithful. In suffering we persevere,

gain character, hope, and it is made clear
that hope in the Lord does not disappoint.
The righteous may suffer but God will anoint
those people who die for that which is good.
It's so very rare, though men often should
die for the righteous. But it is a fact,
Christ died for the wicked. No man will do that!
In Christ's blood we're cleansed, so having been cleaned,
how much more in God's love can goodness be gleaned?
Sin came through man, with death on its heels.
Through Adam man fell. Through Christ, God reveals
Himself to us all. True life can be sought.
Let grace reign in all the Lord's son's blood has bought.

Romans 6 - 7

Baptized by death, we rose from the dead
so we might find new life through Jesus instead.
But in that life we must be dead to sin, so
sin no more, brothers, and let his peace show.
Now you are slaves! So serve and obey.
You offered yourself to the Lord on the day
that you took in His son. It's good to be free
from our sin, so serve righteously for all to see.
In marriage a woman is bound to her mate
till he dies. So the law can only relate
while alive, but you died, then rose, born anew!
Now faith in the Lord, not the law, governs you.
That is not to say that the law is a sin,
but it shows us what's wrong and it binds us within.
The very commandments God meant to inspire
brought passion and lust and sinful desire.
We know it's not right, but it's sin we seek out.
I knew the law well, but was not devout.
How wretched I was. How wretched I am.
But Christ protects me from my sins as a man.

Romans 8

Therefore there's no condemnation for those
who are Christ's, for in them the love of God goes.
The mind of the man is death, but the mind
of the Spirit is life. In that you will find
that if you're controlled by the Spirit, you'll gain
eternal life inside the Lord's great domain.
Therefore, my brothers, it's your obligation
to base all your actions on Christ's strong foundation.
Our suffering now in no way compares
with the glory eternal that God has prepared.
If God is for us, what power can stand
against Jesus Christ and the Lord's holy hand?

Romans 9 - 10

My people, the ones who were promised, are sons
of the patriarch, Abraham. Through their veins runs
Isaac's blood, he of the Lord's promised birth.
Through his line came Christ, to save the whole Earth.
But the firstborn of Isaac and Abraham too,
weren't favored by God. But is it not true
that the firstborn is favored? No man may foretell
whom God is against and whom He likes well.
Pharaoh was under God's power when he
was laid low so all of the world might see
that God's power was the greatest of all.
God sets who falters and who shall stand tall.
So Israel cries, "Why are Gentiles blessed?
God gave us the law, but he loves them best?"
We sought through just works to earn God's delight,
but it was our faith that He sought to ignite.
My prayer is that Israel still may be saved.
They're zealous for God, but the price has been paid.
Christ is the end of the law. They don't see
that God asks His people to simply believe.
If you call on the name of the Lord, He will hear.
But how can you call when you don't think He's near?

They heard the good news, but the message was lost,
and I fear for their hearts; I fear for the cost.

Romans 11

So did God reject them? Of course not, for I
am an Israelite. But they turned a blind eye.
Why does Israel worship false idols and kill
God's prophets? They're stubborn, ignoring His will.
Can they still find grace? Of course, the Lord cares
for His chosen ones, but they should fear and beware.
Though branches are broken, a wild shoot grows.
That's you, and the Lord sees your faith and He knows
your faith has come honestly. Don't boast, for He
knows the root still supports you. You're cut from the tree
He blessed from the start. But they're chosen above
all the others, and they shall retain the Lord's love.

Romans 12

As God's living sacrifice, do not conform
to the pattern of this world, but be transformed.
Don't think that you're better because you are blessed
but use every gift, serving God without rest.
If you prophesy well, then prophesy, man.
If your gift is to serve, serve all whom you can.
To teach or encourage? To give or to lead?
In faith, I say do so with every deed!
Let love be sincere, and cling to the good.
Rejoice when there's joy, and mourn when you should.
Hope and be patient in any affliction.
Bless those who curse you, and without restriction
do not repay evil with evil, lest you
fail to heed God. So seek to pursue
what's peaceful, for vengeance is God's own domain
and He'll repay all who cause His children pain.

Romans 13 - 14

Submit to your rulers, although God alone
is the true ruler. He put them onto their throne.
No ruler holds terror when you do what's right.
Pay taxes, respect them, and shine the Lord's light.
All the commandments are summed up in one
"Love others just as you would want it done
to you." So don't murder, don't covet, don't steal.
Instead we must love, friends, and serve God with zeal.
Accept those whose faith is weak and don't judge,
but let your great faith never waiver or budge.
Let each thought and action seek edification
for your foes as much as your own congregation.

Romans 15 - 16

God glorifies Jews as his promise fulfilled.
God glorifies Gentiles, for it's His will
to show His great mercy for one and for all.
Through Jesus the world will hear the Lord's call.
I have been called to seek out people who
have not heard of Christ. As I brought him to you,
so now I shall bring him to Spain. On the way,
I'll see you in Rome and embrace you that day.
My blessings to all, for my thoughts are with you.
Beware of division and those who seek to
set you against one another, for when
you're united in Christ, you can turn away sin.

I Corinthians 1 - 2

From Paul, to the church of Corinth, I write,
in the peace of our Christ and God's great delight.
I appeal to you, friends, to never divide,
for we as believers should not choose up sides.
One might say, "I follow Paul," while another
says, "I follow Cephas." I ask you, my brothers,
was Jesus divided? Was Paul crucified?
Were you baptized in my name? Am I to have died
and been born again? No! Christ is the one.
And arguing only undoes what's been done.
The death on the cross is meaningless to
all those unbelievers, but to me and you
it's the act that has saved us. Its wisdom is in
the fact that Christ came and has freed us from sin,
and those who don't see scoff at the reward.
But he who may boast, must boast in the Lord.
When I arrived, I didn't say I was wise.
I sought to have nothing but Christ in my eyes.
Put your faith in God, not wisdom of men.
When we speak of wisdom, we speak of what's been
hidden from us that God sought to be
revealed by the Spirit, so all men may see.
No man on this Earth knows God's thoughts or mind,
but in Christ we can see the Lord's plan for mankind.

I Corinthians 3 - 4

You're stuck in the worldly, quarreling when
you ought to be godly, but you act like men.

You're following those who have planted a seed,
but God makes it grow. He's what you need!
Though one man may lay a foundation, it takes
many to build a building. Mistakes
can be very costly if made early on.
You are God's temple. You're perfectly drawn,
and for that, you're sacred, but don't be deceived.
You're not wise, although you have been well conceived.
Stop boasting of that which belongs to this world.
You're Christ's. Let all that is his be unfurled.
Those who are trusted must prove their faith's true.
No one but God can truly judge you.
You're rich! You are kings! In Christ you're made strong.
while all the apostles are cursed and are wronged.
I don't say these things to make you feel shame,
though arrogance doesn't praise Christ's holy name.
I'm sending you Timothy, who will remind
you all how to act. I'm not far behind.

I Corinthians 5

I've heard there's a man in your midst who has taken
his father's wife. Tell me that I am mistaken!
I've heard that you're proud of this fact, when you should
have cast the man out of your group. It's not good
to have such a thing - such an evil - near you.
This is a man that the devil pursues.
His sin will be yours if you all allow
him to poison the church. Expel the man now.

I Corinthians 6

If you have disputes with each other, don't go
and ask unbelievers to judge you. You know
that all your disputes can be solved by the men
in your own congregation. It's so much worse when
you argue in front of those who don't believe.
And why are there lawsuits? You have deceived
your brothers in Christ! Have you not been cleaned?

Why would you let yourselves be so demeaned?
Do not fall into the depths of depravity,
sexual deviance, and immorality.
You are from Christ. Don't taint what is good!
The righteous both know and do what they should.

I Corinthians 7

Now to the matters that you wrote about.
It's good for a man not to marry, no doubt,
but there are temptations a man knows in life
so it's better for most men if they take a wife.
The same goes for women. A husband is good,
and to each they should be as one body should.
I wish every man could be unmarried too,
but not everyone is like me, it is true.
To the unmarried and to the widows, I say
it's good to stay single, but don't go astray.
It's better to marry if you feel the need.
I do not command you, I only concede
that few can restrain from passion's desire,
for in many people it burns like a fire.
To those who are married, I say don't divorce.
The vows of your marriage are strictly enforced.
If you have a wife who is not a believer,
I tell you you're not to divorce her or leave her
for she and your children have been sanctified
through you who was cleansed when the Lord Jesus died.
The same goes for sisters in Christ who are wed
to husbands who don't know that for them Christ bled.
Keep God's command for that is what counts,
for God bought your life. He keeps His accounts.
In marriage you must always think of your spouse,
but if you are single you tend to God's house
much easier since all your worries are less.
Marriage, in my mind, creates so much mess.

I Corinthians 8 - 9

As for food sacrifice set out for gods;
do you not realize that this is at odds
with all we believe? There's one God who's great!
There aren't other gods, nor lords, nor the fates.
Why do I hear people grumble when I
need food? Do you want the apostles to die?
Who serves as a soldier at his own expense?
To not feed those feeding your soul? That's nonsense!
Though I have been freed, I'm a slave to mankind
so each man and woman have their chance to find
the Lord. It's a race, so run for the prize,
so His glory is always in front of your eyes.

I Corinthians 10 - 11

Our forefathers all had been blessed by the Lord,
but turned and rejected the greatest reward.
They reveled as pagans, bowing to fakes.
They tested the Lord and were bitten by snakes.
These deeds were but warnings. Be strong in belief.
Not some simple fool blown around like a leaf.
There's only one body of Christ, so partake.
To challenge the Lord is a foolish mistake!
All is allowed, but not everything's good.
Don't seek what is selfish. A righteous man should
do what's right by others. Let no brother stumble.
Seek glory for others, that you may be humble.
Be proper in worship, in dress and in acts.
The Lord's Supper's not to be some common snack!
It's the body of Christ, and those who forget it
shall know the Lord's anger and soon they'll regret it.

I Corinthians 12

The Spirit was given that we should have gifts
that help us to proselytize and uplift
our brothers and sisters, that they should soon find

Christ's love in their hearts and his words in their minds.
You too have a gift, whether prophet or teacher,
helping or healing, leader or preacher,
miracle worker or speaking in tongues.
These gifts have been given to both old and young.

I Corinthians 13

If I speak in tongues or can hear the Lord's call,
but I have no love, it means nothing at all.
For true love is patient, and true love is kind.
Not envious, boastful, proud, unrefined,
rude or self-seeking, not angered or wronged.
It shelters and trusts, so hope is prolonged.
Love never fails, though knowledge is lost,
prophecies cease, and tongues must exhaust.
When I was a child, I thought as one does.
I turned to a man and all that once was
I thus left behind, and sought what's above,
faith, hope, and love. But the greatest is love.

I Corinthians 14

I wish that you all spoke in languages, though
I'd much rather hear you all prophesy so
that those who could hear would then find the Lord,
for that is the greatest and finest reward.
My brothers, I ask that in worship you seek
to glorify God - whether you're Jew or Greek.
If you are so gifted, then speak for the gain
of God. Let the people all find His domain.

I Corinthians 15 - 16

Christ died for our sins. He was buried and raised.
This is the truth, not the turn of a phrase.
To Peter, the Twelve, and more than five hundred
he came after death. If any man's wondered,
I saw Jesus too. I'm the lowest of all!

For I persecuted the church, until called
to give up my ways. For he was the proof.
The dead shall have life born anew. That's the truth.
From Adam, we die. But in Christ, we shall live.
He showed us the good news: that our Lord forgives
our trespasses. He grants a heavenly new
body to all who believe. Now do you
know that the Lord is with you and your church?
Never cease seeking Him, for in your search
you'll find what is true. I will come when I can.
Till then, I shall pray that God shows you His plan.

II Corinthians 1 - 3

To you, brothers, both I and Timothy write
to let you all know of the news of our plight.
It once had appeared that our lives would be lost,
which we'd gladly give for the faith as our cost.
We take our comfort in Christ, for we know
that the dead are reborn in the place where we go,
but God heard our need, and our lives were both spared.
I'd planned to be with you as I had declared.
But my plans were changed, though I wanted to come.
Because of the danger, I'm sparing you from
the things we endured, so the Corinth church may
continue its worship of Christ and his way.
So I tell you, brothers, forgive those who sin,
for Christ was the only perfection of men.
The rest of us fall far short of the goal.
God cares not for bodies but for a man's soul.
So as you are ministers, seek to lift up
each brother as he takes the bread and the cup.
The glory of God's new covenant shines
for everyone. Don't let your hearts or your minds
dwell on the earthly, for God is above
the Earth and the stars. In Him you'll find love.
Our faces unveiled reflect the Lord's glory.
In Him and in Christ, we know the true story.

II Corinthians 4 - 5

God made the light come forth from the dark,
and so in our hearts, His light left its mark.

And this is our treasure, for we're jars of clay.
No matter what happens to us, night or day,
we carry the joy of the cross and rebirth
in all that we do, throughout the whole Earth.
And we may reveal it so others might see
the glory of God, through you and through me.
Do not lose heart, for the earthly may fall.
We may be burdened, but God heals it all.
The heavenly kingdom can't be touched by men.
To enter it, we must be cleansed of our sin.
That's why Christ came! We've been reconciled
from all that is earthly and all that's defiled
our senses, our minds, our souls and our lives,
so we may see Heaven when judgment arrives.

II Corinthians 6 - 7

Through beatings and riots, in prison, hard work,
in hunger and sleeplessness, let us not shirk
our duties to our fellow man. For our prize
is the saving of those who would meet their demise.
Just as we opened our hearts to you all,
I hope Corinth's church will answer the call
to help men believe, but those who will not
should be cast aside and not enter your lot.
My joy has been great, though I've known no rest,
for Titus and others have shown me how blessed
I am in the Lord. I know in your prayers
I've not been forgotten through all my affairs.

II Corinthians 8 - 9

Last year your church led the way as you gave
in supporting the cause so that others were saved.
I ask that this year, you finish the task.
Be generous. I don't demand it. I ask.
I send to you Titus, for he's good and fair.
I want you to know that I pray and I care
that your gifts be administered properly so

that not only God, but also men know.
Whoever sows sparingly, so that man reaps,
but those who are generous gather in heaps.
Your gifts should be used to the benefit of
those who seek life in Jesus' love.

II Corinthians 10 - 12

Though I may seem "timid" when we're face to face
and "bold" in my letters I sent from a place
that's far from your city and church, as I've heard,
my boldness shall show, both in action and word.
In Christ we build up, but some walls are torn
down to the ground when we are reborn.
Though I preach of meekness and follow the Way,
I cannot sit back while you disobey.
If one comes and speaks of Christ and you see
a teaching that's different than what came from me,
then do you not realize that man is a fake?
You all know the truth! He's just like the snake
that tempted poor Eve, and then paradise fell.
Don't be so gullible. You know as well
as I what Christ did. Don't follow such lies.
Such people are demons in human disguise.
I am no fool, but if you think so,
then let this fool boast. Wherever I go
I'm beaten and flogged, thrown in prison and death
is a threat that's as common as taking a breath.
Three times I was beaten with rods. I was stoned,
but survived to be shipwrecked three times. I have known
a night and a day in the open sea till
I was saved, and that only through God's gracious will.
My countrymen hate me. The Gentiles too.
Why do I have to tell all this to you?
My anguish is nothing, if men may be saved.
So ignore anyone who would lead you astray!

II Corinthians 13

I'm coming and this time it will be the third
time I have seen you, and I'd have preferred
to come in God's joy, but I come to cleanse
the church of those who disobey and cause sins.
Before I arrive, test yourselves. Are you good
and faithful to God? Do you do as you should?
Aim for perfection! Now is the time.
May God dwell within you. Be peaceful and kind.

Galatians 1

From Paul: To the church in Galatia, I send
the peace and the glory of Jesus. Amen.
I'm shocked that you all would so quickly reject
the gospel and turn to what's incorrect -
and by incorrect, I mean it's not real!
The fact that false prophets fooled you is surreal.
Such lies and their liars should all be condemned,
for I speak of God, while they speak of men.
The gospel I gave you is not just invented.
I used to persecute those I resented -
the Christians! But then God revealed unto me
His son. Only then did I finally see.
He told me to preach to the Gentiles so
you would learn about Jesus, and then you would know.
Through Arabia, into Damascus and then
I went to Jerusalem. That, friends, is when
I met up with Peter and James, who's the brother
of Jesus, and everyone asked one another
throughout all the churches why their greatest foe,
now preached the good news wherever he'd go.

Galatians 2

With Barnabas and with Titus, I went
fourteen years later to where the Lord sent
His servant. I spoke to the Gentiles who
were looking for hope, just like all of you.
But snakes were among us. They sought to enslave
those freed by the fact that Christ rose from the grave.

But we were not fooled. As we had agreed
with Peter, both Jews and Gentiles need
the word of the Lord. Yes, people like you!
So I sought out Gentiles; he taught the Jews.
Because Peter drew back entirely from
the Gentiles, I asked him, "Why'd Jesus come?
That all should find hope!" But some fell away.
Even poor Barnabas was led astray.
I asked them, "What then should a Gentile do?
Take on traditions and live like a Jew?
Our faith is not made by observing the law!
Our faith's in the life after death that you saw.
If we become sinners while seeking out Christ,
does that mean that being a sinner is right?
Of course not! I died so Christ could be born
inside of my heart. Why show the Lord scorn?
If righteousness through the law could be reached,
then Christ's death was meaningless. Why should we teach?"

Galatians 3

You foolish Galatians! How were you all saved?
By words that you heard or the laws you obeyed?
I showed you the way but you don't understand.
By faith you'll be saved, not by your own hand.
Was it all for nothing? Abraham knew!
God said, "All nations shall be blessed through you."
Christ has redeemed us so all may be blessed
through Abraham, not just the Jews, but the rest!
The promise God made came hundreds of years
before the law did. Does nobody here
realize why God first established the law?
To stop the transgressions He constantly saw.
Is the law against God? Of course not. It's His!
But now we have Christ, and the new message is
that we're all saved through him. That means that you
were saved through his death, not the things that you do.
So now we are all sons of God, can't you see?
No Jew, no Greek, no slave, and no free.

No woman or man, for in Christ there's no need.
Through him God has made us of Abraham's seed.

Galatians 4

If a child inherits his father's estate,
he cannot yet manage the work. He must wait.
Until he is grown, he's no more than a slave,
just as we were until the Lord gave
His son, born to us so that we could lay claim
to the rights of a son. That's why Jesus came.
Galatians, why have you turned back to old ways,
enslaving yourself as you did in the days
before I knew you? Was my work a waste?
I preached so that all of your fear was erased.
Now where is your joy? And have I become
an enemy to you? I know there are some
who want you to turn against what I've preached,
but you should be zealous for that which I teach.
I'm not mad at you. Instead I'm perplexed,
confused and alarmed and totally vexed.
Don't you remember Abraham's sons?
Hagar, the slave, gave birth to the one
in a normal way, but when Sarah conceived
it was a blessing from God they received.
You are like Isaac, born because God
promised salvation. It's not a façade.
The inheritance cannot be shared by the slave.
You were born free, so take what God gave.

Galatians 5

Those who are saying that your circumcision
is what God requires can't make that decision.
That's from the law, and Christ came to set
us free from the law, or did you forget?!
So throw off that yoke! The uncircumcised
aren't cut off from God or somehow despised.
The one thing that matters is faith shown through love.

That's all that matters to our Lord above.
The law is summed up in one simple way:
"Go, love your neighbor as yourself this day."
Don't be confused or let them provoke
your heart. Do only as Jesus Christ spoke.

Galatians 6

If someone is caught in a sin, gently bring
him back to the fold. Nobody should cling
to pride. Help to carry all those who may need
your help, and, dear friends, do not be deceived.
God can't be mocked, and you reap what you sow.
If you plant a sin, then destruction will grow.
But planting the Spirit reaps eternal life,
so seek to do good. Don't bring about strife.
Those who want you to be circumcised boast
of your flesh, but you'll see that they don't follow most
of the law. Through Christ, we're God's new creation.
Take strength in his hope, and find your salvation.

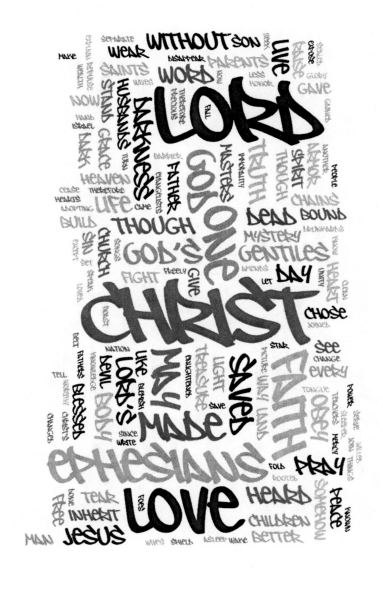

Ephesians 1

From Paul, to the saints of Ephesus, peace.
God has blessed all that we do without cease.
The Lord chose us even before the creation,
adopting His sons throughout every nation
to speak of the Christ. By God's love and will,
we're blessed through His son who was tortured and killed.
Wisdom and knowledge were given so we
would unite Earth and Heaven. It's no mystery
that we were made heirs, predestined and planned
to honor the Lord in each tongue and land.
When you heard the truth, through Christ, you were sealed
with the Spirit so that you were saved and were healed.
Since I heard of your faith in the Lord, I have not
stopped praying for you with each word and thought.
I hope that you know the Lord better each day.
May you be enlightened so you do not stray.

Ephesians 2

You were dead in your sin and the ways of the world,
like all of us were till His glory unfurled
and showed us the way. I too was once dead.
By grace we've been saved, and by Christ we are led.
Do not be confused, you did not save yourself.
It's only through God that you gained so much wealth,
not your works. Do not boast. You're no better than those
who aren't saved, except for the path that you chose.
Therefore remember, you're Gentiles, all!
You were separate from Christ, until you heard his call.

But though you were far, you have all been brought near,
and through Him you'll see that the gates disappear.
He tore down the barrier and barricade
that kept you from knowing Him. Don't be afraid,
for you are now citizens. His is your land.
In Him you shall live, and for Him you will stand.

Ephesians 3

For this reason, though I am bound up in chains,
I write to you so I can somehow explain
the mystery and the vision made known
to me by the Lord. In it I was shown
that Israel and the Gentiles are
brothers through him, born under the star
of Heaven. We share one body, one heart,
and in Him nobody may tear us apart.
I'm but a servant. I'm less than the least.
Through grace I inherit His mercy and peace.
Until Jesus came, you could not join the fold
or gain the Lord's treasure, more precious than gold.
In Christ, Jew and Gentile can serve as one,
the most glorious Father, in whom all was done.
So therefore, don't fret over what I endure,
for in God our treasure is safe and secure.
Before God the Father, I kneel and I pray
that His power and love strengthens you every day.
That your love is rooted, so you are instilled
with the heart to do all that the Lord God has willed.

Ephesians 4

Be worthy in your life. Be humble and kind.
Be patient. Seek love. Through effort you'll find
the unity of both the body and soul.
In your faith and your baptism, you've been made whole.
Yes, Christ descended, so he could ascend.
Only through him may we make our amends.
He gave us apostles, some prophets, and preachers,

pastors, evangelists, and made us teachers.
He taught us to build up Christ's body until
we're united in faith and we do the Lord's will,
so we won't be infants who change with the wind,
but joined in Christ Jesus; one life without end.
Don't live like the Gentiles, though you were one.
Now you've been changed, through God's loving son.
They've hardened their hearts. They are lost in the dark.
You were made new, so in truth we embark!
Don't let the sun set in anger. Don't give
the devil a foothold, or in you he'll live.
Don't tear people down, but seek to build up,
so love and compassion will fill the Lord's cup.

Ephesians 5

Repulse immorality. Turn away greed.
If a man imitates the Lord, then indeed
he's a gift to us all, and a jewel in God's sight.
Though you were in darkness, you now are the light!
As the children of light, shun the darkness. Expose
all sin. Light overcomes darkness and glows.
That's why it is said, "Wake up, sleeper, and rise
from the dead, for Christ shines on you. Open your eyes."
Don't be drunkards or fools, but instead sing Him songs,
for Jesus has saved you from all of your wrongs.
Wives, love your husbands, and husbands your wives.
As Christ loved the church, give each other your lives.
Be washed in the word, so that you may be clean.
Keep one another from all that's obscene.
As a man leaves his parents to be with his wife,
so Christ gave the church all his love and his life.

Ephesians 6

Children, obey your parents, for they
will raise you with love. I tell you, obey.
And fathers, raise your children strong in the Lord,
so they may inherit His promised reward.

Slaves, heed your masters, as you would obey
the Lord. And you masters, treat slaves the same way.
Don't threaten them, for the Lord is the true
Master. He watches and knows all you do.
Wear God's armor, friends, so that you may keep
the devil at bay. Do not fall asleep
in your faith, for the fight is against all that's dark,
so when the day comes you will be without mark
or blemish. Wear truth as a belt so you stand
firm with your faith as a shield in your hand.
Let the Spirit, salvation, and righteousness be
your armor and sword. Your foes will all see
that you fight with prayer. So pray for the saints,
and pray that my letter to you somehow paints
the picture of faith and the gospel. Though I
am bound up in chains, I'm free and I fly,
for the word sets me free. So I freely declare
the good news to everyone and everywhere.
Tychicus, who bears this message, will say
all the things I could not. Peace be yours today.

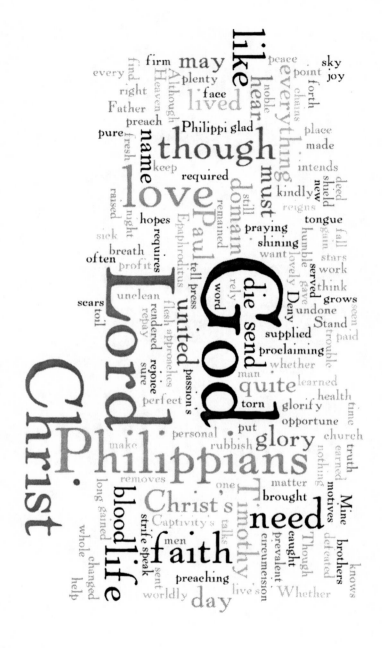

Philippians 1

To the church of Philippi, I, that is Paul,
and Timothy, send out our love to you all.
I'm praying for you. Your partnership in
the great love of Christ has so often been
a joy in my life. For whether in chains
or preaching the word, your faith never changed.
Captivity's brought forth a wonderful yield,
for the whole palace guard knows Christ is my shield.
For him I am here, and for that brothers speak
of their love of the Lord, and their passion's not meek.
Although some would preach for personal gain,
what does it matter? Both make God's name
more prevalent. Whether their motives are true,
Christ's domain grows. And we as the few
must keep on proclaiming, and if I should die,
it's all for His glory. To live's to supply
my efforts and tongue to glorify Him,
and help spread the good news in times that are grim.
I'm torn, for I want to be with Christ above,
but you need me here, and you have my love.
So that's why I'm sure that I will remain,
for God still requires me for His domain.
Stand firm in the Spirit, united as one,
for though you may suffer, you can't be undone.

Philippians 2

Be humble, like Christ, not vain and conceited,
who being like God could not be defeated.

A man, he served men, even up to his death,
with each of his actions and every breath.
For that he was raised, for the Father was pleased.
When we hear his name, we should fall to our knees.
When trouble approaches, be like shining stars.
In Heaven the Lord removes all of our scars.
I hope to send Timothy to you quite soon,
when we find a time that is more opportune,
for though I rely on him, he talks of you,
for now, though, Epaphroditus must do.
You heard he was sick. He quite nearly died,
but God remained with him, and he was supplied
with health, so be glad! His life was saved for
the glory of God and all God has in store.

Philippians 3

I tell you again, circumcision is not
required by God, so do not be caught
up in such fervor. Such faith in the flesh,
was rendered a moot point when Christ made us fresh
and new through his blood. All I've gained in life
is rubbish, for my gift is toil and strife
for the Lord, and in that work my profit does lie.
I gave everything for my place in His sky.
But I am not perfect. I press on each day
in the hopes that when I die, I'll hear the Lord say,
"You are Mine, Paul." Deny what's unclean,
so when you face God, then the truth may be seen.

Philippians 4

I long for you all to be strong and united
in faith. So rejoice! For the Lord is delighted
when gentleness reigns and peace can transcend
everything worldly, as He intends.
What's noble, what's lovely, what's pure, and what's right
is what you should think about each day and night.
Whatever I've taught and whatever you've learned,

put into practice, so Christ's blood is earned.
When I've been in need, you've sent me your aid.
Though you owed me nothing, I've been amply paid.
As I've lived with plenty and I've lived in need,
the Lord will repay you for your kindly deed.

Colossians 1

My friends in Colosse, I, Paul, write to you
with Timothy here addressing you too.
We pray for you all, for your faith and the joy
of Christ in your lives that no man can destroy.
Christ is the image of God who's invisible.
God's will is total and is not divisible.
In Jesus, the Lord reconciled for all
and kept us from what should have been our downfall.
Once you were far from the Lord, and your ways
were not what He wanted, but all of those days
are behind you, for He has established in you
His faith in all peoples. His world is new.
I labor for God and His church. I've become
the mouthpiece for that which has been withheld from
the Gentiles until the Christ came and shed
his blood for us all. Through him, we are fed.

Colossians 2

Though many have not met me face to face, I
still struggle for them. If I live or die,
my message should still lift up anyone's heart.
Although I am absent, I'm with you in part.
Don't be held captive by human tradition,
for Christ didn't come here to bring circumcision
to all of the world! He came so you could
be free from what's evil and seek what is good.
The written code's canceled. The new one's in blood,
so don't be pulled down to dwell in the mud.

Your festivals and what you eat or you drink,
are trivial, no matter what others think.
"Don't handle. Don't taste. Don't touch." What are these?
Commands made by men. They'll pass like the breeze.
They lack any value because they do not
keep us from indulgence, where most men are caught.

Colossians 3 - 4

Look forward, not down at the things of today.
Keep your eyes on the Lord so you're not led astray.
Because of idolatry, earthliness, greed,
and lust the Lord's wrath is coming indeed.
Shun anger and malice, foul language, and lies.
You're clothed and you're new. So let the past die.
Forgive those who sin, as the Lord did with you.
Let the peace of Christ rule, for you were called too.
Pray for us as we proclaim Christ's account.
Whenever you witness to men, make it count!
Let each conversation be full of God's grace,
and preach to each person, each gender, each race.
Tychicus will tell you my news. I send
him and Onesimus, our faithful friend.
I write by my own hand, here in my cell.
My brothers in prison send their love as well.

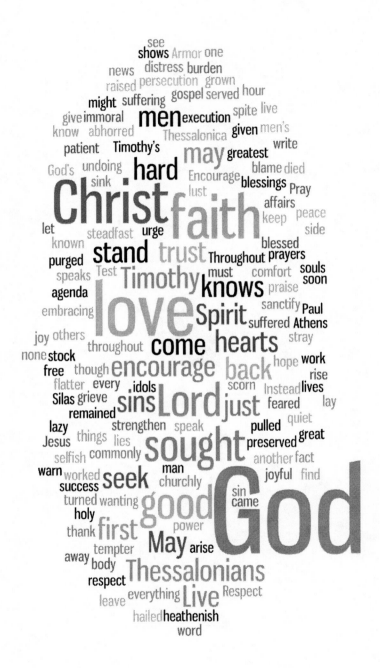

I Thessalonians 1 - 2

From Paul and Silas and Timothy, we
write you, Thessalonica, peace be with thee.
We thank God for you in our hearts and our prayers.
You're faithful in all of your churchly affairs.
The gospel has come to you in word and power.
The Spirit has given you your holy hour.
In spite of your suffering, your joy has grown.
Throughout Macedonia your faith is known.
They know how you turned from the idols you served,
embracing the Lord through whom we're preserved.
Our visit to you is commonly hailed
as the greatest success, for you have not failed!
We all must be men in whom our Lord can trust,
not those who would flatter, be selfish, or lust.
We do not lay stock in other men's praise.
Our faith is in God. That's why Christ was raised.
We sought not to be a burden to you.
We worked hard, which everyone knows to be true.
We sought to encourage and comfort and urge
you to find God so your sins would be purged.
All of us suffered a great persecution,
just as Christ did in his execution,
and though we were pulled away from you, we
have been wanting to see you - none more than me!

I Thessalonians 3 - 5

When we could not stand it, we had to leave,
a fact that in Athens we all had to grieve.

But Timothy came to be with you, because
I feared that the tempter might sink in his claws,
undoing the things that we sought to first do.
But Timothy's back, and he has good news.
Your faith and your love have truly been blessed,
for you've remained steadfast throughout your distress.
May God and may Jesus be first in your love,
and strengthen your hearts by the Spirit above.
Live to please God! Do this more and more.
Control your own body, let sin be abhorred.
The immoral and lustful seek heathenish sins,
and God turns his back on the souls of such men.
Instead seek to live and love one another,
just as a man should love his own brother.
Live quiet lives. Be good and don't stray
so others respect you and trust what you say.
The Lord will come soon and those who have died
in Christ will rise up and stand by His side.
He who says he knows when Christ will arise,
has his own agenda and speaks only lies.
Armor yourselves in faith, love, and hope,
and encourage each other in every scope.
Respect those amongst you who work hard, and warn
those who are lazy that God shows His scorn
for them and their actions. Encourage the weak.
Be patient and joyful in all that you speak.
Pray and give thanks for all that you have.
Test everything; keep the good, not the bad.
May God sanctify you and may you be free
from blame. God's blessings to you from us three.

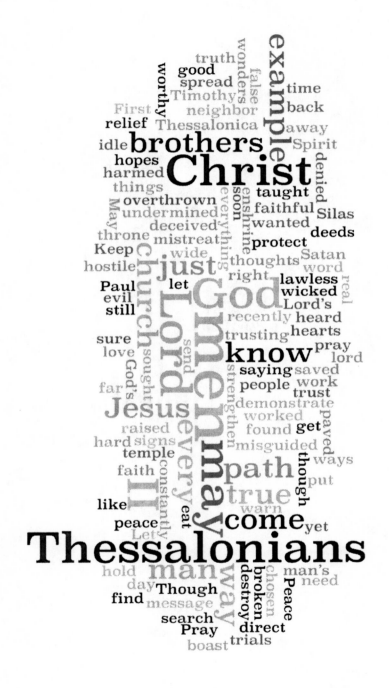

II Thessalonians 1

From Paul and Silas and Timothy to
those in Thessalonica. Peace be to you.
We boast of your church, for in all of your trials
you still love your neighbor, though he is hostile.
You will find relief, for the Lord God is just,
and those who have harmed you will not have His trust.
That you'll be found worthy, we constantly pray.
Be like our lord Jesus in every way.

II Thessalonians 2

As I am sure you have recently heard
some people are saying that it is God's word
that says Jesus Christ will soon come again.
I know that your hopes may be raised by such men,
but don't be deceived, for it's not yet time.
First the most wicked of men shall enshrine
himself in our temple. This lawless man's throne
will be broken by Christ. He'll be overthrown!
Though Satan will send both wonders and signs,
they all will be false and will be undermined
by those that are real, which all come from Him.
God will destroy those who put faith in them.
But you have been chosen and you have been saved!
By trusting the Spirit, your path has been paved.
So hold true to all of the things you've been taught.
Let God strengthen each of your deeds and your thoughts.

II Thessalonians 3

Pray that the message may spread far and wide,
that all of the evil men shall be denied.
For our Lord is faithful and He will protect
our hearts if they're true, so let Him direct.
Keep idle brothers away from your church.
You know our example, you don't have to search
for what is the truth. When we were with you
we worked hard in everything we sought to do.
We wanted to be an example that would
demonstrate Christ and all that which is good.
If a man doesn't work, that man shouldn't eat,
but warn them of their ways and do not mistreat
these misguided brothers, for they are just men
who need to get back on the right path again.
May the Lord be with you in every way,
and may peace be upon you on this, the Lord's day.

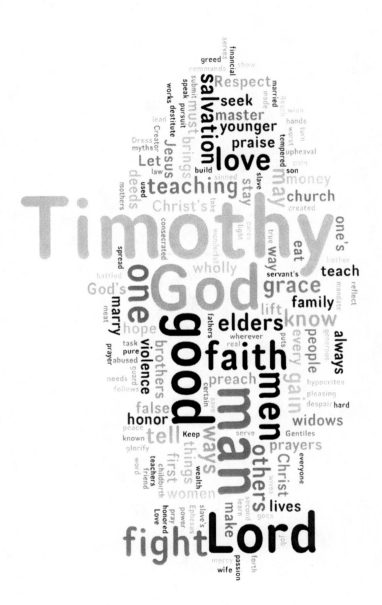

I Timothy 1

From Paul, to my son in the faith, Timothy,
peace and God's grace I wish unto thee.
I urged you to stay there in Ephesus when
I left you to fight all their doctrines of sin.
You battled their teaching. False prophets the lot!
Those who have turned from all that which we taught
want to be teachers, but they do not know
what they're talking about, and they struggle although
the law is not hard if it's properly used.
Unfortunately it's so often abused.
So I thank the Lord who has given me strength
to teach and to preach on the word at such length.
Though I persecuted through violence before,
I've found my salvation - the grace of the Lord!
Jesus' mandate that he set forth first
was to save all the sinners - and I was the worst!
For that may I glorify God all my days,
with works and thanksgiving, honor, and praise.
Timothy, I tell you, fight the good fight
so others may bask in Christ's glorious light.

I Timothy 2

Timothy, pray for the people who rule
that they should refrain from that which is cruel
and be guided by God, for these prayers are good
and pleasing to God. Our prayers always should
include everyone, for all men are under
the Lord and His mercy is not cast asunder

but offered to all. And that's why I am
teaching to Gentiles all that I can.
No one should lift up a prayer in dispute,
but with love and with kindness in every pursuit.
Say to the women, "Dress modestly and
learn to submit to the will of a man."
Adam was first, so it's written and known
that without a woman, a man is alone.
Then Eve was made second and sinned, so the Lord,
through childbirth, shall make all women restored.

I Timothy 3

Those who would watch over our churches take
on a task that is noble. But Timothy, make
sure they are worthy of honor and praise,
with only one wife, and tempered in ways
related to violence and anger. Don't bother
anointing a man who is not a good father.
A man who has power must gain his respect
through Christ's holy love. They must always reflect
his grace, and I tell you these men have to be
deep in their faith and sincere in decree.
No one should look for his personal gain
in the church. The love of one's money brings pain.
In these ways, choose those who will lead people to
salvation through Christ. I know you will do
a wonderful job in picking men out
who are good in their ways and wholly devout.

I Timothy 4

Some will abandon us. They'll be deceived
by the hypocrites who have refused to believe.
They say men can't marry, and say they can't eat
certain foods. Who cares if a man should eat meat
or if he is married? For God has created
all that we see, so it's consecrated.
Point these things out so your teaching is pure.

Keep men from myths. Let true faith endure.
We put all our hope in the one God who lives,
and mercifully He has salvation to give.
Let no one defame you because of your youth.
Devote yourself wholly to Jesus' truth.

I Timothy 5

Respect all your elders as fathers and mothers.
Love all the younger as sisters and brothers.
Reach out to the widows in need, but if they
have family to care for them, show them the way
to lift up their elders so they may repay
their parents and grandparents in such display.
The widow who does not have family puts all
of her faith in the Lord that He'll hear her call.
Help the old widows, the destitute wives
who have honored the Lord in living good lives.
But those who are younger should marry so they
are not gossips who say things that they should not say.
Respect the church elders and all their commands,
and do not be hasty in laying on hands.
People will know if you do right or wrong,
for the deeds of a man can't stay hidden for long.

I Timothy 6

If a slave serves a master and they are both brothers
in Christ, he should serve with more passion than others.
And so in this way, the slave's master knows
his servant's faith follows wherever he goes.
And those who speak false, seeking financial gain
shall find that their greed will ensnare them in chains.
The love of one's money is the root of all evil,
and brings only ruin, despair, and upheaval.
So you, man of God, seek to fight the good fight,
Eternal life's yours, and you're in God's sight.
In God, Lord of lords, and King of all kings,
who is the Creator and rules everything,

tell all of the rich that hope does not lie
in wealth, but in God. And that, friend, is why
they should seek to be generous in all of their deeds,
to build up the real treasure every man needs.
Set a foundation for all whom you teach
and guard what's entrusted to you when you preach.
Timothy, turn from the false and depraved,
and spread the good news so others are saved.

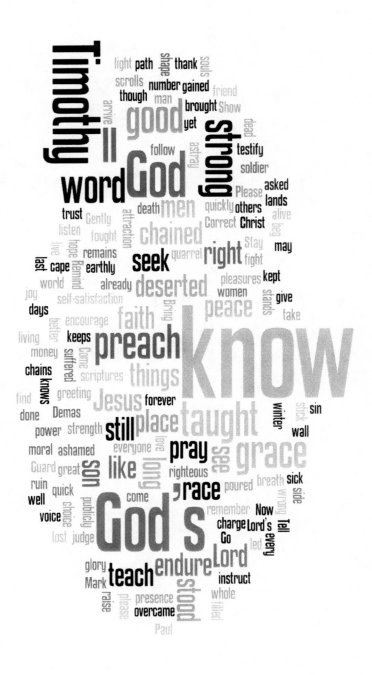

II Timothy 1

From Paul, to Timothy, grace be to you.
I thank God for all that He's asked us to do.
I remember your faith, and the women who taught
you of God's grace so that you were brought
out into the light. Do not be ashamed
to publicly testify God's will and name.
For through His son, Jesus, who overcame death
we gained the great hope that we preach with each breath.
Guard your joy, though. As you already know,
those in the province deserted me, so
I pray for the souls of all who remain,
and those who stood by me when I was in chains.

II Timothy 2

I beg you, be strong. Show others to preach
the things that I taught you, the things that you teach.
Stay strong like a soldier, and know that the race
is not over. We all seek to be in God's grace.
I'm chained to the wall, but God's word cannot
be chained up like men. What Jesus has taught
is if we die with him, we live with him too.
And if you endure, he'll endure with you.
Remind them of this. Tell all not to quarrel,
or ruin will follow. Go teach them this moral.
The Lord keeps His number and knows who are His.
We seek to be righteous. We all know what is
the right path to take, but God gave us choice.
It's better to listen than raise up your voice.

Gently instruct those who don't hear His word,
so they're not led astray, nor are they deterred.

II Timothy 3 - 4

The last days will be filled with sin, and all men
will love money and power. All good that has been
will be lost to the world. Deny the attraction
of such earthly pleasures and self-satisfaction.
You know me well. You know all that I've done.
You know how I've suffered where I've gone, my son.
You know the scriptures, so stick to what's true.
As a man of God, I place my whole trust in you.
In the presence of God, judge of living and dead,
I charge you to preach every word that Christ said.
Correct what is wrong and encourage what's right.
My strength is poured out. I fought the good fight.
I kept strong the faith, and I finished the race.
Now I long for God's peace that I'll find in His place.
Demas deserted me, so please come quick.
Only Luke still remains here while I'm sick.
Bring Mark if you can, my scrolls, and my cape.
Come quickly, my friend, for I'm not in good shape.
The Lord has stood by me. I know He still stands
by my side. How I long to see the Lord's lands.
To Him all the glory forever shall be.
Please give the greeting of peace that's from me
to everyone there. I pray you'll arrive
by winter, so I may yet see you alive.

saved fasting person rest
soul drunkards grace
search governors good sound left
desires seek always
hello people friend believes men
wants call angry obey heirs
twice setting
render consider corrupt
wine passion kings prove
Nicopolis Tarsus day seen
fall encourage observed
gave help finding enticed laws
winter much elderly become
send vine pureness brothers trust
Beware Everyone
control must serve
eyes fruit sent
needed faith Warn
servants things wonderful found
vice love Let contend
used temptation requires everyone know
proves chore one loyalty eternal
receive disciplined Paul change fault
actions despised violent till
Lord Teach everlasting Christ spouse made
decree write let life task
sisters sufficed forever doctrine
ideas slaves temperance disrupt children way
elders church man young drink
God silent bloodlines Now
Rebuke Titus oft

Titus 1 - 2

I, Paul of Tarsus, as one who believes
in life made eternal that we shall receive,
write to you, Titus, my wonderful friend.
I left you in Crete so you could contend
with setting up elders, a chore that requires
finding the people that our Lord desires.
They must not be drunkards or angry or violent,
nor render a man with good ideas silent.
For upright and disciplined men you must search
so they may encourage the rest in the church.
Beware in this task, for some will corrupt
and not seek out faith but seek to disrupt.
Teach them the doctrine; temperance, control,
faith in His love, and the pureness of soul.
Don't let the elderly drink too much wine
and let the young know that the fruit of their vine
is love of their spouse and children, that they
may prove Christ is in them forever this way.
Let all of our brothers and sisters be sound
in faith, so that in them no fault may be found.
Teach servants that loyalty to those they serve
proves trust, for their faith will oft be observed.
Encourage. Rebuke. But don't be despised,
for actions are seen by more than your eyes.

Titus 3

Teach everyone that they ought to obey
what kings will decree and what governors say.

Teach them to always do good, lest we fall
back into temptation and its fatal call.
We used to be slaves to passion and vice.
God gave us salvation which should have sufficed,
but we needed more, so He sent us Christ,
who saved us from all of the things that enticed.
Now we've become heirs to the life everlasting.
Don't quarrel on laws, or bloodlines, or fasting.
Warn a man twice and if he won't change,
consider the person from that day estranged.
Everyone here wants to tell you hello.
This winter I'll be in Nicopolis, so
I'll send you some help, and then you can call
on me, but till then, grace be with you all.

Philemon 1

From Paul, still sharing the good news in jail
and Timothy, who has stayed by without fail.
We're praying, Philemon, for you and your friends,
for I know your church grows as your faith extends.
I could demand, but I'd rather just ask
that you extend help to a man from our past
who hasn't been useful, but now he is quite
important to us and to me in my plight.
Onesimus, whom I now send back to you,
has become a believer and quite useful too.
Show him your kindness. He's not just a slave
but a brother now too, for he has been saved.
And if he has harmed you, charge me the toll.
It should be remembered you owe me your soul!
I know you will do what I ask and then more,
for that is what brothers in Christ are good for.
Keep a room ready for me, as I pray
that I will be freed from this prison some day.
My prisoners and brothers in Christ all extend
their greetings. Christ's blessings be with you, my friend.

Hebrews 1

In the past the Lord spoke to our forefathers through
the prophets, but now He has spoken to you
through His son whom He made the heir of all things.
And when the son died, he was placed above kings
and above all the angels, for when did God say
to an angel, "I'm making you My son today"?
For wasn't it written when Jesus was born,
'Let all angels worship him. Take up your horn'?
The son was set higher to show us the way,
anointed with oil for all to obey.
Christ was thus given the seat on God's right,
and angels are spirits who show man the light.

Hebrews 2

We must pay attention to what we have heard
so we do not drift far away from the word.
God's word is binding, so our violations
of what Christ has taught will deny us salvation.
In Psalms it is written, "Why do you love man
so much You'd redeem them by Your holy hand?"
Though we can't see everything under God's power,
Jesus is crowned, at this very hour!
It's fitting that God, through suffering, made
His son our salvation. Do not be afraid,
for though we will suffer, through that we become
brothers of Christ. Because of this, from
this day and onward, you never need fear
your death. That's the reason why Christ was sent here.

Christ came to be us, in human formation,
to be tempted so he'd release our temptation.

Hebrews 3

Therefore, fix all of your mind and your heart
on the calling of Jesus and never depart.
Moses, so faithful to God, still is less
than Jesus for he is God's son, truly blessed.
Just as a house cannot be judged greater
than its architect who was the creator,
so God has given this house to us all
and gave us His son that we should not fall.
Our forefathers all were tested and tried
because they were saved, but still they denied
the Lord God above. Look into your hearts.
Believe and hate sin, so you may all start
to encourage each other. We're all here to share
in the warmth of the Lord, which is why you must care.
For Moses brought our people out of their chains,
but their unbelieving caused their later pain.

Hebrews 4 - 5

We've all heard the gospel, so do not fall short
as many who've heard but did not support
their hearing with knowledge. Those who believe
know of God's rest, and they will receive
His peace. For it's written, 'When you hear His voice
don't harden your hearts. That's the time to rejoice.'
For God's word's as sharp as a double-edged sword.
It pierces and knows if you're worth His reward.
Everything's bared. We must give account,
but our high priest, Jesus, knows the amount
of temptation, for he came so he'd know and see
that we gain God's mercy in our times of need.
High priests are selected and they are appointed
so they may give offerings and be anointed.
They're gentle with those who are going astray.

They're called by the Lord, and in this same way
Jesus was called by our Lord, who said, "Son,
you're a priest of Melchizedek." So he was one.
He offered up prayers and petitions for all
and submitted to God. And if you recall,
in suffering death, perfection was reached.
You're so slow to learn, so heed what I teach.
You ought to be teachers. You've all heard the word,
and it's elementary, the things that you've heard.
You still ask for milk, for you are but babes,
and solid food's saved for the ones who have made
the time to mature in their knowledge and know
what's good and what's evil. You still need to grow.

Hebrews 6

But let us not talk of the simple ideals
like baptism, faith, and seeking to heal,
instead let's remember that turning away
after knowing Christ's grace is like seeking to slay
him over again. God is not unjust.
He won't forget all that you've done. You must trust
that He will still know you, for that is a fact,
but you must know Him through faith and through acts.
What God promised Abraham, so the Lord gave.
And He made an oath that we should be saved.
Hope is an anchor that's firm and secured,
and Jesus died so that our place is assured.

Hebrews 7 - 8

Do you not know of Melchizedek, King
of Salem and priest of the Lord? Everything
about him is holy, for Salem means 'peace.'
His name means 'The King of the Righteous'. Not least
is the fact that our father, Abraham, gave
a tenth to Melchizedek of what he'd saved.
And in the same manner, Jesus was sent
that we should be saved and we should repent.

The old law's abandoned. It was unclear,
but now we have hope and all may draw near.
Other priests sacrifice day after day,
but Jesus gave once, so he would allay
the sins of mankind when he offered his flesh.
Because of his blood our souls are refreshed.
The law appoints priests, but they are just men,
but through resurrection, we've been purged of sin.
Christ is our High Priest. He sits and he serves
the true tabernacle of God. So observe
that it has been written so by Jeremiah,
that God would choose when He'd send us His messiah.
'The time shall soon come when I'll make a new
covenant with all My people, and you
will see it is different than that which I gave
to Moses when all your ancestors were slaves.
The laws will then be in their hearts and their minds.
No teachers are needed, for each man will find
My grace and forgiveness if he should but look.
And I'll strike man's record of sin from My book.'

Hebrews 9

In our earthly temple, the high priest alone
would enter the holy-of-holies, atone
with the blood of a sacrifice, but we're made new
for now everyone can do what the priests do.
Christ gave his blood. The sacrificed lamb!
He cleansed us so that we may know the I AM.
He does not go in, like priests, every year.
He went just one time. Now our path is clear.
So when the day comes that Christ comes again,
his coming will not be to cleanse us of sin.
Instead he shall come for those in our nation
who wait on him. He'll bring the world salvation.

Hebrews 10

The law is a shadow of good things to come.
God is where all of our real joy comes from.
Christ came because all our offerings were
unable to please God. He would prefer
that we would pursue the Lord in our lives,
and so Christ was given as one sacrifice
that we should be holy, once and for all.
We should be humbled and also enthralled.
We're drawn to the body of Christ to know God
with a heart and a faith that is not a façade.
Let's spur on each other to faith and good deeds,
for He showed us mercy in our time of need.
We've all been insulted in public, and thrown
in prison with our brothers. Have we not grown
in our faith and reward? For we persevere
in knowing the truth. Through Christ we draw near.

Hebrews 11

By faith we know God formed the universe and
all life upon Earth with a simple command.
By faith Abel pleased God, so he was killed.
By faith God warned Noah, and he did God's will.
By faith Abraham followed God's word and hand
and walked as a stranger in far foreign lands.
By faith Abraham was a father, though he
was too old, because he believed God's decree.
By faith Abraham offered Isaac to die,
and so he was blessed for his faith in God's eye.
By faith Isaac, Jacob, and Joseph were blessed.
By faith Moses saved us at our Lord's request.
By faith the sea split. We passed through the swell.
By faith the great wall of Jericho fell.
By faith Rahab welcomed the spies in and cared
for their needs and saved them, and so she was spared.
Shall I speak of those who died by the sword,
were tortured, or saved because of the Lord?

By faith they were promised what we have received...
Jesus! And that's why we have to believe!

Hebrews 12

With all of these witnesses, shouldn't we set
our eyes upon Jesus? Let's never forget
the Lord's discipline is held back from none
whom He loves, nor anyone He calls a son.
As our fathers did, so we must admit
our faults to our heavenly Father. Submit.
Be disciplined, and be assured in the end
we shall reap the greatest award - to ascend.
So make every effort to live and to be
holy in all that do, for you see,
you have come to the Lord and Mount Zion where men
are cleansed in His righteousness. You'll live again.
As it is written, and as the Lord stated,
God can shake everything He has created.
So let us all worship, humbled and awed,
the fire of holiness that is our God.

Hebrews 13

So now, go forth and love one another.
Treat every stranger you meet as a brother.
Keep strong your marriage. You shouldn't fall in
to loving your money, for that is a sin.
God won't forsake us, so don't be afraid.
Follow the path that Jesus has laid.
Give God your sacrifice: undying praise,
so that you may bask in His beautiful gaze.
Timothy has been quite recently freed,
and when he arrives, we will come back to see
your church and sit as a part of your meetings.
From Italy, all of us send you our greetings.

God man James like faith without things good friends God's chair crisis hold deeds judge tongue brothers humble impressed isaac show true need love perfect more merciful who'd high slow sin just judgement Lord one joy Seek dead know wisdom ask suffering Abraham's person set rich away lead poor righteous

James 1:1 - 1:18

As a servant of God and of Christ, I send greetings
to all of the twelve tribes in your holy meetings.
Consider it joy when trials and fears
are faced, for in that your faith perseveres.
When you lack in wisdom, ask and you'll find
He delivers. But doubt and the Lord will decline.
He who doubts God is a wave on the sea,
tossed to and fro by the wind like debris.
The humble man stands higher than those in power.
The rich man will blow away just like a flower
that's scorched by the sun. Be humble and know,
to the faithful the crown of life God will bestow.
God can't be tempted, nor does the Lord tempt.
Temptation is ours and we show God contempt.
Don't be deceived! For God shows us love.
Each of His perfect gifts comes from above.

James 1:19 - 1:27

Be quick to listen and be slow to speak.
Be slow to anger, for God loves the meek.
Bask in the Word, for sin's like a cell
in a prison. Listen and obey as well!
To hear but not do is to look in a mirror
forgetting your own face. Seek to draw nearer.
Watch what you say, and serve those in need.
That is religion! That's why we're freed.

James 2:1 - 2:13

Suppose that a poor man and rich man walk in
to your meeting place. Should you then begin
entreating the rich man to sit on a chair
as you force the poor man to kneel where it's bare?
No! Don't show favorites! You are not to judge.
To the poor and the weak, do not hold a grudge.
God sets them up in faith above those
who'd judge them by money or status or clothes.
Go! Love your neighbor, as you love yourself
and set sin and pride high up on the shelf.
Be merciful, friends. Put judgment away,
or you won't see mercy on your judgment day.

James 2:14 - 2:26

What good, my brothers, is faith without deeds?
If one who has faith sees one who's in need
of clothing and food, but lends him no aid
what good does it do if the righteous man prayed?
So faith without deeds is dead! It is true.
Show me your faith; I'll show what I do.
If you ask for proof, I'll point to our past.
Abraham's faith is still unsurpassed,
because he was willing to give up his son,
Isaac, to God. What Abraham's done
is show us a faith that was honest and true.
You believe God is one? Well demons do too!
The prostitute, Rahab, had true faith. Do you
back up your faith with the things that you do?
As a body's a corpse once the spirit has fled,
so faith without deeds is a faith that is dead.

James 3

Would you be a teacher or rabbi, my friends?
Seek not to be, for we in the end
will be judged more strictly than those who would learn.

We are not perfect. For God's love we yearn.
The smallest of things can set a new course,
like a ship's rudder or bit for the horse.
A man's tongue may lead him down paths undesired,
and corrupt a whole person and set him afire.
You have seen birds and beasts that are tamed,
but the tongue is so restless with all of its claims.
Both curses and praise our mouth seems to know.
And from this fresh spring, salt water may flow.
So let those amongst you who'd lead a good life
not harbor the evil that cuts like a knife.
The wisdom of Heaven is peace-loving, pure,
considerate, merciful, kind, and secure.
So seek out such wisdom and follow the Lord,
so someday you're given the greatest reward,
for peacemakers out sowing peace always raise
the harvest of righteousness all of their days.

James 4

What causes fighting among you? It's sin!
You ask but don't get, because deep down within
your request was for something to spend on your pleasure,
but you should ask so you increase the Lord's treasure.
Submit yourselves now to God up on high.
Wash your hands, sinners, then go purify
your heart. And don't slander or judge for there's one
Lawgiver. God can't be tried or outdone,
so do not predict what the future will hold.
Your life's but a mist! Do not be so bold.
Only God knows what tomorrow will bring,
so you must rely upon Him in all things.

James 5

You who are rich, you have been warned.
Oppressing the innocent, poor, or the scorned
has fattened your pockets while harming the rest.
God's not impressed by the things you possess.

But those who are suffering, you should not stop
believing, for just like a farmer with crops
waits for the rain, so we are in wait
for the Lord. Take joy in your suffering fate.
Have patience, my brothers, you must persevere.
In prayer and confession God takes away fear.
Turn just one sinner to God and you'll stand
as the person who saved and cleansed that poor man.

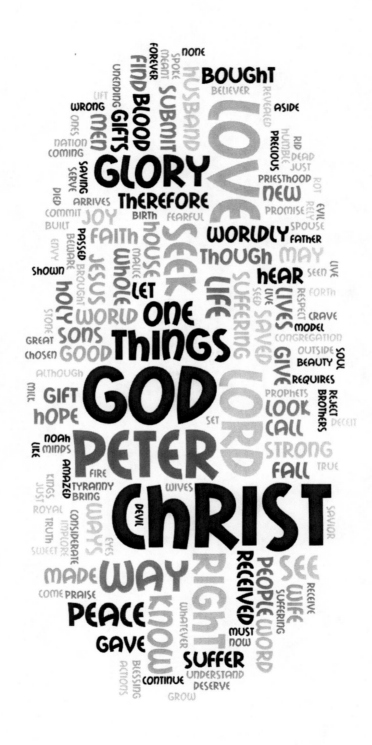

I Peter 1

From Peter, apostle of Christ, to you all,
the elect, though you're strangers to me, hear my call.
Praise be to God, the Father, who gave
us new birth in Christ. Through his blood we're saved.
And through it we gain the inheritance we
could not have received through acts or through deeds.
Though you have been made to suffer in fire,
the faith we receive is our one true desire.
Show it is genuine in all you do.
Though you haven't seen him, I promise to you
that your love and your joy in Christ made you whole.
The goal of his coming was saving your soul!
The prophets who spoke of the grace that would come
meant Jesus, his suffering, and all that's from
the Spirit in Heaven. So therefore prepare
your minds; be controlled, and also beware
of conforming to that which is evil. Obey!
Be holy in all that you do and you say.
Be reverent and fearful, because you were bought
by blood from our Savior, not gold or such rot.
When Jesus was with us we all were amazed.
He was revealed when he died and was raised
so you would know hope and be purified.
You're born again out of a seed that can't die.
The word of God lives! For as it was said,
'Man's glory will wither, will fall and be dead,
but the word of the Lord stands forever, all days.'
These things were passed down, so you'd know them always.

I Peter 2

Do not seek malice. Be rid of deceit,
hypocrisy, envy, and crave what is sweet.
Just like a babe, seek the milk God can give,
so you may grow strong; so that you may live.
You are a stone in the house of the Lord,
built so that all of us can look toward
His glory. Although other people reject
the Builder, we bow down and give our respect.
You who are chosen as His holy nation,
His most royal priesthood and His congregation,
here in the world, you're alienated.
Do what is good, so those who have hated
you and your ways can see you're above
this worldly life. Let them see your love.
Submit yourselves unto their worldly kings.
Let no one say, 'That man rebels in all things.'
For if you do right but are beaten, you stand
above tyranny, so men understand
you suffer their insults as Christ did the same.
In this way you honor the Lord and His name.

I Peter 3

Wives, in the same way submit to your spouse.
If they aren't believers, they see in their house
a model of Christ. Your beauty is shown
through faith, not through necklaces or precious stones.
Your gentleness and your spirit are gifts
in the eyes of the Lord, and if they can lift
your husband to be a believer as well,
then you'll be the cause of the joy that will dwell.
And in the same way, a husband must be
considerate, loving his wife so that she
can inherit the gift of an unending life.
Be good in all ways, and in Christ love your wife.
You cannot right wrongs with a wrong, so seek to
bring peace to your brothers, and peace shall find you.

Suffering for what is right is a blessing.
Don't still your tongue. Continue professing
the truth and the hope to all sons and daughters.
You have been saved, just as from the waters
Noah brought forth a new people to serve.
So Christ bought us life, which we did not deserve.

I Peter 4

Live for the Lord, not for your desires.
You've lived as a pagan, but now God requires
your actions to match the gift you received.
You left behind darkness when you first believed.
The end of all things is nearing, therefore
be clear in all things, seek love, and implore
those who don't know him to find peace in all
that Christ does for us, and thus hear his call.
The gifts that God gave you should be used to do
His bidding. In suffering, you shall renew
the glory of God. Commit your whole lives
to doing what's right till His judgment arrives.

I Peter 5

To the elders, be shepherds and watch with great care
as your flocks look to you. And make them aware
of Christ's love so none of your sheep are afraid,
for his glory is present, and it does not fade.
Young men, in the same way submit to the ones
who are older, as if you were fathers and sons.
Be humble, my friends, and wary that you
don't fall to the devil, whatever you do.
Be strong and be steadfast, for God set aside
each one of you from the world outside.
She who's in Babylon, Silas, and I
send you our love, and on you we rely.

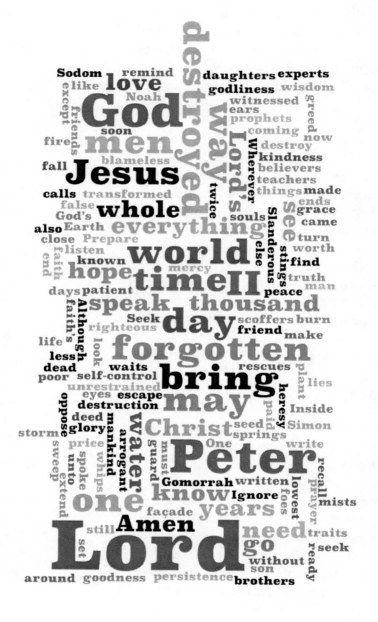

II Peter 1

From Simon, now Peter, apostle and friend
of believers, I write you, that I may extend
peace and God's grace through Christ, which we gained
through Jesus' death; a hope unrestrained.
Jesus has given us all that we need
to be godly in life. So go plant the seed
of goodness through faith, your own self-control,
and wisdom, persistence, but to be made whole,
you also need godliness, kindness and love.
These traits bring you close to the Lord up above.
If not, you've forgotten the price that was paid
and your faith's a façade; a poor masquerade.
Although you may know this, I still must remind
you, brothers. When you look around you may find
you've forgotten the truth and you listen to lies.
These are not myths! For with my own eyes
and with my own ears, I witnessed God say,
"This is My son whom I love."
In this way,
the prophets who spoke long before Jesus came,
did not speak as men, but in the Lord's name.

II Peter 2

But there are false teachers who speak heresy.
They'll soon bring destruction on all that you see,
for God has no mercy for those who oppose
His will and His way. He wipes out His foes.
The Lord destroyed Sodom, Gomorrah, and He

destroyed the whole Earth, except Noah. You see?
Slanderous men are worth less than these things.
They will not escape the Lord's whips or His stings.
God rescues the righteous. The arrogant fall.
These experts in greed are the lowest of all.
They're springs without water; mists in the storm.
Only through Christ can our souls be transformed.

II Peter 3

I've written you twice. I hope you'll recall
that in the end days, before the Lord calls
the scoffers will say, 'Where's the coming you said
would be here?' Inside, their hearts are all dead.
But they have forgotten the time when the water
destroyed all the world, its sons and its daughters.
In the same way, fire waits for its turn
to destroy everything, so this world shall burn.
Ignore everything else, but do not forget
that unto the Lord, no time has been set.
One thousand years is a day, and one day
is like one thousand years. Not one man can say
when He shall make His will known to mankind.
He's patient with us, but in His own time,
the day of the Lord will sweep down. Prepare!
Be ready for Him in deed and in prayer.
Seek to be blameless as we cannot know
when the Lord ends the world. Wherever you go
be on your guard, and seek to bring men
to the glory of God. Amen, friends! Amen!

I John 1

From the beginning, all we have heard,
and all we have seen and touched - all the Word
of life, we will testify. It is eternal!
In fellowship with the One who's paternal
and He who's the son, we write you this text.
Our joy is complete, no matter what's next.
This is the message: God is the light.
If we say we're with him but walk in the night,
we lie to ourselves. But gifts from above
abound when we walk in the grace of God's love.
Truth is the key. No man's free of sin.
Confess and the Lord will then welcome you in.

I John 2

I hope you don't sin, but every man does,
so ask Jesus Christ to save you because
he'll speak on behalf of you. He will atone.
For all of us he gave his flesh and his bone.
Seek out the truth and make it complete.
To walk as Christ did is an admirable feat.
This command, friends, is not new, it is old!
But now in the light it is made manifold.
If you claim you love, but you hate your own brother,
then you're in a darkness unlike any other.
I write that you've sinned. I write you're forgiven.
I write so through Christ, the evil one's driven
away from your heart. Do not love the Earth!
The worldly passes, as death comes from birth.

He who loves God and does what He willed,
has life everlasting and shall be fulfilled.
Lo, but you've heard the hour is near.
The antichrist comes! Right now he is here
amongst our own ranks! But bask in the truth,
exposing the liars, the cruel and uncouth.
Those who deny the Son don't know God.
So let people know that the Lord's love is broad.
I write so my friends are not led astray.
Ask what would Christ do? What would he say?

I John 3

How great is His love, that we are God's children!
They didn't know Him, for He hadn't filled them
with love till we came. Now He'll purify
the people, but still there are some who would lie.
Do what is righteous and He'll fill you too.
Sin and you'll find that the Devil owns you.
Love one another, do not be like Cain,
and don't be surprised when you're met with disdain.
Jesus laid down his life for us all.
To do that ourselves is our Lord's highest call.
If you have possessions, but someone does not,
do something! Actions speak louder than thought!
Those who obey will ask and receive.
Those who do not are quickly deceived.
Do what you should, lest you are condemned.
Those who obey these commands live in Him.

I John 4

It's true that false prophets abound and will say
spirits have told them to follow a way
that does not match up with what Jesus taught.
You are from God, so do not be caught!
Those liars are worldly, they do not speak
of love, for that trait is what's truly unique
to those who are God's. Love one another.

This single quality makes you Christ's brother.
God showed His love by sending His son
to die for us all. He had only one!
No human can ever show love that's so grand.
So love, friends, just love. That is God's one command.

<u>I John 5</u>

To love's to obey, and that is not hard.
God made His rules simple in that regard.
And through Jesus Christ you shall all overcome
the world, for that is not where He is from.
He is from water and also from blood.
He is the truth while liars spew mud.
Life is eternal because Jesus came.
He is the one who lived life without blame.
I love each of you, but this part is vital.
Keep all of your brothers from worshiping idols.
I've said it, but I shall now say it again;
seek in your life to be without sin.

love
grace
Though
walking
truth Deceivers
one chosen live
soon way
Christ children 'll Always
elder commanded
mother another important
quite sight teachings
monsoon peace
must
thoughts
lose John
now see like
speaking Let
mercy God
choose glad
write

II John 1

To she who is chosen as elder, and to
her children, I'm so glad to write this to you.
Let mercy and grace and peace from above
be yours as we live in truth and in love.
I see that your children are walking the way
that God has commanded, so now I must say
to God what's important for you as a mother
is that you and yours should love one another.
Deceivers are speaking, but you must not lose
sight of the teachings of Christ. Always choose
love. Though my thoughts are like a monsoon,
I'll write no more now, for I'll see you quite soon.

sure face God's see

Let soon imitate true

temperament

ink slandering brother pure

friend good

kind quite holy

manger seek

strangers likejust now

actions speak Lord

follow Peace John

faithful

faith grace Treat

soul finds Gaius Ill think Go

evils may manner

health banner pen

want born

desire brothers

hear purposely unite

talk pray

Diotrephes

<u>III John 1</u>

To Gaius, my friend, I pray that this finds
your soul in good health and your temperament kind.
I hear what you do for those who are strangers.
You're faithful, like he who was born in the manger.
Treat all of our brothers in just such a manner
that we may unite under God's holy banner.
I pray you won't be like Diotrephes, who
is now purposely slandering both me and you.
Let us not imitate evil, but seek
to follow the Lord. We should do and speak
that which is true and that which is pure
so in all our actions our faith may be sure.
How I desire to share what I think
but don't want to do so with just pen and ink.
I'll see you quite soon and we'll talk face to face.
Peace to you, brother. Go with God's grace.

desire Gomorrah Cain fault
instead forever started seek
just Christ's glory fire
pray frustration represent Sodom
faultfinders rain
Amen lead sin Clouds fruit
whose destroyed foretold power
Woe immorality Jude God's try
Remember must acting faith
giving God
enslaved
like saved scoff
brother depraved true now evil
trees One amen apostles ranks
yet men amongst
wish mercy salvation
peace neither
build thanks way
James without halt
lie Egypt
still Christ
doubt friends
Lord overcome keep Torah led write
Keep divide
eager able grumblers
love

Jude 1

From Jude, a brother of James, I wish true
mercy and peace and love upon you.
My friends, I was eager to write of salvation
in Christ, but instead I write in frustration.
For there are now men who lie in your ranks
and represent evil as giving God thanks.
Remember that God destroyed those he'd saved
from Egypt, when they started acting depraved.
So those men amongst you are Sodom, Gomorrah!
They love neither Christ, nor God, nor the Torah.
Woe to them, they seek to be just like Cain.
They're trees without fruit. Clouds without rain.
They're grumblers and faultfinders, led by desire,
and if they lead you, it's into the fire.
But as the apostles foretold, 'Those who scoff
will try to divide you and then lead you off.'
And so you must build up your faith now and pray.
Keep to Christ's love and keep to God's way.
Those who still doubt can yet still be saved!
But through immorality men are enslaved.
The Lord God is able to keep you from fault;
the One in whose glory all evil must halt.
His mercy and power will overcome sin,
now and forever. Amen and amen!

Revelation 1

This revelation, which was thus revealed
to John by an angel of Christ, is unsealed
that those who should hear it shall take it to heart,
for the things that are written are nearing their start.
To all seven churches in Asia, peace be
unto you, for by the Christ's blood we are free.
We have been set as his kingdoms and priests
by the power that governs the most and the least.
Lo, he is coming in clouds and each eye
will see him, including those who let him die.
"I am the Alpha and Omega in sum;
Who is and who was, and who is yet to come."
I, John, your brother who's suffered, enduring
this exile, tell you I saw visions during
the Lord's day and heard a voice say unto me,
"Write down each one of the things you will see.
Send them to all of the seven."
I turned
and there seven lamp stands appeared and they burned
with the Son of Man's figure among them. The light
was too much to look at. His face was so bright.
His head and his hair were as white as new wool.
His feet glowed like bronze. His voice was as full
as the great rushing waters. His eyes were ablaze.
I stared at my lord, and I was amazed.
He held seven stars in his hand, and then out
came a double-edged sword, pulled right from his mouth!
I fell on my face, as if I were dead,
then he placed his right hand upon me and said,

"Do not be afraid. I'm the First and the Last.
I'm the dead who was raised. I'm the future and past.
Write what you see and what's yet to come."
His face was as bright as if touching the sun.
"The lamps are my churches to whom you will write.
The stars are the angels I send to give sight
to all my believers. Although I was dead,
behold! I'm alive! Through me, men are fed."

Revelation 2 - 3

"To Ephesus write, you all persevered.
Though false prophets came, whom others revered,
you remained true, and yet you forgot
to honor your first love. If you do not
return to the things that you used to do,
I will remove my lamp stand from you.
To those who can overcome hardship, I give
the tree of life's fruit so that you may live.
To Smyrna, write this. I know you are poor
and impoverished. But truly you're rich! For in your
own land there are devils who'll persecute you.
Still each one of you must be faithful and true.
Even if death should be your reward
for faith, know that you are so loved by the Lord.
The crown of life comes at a very high price.
Overcome! I promise you will not die twice.
To Pergamum write, I know Satan's throne
is among you, yet you are as steadfast as stone.
You did not renounce me, though many were killed,
but there are still things you have not fulfilled.
People among you still hold to their Baal's
and perversions. Repent, lest you be impaled
on the sword of my mouth. But the faithful, I'll claim
with my manna. My children shall have a new name.
Thyatira, your faith and love have improved,
but still there are things which I do not approve.
The prophetess, Jezebel, misleads the free
with sexual acts for her idols to see.

She will not repent, so I've made her a bed
of suffering. I'll strike her children all dead.
And those who adulterize with her shall know
her suffering too. Do not fall so low!
Those who repent shall rule over nations,
with scepters of iron and authorization
to shatter the wicked like pottery jars.
And I'll give to him the bright morning star.
To Sardis, you act like you live, but you're dead.
Wake up! Remember all that has been said.
The few who aren't soiled will walk dressed in white,
but the rest will be struck from the great book of life.
Philadelphia, though you are weak, you've been strong
in keeping my name and refraining from wrong.
Because you've been true, though liars defiled
my name, you won't see the hour of trial.
In the temple of God, be a pillar that's true,
for a new Jerusalem's coming for you.
To Laodicea, so lukewarm with doubt,
be cold or be hot! I should spit you out,
because you are nothing. Nor for or against.
Be something! You're nothing, which makes me incensed.
You say you are rich in your wealth, but you're blind
and naked and poor. Come seek me and find
gold from my fire and clothes you can wear
and salve for your eyes. I'm standing right there!
I've knocked at your door. Will you let me in?
He who would eat with me, I'll eat with him."

Revelation 4

After these words, I looked and I saw
a door in the heavens. I listened in awe
as I heard a voice that spoke, telling me,
"Come up and I'll show you what you are to see."
Suddenly I was in front of a throne
where One who appeared to be made of bloodstone
sat there, encircled by rainbow-like jewels,
and twenty-four smaller thrones all sat there too.

On them were twenty-four elders in white,
and from these came thunder and flashes of light.
Seven lamps blazed. And stretched out before
the thrones was a sea made of glass as the floor.
Around the throne, four creatures covered in eyes
were praising the Lord with their shouts and their cries.
"Holy is God, who is, was, and shall be."
The creatures were strange that had gathered around me.
One beast like an ox, one a man, one a lion,
and one like an eagle, though never in Zion
or all of the Earth, have men seen such things.
Each of these creatures had six separate wings.
And all of the elders fell down at His throne
crying, "O Lord, you've made all that is known.
You're worthy of honor and glory and power,
each second, each minute, each day, and each hour."

<u>Revelation 5</u>

The Lord held a scroll with seven great seals.
An angel with Him then made this appeal,
"Who here is worthy to open the scroll?"
I wept, for on Earth and in Heaven no soul
was worthy. But then an elder said, "Hold,
the Lion of Judah is great and is bold.
He'll open the seal."
Then there was a Lamb,
standing in front of the throne of I AM.
It looked as if he had been slain, and I saw
it had seven horns, seven eyes, but no flaw.
He took up the scroll from the One on the throne
as the four other creatures bowed down as they droned
a musical song with harps and incense.
They sang, "You gave your life in mankind's defense.
Because you were slain, you're worthy to be
the one who will open the scroll and set free
its wisdom."
And suddenly angels appeared.
Thousands were singing to God as they neared.

I heard every creature on Earth sing in tone,
"All glory and praise to the Lamb and the throne."

Revelation 6

He opened the first seal, and then white as snow
came a horse and his rider was holding a bow.
He was given a crown as a conquering king,
bent upon conquest of all living things.
The next seal released a horse red as fire.
His rider was filled with a single desire,
to take peace from Earth, and bring upon war.
He took up a sword, and off the horse tore.
The third seal, a black horse's rider who sat
with scales to measure the grain in the vat.
The four creatures said, "A liter of grain
per denarius," but they chose not to explain.
The fourth seal was broken. A fourth rider came
riding a pale horse. Death was his name.
He was followed by Hades, with power to kill
by famine or plague or whatever they willed.
The fifth seal was opened, and I saw the souls
who had died for the word, begging to be consoled.
They were saying, "God, free us!" and, "God, You are great!"
But He did not free them. Instead He said, "Wait."
The sixth seal was broken; the sun turned to black.
The moon turned to red, and the Earth shook and cracked.
The stars fell to Earth and the ground split apart,
and nothing remained as it was at the start.
Then the people of Earth, from the kings to the slaves
ran into hiding, to mountains and caves.
They screamed, "Oh, the wrath of the Throne and the Lamb!
The great day has come. The end is at hand!"

Revelation 7

Then I saw the four angels who held back the wind
and seas that were set to bring on the Earth's end.
Then a fifth angel came from the east and appealed,

"Hold back destruction, till I place the seal
on the one hundred forty-four thousand souls who
are the servants of God. Then I'll call upon you.
Twelve thousand from each of the twelve tribes will be
marked for the Lord, and they shall be free."
Then a great multitude dressed all in white
stood at the throne crying out in delight,
"Praise to our God who sits on the throne."
The people and creatures and elders fell prone,
worshipping Him, "Great glory and power
to God the Almighty in His greatest hour."
Then one of the elders said, "These are the ones
who through tribulation knew God and His son.
They all washed their robes in the blood of the Lamb
and now they will serve day and night the I AM.
The Lamb is their shepherd, no tear makes them blink,
for he leads them to living water to drink."

Revelation 8

Then he opened the seventh seal and there was silence,
a lovely respite from the noise and the violence,
and then seven angels with trumpets stood round
as one threw a fiery censer straight down.
It struck the Earth hard, causing earthquakes and lightning.
The trumpets produced a great noise that was frightening.
The first trumpet brought forth fire and hail,
mixed up with blood. Chaos unveiled.
A third of the earth and the grass and the trees
were burned up at once like a flaming disease.
As the second one blew, a mountain ablaze
fell into the sea. In this second phase
a third of the sea turned to blood, and a third
of the ships and the beasts of the sea ceased to stir.
As the third angel sounded his trumpet, a star
named Wormwood fell down to the Earth from afar.
It poisoned a third of the waters and springs,
and all died who drank of it, peasants and kings.
The fourth trumpet blared and a third of the sun

and the moon and the stars were completely undone.
A third of the day and a third of the night
were darkened, and I saw an eagle in flight.
"Woe," said the eagle, "to all who survived,
for the three trumpets left shall leave few men alive."

Revelation 9

The fifth trumpet blew and from the Abyss
poured smoke as if from a great furnace. Then this
was followed by locusts who stung with the sting
of a scorpion. These bugs ignored everything
except for the people who had not been marked
by the seal of the Lord, and every sting sparked
a torture that lasted for five months. Men cried
for death, but not one of the suffering died.
These locusts looked like tiny horses with crowns;
their faces like humans, their hair woven round,
and teeth like a lion and armor as well.
They bow down to Abaddon, he who rules hell.
The sixth trumpet sounded and then a voice said,
"Release the four angels and let them cause dread."
The four angels all were unleashed and they sent
an army to kill wherever they went.
The riders wiped out one-third of mankind.
They killed the unmarked, as they'd been assigned.
Out of their mouths came sulfur and fire,
but even this didn't stop people's desire
to worship their idols of silver and gold.
Their hearts had been hardened. Their souls had gone cold.
They did not repent for their immoral deeds,
their murders or thefts, their lust or their greed.

Revelation 10

An angel enveloped in clouds then descended,
and burned like a sun, both frightening and splendid.
He held a small scroll inside of his hand
and stood with his feet in the sea and on land.

He roared out and all seven thunders spoke then.
But a voice told me, "Now you must put down your pen.
Do not write down that which the thunders extol,
but go to the angel and ask for the scroll."
I did so. The angel said, "Eat it and learn.
Though it tastes like honey, your stomach will turn."
I ate up the scroll, and just as he'd said,
it was good in my mouth but my stomach was lead.
Although I was soured, a voice told me, "You
must do everything that I tell you to do.
You must prophesy about kings and of nations
and people and languages without cessation."

<u>Revelation 11</u>

I was given a reed like a measuring rod
and was told to measure the temple of God.
Outside the wall, the Gentiles would
trample the city and all that is good
for forty-two months. But there would be two
voices to ring out and say what is true.
For more than three years they would prophesy so
that the world might learn and the world might know.
Fire will come from their mouths and destroy
their foes. They will both have the strength to employ
diseases and plagues, but after their time
the beast will destroy them. They'll lie in the grime
and the muck of the gutters as all the Earth cheers,
saying, "They plagued us for more than three years.
Celebrate this day with presents and gifts."
But after three days, the Lord will then lift
the two men back up, so they live again.
The world will watch as the two men ascend
to Heaven, and then an earthquake will come
to the city where they crucified the Lord's son.
A tenth of the city will crumble and fall.
Though it will be terrible, that is not all.
The angel then sounded the last trumpet and
the voices called out, "The time is at hand.

Earth will become now the kingdom of Heaven.
The trumpets have blown. We've sounded all seven.
The Lord and His Christ will reign."
Then they fell
on their faces and said, "It is good and it's well,
for He's come. It is now time for judging the dead.
We will reward those who put You ahead
of all that is earthly. But we must destroy
the destroyers of Earth, for they have no joy."
Then the temple in Heaven was opened and there
was the ark of the covenant up in the air.
Lightning and thunder, earthquakes and hail
came out of the ark, for the Lord would prevail.

Revelation 12

Then a great sign appeared, a woman clothed by
the sun, with the moon at her feet. Then the sky
was darkened for all of the stars crowned her head.
She was giving birth, when a great dragon, blood red,
with seven heads, and seven crowns, and ten horns
swept down to eat up her child, once born.
A son was born to her to rule over all,
and God swept him up just before he could fall
in the mouth of the beast. Then the woman ran in
to the desert where she would be cared for. But then
a war began between the dragon and those
angels that backed him and those whom God chose.
The dragon, that beast, was hurled to Earth,
unable to murder the one that she'd birthed.
And all of the angels who'd been on his side
were cast down along with him. They had denied
the Lord. Then a voice said, "Now it has come
that the kingdom of God has defeated the sum
of its enemies. Now comes the time of salvation,
through Christ for our brothers within every nation.
Through the blood of the Lamb, their lives are reclaimed,
though they gave them up for the Lord's holy name.
But woe to the Earth, for the devil is strong.

He's angry for he knows his time is not long."
The beast chased the woman, and his fury flared.
She ran to a place that the angels prepared
where she would be safe for more than three years.
Until that time she would not know any fears.
The serpent spewed water to sweep her away
but the earth swallowed it. So knowing his prey
was outside his reach, he turned to make war
on all the believers. His wrath was outpoured.

Revelation 13

I stood on the shore of the sea as a beast
came out of the sea, and the dragon unleashed
his power so that the beast could control
his authority for the two's mutual goal.
The people all followed the beast and bowed down
to the dragon, for in him the beast's strength was found.
"Who could defeat such a beast?" they all said.
"Those who oppose him will all end up dead."
He blasphemed in pride, and slandered God's name.
He defeated the faithful throughout his whole reign.
Then out of the earth, a two-horned beast rose
who had the same power and fought the same foes.
He made all the world bow down to the one
who had come before him, and all he had done.
He sent fire down on the cities like rain.
To those who defied him he brought only pain.
He set up an image to worship, then said,
"Each person must now bare a mark on their head
or hand, if they want my permission to trade."
On the mark the beast's name and number's portrayed.
Now this calls for wisdom. The beast's number is
the number of man. Man's number is his.
Now calculate with your mathematical tricks,
for you know his number...it is six-six-six.

Revelation 14

I looked at Mount Zion and there was the Lamb
with his one hundred forty-four thousand at hand.
And all had the Father's name on their foreheads,
and a song came from Heaven, but what the song said
was not clear to any except those who stood
with the Lamb, pure and perfect. They all understood.
Then an angel was flying, proclaiming the word.
No matter your nation or language, you heard.
"Fear God! Give Him glory! His judgment has come,
for He is the one that all things have come from."
The angel was joined by another who said,
"Babylon's fallen! Her madness is shed."
Then a third angel yelled, "If you worship the beast,
or you honor his mark, then you'll drink in the feast
of God's fury. You'll burn in the presence of all
that is holy. The Lamb will not stop your fall.
But those who love God shall find peace in the Lamb.
and know that he comes from the wondrous I AM."
Then a voice came from Heaven.
"All those who die now
for the Lord will be blessed, for the Lord can see how
you have suffered for Him. All your deeds have been seen.
In the blood of the Lamb, the faithful are clean."
As a white cloud came down with the Son of Man crowned,
an angel said, "Now you shall reap from the ground.
Swing your great sickle."
He did and he drew
all the good and the holy. A new angel threw
all the sinners down into a winepress and blood
flowed over the world to mix with the mud.

Revelation 15 - 16

I saw seven angels there standing in Heaven,
each with a plague, and the plagues numbered seven.
Below was a sea of fire and glass
and there on the shores were the ones who'd surpassed

and beaten the beast, his number and name.
They sang out a psalm to the Lord's mighty fame.
I looked up and saw the four creatures then hand
each angel a bowl for their plague. The smoke fanned
across the great temple. A voice said, "Go pour
your plagues on the Earth." The first one was sores.
It only affected the ones with the mark
of the beast. Then the second bowl turned the seas dark
like the blood of the dead. All the life in the sea
was destroyed. Next the lakes and the streams ceased to be,
for the third bowl was poured. The fourth one came too.
Their hearts did not change though their suffering grew
as the sun scorched the earth with fire and heat.
The marked cursed the Lord, even in their defeat.
The fifth poured his bowl on the throne of the beast,
and darkness ensued as their anger increased.
The sixth poured his on the Euphrates which dried
the river up. Now there was nowhere to hide,
and the kings from the East could attack as they pleased.
Then three spirits came from the mouths of the beast,
the false prophet, and then the dragon as well.
They went to the kings of the world to tell,
"Go gather your armies. The battle is on
at the hill of Megiddo." Their swords were all drawn,
when the seventh one poured out the plague in his bowl.
A voice said, "It's done." I saw the death toll.
An earthquake destroyed the great city and then,
the Lord punished Babylon for all her sin.
The cities and nations all perished that day.
The islands and mountains were all swept away.
Hailstones destroyed every woman and man,
as they saw their final destruction at hand.

Revelation 17

"Come," said an angel, "I'll show you the way
the great prostitute will be punished today."
So he took me out to the desert and there
was the woman, and I could not help but to stare.

She sat on a beast with blasphemous names.
Its heads numbered seven, and she held the reins.
She was dressed up in scarlet and purple with gold.
Her chalice held sins too corrupt to behold.
Across her head was written, BABYLON, WHO
IS THE MOTHER OF WHORES AND OBSCENITIES TOO.
And the harlot was drunk on the decapitations
and slaughter of saints. Her foul desecration
of all that was righteous left me quite astonished.
The angel told me, "She will soon be admonished.
But why are you shocked? Let me explain some.
The beast who existed is gone. Yet to come
is the one she's atop, out of the Abyss.
Surprise to all those who don't think he exists.
The seven heads are seven hills; seven kings.
Five fell, one is now, one the future shall bring.
Ten horns on its head are ten kings of the beast.
Their goal is to see the beast's power increased.
They will war with the Lamb, though he is Lord of Lords.
Through him all the faithful will find their rewards.
The beast and his horns can never be sated,
and so they'll despise her; the harlot who's hated.
They'll ruin her, burning the flesh of the girl,
for she is the city that rules the whole world."

Revelation 18

A new angel came, proclaiming the news,
"Babylon's fallen! The land that's suffused
with all that's detestable, all that's unclean,
excessive, adulterous, cruel, and obscene."
A new voice from Heaven said, "Let people come
to me from her walls, for I know there are some
who don't share her sins, her plagues or her crimes.
The Lord pays her double for all of the times
she has sinned against Him. All her torture and grief,
is proof to you all you're to put no belief
in the earthly. All faith is for God, and they'll say,
"Babylon, how far you've fallen today."

The merchants shall weep when her riches have vanished.
The good have all left, as the evil were banished.
The sailors will see the smoke far away.
"Was there one like that city?" they'll mutter and say.
Then a great angel picked up a boulder and threw
it into the sea, and it started to brew.
"With this kind of violence shall Babylon fall.
And never again will she hear trumpets call.
The light of the lamp shall go out of that town,
for the blood of the prophets tore all her walls down."
Her magic spell led all the nations astray,
so now let her name be the name of decay."

Revelation 19

Then the multitudes roared. "Hallelujah!" they called.
"He condemned the great harlot, the one who has crawled
amongst men, corrupting them with all her sin."
Then the four creatures fell down and all worshipped Him.
They sang out in praise, "Let the Lamb's wedding be
the most wondrous of all."
Then an angel told me,
"Write down that all who are invited as guests
to be at the Lamb's wedding supper are blessed."
I fell down to worship him. He said, "Please rise.
I'm a servant like you. Worship God with your cries."
Then the heavens split forth and a white horse came through
with his rider, and his name was Faithful and True.
With justice he judges, his robe dipped in blood.
He throws all the evil ones down in the mud.
He is mighty indeed, and they fall by his sword.
On his thigh's inscribed, 'King of Kings, Lord of Lords.'
And an angel called out to the birds, "Gather round
to eat up the flesh as it falls to the ground."
The armies collapsed. The false prophet and beast
were thrown in the sulfur, and all fighting ceased.

Revelation 20

Then an angel came down with a lock and he bound
the dragon (that's Satan), and then threw him down
into the Abyss for a thousand long years
during which time, the Earth knew no fears.
At the end of that time, he would be set free
for just a short time, which was God's decree.
Then the ones who had not fallen prey to the beast
would be resurrected to live in Christ's peace.
When the thousand years end, Satan will then deceive
the four corners of Earth as he hopes to achieve
a victory over God's people, but they
will be saved by a fire from Heaven that day,
and Satan will drown in a sulfur lake too.
The book of life knows everything that we do.
We'll be judged, if the book does not hold someone's name,
like Hades before them, they'll soon know the flame.

Revelation 21

Then I saw a new Heaven. I saw a new Earth.
For the old ones had passed, when new ones gave birth.
A Jerusalem, new and better, came down
from the heavens as bright as a bride in her gown.
I heard a loud voice say, "My new domain
has come. No more death, nor mourning, nor pain
will exist now, for I'm the beginning and end.
The Alpha and the Omega. To him
who thirsts I shall give the true water of life,
and he'll be My son. He'll know no more strife.
But unto the vile, immoral, and cruel,
they all shall be tossed in the great sulfur pool.
and this will be their second death," said the Lord.
"And they'll join the sinners as one of their horde."
An angel said, "Come. Let me show you the bride
of the Lamb," as he then pointed up with great pride.
The great, new Jerusalem gleamed like a gem.
And the new city pulsed with the glory of Him.

Twelve gates and angels, upon twelve foundations;
each tribe and apostle etched like invitations.
But there was no temple, for there was no need,
for the Lamb and the Lord were the temples indeed.
No sun and no moon, for the Lord gave it light.
Its gates never shut, for there's never a night.

Revelation 22

Then the angel showed me the life giving spring,
and said, "I was sent to you so you might bring
these words to the people, for these things shall come
to pass very soon. Know where they come from.
Behold, I am coming soon! Blessed is he
who keeps these words."
I kneeled at this prophecy.
"Do not worship me. Worship God, Lord of all!
For I'm but a servant. At His feet I fall.
Don't seal up the words of this book, oh my son,
for each man I'll give him back what he has done.
The good shall get good, and the bad shall get bad.
And all who pass in through those gates will be glad,
for they'll know their goodness has thus been repaid
by God, but not those who have turned or betrayed.
They'll stay outside just like the dogs, all the ones
who have worshiped the earthly or bowed to the sun.
And I, Jesus, sent you my angel to give
these words to the churches so that they may live.
I'm the Root and the Offspring of David. I stand
as the bright Morning Star, and I offer my hand.
Do you thirst? Come and drink of my life-giving waters.
This is a free gift to my sons and daughters.
If anyone adds to these words, then you'll gain
the plagues, and if you take away, then the same
shall be done to you. God takes from your share
of the tree of life. That person won't be an heir.
I will come to you soon, but no man shall know when."
May the grace of God be with His people. Amen.

amen

ACKNOWLEDGMENTS

All glory is God's. He made this happen. I pray that all I have done in this process is pleasing to Him!

My beautiful wife, Kim, who has supported my work on this project for three years...and continues to support me today! And my sons, Noah and Jonah, whom I love so dearly.

Bryce, you inspired me to think I could even start a project of such a size. Thank you for your honest critiques, your wisdom and advice, and for being the best brother I could have ever hoped for. Amanda, what a great supporter you've been, and a perfect match for Bryce.

Mom and Dad – I love you guys so much, and am so grateful for all you have done for me.

Jon and Katie Davis – Your support and friendship has been so powerful.

Tim McCabe – Thank you for being a great friend and a wonderful artist.

My friends at church who have been bastions of faith: the Andersons, Beveridges, Bohns, Chartiers, Ciordas', Clarks, Conards, Davids', Duncans, Entwistles, Fraziers, Jones', Kirklands, Meads, Monahans, Sears', Smiths, Souans, Swaggerts, Swartzes, Thiels, Townsends, Van Utrechts, Whaleys, Wisdoms, Woelks, and everyone else!

My Facebook friends and fans – Thank you to all of you who have passed *The Bible in Rhyme* on to others. You've supported my efforts, and even helped me choose my cover art. You all rock!

Everyone who has downloaded The Bible in Rhyme – Your messages and comments...and just the fact that you downloaded it...have been so encouraging!

And I especially want to acknowledge, remember, and give thanks to the men and women who wrote and passed the Bible down for generations. They laid the groundwork for all men and women of faith today.

ABOUT THE AUTHOR

Kyle Holt owns and operates a software development company in Overland Park, Kansas and writes faith-based books, scripts, and blogs whenever possible. *The Bible in Rhyme* is Kyle's first book, and he is already at work on additional literary and multimedia projects. Kyle is blessed by his beautiful wife, Kim, and their sons, Noah and Jonah.

www.thebibleinrhyme.com

CPSIA information can be obtained at www.ICGtesting.com
Printed in the USA
LVOW060855220911

247365LV00001B/299/P